The Interest in Disinterestedness

Pierre Bourdieu

The Interest in Disinterestedness

Lectures at the Collège de France (1987–1989)

Edited by Julien Duval

Translated by Peter Collier

polity

First published in French as *L'intérêt au désintéressement. Cours au Collège de France 1987–1989* © Éditions Raisons d'agir/Éditions du Seuil, 2022

This English edition © Polity Press, 2024

The editor extends his thanks to Louis Gabrysiak and Thibaud Izard for their work in transcribing the lectures, as well as Bruno Ambroise, Johan Heilbron, Louis Pinto and Yves Winkin for their help during the editing of the final text and the notes.

Polity Press
65 Bridge Street
Cambridge CB2 1UR, UK

Polity Press
111 River Street
Hoboken, NJ 07030, USA

ISBN-13: 978-1-5095-5511-6 – hardback

A catalogue record for this book is available from the British Library.

Library of Congress Control Number: 2023948032

Typeset in 10.5 on 12 pt Times NR MT Pro
by Cheshire Typesetting Ltd, Cuddington, Cheshire
Printed and bound in Great Britain by CPI Group (UK) Ltd, Croydon

The publisher has used its best endeavours to ensure that the URLs for external websites referred to in this book are correct and active at the time of going to press. However, the publisher has no responsibility for the websites and can make no guarantee that a site will remain live or that the content is or will remain appropriate.

Every effort has been made to trace all copyright holders, but if any have been overlooked the publisher will be pleased to include any necessary credits in any subsequent reprint or edition.

For further information on Polity, visit our website:
politybooks.com

Contents

Editorial Note

This book continues and concludes the publication of Pierre Bourdieu's lectures at the Collège de France. A few months after his last lecture at this institution in March 2001, Bourdieu had published a concise version of the last year of his course (2000–1), under the title *Science de la science et réflexivité* [*Science of Science and Reflexivity*, 2004].[1] After his death, *Sur l'État* appeared in 2012 [*On the State*, 2014], followed by *Manet. Une révolution symbolique* in 2013 [*Manet. A Symbolic Revolution*, 2017].[2] The publication of the 'Cours de sociologie générale' that Bourdieu gave during his first five years of teaching at the Collège de France, between April 1982 and June 1986, was then launched, with a first volume combining the lectures of the academic years 1981–82 and 1982–83 issued in 2015, and then a second volume in 2016, containing those of the following three years.[3] The lectures given in 1992–93 that Bourdieu had entitled 'Les fondements sociaux de l'action économique' were published in 2017.[4] Our present volume combines the lectures given in 1987–88 and 1988–89 under the title 'À propos de l'État' [On the State]. The first year comprised five sessions, each lasting about 1 hour 50 minutes, which were held weekly on Thursdays at 11am in March and April 1988. The second year collates two lectures given in Lyon[5] with five lectures given in Paris on Thursdays in January and February 1989.[6]

The present edition respects the editorial approach chosen for the publication of the lectures on the State, aiming to reconcile faithfulness to the text with readability.[7] The text reproduces the transcription of the lectures as spoken.

As in the previous volumes, the transposition from oral to written has involved some superficial rewriting, which is careful to respect the criteria applied by Bourdieu himself when he revised his own lectures and seminars: stylistic corrections, smoothing over rough patches in

Contents

vii

the oral discourse (eliminating repetitions and other linguistic tics, etc.). On the rare occasions that passages were more or less inaudible, these have been indicated by ellipses between brackets. Here and there a word or a part of a sentence has been added by the editor in order to facilitate comprehension of the text or clarify elliptical formulae; since they were not spoken by Bourdieu, they have been placed between brackets.

The divisions into sections and paragraphs have been provided by the editor, as have the subtitles and punctuation.

The footnotes are mainly of three kinds. Some notes indicate the texts explicitly (or sometimes implicitly) referred to by Bourdieu, wherever it has been possible to identify them; in cases where it has seemed useful, we have added short quotations from these texts. Other notes aim to alert the reader to texts by Bourdieu, whether published before or after these lectures, that include developments of the topics discussed. Finally, there are notes that provide contextual information, for instance to explain allusions that might seem obscure to contemporary readers or those not fully aware of the French context.

Lecture of 10 March 1988

Internal reading, external reading and autonomy – Forgetting the microcosm – The coherence and normativity of the law – The space of works and the space of positions – A canonical text by d'Aguesseau – The invention of the public as a new sovereign

[The recording at our disposal lacks the start of the lecture. The length of the missing passage is difficult to estimate. To better understand the starting point of these lectures, it is helpful to refer to Julien Duval's essay situating 'Pierre Bourdieu at the Gates of the State', below.]

Durkheim said that there is one serious problem which the sociologist cannot approach without fear and trembling, which is the problem of the State.[1] This problem is all the more difficult because people are constantly giving their often wrong-headed opinions on it, and I fall back on this argument: the particular difficulty of sociology, as Durkheim himself said,[2] is that we are all amateur sociologists; we all think we have the answers to even the most awkward scientific questions. The problem of the State is inherently difficult, but in addition the State has never been such a subject of debate as it is today (nor the subject of so many silly opinions). This leads me to approach the problem in a negative manner,[3] obliquely, moving gradually inwards towards what I believe to be its centre.

After a certain number of preliminary considerations, I shall approach the problem of the law and more precisely the problem of how a group may come to proclaim how the world should be. For indeed it is of the essence of the corps of jurists to be socially mandated – and partly self-mandated – not only to state the facts of life, but also to proclaim what these should be. We are so used to them taking this upon themselves that it appears to be self-evident, but if we stop to think for a moment, there is something scandalous, extraordinary and astounding here: how can a group, however respectable, come to feel authorized to say what should happen in the social world? How can it mandate itself, or be mandated, to decide on questions of life or death? In other words, what right do they have to say what is right and lawful, or (the question that was raised in May '68, among other very good questions),[4] who is to judge the legitimacy of the judges?[5] Are the judges best placed to decree their own legitimacy? But put in these terms, the question is inadequate. It voices the rather ironic tendency which often motivates sociology and is its primary instinct. Although this critical tendency to look behind the scenes, to be suspicious of all wearers of wigs and gowns, does allow us to take the first steps towards establishing a science of the social world, it then becomes an obstacle to attaining a rigorous knowledge of that world. This is one of the questions that I would like to raise (but there will be others).

Before I launch into the details of my analysis, I would like to say that a social space like this one [the lecture hall of the Collège de France] is not very suitable for discussions and questions and answers, as you can imagine. And so, in order to promote a form of exchange that I would find extraordinarily useful, I propose to ask you, as I have always done in the past, to place on my table, during the break for instance, a piece of paper, either signed or anonymous, with questions or objections for me to answer. If it seems possible and easy to do so I shall try to answer straight away, or otherwise in the next lecture. In any case I find it psychologically important [to proceed like this], because all speech raises the question of its own legitimacy, and one way of feeling some slight justification in monopolizing speech is to have the feeling that you are answering people's questions. You will see that one of the texts which I intend to comment on today resorts to this form of legitimization, and even if we may doubt its scientific validity, this legitimization does have a psychological validity. So if you have any objections or questions, I encourage you very strongly to write them down on a piece of paper and place it on my table so that I can try to reply. I should point out that this procedure is important because, for reasons of time or professional discretion, I shall constantly suppose that you know things which you may possibly be ignorant of. So I insist, don't hesitate to raise questions even if you think they may be trivial or I: I questions are often the most fundamental ones and they might oblige me to fill in details or plug gaps I have left in my argument, or, as often happens to me, to admit that I simply don't know the answer.

Internal reading, external reading and autonomy

Now to start with, I want to recall the text that the different speakers at the seminar agreed to discuss:[6] it was an article on the notion of the juridical field that I had published under the title 'La force du droit' (The force of the law) in *Actes de la recherche en sciences sociales*, number 64.[7] The article is rather [*Bourdieu hesitates in choosing his adjectives*] defensive, abstract and obscure. I shall try to summarize its substance very briefly, as an introduction to the problem that I want to deal with today, while attempting to take the argument further.

In this text I try to show that the law raises an issue common to all learned discourse, or any discourse with claims to being universal, including philosophical and even scientific discourse, and, more generally, all forms of expression (such as painting and literature, for instance): to understand these particular forms of expression we need to avoid the alternatives that have shackled scientific debates up until now. For instance, in the area of philosophy, or even more in the area of literature, which have been relatively spared by objectifying analysis, two camps confront each other in a crude alternative based on the 'either–or' principle. The first position, whose recent form is what they call 'semiology', is occupied by internal analysts who claim that to understand a juridical or literary corpus, a poem, the work of a painter or a philosopher, you need to study the work and nothing but the work itself. The internal reading of the text taken in itself and for itself, considered as a coherent whole, must reveal what the text contains. The opposite, antagonistic position takes as its object of study not the text itself but the context, that is, the social space in which the text, or more simply the author of the text, is produced. This tradition has been illustrated by people like Lukács, Goldmann or Adorno on the subject of Heidegger, for example.[8] To simplify, this manner of proceeding consists in seeing the texts as reflections and, in the case of law, as tools: their discourse, corpus, codes and laws are considered to be reflections of social institutions or forces (society, the dominant class, etc.) and, as such, to serve as instruments for the social groups that they express.

In the case of law, the internal readers are to be found in the camp of the doctors. This is a property that law shares with philosophy: in both cases the specialists have monopolized the history of their discipline. In practice they are the only two corps that have established the history of their discipline as a separate science. The history of philosophy is an empire within an empire, it is independent, it is not taught in history classes. It is taught by philosophers in a very special manner, that is very different from the manner of historians. This private domain is one of the means whereby a discipline works to preserve its autonomy: none shall enter here if not a philosopher, none shall enter here if not a jurist. The history of law, like the history of philosophy, is monopolized by those who have paid their entrance fee to join what I call a 'field' and who accept the fundamental preconditions that you accept on entering the corps of philosophers or jurists. You don't even think about it; you find it natural for the history of law to be written by jurists or the history of philosophy by philosophers, and only philosophers, who rise up and cry scandal, denouncing reductionism or positivism, as soon as anyone who is not a declared philosopher ventures to study that special object, philosophy. This kind of postulate of autonomy is very important, and one of the objects that I shall investigate today is the constitution of an autonomous cultural universe and of a corps of people who are, almost literally, bound up with this autonomous corpus. [. . .]

[It is often useful?] to take an expression literally: when we speak of an 'internal reading', 'internal' signifies that the text is taken in itself and for itself, that is, read by people who are on the *inside* of the group of those who know that the text should be read for itself and in itself. The internal reading is the reading performed by those who accept the precondition according to which a text by Descartes, for instance, has been removed from history once and for all time, and I have the right to read it without having any idea who Descartes was. I can even profess that it is important to have no idea . . . thus Heidegger kept repeating that you should not take an interest in the author's world, that this world was of no importance, and he had a certain interest in saying this.

To be more precise: the internal, formalist reading is a reading that focuses on the text itself with its unique form, and only this. Internal readings are formalist readings that find their complete expression in pure theories. We should look into the possibility of a sociology of pure theories and the properties common to pure theories (Walras's pure theory of economics, Kelsen's pure theory of law, the pure theory of the State . . .). This topic would be worth developing at length.[9] Suffice it to say for the moment that these pure theories share a common affirmation of the pure autonomy of form (juridical, literary, etc.) from the social world in which it is produced, whereas, opposing them, the upholders of external reading, the reductionist approach, deny this autonomy of form, and claim they have the right as it were to pass through form as a sort of screen, in order to find what is being expressed under cover of this form. To affirm the legitimacy of an internal reading also means affirming the existence of a specific mode of thinking inseparable from a specific mode of expression, a specific form, and affirming the irreducibility of any pure discourse to its translation into any other language. To exaggerate a little, to make this easier to understand, we might say that ultimately the only legitimate discourse is a faithful paraphrase: we ought perhaps to analyse the discourse of the philosophical commentary and the role played in it by linguistic and syntactic mimicry . . . Thus they affirm the existence of a specific mode of thinking irreducible to the social conditions of its production.

One last property: this specific mode of thinking and this specific mode of expression derive their foundation from within themselves. As Kelsen said, there is no need to seek a norm outside the juridical world:[10] it is from within the law itself that the law finds its roots. This is another of the problems I need to consider: by proceeding in this way we solve the paradox of Baron Munchausen, which is I think the historicist paradox par excellence – founding a positive discourse on the social world, such as the legal discourse, without appealing to some ground outside this discourse, is to pull oneself up by one's own hair, and stay up there hanging in the air.[11] I am saying this in a rather caricatural way, but I think that the question of foundation, which is one of the noble and primordial philosophical questions, can be re-translated into this picturesque language, which is not without foundation (!). Pure theory is the ambition to suspend the system in the air by very force of the system. In the case of the law another *coup de force* is the passage from the positive to the normative, from the observation 'this is how things are' to the normative, from the sociological (or the positive and the observed) to the normative, from being to what should be.

This then is the opposition, reduced to its most simple, not to say simplistic, form. A remark in passing: the partisans of external reading display their indifference, whether voluntary or involuntary, to form, that is, to anything that might draw attention to an internal reading. The external reading tends to miss and even to ignore the specificity of different modes of expression, the specificity and irreducibility of form. For instance, one paradox of this tradition is that Marxist-structuralists like Althusser have paid no attention to the structure of the discourses that they sought to explicate using theories such as the theory of the State apparatus;[12] in short, the force of traditional reflection theory, of ideology, is such that, even in a structuralist period, this approach tends to cast form and the structure of symbolic systems aside, to focus above all on function. To put it in banal and elementary terms: the sociology of religion reduces religion to its function as 'the opium of the people';[13] it ignores the question of the very structure of the message that fulfils this function, as well as the more sophisticated question of knowing whether the structure of this message might facilitate the fulfilment of its function and whether it is not through, and only through, this structure – which might have the function of hiding the function – that the function is fulfilled (I am not being complicated on purpose; I remind you that these things are complicated).

If I insist on this simplistic opposition [between internal and external reading], it is because all you social subjects present in this room have it imprinted in your minds as an unconscious pattern; one difficulty in practising social science being that we have in our minds a whole host of oppositions of this kind which function continually and which serve as a screen filtering all the messages we receive: everything that I say will be perceived through this opposition, and while I am speaking you will continually be consciously or unconsciously changing your minds as to whether I am situating myself at one pole or the other, whereas I shall be trying to overcome this opposition, which does not mean that I shall totally succeed, because I too have had this pattern in my mind. We need to overcome this opposition, not in a syncretic manner that judges both camps to be right, as in philosophy essays (where the third part offers a kind of soft synthesis of the first two [*some laughter*]), but by finding a way of avoiding the alternative.

Forgetting the microcosm

This preamble was important because it helps me introduce the idea that, to understand science, philosophy and, in this particular case, law, what enables us to escape this alternative is taking into account what I call 'the field of production' (here, the judicial field). For the two camps that I have described do have in common their unconscious ignorance of a social reality that is extremely important for understanding the workings of a text – the space where it is produced, debated and commented upon, the space where people fight over books and paintings, etc. The internalist tradition generally mentions this space only rapidly and partially, in snippets: for instance, discussing Renouvier's philosophy, they will mention in passing the fact that he was a student at the École normale in some particular year, when X was one of his fellow students.[14] You might expect the external readers to be more attentive to this universe, but in fact they too pass over it in silence, they repress it just as much, as a psychoanalyst would put it, because, following what I call the logic of the short-circuit, they move directly from the texts to society in general or, as certain jurists would say, to the 'social groups' (this is the expression to use when you don't want to say 'social classes'), strangely consigning to silence the social universe where the special truths promulgated by learned discourse are produced.

In the case in question, this social universe is what I call 'the juridical field'. There are various possible definitions, but I shall give you only a few, complementary ones. The juridical field is a social universe in which people struggle to say who has the right to say what is right and lawful. It is a social universe whose business is the law: the law is a business, it is an important affair; those inside this field have law as their business, as opposed to those outside the field who have nothing to do with it, who are indifferent to it. Being inside the field means being able to tell the difference between two statutes, being ready to die for the difference between two decrees, whereas somebody outside the field would not even grasp the issue. In a philosophical field, it's the same thing: people will stake their lives on an ontological difference. Ontological difference is a very serious problem and I understand why people are ready to die for it, but what I am driving at is the fact that when you are in a field you are fashioned by it. It would take too long for me to do it today, but it is very important to tease out the implications of what it means to be the member of a field, what it means to 'belong'. One property of membership is the fact of not being indifferent, of not saying, 'I don't care', 'it's all the same to me', 'I can't tell the difference'. Conversely, those who lack the cognitive and judgemental faculties to detect and tell the difference, are indifferent; they attribute no more value to one thing than another, they are like Buridan's ass.[15] This indifference is a sign of non-membership, whereas not being indifferent, but investing in the business of the field, is on the contrary a sign of belonging.

This means that having interests in the game is a sign of membership. My use of the word 'interest' is often misunderstood, which leads people to quote me saying some very silly things on the subject. So I shall speak in Latin [*some laughter*]. (As I always say, language is one of the great problems faced by social scientists: they are obliged to speak in a language that has been devised in order to avoid describing things as they really are. Sociology has to fight against the language that is the vehicle of discourse on the social world but at the same time masks it. . . .) Since the word 'interest' immediately makes us think of Bentham or Stuart Mill, among others, I shall prefer to speak of *illusio*, drawing on a false etymology (I am repeating something that some of you may have heard me say before)[16] that has been attributed to Huizinga. In

Homo Ludens, Huizinga said that we may understand *illusio* as the fact of being invested in a game, of being involved in a game, of being interested in the stakes that are at issue, that are in play, in a game.[17] This is precisely what I mean by a specific interest (for there is no other kind of interest – when people read me, they always forget that I point out that I am referring to a '*specific* interest'). It is because of his specific interest that the jurist is not indifferent to what is at stake in the juridical game; he has a specific competence, a specific capital, since competence may also function as capital, to tell the difference where others would not, and at the same time to invest in the game (the word 'investment' may be taken in its economic sense). When a field is in crisis this means that its specific capital is threatened. If for example the teaching of Latin in *lycées* is suppressed, its value as cultural capital collapses. This specific competence is what enables us to distinguish differences, and thereby leads us to invest, in the economic sense. The acquisition of a juridical culture is thus an investment that will bear profit over a lifetime. This economic investment is at the same time a psychological investment, but I shall not develop that point here.

That is more or less what I mean when I speak of a field. Both internal readers and external readers forget the existence of relatively independent social universes that we might qualify as 'microcosms' (the 'political microcosm' described by you-know-who[18] is one of these universes). For once this is a good metaphor: a field is a microcosm that is relatively autonomous in relation to the social cosmos; it has its own logic, it doesn't exist in a vacuum. The illusion of the internalists is to believe that this microcosm is entirely autonomous, as if it existed outside of space and the force of gravity. A microcosm is relatively sheltered from external pressure and demands. The law is relatively independent of the demands of the prince and the public. Inside this universe, as I have just said, specific interests and forms of capital and power develop; those possessing the rare competences that are engendered in this universe acquire an instrument of power in this universe and often beyond it. Fields, then, are the site of the production of specific forms of capital, of specific authority and rarity. They are also the site of specific power relations which are not relations of brute force between classes, as the externalists would have it, but power struggles taking the form of conflicts of competence, [even if?] ultimately there is no philosophical struggle, however abstract it may appear, that does not bear some relation to social conflict.

The coherence and normativity of the law

The jurists affirm the autonomy of their juridical norms. They speak of a juridical science [. . .]. I shall not develop this point here, because it was developed at length in the article I drew your attention to, but one property of this rule-bound game is to produce coherence. To different degrees and in different guises according to the times and the society, the juridical field is organized in such a way that the interested (in the sense of betraying a specific interest) struggles that arise there tend to produce coherence insofar as they are placed under the sign of recognition of the systematic nature of the corpus of rules in the name of which we fight, and insofar as, to have the last word in a juridical struggle, you need to have the system, coherence and the law on your side. A juridical struggle is defined by the fact that it is a combat which you can only win if you have the law on your side; to participate in a juridical struggle is to accept the tacit rule of the game, that you leave violence at the door and you fight with the laws as your weapons. Just as in mathematical struggles you don't act like the Roman soldier who kills the mathematician or the physicist,[19] so in juridical struggles you use no force other than the force of the law. They are struggles in which you recognize the force of the law and you reinforce the law by using no force other than the force of the law. This is the paradox of the juridical field. These properties that we find affecting the system, meaning that these systems are apparently motivated by a kind of tendency to self-compression, to increasing systematization, are properties that the internalist readers, succumbing to a Hegelian vision, place *inside the system*[20] (this remark would also be valid for mathematics, for the notion of *épistémè* . . .):[21] there would be a *Selbstbewegung* of the system, a self-development of the system in the direction of systematization. But this problem is not inherent in the system: it occurs in the system when it is at stake in the struggles between people who recognize the system as an instrument of struggle. And it is because you have to choose to use the system if you want to struggle in the juridical field, that you work on the coherence of the system. I shall not take this first point further here.

The second point is more complicated. It deals with normativity. How is it that the juridical system produces what has always been considered, in particular by philosophers since Hume,[22] something like a *salto mortale*? How is it that we can pass from 'this is' to 'you should' or 'you must'. We could say that the juridical field, like all fields, is a site of social alchemy, of a sort of transmutation: on entry you have social forces and arbitrariness, and at the exit you have the universal.

(I am simplifying somewhat, but if we can't simplify for oral discussion, when can we? One virtue of oral communication is that it enables you to say rather simplistic things, then correct them or say that they are simplistic. That is why I don't want to be recorded [*laughter*]: in the recording, particularly in the playback, you only notice [the simplistic things].)

This social universe in which the norm is produced has to face the question of its own foundation. Kelsen, who is one of the major founders of the pure theory of law, has followed a Kantian logic in trying to construct a pure theory of law, refusing to import any positive, positivist ideas. He sought out the fundamental norm, the basic norm, the famous point that you could use to pull yourself up by your hair.[23] For my part, I would say that the fundamental norm is the law of the functioning of the field: it is in the law of the functioning of the field that we find the only possible historical foundation of the provisional originality of the law, and the same is true of philosophy and science, for instance. To try to justify what I have just declared, I would refer very briefly to Kant's *Conflict of the Faculties*, which I often invoke as being what I consider an important contribution to the sociology of science.[24] Here Kant distinguishes what we might call temporal faculties (the faculties of theology, medicine and law) from what we might call spiritual faculties (arts, philosophy and the sciences) and he opposes these two classes of faculty according to the grounds of their authority. (I am giving you my rereading of his text from memory, but you can refer to the original yourselves.)[25] The authority of the temporal faculties is based on a delegation of temporal power: the doctor, advocate, judge and theologian are mandated by a temporal power to do what they do; ultimately they are mandated as delegates or plenipotentiaries of a power. Kant's text provides an inkling of a sociological foundation for the emergence of the question of foundation. The non-temporal faculties, on the other hand, are not mandated. Having no foundation outside themselves, they are obliged to face the question of their foundation: how to found my authority if I can't say 'I am mandated', 'I am authorized', 'I am guaranteed to conform', by the State, for example, which has them in its gift? The spiritual faculties could not evade the question, and Kant's merit, historically speaking (afterwards, things became metaphysical, with this notion of *Grund* [foundation] inspiring pathos), was to face up to the kind of destitution that the spiritual faculties find themselves confronted with once they know that they are no longer delegated and can no longer derive their foundation from within. In this sense Kelsen is very Kantian: he confronts the problem in the case of the law, which, of all the cases concerned, is no doubt the most difficult to find a pure foundation for. The jurist may well avoid asking himself the question faced by the mathematician or the philosopher. But Kelsen does put the question: he looks for a specific mode of argument, an absolute beginning, the equivalent of the *cogito*, a first fixed point giving us a starting point from which we can elaborate a chain of reasoning.[26] He attempts to found a general theory of norms by making the jurist the founder of the fundamental norm from which he deduces all the particular norms. Ultimately, the central idea of what I am arguing is based on the theoretical work of Kelsen.

As often happens in the autonomous fields, Kelsen raises to the level of a conscious and explicit programme of research something that is an ongoing process in the field of production, and what I now want to show is that the juridical field established itself progressively over a period of time as a self-founded or self-founding universe, bearing its own foundation within itself, through a whole series of struggles with the Church, the princes and the royal powers, etc. What we call the autonomy of a juridical field has been the product of a collective process of representation and a collective conquest, which Kelsen retranslates into theoretical terms and tries to reproduce on the theoretical level. Retracing the whole history of the process of autonomization of the juridical field would be an enormous undertaking, and I cannot do this in a few lectures. I shall simply use two or three examples to characterize the logic of this process of autonomization, emphasizing two aspects that seem to me to be equally indispensable for a field to become autonomous and self-founding, or at least for it to be capable of giving both those who participate and those who don't the illusion that it is self-founding. On the one hand a corps and a field become autonomous, and the corps that become autonomous as they produce the field produce precise norms which they use to break off their relation of dependency on external authorities. The jurists work to establish the juridical field as a juridical order (the word 'order' is important: think of the Order of Advocates, the Order of Doctors); establishing the autonomy of a discipline requires an effort of self-discipline in all the senses of the term. This work has a long history. We could give an almost yearly account of the relentless work of codification of the rules of the game in the juridical field through which that field provides itself with a collective and autonomous foundation. This is why I want merely to mention it: there are immense treatises that I have only been able to thumb through superficially. On the other hand there is a symbolic work at the level of representation which is no less important ([ignoring this] is yet another of the illusions of primary materialism) and which leads to giving the social agents engaged in the juridical field (advocates, magistrates, etc.) a mental representation of their practice.

The space of works and the space of positions

Thus I distinguish two levels. There are codes, texts and laws, and social agents who handle, benefit and profit from them. Exponents of the most pure anthropological tradition nearly always confuse culture as an objectification of mental structures – an ensemble of tools, practices, techniques and styles of thinking – with culture as the social space within which mental structures are used[27] (I am saying too much or too little, but I could not avoid saying at least something). In relation to this tradition, the notion of field has the merit of saying that it involves a social level: there are judges, magistrates, barristers, advocates general, prosecutors, institutions and associations and struggles between these institutions, and these agents fight over posts, rewards, specific stakes and monopolies, etc. Within this social universe, where a whole lot of social action occurs, we see the emergence of a universe of discourse, produced, reproduced and transformed with its systemic properties (properties such as coherence, the tendency to persevere in being, to continue and perpetuate its existence), properties that it owes, I believe, to the logic of action on the social level of struggles, conflict and competition, but the two levels should be clearly distinguished. To clarify: I distinguish between the space of positions and the space of stances adopted, that is, the space of positions held by the agents in a space. If, for example, you describe the philosophical fields in France, you will note that there is a hierarchy of academic positions and then, alongside these university positions, there are journalistic positions; some philosophers hold only a university position, others hold at the same time positions in journalism, etc. We can also undertake a sociology of the space of positions and the power relations between the agents who hold these different positions, with the hypothesis that knowing this space of positions provides a basis for understanding the standpoints they have adopted, that is, what they variously write, the forms or styles they use and the quotations and references they make, whether some of these are in German or English, etc. So we need to distinguish these two universes quite clearly and not exclude the hypothesis that the universe of standpoints may be independent of the universe of positions, since it is through this independence of the standpoints from the positions that a cumulative progress towards the universal may be engendered. I would even go further: if cumulative progress there is (as there evidently is in the scientific fields, but also in a philosophical field), it is because the tacit entrance fee to a learned field is mastery of its past and present standpoints, mastery of the specific culture needed to be able to play the game; it is through mastery of this specific culture – which itself becomes an instrument and a stake in the struggles between agents who, having paid their entrance fee, are engaged in the field – that cumulative progress can be produced. Here is a simple example: a motor of 'progress' in a field may be the tendentiously universal posture that leads new entrants to challenge the dominant in the name of those properties of the space of standpoints that the dominant have repressed or downgraded. I can use a simpler language if I take the case of the religious Reformation. The reformists make use of the specific capital (the gospels and other canonical writings) to proceed to a return to the sources, to the pure and the foundational, and thus produce a revolutionary effect in the name of the truth of the tradition. This form of change is I think the most frequent in the fields of cultural production;[28] it consists in playing on the independence of the space of standpoints from the space of positions and drawing on the thesaurus of knowledge acquired by the collective memory of the field to produce subversive effects within the field of positions.

What is important for the analysis that I offer, which differs from the theory of systems,[29] is my very clear distinction between the space of the works whose corpus forms a quasi-system and aims in fact to be systematic, and the space of positions within which the strategies of the juridical agents, liable to use a reference to the system with its coherence and rigour as a weapon, are defined. [. . .] For me, the system of juridical forms, or at least the ensemble of norms that claims to form a system, is independent of the space of positions. Incoherence is one of the weapons that can be used against a system claiming to be systematic: its claim can be turned back against it. It is through such cunning that the universal progresses. We could speak of the cunning of reason[30] (because what is at stake is understanding how reason is born in history). The major cunning of reason in the social universes as I describe them is to turn back against a system the weapons that the system itself provides, to turn back against it the identity which it claims as its own. When the universe claims coherence, the chief means of attacking it is to criticize its incoherence, or to pursue the consequences of coherence to an extreme which could enable conclusions to be drawn that would not normally follow from the premises.

So we have a system. Or a quasi-system. The notion of quasi-system is relatively important. Religions, for instance, are quasi-systems;

vague, fuzzy systems which achieve their impact both through their fuzziness and their systematicness: if they were completely systematic or completely incoherent, they would not function effectively. I think that this is true for the law too. In fact you could no doubt establish a hierarchy of quasi-systems, from the most fuzzy to the most precise, where I would place law in the middle. In juridical struggles, accusations of incoherence play a crucial part, and among the side effects of defending their honour (another example of the cunning of reason) when a corps of scholars is entangled in the rules of their own game, the claim of deduction arises. In the article that I have mentioned,[31] I also quote two or three texts that are splendid examples of the professional ideologies of self-promotion of the corps: jurists with philosophical pretensions attempt to show what is the proper mode of juridical argumentation; they attempt to found juridical deduction as a totally rigorous form able to subsume particular cases encountered by the magistrate under universal rules. Nine times out of ten this juridical deduction is an *ex post* deduction (they have taken the decision first and they make the deduction afterwards), but it is an example of the cunning of reason: presenting as the result of a deduction what has been the result of an intuitive decision by the habitus is an extraordinarily important phenomenon. Ultimately everything I am saying could be summed up by the famous proverb: 'Hypocrisy is the tribute that vice pays to virtue.'[32] During the recent seminar, on the subject of the Cour de cassation (Supreme Court of Appeal), Alain Bancaud spoke of what the jurists themselves traditionally refer to as a 'pious hypocrisy'.[33] In fact my whole reflection turns on wondering whether pious hypocrisy, as the tribute paid to virtue by vice, might not be a contribution to the progress (still provisional and historical, of course) of juridical virtue.

To consider this point for a moment: we have a quasi-system of quasi- or semi-coherent norms, or norms claiming at least to be coherent, then a regulated universe of people playing for stakes and struggling for power in the ambit of this system, with the rules of the game forbidding them from spurning pious hypocrisy and saying: 'All that is not worth a penny.' The Roman soothsayers couldn't watch each other at work without laughing,[34] but (a very important rider) [only when they were] alone. This cynical view makes us laugh and helps us understand, but it also falsifies [our understanding], for in order to be effective, the Roman soothsayers had to believe in it and not even think for a moment: 'Hang on, this whole set of rules is senseless.' Having taken a decision according to their laws which flout coherence, regulations and laws, they need to strive wholeheartedly to clothe their decision with nominally juridical reasoning. They had in a way to appeal to the logic and coherence of the system. In so doing they did something extremely important: I think that whenever we accomplish one of these pious but hypocritical acts we make a little progress towards the universal. This is something that I had not appreciated at first. In fact it is difficult to understand, because we practise sociology at first for the Nietzschean pleasure afforded by a semi-skilled demystification; it is only with time that we accede to a third level of initiation. The semi-skilled forget that we can't produce representations of the universal without involving ourselves in the game of the universal.

To sum up. The construction of an autonomous juridical field is the product of an extremely long collective labour, which does not see itself as an end in itself. This last point is essential if we are to avoid succumbing to the illusion that I call worst-case ('the dominant class is becoming more and more dominant') or best-case ('it's the progress of reason') functionalism or finalism. Sociology leads us to clarify the effects of actions, but it never says that these effects have been posited as ends by the agents who have produced them. The most powerful social effects are often those that have never been consciously posited by any subject, and all the effects that I am going to describe have as their subject not individual social agents but the field. (So then you will say: 'What is this field? It is monstrous.' Nowadays we might say 'It is totalitarianism.' I leave to those who say this kind of thing the responsibility for what they are saying, that is, the utter irresponsibility of their comments.) It is (almost physically) difficult to write a rigorous social history, because linguistic habit leads us to say, 'X did this, for that reason', whereas we ought to invent another kind of language, along the lines of 'this occurred, and its effects were . . . and he entertained intentions which . . .'. It was Max Weber who had the most acute intuition of this logic of the historical process. He somewhere compared history to an absent-minded little girl who intends to go somewhere but goes somewhere else, and while on the way forgets what she meant to do or decides to do something different from what she thought she had wanted to do.[35] This metaphor gives an idea of what needs to be done, but in fact things are much more complicated: we have to remember that there are a lot of people who are doing a lot of things, who are doing things that they don't realize they are doing because the space in which they are doing them, which they have helped to form and continue to form by doing what they are doing, has a logic that transcends what they are doing and thereby constantly escapes what they think they are doing. That doesn't mean they are stupid and don't know what they are doing: they have intentions and from time to time they have a quasi-sociological view of their universe.

From time to time, some people do understand. In any case the people who dominate such complicated fields have a practical mastery of what I am describing; for instance, Heidegger could only do what he spent twenty years doing because he had a prodigious practical mastery of the philosophical field whose existence he denied until his dying day; he could have borne exemplary witness to this process.

This then is the logic of what I shall attempt to describe: in these social universes a whole lot of things occur that are regulated, without people following any regulations. They are places of regularity where there is no person as a subject; which does not mean there is no subject, for this is not structuralism: agents do do things, they constantly have aims, projects and intentions, they are not robots. But the systems of action in which they move are so complicated that the effects are irreducible to their intentions and the sum of their intentions; we need to take into account the structure of the universes within which these intentions are deployed. For this reason the least worst formula, even if it is simplistic, is still the one that I used just now: if there is a subject, it is the field.

A canonical text by d'Aguesseau

To return to the main issue (I am constantly obliged to digress, because that is the price to pay for successful communication). A relatively autonomous space that I call the 'juridical field' gradually establishes itself. It is a site of struggles in the name of the law and through the law, and its autonomy will be a gradual conquest: the juridical field will become a closed field, the gate and the boundaries will gradually close, and the entry fee be raised ('Let none but geometers enter here':[36] you don't enter if you don't know your maths, you have to pay the entrance fee; if you try to solve a theorem with a revolver they will eject you, if they can [*laughter*] . . .). The jurist will place barriers at the entrance and display a representation which will be the entrance fee: you will not enter unless you believe that what we call the legitimate representation of the law is true.

I had planned to start by telling you very briefly how the rules concerning the profession of jurist evolved, but I think in the end that it is more interesting to start with an example of the learned elaboration of juridical discourse and the representation of juridical activity. I don't want to disguise the fact that I am not a great specialist in the history of law, but I have been struck in my research over the last few years by the fact that the magistrates and judges often refer to a famous text written by a magistrate, the Chancellor d'Aguesseau. This text must be very special to have become a sort of canonical scripture, a sacred text for people to quote. I went to consult this text and was astonished at what I found there. I shall give you the reference because obviously I won't be able to give you all the details. The author is the Chancellor d'Aguesseau. [*Bourdieu comments on the name as he writes it on the board*:] It was originally written 'Daguesseau' as one word, then it was written with a 'd'': that is part of the sociological make up of the character [*laughter*]. His first name, Henri François, is also important: he belonged to a family of jurists, for canonical writings were not the province of a newcomer. The text is taken from a work in twelve volumes.[37] I shall not pretend to have read them all: I have read this major text, and then a few others whose titles seemed interesting to me. This text was an inaugural lecture for the opening of parliament held in 1693. Its theme was the independence of the advocate,[38] the advocate being a sub-category of a larger category, the parliamentarian, the man of the gown. In fact it is a text on the autonomy of the advocate.

Since philosophers have started to write history, we have tended to consider texts taken right out of context: we found them somehow or other in the Bibliothèque nationale, we give the date of the text, then we read it and comment on it. This is a typical internal reading. I myself have made only the minimum study of the context, but I did at least go to look into who this personage was. To be absolutely true to the method that I preach, I should situate him in the juridical space, track down the sources he refers to, see what the allusions he makes signify, etc. I did just enough work to give an indication of what ought to be done and to feel authorized to distinguish myself from those who practise random readings of texts taken out of context. (You can imagine the advantages of diving into a very rare document – nobody knows Chancellor d'Aguesseau, apart from some jurists who aren't here with us. This is one benefit of the autonomy of fields: it is a text that is very banal for one discipline but very rare in another. If we apply the traditional technique of philosophical reading to it we can pull a number of rabbits out of our hat and thus offer a type of cultural production which is widely practised in France today, but which I don't rate very highly. I am telling you this in passing because after all it is an opportunity to say what I think in public and because other people very often say what they think about what I say, when I can't answer back [*laughter*].)

Who was the Chancellor d'Aguesseau? To put it briefly, he was of noble legal lineage: there were three generations of magistrates and intendants in his ancestry. His father was an intendant and counsellor

at the Parliament of Metz, and then Counsellor of State (this is important, you will see why), and he had married a woman born from
another line of magistrates, the Talon. The chancellor himself married
a woman from the legal nobility, the d'Ormesson. The fact that some
of these names are still current is not without interest.[39] In fact (to
anticipate my forthcoming argument a little), I think that this argument will help to establish a theory (that is implicit in my argument)
whereby public service and public welfare at certain moments suit
the interest of certain social categories, and these social categories
(people whom we call 'technocrats' nowadays) are interested parties in
serving the general interest as they themselves define it, and in so doing,
can help to express things that go beyond their immediate interests.
(I think that, at least when we are speaking of the social world, we only
say things that suit the general interest if we ourselves have an interest
in them – which raises the question of the interest that I have in saying
what I am saying: since I have just realized this, I feel bound to tell you
[*laughter*] . . . I think that I could answer [that question].)

My information comes from a canonical book by Marcel Rousselet,
Histoire de la magistrature française, des origines à nos jours:[40] the
Chancellor d'Aguesseau was one of the most famous magistrates in the
history of France. He was a 'brilliant student', as [Rousselet] says in
his book, with prowess in Greek and Latin from a very early age: this
precocity is also an important property for understanding his discourse
(I could have done it the other way round: read his discourse and then
revealed the properties of the author, but I had to choose the order
. . .). He completed all the canonical studies, but also some stranger
things: Hebrew, and modern languages, which were not studied in
those days. He received a very strict moral education from his father,
as described in detail in [Rousselet's] book. He was very precocious:
he started to study Roman civilization when only seventeen, and the
discourse which I am going to comment on was pronounced when he
was twenty-two or twenty-three; he became Advocate General and
finally the equivalent of Minister of Justice. He considered Justice to be
something sacred. He made his name in 1696 through his role in a very
famous trial (which is important in relation to the text that I am going
to comment on) which opposed the prince de Conti and the duchesse
de Nemours. This was a trial between two grand figures, that is, a
situation where Justice rises above temporal grandeur, where judicial
dignity is able to affirm itself as superior, while showing respect, and
on condition that it shows respect. D'Aguesseau takes the opportunity
to pay homage to the great names, but he says: 'Stripped in its presence
of their external advantages, they come to lay at its feet [*Bourdieu clari-*

fies: at the feet of Justice] the radiance of their dignity. They submit all their grandeur to the empire of the law, to hear from its oracle the certainty of their fate.' He continues: 'Let us then leave to those who are lucky enough to be simple spectators of so illustrious a dispute, the pleasure to note that an individual affair seems to have become a public cause; that the interest of the one is taken to be the interest of all; and that if judgement is divided, at least the intentions and wishes are conjoined.'[41] In fact this marks the triumph of the jurist who consecrates the universalization of individual interests and the transcendence of juridical interest over temporal powers. He develops a long argument about the fate of families. Commentators have noted the most conventional points, and those linked to his background and training: the rise and fall of great families, the shame it is that we have to discuss acts perpetrated by the descendant of a great family when he has lapsed into senility, etc. But in fact the true intention of this debate is to affirm the superiority of justice and the *dignitas* of justice (whose origins have been traced by Kantorowicz)[42] over the temporal dignities represented by the nobility. D'Aguesseau was finally appointed Lord Privy Seal and Chancellor, in acknowledgement of his merit as a technocrat.

I was looking for something else when I came across this document from 1693 rather by chance, and there are probably many other documents that could help us reconstruct the progress of the ideology of the public good and public service, which seems self-evident today and is even taught at Sciences Po (somebody should research the history of the origins of the public good). I am now going to try to describe how the procedures used by the text work. On a first reading, there is a screen of Ciceronian rhetoric, which leaves the impression of a pompous, tedious discourse in a judge's wig, opposing vice and virtue, passions and interests. When you have read Hirschmann,[43] the text appears very typical of the seventeenth century, and you see the emergence of the notion of interest in the modern sense of the term. D'Aguesseau does oppose passion to virtue, but he says that we can only fight a passion with another passion, that there are rational passions that should be used in the service of reason to advance reason (which is more or less what I have been saying) . . .

However, when you read the text more closely, one thing does capture your attention: the word 'public' occurs a dozen times, used in a very modern sense. And this makes it slip by quite unnoticed, although in fact it is very strange in this context. This anachronism is a trap that sociological analysis easily falls into: when we try to reconstruct the origins of a field, the most important words are the most modern ones, and for this reason they are the most likely to go unnoticed, because we forget that in their [original] context they were extremely rare. It is the same when we try to understand Manet, despite the fact that he is relatively much closer to us: we apply to people who have achieved a symbolic revolution the categories of perception produced by this revolution.[44] In the present case, when this man who fought to give an entirely new foundation to Justice (invoking neither God nor king) says 'public', it seems self-evident enough to us; but this is partly because so many people have repeated: 'As Chancellor d'Aguesseau said, the only foundation for Justice is the public, Justice belongs to the public.'

If we take another look at the word 'public' in this context, its usage is very strange: 'He can no longer take any rest without it being fatal to the public.'[45] This is a variation on the theme of the misfortune of the great, who are reduced to voluntary servitude, who don't have a moment's spare time for themselves (a theme that we still hear today [*laughter*]), their life is one long servitude. There we have a first strange indication. The magistrates, who are one of the categories who suffer this great stress of having no time for themselves, suffer from this lack of time because they have the feeling that any time they take to look after themselves, or their children, etc., is stolen from the public. There is already between the lines the idea of a total service, of a total gift to the public. Today they would say, 'I have gifted my person and my time to the State',[46] but in d'Aguesseau's day it was not to the State but to the public, and it was against the State that this public service needed to be constituted. 'He can no longer take any rest without it being fatal to the public: he reproaches himself with taking the most innocent pleasures, because he can only enjoy them by taking time away from the time devoted to his duty.' *He is a slave*, 'glory brings even heavier chains to bear'.[47] This sentence seems once again to trigger a rhetorical opposition: 'glory' is straight out of Bénichou's *Morales du grand siècle*,[48] where the great pay for their access to glory by being in chains. It is against the egregious servitude of the ordinary great, that is, the nobility (whence the importance of the 'd'),[49] that true greatness will be constituted, the greatness that suffers from not having enough time for the public. The ordinary great enjoy an illustrious servitude to society values and games. This anticipates Norbert Elias, whose famous argument in *Culture and Civilization* draws on Kant, among others, to describe very well the inversion of society values in the small German courts, the discovery of the serious and the profound, of academic values against the values of civilization.[50] (I shouldn't have mentioned that, it's too soon, but still you might now read Elias, thanks to me.)

[In d'Aguesseau's opinion] there are on the one hand the chains of servitude which lead to the accumulation of social capital, at the expense of some social effort, since you need to maintain your connections. I refer you to a recent article by Monique de Saint Martin:[51] even today an aristocrat like the duc de Brissac has to work quite hard to reproduce his aristocratic capital; it is servitude and chains; his lustre, glory and brilliance have to be paid for and require a certain expenditure of time. On the other hand, there are those who accumulate economic capital through business and who enjoy a less illustrious servitude. And then there is another character: the 'philosopher', for whom the price of freedom is obscurity. How do we square the circle? The magistrate's position of representation requires brilliance, he absolutely must dazzle, he cannot gain freedom through obscurity. He cannot achieve his freedom through obscurity, but only through public service, and he will gain that independence by his joint refusal of worldly commerce and commercial business, through a double asceticism regarding social intercourse and business affairs. This double opposition will be based on what is commonly called virtue, without any qualification, but which becomes explicit if we look at the text in the light of the notion of disinterestedness. In fact the collective foundation and the norm for the juridical microcosm, as d'Aguesseau defines it, is disinterestedness. The fundamental law is: 'You will be free if you are collectively disinterested.' It is not a Kantian, individual virtue, but a virtue that we might call Hegelian: it is conformity to the order of the jurists. The order of the jurists imposes the rule of disinterestedness on the corps of the jurists, and it sanctions any lapses from disinterestedness, that is, those who succumb to the temptations of money and sex, the two being closely linked, as they are in all the orders of the clergy who pay for their right to freedom with their virtue in these two domains (as we see in the extreme case of the monk with his tonsure).

How can the magistrates win their independence collectively? (I would like to keep quoting the text but it would take too long.) They can do it through virtue, that is, by enslaving themselves to justice. And they are predisposed to do this because they owe their position to their merit alone. There is then an ideology, an explicit eulogy to merit which in our day would be based on the invocation of academic achievement or educational distinction. Here [the magistrates propose] a combination: 'We are serious people, we work very hard, we owe our rise only to our work, we are the "self-made-men" of virtue, disinterestedness, sacrifice and study, we share with the philosopher the fact that we have paid for our symbolic exhibitions of eloquence copiously with our obscurity, labour and erudition.' In passing, there is a very fine passage where d'Aguesseau contrasts eloquence with erudition:[52] he says that not everyone possesses the gift of eloquence (he doesn't use the word 'gift', but we can read it between the lines) that makes the great magistrate or the great advocate, but the opposition between the advocate general, who in those days prepared the dossiers but did not appeal at the bar, and the advocate is artificial: erudition represents virtue as much as eloquence does, even if one requires genius and the other hard work.

> We are then the fruit of our labours, and as such, we embody virtue, [which] can render noble even a man without birthright, rich a man without possessions, elevated a man without dignities [*the temporal 'dignities' are the privileges of the nobleman*[53]], happy without the assistance of fortune [. . .]. Virtue is the principle of your independence [*this is the key axiom*]. Merit is inseparable from glory [*whereas for the ordinary nobleman glory is a glory without merit*]; [. . .] the man who is the sole author of his elevation holds all other men in the dependency of his enlightenment [*here we detect the emergence of educational capital ('enlightenment')*]. Those distinctions founded only on the chance of birth, those great names that flatter the pride of common mortals and dazzle even the wise, become useless resources in a profession where virtue is the source of all nobility, and where all men are esteemed not for what their fathers achieved but for what they achieve themselves. When they enter this famous corps, they leave behind them the rank assigned to them by worldly prejudice, to attain the rank that reason assigns them in the order of nature and truth.[54]

Here there is a symbolic process of constitution (this word is important): a group is constituted through the constitution of its fundamental norm, and the constitution (in the juridical sense) of the group of jurists is: 'The principle of your value is your virtue.' To continue: 'Justice, which opens the way to the bar for them, erases even the memory of this discrimination that is injurious to virtue, and makes no distinction other than the degree of merit of those that she calls as equals to the functions of the same ministry.'[55] They are then equal: theirs is a collective virtue, subject to collective sanctions, and any infractions are collectively punished.

The invention of the public as a new sovereign

Riches may gild another profession [*the parallel with our educational meritocracy is patent: while avoiding anachronism, I do think that this is an ancestor of the École nationale d'administration (ENA)*]; but our own profession would blush to owe its prestige to them [. . .] Work shall give you what nature has withheld [. . .] Freed of the yoke of avarice, you will aspire to goods that are not subject to its domination [. . .] Merit, which is our only ornament, is the only good that cannot be bought; and the public, whose vote is always free, bestows glory, but will never sell it.[56]

This passage is very dense and very modern. For us today 'the public' evokes 'public opinion' or the audience in a theatre, but these notions did not emerge until the eighteenth century (an American historian has shown how the press and the tradition of the salons brought a sort of public opinion for painting into being, constituting a lay judgement for matters of taste),[57] so we need to be careful [not to project them onto this text]. 'Merit, which is our only ornament, is the only good that cannot be bought; and the public, whose vote is always free, bestows glory, but will never sell it.' This is how the process of symbolic constitution works: you create a transcendental reality which then becomes the objective foundation of a judgement concerning your nature: 'I declare that an irrefutable agency, the public, says that I am what I say I am.' This is an operation of alchemical transubstantiation ('the public, whose vote is always free'). What is important are the virtues that are attributed to the public. Firstly, as I have just noted, the public replaces God and the king. The public becomes the focus of a conjuring trick (which isn't one, because it has succeeded) which amounts to saying that the public is always right, that the public has the right vision because, being free and virtuous, it is able to freely recognize virtue; in the public we [the magistrates] find support. This is the famous Baron Munchausen syndrome: the public provides the Archimedean point which will enable us to leverage our microcosm out of the path of historical contingencies.

The word 'fortune' is also interesting. This is another very ambiguous word; its origin is Latin,[58] and it is used rhetorically. That said, once it is used in an opposition it becomes perfectly clear. One key that I often use is a very amusing concept used by the philosopher Austin, the 'trouser-word':[59] certain words ('real', 'serious', 'virtue', etc. – all words needed for marking dissertations)[60] only take on their full meaning when used with another very important concept, which is not named but 'wears the trousers', and which through its existence will determine the sense of the concept used. Thus the word 'fortune' is a subordinate concept which only takes on its full meaning in relation to the trouser-word that determines it: 'fortune' is opposed to 'public', 'merit' or 'virtue', depending on the context. Fortune is something that falls from the heavens, something not merited, something that happens to noblemen. It is distributed without regard for merit. It is venal, it does not reward virtue. The public then is the anti-fortune: it celebrates the merit of a person; so that in celebrating it we are celebrating an agency that is just, and we constitute ourselves as just, because we are celebrated by this just agency that celebrates us. We understand what is meant by the fact of saying that we respect the public good or that nothing is more legitimate than serving the public . . . Since the public good – which I may discuss in more detail next time – is both what is good *in the eyes of* the public and what is good *for* the public; the idea of public service recalls the Platonic idea of the philosopher king who knows better than the people what is good for the people.[61] In fact the technocrats and epistemocrats[62] use the name of this new sovereign, the public, the *vox populi*, to say what is good for the public, and the public cannot object, because it is they who have lent it a voice. This is what I call the 'oracle effect'[63] exercised by the intellectuals (we should always be suspicious of the intellectuals when they say 'the people think . . .'). This effect alerts us to the suspicions which I mentioned just now, and which are useful for this analysis (but, to avoid seeming to contradict myself, I repeat that through this oracle effect, the Pythias are hoist by their own petard; they are obliged to reply in a certain way, which circumscribes their responses).

To continue for a moment in this vein. The public is able to distinguish between true and false foundations of reputation. It is able to recognize people who owe everything to fortune and absolutely nothing to merit.

> The public, who know what your time costs, dispenses you of the duties that they demand of other men; and those whose fortune always attracts crowds of admirers come to offer you the prestige of their dignity and submit themselves to your decisions, and await from your counsel the peace and tranquillity of their families.[64]

> All your days are marked by the services that you render to society [*Society is the public*]. All your occupations are exercises in rightfulness and probity [. . .].[65]

Bancaud, in his seminars,[66] insisted strongly on the rightfulness of the jurists: to have the right to lay down the law, you must be law-abiding. I shall give plenty of examples of sanctions against the failure to be rightful.

It is still the case however that we may wonder how to situate this new sovereign, the public, in relation to the real sovereign. A properly trained historian cannot fail to think of this. That said, a forceful text stands out from its context. A well-constructed text becomes self-sufficient, and it takes a lot of contrary energy to manage to read its unspoken message. For example, this text does not mention God. How is this possible in such a Christian era? In fact it does mention God, but in such a strange manner that it is worse than if it did not. It is impossible not to think that it is saying: 'As an independent corps, we know that we are virtuous, and that we must be virtuous, that we are subjected to the public, but other corps might forget this.' It does say this in so many words, but its objective tone is in fact normative, which is another cunning of an ideological discourse: 'Man is never more free than when he has submitted his passions to reason and his reason to justice.'[67] We say, 'What rhetoric!', but he goes on to develop a whole argument about the nobility and kings: 'The most noble images of divinity, the kings, that the scriptures call our earthly gods, are never greater than when they submit all their greatness to justice.'[68]

At a time when powers emerge that could be foundations external to the juridical corps (they could invoke delegation, for instance: I hold my power from God or the king, or from the divinely empowered king), the public comes to fill the gap: 'God is dead, the king is dead, long live the public good!' I (i.e. d'Aguesseau] speak indirectly of the king to say that he is himself subject to justice and that he is never so great as when he comes to submit to justice and the public good. If he does so, it is because he recognizes (a term which I use here in the Hegelian sense) the legitimacy of those who lay down the law, because he recognizes their virtue, and it is through their virtue, that is, through the discipline they impose, that they impose recognition of the discipline they impose. I shall stop there, but it would be as well if you could read the document for yourselves.

Lecture of 17 March 1988

Common sense and the feel for the game in a field – The transfiguration of common sense into specialized meanings (sequel) – Producing a love for the game – Two other questions – The double historicization – The Jansenist influence and the problem of self-love – Inventing the public: the oracle effect – Producing the universal with individual interests

Common sense and the feel for the game in a field

I shall not reply to all the questions that I have received, firstly because there were some that I was unable to read (I must ask those who are writing little notes to make the effort to be legible), and then because in some cases I think that I have already replied, or intend to do so.

A first question, which is too long for me to read out, is about agents belonging to more than one field and the question of belonging to fields as opposed to belonging to the ordinary world. The question may seem rather technical. One property of the audience here [at the Collège de France] is its great diversity and I obviously tend to be interested in the questions that I find most interesting because they inhabit a universe of problems close to my own. This question, then, concerns the relation between an analysis of the function of the fields and an analysis of everyday life of the kind that ethnomethodologists propose when their project is to describe the experience of everyday life. This question alone could take hours and hours to answer but I shall try to reply rapidly: the little that I shall say will be better than nothing, at any rate for the person who is asking the question and for those of you who share the same interests. The same person has drafted another question, concerning the place that sociology can allocate to emotions and passions: are the passions included in the analyses that I have accomplished? The two questions are obviously not disconnected. They draw on a problematic that is slightly different from mine, and they can only be raised within what certain contemporary epistemologists would call another paradigm.[1]

[I shall start by making clear that] what we call 'competence', the ensemble of learned skills that social agents deploy in their everyday practice and which enable them to avoid being run over in the street or to predict in a more or less reasonable (I won't say rational) way the behaviour of other agents, has been very well described as early as Aristotle (sometimes the philosophical reference is a useful way to silence the babble of certain false claims to be original). In fact, this practical competence which in my language I would call the 'sense of practice' is what Aristotle called *phronèsis*[2] (conventionally translated into French as 'prudence',[3] but this is not a very good translation). It is the mastery on the practical plane of patterns of perception, action and appreciation which, briefly put, allow us to make our way in the world. We can also call this sense of practice a 'feel for the game', but there we are moving on to something that applies more to the specialized social fields: the sense of practice as a feel for the game enables us to anticipate the unfolding of events in a social universe. It is a kind of adjustment to the procedures of the social world and its immanent tendencies. This anticipation is based on an unconscious adjustment (which is expressed in the notion of 'habitus') and allows us for example to be in the right place at the right time. So we can talk of a sense of 'placing', emphasizing the double meaning of the word 'placing', both in terms of the 'place' of a sportsman (on the pitch) and in terms of 'placing' an investment in the stock market.

(Such play on words is not a Heideggerian tease. It is useful because one of the problems with these notions is the fact that they designate something that is traditionally ignored in philosophical language. My reference to someone as ancient as Aristotle was no accident: in fact philosophy has paid very little attention to practice. I shall speak off the cuff for a moment and no doubt shock some of you once again, but even the Marxist notion of *praxis*, which seems to talk of practice, says very little about it. When my German translator asked me about the title of my book *Le sens pratique*, I rejected the word *praxis*,[4] because in my eyes *praxis*, at least in its usage by those who speak so much of *praxis*, is almost the opposite of what I call 'practice'. That was a brief parenthesis, but I think that these little digressions, which use a kind of metadiscourse to express the deeper intentions of my work, are likely to be of interest to some of you.)

 Lecture of 17 March 1988

Since the philosophical tradition has been erected in opposition to what we designate today as a 'sense of practice', this latter becomes difficult to name and even describe. We could trace a genealogy in the history of ideas of the opposition between theory and practice, between the philosopher and the man in the street. There is a whole philosophical tradition based on these oppositions, which have become mental structures and topics for students' essays – which are one of the media through which topics become mental patterns. The difficulty in thinking of practice lies in the fact that we have to probe more deeply behind these categories of perception of the social world. This is something that I believe I share with the people called 'ethnomethodologists'. I did some work along the same lines as Garfinkel, at about the same time, in a book called *Le sens pratique* [translated as *The Logic of Practice*],[5] which has not found very many readers (for those of you who don't know it, and are interested in that aspect of my work, it is the book where I tried to explain a certain type of theoretical foundation of my research). When we want to think of practice, we lack theoretical resources, and for good reason: the theoretical tradition has been constructed in opposition to it. Luckily there are one or two fellow travellers. Heidegger, for complex reasons that helped to make him a Nazi, took an interest in some things that had been abandoned by the philosophical tradition, in particular our practical relation to the world, which the theoretical tradition leaves aside.[6] People like Wittgenstein have also reflected on things that are fundamental for a sociologist or an ethnologist, and perhaps even more for a sociologist of law or a jurist: What does it mean to follow a rule or obey a rule? Does having a regulated way of life necessarily mean that one obeys the rules? Is all regulated behaviour the result of following the rules?[7] The notion of a sense of practice aims to reply to these questions[8] and to remind us that we have a non-theoretical mastery which does not take the form of explicit knowledge, but does make our social world liveable in. Moreover, one of the tasks of sociology or anthropology is to help indigenous agents explicate their practical mastery of the immanent laws of the social universes which they navigate, and in which they show reasonable (not necessarily rational) behaviour, insofar as they have more or less successfully internalized the logic of these universes. The prime example is our practical mastery of the mechanisms of language: we know how to say 'here' and 'there', how to use deictics correctly, and this mastery is so extraordinary that it would sometimes take several hours to explain a specific use of the word 'here'. In other words, we bring to our practice, without knowing how, an immense pre-knowledge that the phenomenologists would call pre-reflexive and non-thetic, and I agree with the ethnomethodologists that one of the great tasks of the social sciences is to render these things explicit.

But the question that has been put to me raises an issue where I differ very markedly from the ethnomethodologists (I am not seeking deliberately to distinguish myself, for I had never thought of this relation before reading this question – which is why I find it useful). What is the relation between the sense of practice employed by the agents who harmoniously navigate fields such as the political, scientific or intellectual ones, and the sense of practice that the same agents would call on in their daily lives to cross the road? The virtue of the notion of a field and the use of this notion by sociology is to remind us that the social world in which we live is differentiated. The analyses that I published in *The Logic of Practice* were essentially anthropological and ethnological, and were based on anthropological material – research into Kabyle society. I relied on the practical mastery acquired by social agents in an almost undifferentiated social universe where there is not, for instance, a juridical system or field, and where, since the major division is the division of labour between the sexes, there is no division in the work of domination. In such a universe, the practical patterns that orient practice are not constituted as scholarly schemata, they are not transformed by the kind of alchemy that the different fields operate. We could then say, in the language of the question put to me, that in such societies the sense of practice is a common sense:[9] what you need to know to live in this type of society is to a certain extent evenly distributed. In fact this is never entirely true, since there is already a division in the labour of symbolic production. I had underestimated this point at the time I was writing *The Logic of Practice*. I discovered it a little afterwards, in particular in my conversations with Mouloud Mammeri, a Francophone Kabyle poet whom some of you know and who has worked hard to make what is called popular Kabyle poetry known.[10] He has discovered a popular poetry which has all the properties of learned poetry: you only have to translate it to think of Mallarmé, which should present a problem for those who think that 'popular' means 'simple'. So on this occasion I discovered something that I had vaguely intuited but had not found room for in my analyses, largely because I had internalized the unconscious models that ethnologists import into their objects ('they are all the same', 'their universes are hardly differentiated', 'there is no initial accumulation of cultural capital', 'culture is more or less evenly distributed', 'everybody speaks in more or less the same way, in the same language', 'everybody is fairly equally well-informed', etc). In these societies, there is already a primitive form of accumulation of cultural knowledge, and, for example, an elementary division of religion work between the shamans and the ordinary people. In the case of the Kabyle, alongside the ordinary people, there are poets capable of 'giving a purer sense to the words of the tribe'.[11] They are capable of playing with words, of doing a Heidegger on Kabyle proverbs; they do things that are highly sophisticated, intellectual and refined. (I am going from digression to digression, but these digressions are not disconnected from what I intend to say.)

I think nevertheless that we could say that the sense of practice is a common sense in societies of this type. Certainly in these societies there does exist a division of labour in symbolic production, but it is not very pronounced, and the difference between the poet and the non-poet, between the most specialized and the most ordinary of men, is not radical. It is not comparable with the difference that today separates a professional jurist and an ordinary plaintiff pleading his case, or a layman and a specialist. These trivial things are important. Max Weber has written remarkably about the fact that in our societies we can only master the world by proxy, through delegation to specialists; for example, at the moment of death, we entrust ourselves to the scientists.[12]

These apparently trivial considerations are also significant for the understanding of the problem I am discussing: what is the relation between a science studying common sense, as ethnomethodology might, and a science studying the specialized common senses which are implied by a theory of fields? (These are complicated problems, but now I have started, I might as well continue. . . .) It seems to me that the sense of practice used in everyday life has something in common with the sense of practice used in the specialized fields; you can only really find your way around a specialized field if you master the immanent laws of everyday life; you have to elaborate the strategy of a career just as you learn how to cross the road, feeling that it 'goes without saying' and not elaborating it as a conscious strategy or a rational, calculated, intentional and interested project. Moreover, I still find that ethnomethodology gives the impression that it studies things on a more universal level [than my way of proceeding]. This is why, rather like anthropology, it touches some philosophical nerve. If I tell you that I am going to describe the functions of the juridical field in d'Aguesseau's day and age, which I mentioned last time, you will find my project historical, or historicist. The intention to explicate the fundamental structures of the practical competence deployed by any agent in safely negotiating the everyday world seems, to put it naively, more philosophical: it seems to discuss things that are more universal,

fundamental and general, and it appeals to a tradition (Husserl, etc.)
... I think that the special charm of this mode of thinking depends
partly on the fact that it glosses over the (equally anthropological)
question of the different forms that this sense of practice will take, in
different universes.

That is what I wanted to talk about. Our societies are differentiated
societies, and one of the fundamental processes producing them is
the process of differentiation (not to be confused with the process of
division into classes) which gives rise to their separate universes, their
orders (one of the aims of these lectures is precisely to say how the
juridical *order* came to be constituted), and the small empires within
empires of the social world, sub-universes which have their own laws.
The principal difference between the societies that ethnologists study
and those that sociologists study seems to me to turn on this question
of differentiation. But taking note of this process of differentiation
leads us to devise a theory of the constitution of these universes, to
study first of all the process of autonomization and the specific logics
of these different universes before going on to enquire whether there
might not exist invariant trans-field laws between fields, such as the
mathematical and the juridical, for example.

There remains the fundamental problem of the relation between
the specific competences employed in navigating these fields and the
competence employed in navigating the ordinary world. I have been
thinking about this for some time but I do not find the expression
'common sense' entirely clear. This banal expression, which seems to
have lost all meaning, can take on a stronger sense if we remember
that everyday experience and the practical competence that we employ
in navigating it may perhaps not have exactly the same status as the
practical competences that we employ in the other fields. The former
has a certain priority, which is what makes the ethnomethodologists'
research interesting: it is the basic competence which the various specialized fields draw on, more or less totally, depending on the degree of
separation of the fields.

To explain. I often say that certain types of intellectual construction
should be related to the intellectual field where they are produced, and
I insist on the fact that these intellectual constructions, in particular
in their linguistic dimension, are often based on a false delineation.
I don't want to rehearse the details of my argument on Heidegger[13]
(knowing that we could choose other examples), but I did show that
he used quite a complex network of meaning based on phonologi-
cal and semantic play (on the word *Fürsorge* ['solicitude'/'welfare'],
etc.), and that this intellectual play with meaning gave an impression

of autonomy: Heidegger's philosophical discourse claims to be self-sufficient, and irreducible to what is ordinarily expressed using the same words. Heidegger, who had a fine sense of social strategy, often said: 'Don't make me say what I am not saying; when I say *Fürsorge*, I am not saying "Social Welfare".' He denies it, but his text keeps repeating it. In fact it constitutes a discursive network that is partly independent, with its own oppositions that oppose, not the large and the small, but the authentic and the inauthentic (an analysis of the juridical system would give exactly the same result). This kind of symbolic system produced by specialized fields based on a partial or even a false division retains an organic link with common sense: the oppositions of common sense remain present. A philosopher of law whom I quote in my article on law[14] understood this, and said that you cannot understand legal language if you don't have a mastery of ordinary language, just as you cannot understand the shamanic language of a traditional society if you have not mastered that society's ordinary language. That said, the common language is alchemically transfigured, and passes from the exoteric to the esoteric. The semi-autonomous fields are rooted then in everyday experience, and the 'symbolic' (rather than 'ideological', a word devoid of meaning) effects that you can produce with a poetic, philosophical or political language are nearly always based on a kind of double play on the esoteric and the exoteric meanings, that is, on its meaning within the field and its meaning outside the field. In an article entitled 'Le champ religieux'[15] [*the audience laughs when Bourdieu spells the word 'champ' (field) to avoid confusion with the 'chant religieux' (religious song)*], I try to show that the fundamental oppositions which form a religious quasi-system can only function properly because they are rooted in everyday oppositions such as large/small, weak/strong and dominant/dominated, while giving the illusion of being autonomous. There is more of a problem with fields that are much more autonomous. It seems to me that the symbolic systems within the very advanced scientific fields, such as the space of mathematics, for instance, are open to an ordinary sociological analysis, without forasmuch being directly reducible to the oppositions of everyday life. Here we can no longer make a direct reduction and choose between two scientific theories, even biological ones (this did happen a few years ago . . .) by using oppositions taken from everyday life (I don't want to expand on this, but I did want, as on other occasions, to mention this problem because there is bound to be someone among you who might think that I hadn't thought of it [*some laughter*]).

To return to my problem, which I don't think I have lost sight of. The problem posed by the existence of fields is the articulation of the sense of practice germane to these fields with the practical competence current in the ordinary space around them. Ethnomethodology does not even posit the problem, because it fails to acknowledge differentiation, and therefore constitutes the ethnology and construction of everyday experience as the alpha and omega of social science. Which in fact makes it very primitive, despite its rather sophisticated airs. I am saying what I think . . . (even if I do also have very positive thoughts about this important and interesting tradition). Those of you who are particularly interested will certainly have further questions: you can pass them over during the break and I will reply on another occasion.

The transfiguration of common sense into specialized meanings (sequel)

I shall now move on to the other set of problems, which is not unrelated to the first, and which leads more directly to the problem of disinterestedness which is the underlying theme of these lectures (as I was saying, one of the aims of my research into the genesis of an autonomous juridical field is to discover the procedure leading to the constitution of a universe where people take an interest in disinterestedness). The author of this question asks me: 'How can we practise a sociology of the passions, emotions and affections, while accepting an analysis in terms of the field? Do the emotions result from the agents incorporating their interests into the games and stakes of the field, which they experience in the guise of emotions?' [*Bourdieu notes that he may have misrepresented the question, because he was unable to read it*] . . . The question contains part of the answer, and that may be why I approve of it [*some laughter*] . . . It reminds us how naive it is to denounce my work for its theories of interest or neo-utilitarianism.

I must point out in passing that this criticism makes no sense. Yet I do understand why people may say things that I find nonsensical: I try to overcome the opposition between interest and passion, and I find people putting a question based on the difference between interest and passion. As I so often have to say, it is the fate of efforts to overcome common-sense oppositions (as I have just defined them) to be constantly kicked back into the ball park of common sense by 'intellectuals' who are applauded by the upholders of common sense because they wind the clock back to zero. This is a strategy of the type that I was describing in the case of d'Aguesseau: they appeal to the public's understanding to call into question what I see as scientific facts, which are inevitably acquired at the expense of common sense. This is one of the specific difficulties facing the social sciences. I hesitate to say more, for fear of straying too far from my programme, but this is relatively important. The social sciences find themselves in a distinctly peculiar situation, which exposes them to forces attempting to drag them downwards. This is how I see things: the specialists attempt to rise above common sense. As scientists always have done, they attempt to rise a little by casting off the guidelines of accepted ideas, ordinary oppositions, presuppositions and preconstructions. But this effort to call common sense into question, which has its place in the French epistemological tradition (Bachelard said that 'primary truths are primary errors'),[16] is particularly awkward for the social sciences. Common sense was on the defensive in the age of Galileo ('The Earth does not turn, it's impossible, we would know', and so forth), but when the social world is at stake it is much more energetic, firstly because the stakes of the enquiry are vital (they are real, worldly stakes, they are interests in every sense of the term: as Marx said, the interests of the Church of England are at stake),[17] but also because there is a permanent alliance that I have just briefly mentioned between common sense and bad scholars – to state my opinion frankly – those who cannot fly can always call on those left on the ground for help in saying that those who have taken to the air are in the wrong . . . and it works! [*laughter*] You will find numerous examples concerning sociology in the weekly and daily press. (I could make a subtler argument, but I prefer to express myself more polemically and aggressively, to make sure that I am understood, and to avoid appearing to plead my own cause . . . That was a parenthesis.)

Common sense is a special case because it constitutes the common ground. Here we could encounter phenomenologists, who in fact understood this much better than their wretched American disciples (here again, I reveal my personal opinion). Speaking of a common ground, of an ordinary, native ground, has Heideggerian connotations which are not always very appealing, but it is important. Common sense is the place where fundamental experiences are rooted, where the founding patterns of perception are constituted (large/small, high/low, masculine/feminine, hot/cold, etc.) and continue to function, in forms transfigured by the specific alchemy of each field, in the individual universes, or, to use Husserl's language, in the regional spaces. This is why an analysis of the ordinary sense of practice in the form of common sense is particularly important, as long as it is conceived, not as an exercise in style for campus revolutionaries,[18] but as an analysis of the *doxa*, that is, of everyday political experience. Common sense is full of politics, and phenomenology as I describe it here is one of the foundations of a science of politics. It is against a background of *doxa* as experience of fundamental values and beliefs that the operations of political alchemy unfold. You only have to think of the passage from *doxa* to orthodoxy, which consists in a transformation of beliefs in a practical, non-thetic, unconscious state into explicit, justified beliefs (I shall not develop this point, because I have often discussed it here before).[19]

I think that I have said not only what I think of this common sense but also the significance I attribute to ethnomethodology, which we should have encountered twenty years ago but has only now turned up to wreak its havoc in France[20] . . . As always, France is one of the countries where people are least ready to read those things that need reading, when they need reading. I'll return this on another occasion.

Producing a love for the game

I have not lost track of my argument. As I was saying, the question about the sociology of affectivity contains its own answer. The other day I said that instead of saying 'interest' we might just as well say '*libido*', '*illusio*' or even 'investment',[21] but the word 'interest' indicates more of a break. Chancellor d'Aguesseau teaches us that Pascal's self-love is simultaneously love for the fatherland,[22] and that there is no function finer and more admirable than his, in the service of justice. Saying that it is in his interest to say so is obviously rather rude and reductive. It is what I would call a semi-skilled work of reduction. But it is nonetheless very important, because otherwise we accept the flood of words (even more so if it is a philosopher speaking) that sweep us into playing the game of misrecognition, that is, of recognition and legitimization. Let us say that there are cases where it would be in our interest to say: 'he is interested'. That said, the word 'interest' is dangerous because we give it the very limited significance that emerged with the utilitarians in the eighteenth century, exactly the period that I have evoked very superficially through d'Aguesseau, and which is a historical invention associated with certain societies and certain moments.

In which case, it would be better to use a more general word, like *illusio*. The *illusio* is the relation that arises between a social agent who has a feel for the game, and the game, which leads him to ascribe value to the game for the simple reason that he is born in the game and he wants the game to continue so that he can continue to play and largely dominate the game, for instance. It is a form of interest, but it can be extraordinarily disinterested. This kind of analysis enables us to understand why, for instance, you can 'die for the fatherland' (the very fine title of a book by Kantorowicz)[23] or, as d'Aguesseau is basically saying, die for justice. There is no act more disinterested, but there is an interest in dying for your country (sad to say, but I have to say it . . .). It is however a very peculiar type of interest, which is lived as a passion, and can be experienced in the manner of an unconditional, absolute espousal of a habitus and a field, in a kind of mysterious, quasi-organic reaction. Here we might use Heidegger's language: it is a relation of ontological complicity between two forms of the same thing; that is, between a field and a habitus which has resulted from internalizing the rules of the field. When a feel for the game encounters the game, the players at every moment make the exact moves required by the game; they are pleased to do so, and the fact that they are pleased contributes to their success. It is plain to see that a love for the game (as implied by the notion of *libido*) is one of the conditions of their success in the game. I hope that you can see what connects these comments; I am rather afraid you might think they are random, whereas there are links . . .

For instance, the procedures of co-optation which the dominant in a field tend to use to reproduce the position that they hold, and which are fundamental to the reproduction of the corps, in the social sense of the term, very often take as their criterion a love for the game: what the candidate needs to show at the entrance exam for the *agrégation* or the ENA is a love for the game that he is going to have to play. One way of producing a love for the game is to select players who are born in the game. For instance, a considerable proportion of those who end up as inspectors of finance are sons of inspectors of finance.[24] The Claudel-type puns that went the rounds of the *khâgnes* [preparatory classes for the *grandes écoles*] on 'connaissance' as 'co-naissance'[25] [knowledge/ in the family] could be relevant here: you know the game because you are born into it, and because you are born into it, you find the game natural and innate, you have the gift, which is not just a specific competence, but a disposition. Your love for the game can be detected from imperceptible signs: your tone, style, manner of speaking, accent, etc. The love for the game is what is demanded above all by the group, because someone who loves the game is not going to upset the apple cart; he will be a very good propagator of the game and will help to perpetuate it because all of his behaviour is predicated on the future of the game; he will rejoice in this future and anticipate the future of the game in advance.

We should realize that it is also a passion (even if this is not my normal idea of what a passion is). In *Homo Academicus* I present the book in passing as a 'treatise on the academic passions'[26] [*laughter*].

It was a way of amusing my colleagues and getting them to swallow the pill (a noble reference makes it go down more easily),[27] but I also think that it is true. A sociology of the university world[28] studies trajectories, careers and investments: it asks why you would want to be a member of the CNU [Conseil national des universités], the CNRS [Centre national de la recherche scientifique] or a board of examiners for the *agrégation*? Why do you accept under duress, saying that you were not able to refuse? Social agents do not rush to take these positions by force; they are so predisposed to fill these positions the social world obliges them to take, that they can claim to be sincerely disinterested. I am very annoyed to be so often treated as a kind of purposive sociologist (you know: 'As soon as he entered secondary school he was aiming at the Collège de France' [*laughter*] . . . that was not a random example!). This passionate disposition seems to me to merit the name of a 'passion'. We need a broader definition of affectivity: there is an academic affectivity born of the relation between academic dispositions and an academic field, and there is a scientific affectivity, among others. We return to the problem of the relation of specialized common sense to intellectual common sense.

Why might a general sociology of the passions not be a sociology of the invariant mechanisms that we find in the different nosologies of the passions that correspond to the different fields? That would be a way of studying the problem of the relations of sociology as I conceive it to psychoanalysis (I don't know what is happening to me, I didn't intend to say all that and I surprise myself). If it is true that there is a founding *libido*, which proposal I don't judge because it is not my concern, and that there are regional *libidines*, that is, forms of the founding *libido* that are alchemically transformed, then we can understand that the patterns of analysis borrowed from psychoanalysis often clarify very well what happens in the specialized fields, without psychoanalytic analysis being forasmuch sufficient or suitable. If you bear in mind that the essence of the logic of the fields may well be to function on the basis of the common drives and conventional strategies employed by common sense, then we can understand how we might be led to practise differential sociologies of the *libidinal* urges motivating the strategies of the different fields, and that these regional sociologies also call for a sort of general sociology of the passions, which might unearth a number of things that psychoanalysis takes for granted. I don't know if you have found all that completely clear – I haven't! [*laughter*] . . . That said, I think that this sociology of the emotions might allow us to investigate in a contrary direction: rather than start out from a sociology of the common sense emotions of the ordinary *libido* in order to understand the *libido sciendi* of the scholar, it might perhaps be better to start out from these regional *libidines* ... You are going to say that this is perverse, but that is the problem with attacking common sense: you need to upset some things because the alternative process is too easy and has so often failed. My topsy-turvy way of approaching the problem may in the end be a more natural research project. At the same time I should explain more fully how the specific *libido* is constituted and through what alchemy the interests are constituted as passions for the subject himself and for others. This is something that I intend to do in studying the Chancellor d'Aguesseau: I shall try to show that, in order to reveal a sincere experience of individual interest in the general interest (which is what d'Aguesseau's text discusses), we must firstly have the institution of a game – where the general interest attracts our interest because love for the general interest is positively rewarded by glory – and, secondly, a love for the game. The interest in being disinterested, experienced as a passion for disinterestedness, is the junction of these two processes, which in this particular case produces a juridical *libido* and a universe in which this *libido* (which does exist) is rewarded. This dual analysis would have to be applied to every social universe. I shall return to this point.

Two other questions

That then was my reply to the first question. Don't ask me this kind of question every time . . .! I shall answer the others quickly, before taking a break. Someone is asking me: 'Why not a sociology of sociology?' I was going to give a euphemistic reply, but time is pressing, so I shall just say that this is a typically semi-skilled question. I am constantly giving hundreds of signals: what I am saying applies to me, the speaker, and to the universes in which I am saying it. I would even say that the main interest of studying universes homologous to the one you work in is that you can do with them things that would be more difficult in the case of a universe where you have too many interests and passions invested. Studying universes that are close enough for the analogy to work but distant enough to avoid things becoming too painful, you can hope to find things that you would not otherwise find. The person who put this question about 'a sociology of sociology' should look at my book, *Homo Academicus*.

A more complicated question: 'Is there a science of law?' In fact, everything that I am going to say will render this question irrelevant. That is not to say that the question will not arise, but that we need to investigate the 'science of law' as a social fact: who believes that there is a science of law, what is their interest in believing it? What I am pursuing is a science of law, but it is not a juridical science of law: the science of law is the site of a struggle, within the law and outside of the law.

Another question concerns the infinite regression: who will judge the legitimacy of the judges, and so on? This is the essence of the learned fields and it is the Baron Munchausen problem:[29] what is the foundation of the foundation? The question of the ultimate foundation, of Kelsen's *Grundnorm*, looms large in all the fields, even including scientific fields like mathematics. Wittgenstein for instance resolves the problem of mathematics with a solution very close to the one that I propose, by saying that the foundation of mathematics is the fundamental norm of the field of mathematicians.[30] I think that there is no other foundation, unless you are a Platonist and believe in eternal essences. Sociology does not overlook this problem, but since it cannot take up a position, it does not discuss it, even if that lays it open to accusations of positivism.

The double historicization

I now return to what I was saying about d'Aguesseau last time. I came across him more or less by accident, and I must say that I did not know what lay in store for me; I made discoveries as I went along. As you all know, the tradition in this house is not one where the teacher dictates a structured pedagogical spiel that you note under (a), (b) and (c). Here I am going to stray even further from educational tradition and offer teaching that is closer to what I believe it should be according to the historically defined tradition, that is, teaching based on research where the professor is not content just to recount the state of the problems or the established standpoints, but tries to present the state of his research, including all its uncertainty and even confusion. The example of d'Aguesseau is typical: I found his text almost by accident, as always happens in research. Coming across so many references to this character that I knew nothing about, I wanted to read some of his writings, and that was when I discovered things that fitted in with the overall orientation of the research that I had presented here some years ago on the genesis of the notions of public well-being and the general interest.[31] Within the limits of the time at my disposal since the last session, I have tried to understand better who d'Aguesseau was and the universe in which he evolved. That said, I initially considered analysing this text as a contribution to what we might call a professional spirit, a juridical spirit that seemed to be an important element in the genesis of a field (often when we talk of a 'spirit' – a 'mathematical spirit', a 'juridical spirit', etc. – we touch on things of the type that I have been trying to describe [on the subject of the constitution of fields]). The work of d'Aguesseau seems to be an important contribution to the elaboration of a juridical spirit and, more generally, the elaboration of an 'ideology' of public service.

I did not realize how right I was, because what I have come to learn about this character has led me to discover a work that the history of ideas has unfortunately not explored very much. This work began in the Renaissance and mobilized very different people, from Montaigne to Rousseau, and including Charron. These extremely different people are in fact never studied in this light, at least in France, largely because of the divisions between disciplines: some, like Montaigne, are studied in literary history; others, like Rousseau, are shared between literary history and the history of philosophy; authors like Charron belong to nobody; d'Aguesseau is studied in the history of law, Bodin belongs to Sciences Po . . . There is then a universe of things that I find formidably and fundamentally connected, and a space of standpoints that is never studied as such. This happens frequently in what we call the history of ideas. The inertia of academic traditions which continue to accept studies of the 'life and works of' kind means that we can know everything about the relations of a particular agent with a system, without ever knowing the system, which leads us to know nothing, because the nature of a standpoint is to exist in a space of standpoints and not to tolerate standing in isolation. That does not mean that the biography of d'Aguesseau that I have consulted, for instance, is completely useless. (I am saying things rather abruptly, to strike you, because in my eyes one of the roles of education is to try to make some changes not only to academic mores but also to scientific mores. For instance, the bibliography that I have found useful is nearly all in the English language; my disappointment is not motivated by any nationalism, it is merely an objective observation. . . .)

When I read [d'Aguesseau's] text for the second time, armed with some better knowledge and a little more historical culture, I discovered a whole field. Last time, I told you that d'Aguesseau mentioned the 'philosophers', but I think that this is a rhetorical device: these 'philosophers' had personal names, even if they are not named. D'Aguesseau spoke of these people in rhetorical terms no doubt for reasons of euphemization, because we know only too well who he is referring to, but this leads us to read these texts [today] as if they were timeless. This encourages a literary or philosophical reading which claims to be a-historical but is quite simply anachronistic. There is an anachronism specific to historians and I think that few sciences are more inclined to anachronism than the science of history (may my historian colleagues forgive me . . .). The texts that we find interesting (we should be interested in the word 'interesting' in this particular case) and which excite our passions are often the texts which speak to us immediately, which have something interesting to tell us about the problems that we are facing today. This is already a source of anachronism, because the questions that we ask them were no doubt not those that they themselves were asking. What I am saying is banal. Ethnologists have this kind of question constantly in mind, but historians much less, particularly when they appeal to ethnology, which happens frequently nowadays. Intuitions founded on the projection of questions are a trap laid by ancient texts, and I think that it is a sociology of reading based on the notion of the field that can help us understand the motivation of an interest that feels itself to be universal, timeless and transhistorical.[32]

Let me make things clear with an example: in former times (today it only happens in disguised form) they gave you a quotation from Pascal or Voltaire to discuss in your dissertation, and you were asked to take sides, or to comment and discuss, and so on. You could answer with the minimum of *libido academica* that was needed for a dissertation but, if you invested in the dissertation and you made a stand, I suspect that it would often be on the basis of a homology of position: you argued against somebody as Pascal argued against Voltaire. To be more precise: the most transhistorical things are the structures (which makes sense if the notion of the field is true), that is, the oppositions. Chancellor d'Aguesseau and a student at the ENA have nothing in common, the latter is wigless and has no Latin, etc. But the differences of condition (the salary, the lifestyle and conditions, the manner of speaking, etc.) can have radically changed without forasmuch the properties of position, that is, the structural properties in the social space, having changed. I like to take a simple example: when Proust takes sides with Balzac against Sainte-Beuve,[33] it is on the basis of a homology of position. He argues [less against Sainte-Beuve than] against the critic who fails to understand what he is doing. The classic procedure of 'rehabilitation' has to be analysed afresh in the light of this logic. The operations involved in rehabilitating the *Iliad*, which had been scorned by a generation of professors, or making 'restorations' (the Musée d'Orsay,[34] etc.) in every sense of the term, are often performed on the basis of a homology of position involving an affinity of interests ('interests' in the very broad sense of the term that I constantly use).

If we can naively take a stand on the texts of the past, then, it is often because the oppositions expressed in these texts are still alive for their readers and commentators. This is where a sociology of sociology is crucial and where we need to practise what I call a 'double historicization'. I am not the first to say so, Gadamer has said it too, but with a very different emphasis.[35] It seems to me that, very strangely, the only way of escaping anachronism is to historicize both the source material (the text and its author, etc.) and the reader of the text, particularly in order to be on the lookout for the effects that I was talking about: an immediate understanding on the basis of a unchecked relation. (Since examples of this kind of error are bound to be very polemical, I prefer not to give one, but I can assure you that the greatest scholars are liable to fall into the trap that I have just described in abstract terms.) It seems to me that what I have just told you needs to be really taken to heart by those who are researchers or aspire to be.

Let me explain this 'double historicization' a little more, to avoid it becoming some kind of slogan. To start with, I have to say, unfortunately, that the methodological programme contained in these two words is almost infinite: we rarely have a culture profound enough to put this concept completely into practice (which means that history will continue to make progress . . .). The object continues to transcend the person attempting to know it, for in order to escape the trap of anachronism we would have to know so much that we would often capitulate before we get to know enough. But I think it is important to remember that ideally we would have to know a multitude of things to understand a text, whereas it is comparatively easy to show off and appear to be clever . . . What I am saying here runs against the whole tradition of textual exegesis that transforms the limits inherent in the condition of the teacher, and the obligation to start explicating a text on a Monday morning, into methodological precepts. It is not true that 'it is enough to be able to read'. On d'Aguesseau there is a whole programme of research, a whole universe of erudite research that I have seen open up before my eyes, despite using only the paltry erudition that I was able to acquire in a week. That is what I wanted to get across to you, to get you to feel how much you ought to know to be able to comment adequately on a text. I shall return to this notion of public well-being in the lectures to come, and perhaps in a year or two I may be better able to present you with the successive states in which these notions have been produced, both the states of the field of standpoints and the states of the field of positions.

I must also tell you that double historicization supposes that first of all we reconstitute at the level of the text (it would be the same for a monument, a document or a statistic, etc.) the space of contemporary standpoints ('contemporary', that is, temporally related in the broadest sense, relevant to the moment under consideration). The reconstitution of the space of the contemporary standpoints that were effective, active and relevant corresponds to what is traditionally done in a good history of ideas: you need to know what A or B thought, identify who d'Aguesseau meant by 'the philosopher', and so on. Having reconstituted the surrounding discursive space, you need in a second phase to reconstitute the space of the agents who fought over and around these debates, and produced the discourse. I said at the start that it was in d'Aguesseau's interest to universalize this notion of interest. Being identified with a public function, he was the spontaneous ideologue of public service. But much more needs to be cleared up. Is there a genesis of the position? Does the fact that d'Aguesseau was influenced by the Jansenists for instance indicate an affinity between Jansenist discourse and interest in public service? You need to reread Goldmann,[36] who studied a small fragment of this enormous universe. So you can see the culture that this requires, all the more since the fragments of culture that we have acquired are constructed quite differently, and need to be completely rethought. For instance, the scholarly Montaigne is of no use for this work; we need to rethink Montaigne using secondary phrases (such as 'I, Montaigne, mayor of Bordeaux', which is an extraordinary thing, with its private/public mixture). We need therefore to rethink the whole of traditional philosophy . . . Some of you must be finding this superficial and wondering why I am making such a fuss about such obvious things . . . But I have the moral conviction that they are important and I want to convey this to you.

Thus the double historicization consists in first historicizing the object, placing the text in the space of texts and the producer in the space of producers, and then historicizing the reader and the space of readings: the reader is the product of a certain system and a certain culture; they inhabit a space structured by divisions, for example divisions between disciplines, which are objective but also mental boundaries (I may entirely forget 'Maître Thomas', either because I have never heard of him or, if I do know about him, because I thought he was of no interest . . .). Luckily, the two historicizations are conducted at the same time.

What use can we make of my suggestion? As always, methods themselves are not much use, they don't prevent us from making mistakes. They just flag up problems, like notices on trains: 'Do not open the doors.' That is all, but it is still a great improvement, and in the event it might even inaugurate a new intellectual tradition. For instance, I said that I was sad to note that the French bibliography on this question was hopeless. This is not at all due to some national, anthropological flaw. It comes down to sociological conditions, and I think that a sociology of the historicization of the fields of production and discourse would be able to account for the specific obstacles, which arise from the structure of the faculties and their divisions, the representation of positions, the division between philosophy and the other disciplines, the claim of philosophy to play the role of supremely authoritative science, all sorts of things that are rampant in the academic systems of the western world and which are particularly powerful in the French system. I conclude this topic by inviting those of you who are still at the beginning of your scientific careers to be conscious of the limits imposed on you by historicity, being students within the French educational system. If there is one thing that I hope to get across, it is this warning: don't let yourself be trapped within the false premise of your national destiny. If you want to practise science, it is not a historical advantage to be born French [*laughter*]. I have thought deeply about this, and it is perhaps the most useful thing that I can say to those who are willing to listen.

The Jansenist influence and the problem of self-love

To return to d'Aguesseau, I shall first of all recapitulate what I had been saying last time. D'Aguesseau, in this text designed to affirm the independence of judges, magistrates and parliament, strives to establish the transcendence of justice over all other forms of grandeur; the hereditary dignitaries (the nobility), the temporal power (the king), God (he does not mention him, except in a kind of reference *a contrario*) and trade (which is a form of servitude). Thus he identifies different forms of servitude ('voluntary servitude' is an echo of La Boétie:[37] there are all sorts of contemporary stereotypes and *topoi* here), and also opposes justice to philosophy. Here a little historical insight helped me to realize that the expression 'the philosopher' did not in those days designate someone abstract, but someone very concrete, that is, 'the libertine' (which I need to verify, however). I think that this philosopher, who is free while others live in servitude (commercial or noble, say), is in fact a libertine, that is, indifferent to the world and worldly value, and above all to collective interests; he pays no attention to society. There are some very fine passages in the rest of the work that I have not yet scrutinized where d'Aguesseau says that the philosopher is indifferent to the public interest. In the text in question he said that the libertine's freedom was rewarded with obscurity, inefficiency and impotence,[38] whereas the magistrate was strikingly free, his freedom being autonomy. If we think of the libertines, that is, the people who profess their indifference towards political affairs, we understand much better; we would find people who, like Montaigne, said that basically the only way of surviving was to make a clear separation between private and public interests. One focus of the ideological process at work at the time consisted in setting up the oppositions that we still live by: public/private, individual/collective, individual/general interest, private/public welfare, family/Republic, etc.

The philosopher then is not the allegorical character that I had imagined, but a very precise person, affirming his indifference to the public interest.

Against the philosopher, d'Aguesseau affirms the existence of those brilliant, free professions that are based on merit, and not on financial or aristocratic fortune (which share a common origin in chance, being gifts of the gods, obtained without merit). It is merit that makes the illustrious servitude of serving the State a 'vocation' (the word is not mentioned, but I think that this is what is being invented here), a 'calling' (the German word *Beruf* [sometimes translated as 'vocation'] designates something to which one is called).[39] An American author whom I have read says that this text is bathed in a Jansenist atmosphere, and that ultimately the whole of d'Aguesseau's work is a commentary on Domat.[40] Now Domat (to link the history of ideas with the social history of the producers of ideas) is a Jansenist who starts out from a Pascalian philosophy of the human condition (man is driven by self-love and the search for glory – those of you who have read it can refer to Bénichou's *Morales du grand siècle*).[41] Spontaneously, Domat tends to see the world as a place of perdition in which self-love can act only as a sort of poison, as it turns into an interest for glory. He gives the example of Alexander the Great, who is as it were the incarnation of pathological self-love, dealing with the world only in order to accumulate personal glory. Here we have a denunciation of the wrong kind of glory, the love of glory for glory's sake. If you remember your Bénichou, this is the Cornelian scenario of purely egotistical self-love generating the vain pursuit either of distraction or of the accumulation of symbolic capital.

That said, Domat elaborates the problem, since he is considered to be one of the representatives of constitutionalism who developed theories of absolute power, of which Louis XIV was the incarnation. Constitutionalism was very strong in the Jansenist milieu (which was typical of the milieux of the gown, like d'Aguesseau) and these people had a problem: how to reconcile the pessimistic Pascalian theory of human nature based on self-love with devotion to public well-being? Since self-love may lead to perversions such as the pursuit of glory for glory's sake, they develop a psychological casuistry in the style of [La] Rochefoucauld, who inhabits the same ideological universe and for whom one of the ruses of self-love is that, in many cases, self-love leads to charity: there are ways of loving yourself in other people which generate altruism. As far as I understand it (I don't have a complete mastery of these texts but I hope that what I have to say is better than nothing . . .). Appealing to this ruse of egotistical reason that engenders an altruistic reason, Domat starts out from the need to create bodies of civil servants whose motivation would be this kind of self-love redesigned as charity. His starting point, then, like that of d'Aguesseau, is a pessimistic philosophy of interest. Thus 'interest', in the utilitarian sense of the term – as far as I can verify it within the limits of my historical competence – is constituted at the same time as the problem of 'the general interest'; the two are not at all incompatible.

The problem faced by these people is an ethical, and even a theological one, but it is also a sociological problem. Their manner of formulating it is not far removed from the manner that I have adopted to situate the genesis of disinterestedness: they ask how to turn self-love into love for the fatherland and for the general interest. How to transform men of self-interest into the servants of public well-being, into the 'functionaries of mankind', as Husserl called them,[42] into agents of the universal? It is an agonizing problem for the Jansenists, who had such a radically pessimistic philosophy of human nature. So we find them converting the interest for glory and self-love (there is the famous example of La Rochefoucauld, the pardon of Augustus),[43] transposing a theory of self-love onto a theory of the charity of public service, thus elaborating a constitutionalist theory in which the king himself must submit to the rules that are promulgated and guaranteed by the functionaries. It is the Hegelian theme (which I shall say more about) of the prince who does no more than dot the 'i':[44] the civil servants prepare the files, so to speak, and the prince adds his signature, he dots the 'i'.

This is where a universal class starts to be organized.[45] I do not have enough information and I hesitate, because I am afraid of basing my interpretation on guesswork, but I believe intuitively that we see a class in the ascendant that is challenging the nobility, attacking birthright. It is in the interest of this rising class, which owes its rise to the accumulation of economic and cultural capital, to universalize its own destiny. In his sociology of law, Max Weber says that rising classes are always on the side of natural law,[46] that is, of laws that uphold the universality of human nature against the particularity of historical conditions. Rising classes are interested in the universal, firstly because they have an interest in universalizing their ascent and its legitimacy. For you to understand the scope of this axiom of Weber's, I could simplify, and say that a rising class is most often left-wing, and anti-racist.[47]

D'Aguesseau fits into this context, and research has shown that there are things in his work that recall *The Spirit of the Laws*,[48] making him a likely precursor of Montesquieu. In some of his writings that I have not commented on we find Jansenist themes: the condemnation of amusement and of people who cannot stay at rest; the Platonic topos of *pléonexia*[49] (they never have enough, they constantly want more); the theme of anxiety and agitation (which was there in the text that I read out to you, but which I had not noticed, due to a flaw in my historical perception once again); and he recommends moral severity, etc. Then, through an alchemy analogous to that described by Domat, he shows in 'L'Amour de la patrie' ('Love of the Fatherland'), a text written in 1715, later than the one I commented on, how love for the fatherland is almost natural in man: it is a sentiment 'that we know from sentiment, that we praise from reason, and that we should pursue from interest'.[50] Here we see the emergence of a very modern notion: interest well understood as the interest of reason, and the interest in reason which is the true interest of reason; there is an extraordinary sentence on the love of the fatherland: 'Love of the fatherland becomes a kind of self-love.'[51] We can detect the presence of Domat behind all that.

I shall continue rapidly. The love of the fatherland is betrayed by those who are preoccupied with their leisure, their amusements or their interests, it is betrayed by 'the philosophers', who do not merely ignore but condemn interest in the fatherland (I think that this really must refer to the libertines). D'Aguesseau wants to defend the idea that we should devote ourselves to the task of serving the public, which is demanding but brings liberation and is grounded in the hope of having an effect on the well-being of the public. Here I think that the Jansenist theory of good works and grace emerges. This form of worldly reconciliation of egotistical interest with a general interest in public well-being is one of the routes towards liberty and salvation. D'Aguesseau is a great defender of parliament and the constitution, since the constitution was charged with a kind of coordination of self-loves (as was more or less formulated in the text that I read out to you last time). The formula is not d'Aguesseau's, but it could be; it is a Machiavellian-Hegelian theme: the role of the civil servant as servant of mankind, as a force for mankind; not to beatify the soul, but to take self-loves and egotistical interests into account and orchestrate them, by subjecting recognition of these individual interests to a mastery of general interest inspired by virtue. Here we find all the themes introduced by d'Aguesseau.

Inventing the public: the oracle effect

In this context we can understand what I was saying last time: the civil servant (the term does not appear; d'Aguesseau mentions magistrates, members of parliament and judges) is at the disposal of public well-being, and because of this he receives public acknowledgement. He is legitimate because he is plebiscited by the public, the word 'public' being understood in the sense of the user of public institutions (the public frequenting a museum, or, better, the institutions that serve the public: the customers of the Post Office or clients of the Inland Revenue). The 'public' designates an ensemble of agents who need these services of coordination, who expect something from the magistrates, at the same time as they engender a specific legitimacy, distinct from theological, theocratic or autocratic legitimacy. They deliver a judgement that is free and independent of individual interests to the extent that it is a judgement capable of recognizing the merit of dispassionate servants of the public. The ideological process that I have mentioned leads to the creation of a new profession whose particular interests transcend the particular interests of other categories. It is free insofar as it deliberately chooses virtue, that is, disinterestedness, distance from the ordinary egotistical motivations of commerce or society. This universal estate bases its legitimacy on a kind of social phantasm known as 'the public', which it invents in order to legitimize itself.

The 'oracle effect' that I spoke of last time is extremely important: a group cannot set itself up as universal unless it gets the other groups to speak of it as being the true bearer of the universal. This is a fundamental law of ideological alchemy: a group can only universalize itself by establishing itself as the mouthpiece of the universal. Here the 'public' is what they invent to legitimize their function and their interests. The public is an abstract, unreal and secular ally, as opposed to God or the king, and its invention serves to legitimize the function of public service. The Pascalian notion of self-love was missing from my analysis, but it is important in order to understand what is at stake. Basically what they are inventing is a kind of State altruism, and, to coin a phrase, I could say that it is this State altruism that founds the state of altruism, meaning that you cannot be altruistic all by yourself.

In which sense this political theology (for it does in fact remain a theology even if the directly theological references have been erased from the discourse) comes very close to being a political sociology.

(This is an example of a case where I could have undertaken an inspirational [a-historical] reading . . . I point this out because one way of making a very good history of philosophy is by finding your own philosophy in a past philosophy. Many very good historians of philosophy of this period whom I truly appreciate[52] would not know how to answer the question as to whether it is Pascal or his historian who is saying what they are saying. Is it I, for instance, who am finding a theory of 'symbolic domination' in Pascal?[53] The question is important if you think back to the double historicization. I could have presented you with a reading of d'Aguesseau's text suggesting that he was doing a Bourdieu. That would have been really classy. It is one of the great academic strategies of rehabilitation, a way of showing how original you are: 'Look what I have discovered, and yet it is consecrated, it is canonical . . .'. But this is extremely dangerous: the slight slippage introduced by my tentative attempt to historicize – which remains very inadequate, as I am not very sure of myself – creates a gap, a distance that reminds us that this vision of History and of the State, this vision of public service, is historically situated, and what we have to understand are the historical reasons which may possibly enable it to be transhistorical. I don't know if you have followed my argument. . . .)

Producing the universal with individual interests

It seems to me that there are specific historical reasons why, in their historically situated effort to universalize their individual interests ('universalizing an individual interest' is a basic strategy, according to Marx),[54] these people produce something universal that, as a sociologist claiming to describe universal logics, I can perhaps take on board today, not as a theory of a specific case, but as a true theory of the interested/disinterested relation that lies behind the service of the public. I say 'these people' because they are a collective, a group of people at a certain moment in time.

This man [d'Aguesseau] is situated in an initial phase, and don't forget that my social history of the genesis of the juridical field is only a provisional sketch. A famous saying by Lévi-Strauss speaks of the 'admirable grandeur of beginnings',[55] and I have often noticed that, in the periods when a field was being constituted, the historical founders have particular difficulties in formulating what later became self-evident,[56] what became the scholarly common sense of the scientific field or the artistic field, what would become so obvious that it became the *doxa*. In later periods it takes an extraordinary effort to locate the fundamental presumptions on which a field is based, because these presumptions were the price to pay on entry into the field, and if they had not been absorbed, we would not be where we are today. In the initial phases, they are almost explicitly theorized. The double historicization and the historical gaze are not simply a coquettish academic attempt to be modish, but the condition that reveals the interest of the history: the beginnings give an exceptionally helpful route of access into the fundamental presumptions of a field. The method that I have been trying to use for some years now leads me to study the specific fundamental laws of the different fields (the artistic field, the field of public service, etc.), but also, within the limits of my competence and the time and opportunities available, the social genesis of the field. How for instance was the artistic field constituted before Manet? The beginnings, with their difficulties and their 'admirable grandeur', have this virtue: that so many things which the passing of time renders tacit, implicit and self-evident (as the ethnomethodologists would say), are still transparent, because their authors are working, suffering and fighting, and riven with contradictions. So we can understand why their ideology is almost a sociology. If today I could interview Manet, I would learn infinitely more about the artistic field than by interviewing any contemporary avant-garde painter (and I have interviewed many) or, *a fortiori*, any art critic. Manet was in a way paid to know what it is to make an artistic field, with the breaks and anxieties and suffering that it implies, and this led him to attain some lucid insight.

This would also be valid for the history of the sciences. The report of the Collège de France insisted on the fact that it is impossible to study the sciences without a history of the sciences.[57] The genetic approach has an extraordinary virtue: things which have become obvious, and thereby masked by professorial discourse, are still transparent in the founders. A double historicization enables us to fight this false eternity, the *philosophia pérennis* (as you might say), according to which a text can be commented on as if it contained eternal truths, as in the example of the philosophy teacher who comments on modern political events using a text by Plato on the *agora*. Once we have denounced this illusion of eternity, we do not find ourselves confronted with the void or condemned to pure historicism. On the one hand we find ourselves facing the question of the specific historical conditions that make a specific historical context liable to be particularly revealing of something that is not historically situated (which is what I have just done). On the other hand, studying the genesis of a social universe in which the norm of the universal is in the process of emerging, we can acquire the means of understanding what in my eyes is the only source of the universal, that is, the historical genesis of the transhistorical, which is one of the objects of my research.

I shall say only a few words about this, because once again I have been going much more slowly than I had intended, hoping to help you to understand my manner of working and the goals that I have set myself. Why have I taken an interest in d'Aguesseau's text, when I could have continued my general discourse on the passion for the universal, the interest in the universal, the individual interest in the universal interest? But this would still have been a general topos. By studying, even within the limits of my historical competence, someone who is engaged in this work, we can better understand the alchemy through which at a certain moment in time some agents (magistrates, members of parliament, *une lignée de parlementaires*, etc.) will defend their particular interests as a hereditary caste and produce norms that go beyond their interests as a hereditary caste, norms which can even at a certain point backfire against their immediate interests as a hereditary caste. Their descendants could be guillotined in the name of the universal that they have engendered. In any case, in their everyday struggles, they were always vulnerable to those turning against them the universal that they invoked in order to advance their own class interests claiming to be universal. To my mind this is the concrete solution to the antinomy of the individual interest and the general interest that people constantly oppose.

Ultimately, d'Aguesseau or Pascal had the same problem as our sociologist: how to find a way out of this radical historicization? In their case, the question had its practical implications, but it is also a theoretical problem: What are the historical conditions that encourage the establishment of the games, objective laws, systems of sanction, reward and exclusion which have as their official rule a form of universalism (the law)? How are these systems of dispositions which lead agents to participate in the game, anticipating acceptance by the institutions and the rewards offered by the game, produced? Their initial phases show that the two are constituted at the same time: these people work at making their interests explicit by giving them normative forms, and inventing institutions to house them.

Next time, I shall discuss a treatise for advocates dating from the 1880s, which draws on earlier treatises that go back to d'Aguesseau's time, and I shall tell you about the rule of the corporation of the Order of Advocates (I shall not take long, although reading this material did take up a lot of my time, but I can't expect you to suffer all I had to suffer . . . [*some laughter*]). So as not to be too abstract, I shall read you an extract from Mollot, a big fat volume that has often sent me to sleep:

> The disinterestedness recommended by the profession means that the advocate should establish moderate honoraria; it means even, if the client is not in a position to make him an offer, that the advocate should lend him his ministrations gratuitously with as much care and zeal as he would for the richest of persons. Moreover, we have proven that the ministrations of the advocate are not characterized as a mandate, nor much less as hired labour, in the legal sense. The honoraria that the client offers him are a reward for services rendered (as a gift), a testimony of gratitude. They cannot therefore attract taxation or obligation.[58]

Another sentence: 'The word *honorarium* is derived from the fact that advocates in Rome in former times were paid for their services, not with money but with honours.'[59] Then he goes on to give all the rules. In the forthcoming sessions I shall try to show how a nomological system was elaborated and became a corpus of doctrine, an ethic (what we would call a 'deontology' today), and how, in parallel, professional rules of exclusion, sanction and revocation were established. I shall make a very interesting comparison with the United States, which took a different path and where the same problem was treated differently. I think that I shall be able to communicate most of what I want to communicate . . .

Lecture of 24 March 1988

What is a quotation? – The effect of the social sciences on the social world – From interesting conditions to disinterestedness – The principle of sufficient reason and its suspension – Logical logic and practical logics – Conditions creating interest in disinterestedness – Spontaneous submission to the rules of the field – Genesis of the rules of the juridical field – Business law and pure law – Cross-checking – The force of the ideal – Escaping historicism

What is a quotation?

There are two questions [put by members of the audience] that I would like to refer to very briefly because they follow on directly from what I was saying last time: 'Does the incitation to treat texts from a doubly historical viewpoint not make any quotation impossible? Otherwise, should we not imagine and accept that there are two strategies of reading which have different uses and functions, one contextualized and doubly historicized, the other decontextualized and kleptomaniac, where the author pressed into service is extracted from his place of origin?' I have partially answered this question, but it has the merit of drawing attention to the important problem of quotation. Quotation is the epitome of a traditional, ritual act that we practise in the educational system from childhood on without really knowing what we are doing. In fact it is a complex act, laden with presumptions, in which we unwittingly engage a philosophy of history, a history of philosophy and a philosophy of the history of philosophy. If through my reflection on the notion of double historicization I have at least drawn your attention to what is implied in the most elementary act of scientific life, I shall not have wasted my time, nor yours in listening to me. This does not mean that quotation becomes impossible but it does mean that we have to know what we are doing when we use a quotation, whether from a contemporary author or an author from the past (which are two different cases).

In sociological research a quotation from a respondent or an enquiry (which are not the same thing) raises exactly the same problem, which cannot be swept aside by the fact of respecting the norms of positivist science; it is not sufficient to give information about the respondent (age, gender, occupation, etc.) – and even that is not observed by so many in our profession – to be finished with it; respecting the positivist rules is often an alibi for not putting more fundamental questions: Is a quotation by a respondent a proof? Are the propositions that I make about an institution, for instance, confirmed by the simple fact that somebody has formulated them? That would raise the problem of how representative the information given by a particular informer is, and how far the sociologist judges their information according to whether it matches what they have found out for themselves. It is a very difficult and important question.

I raised this question in the last lecture, in the particular case of d'Aguesseau: How is it that this man says almost exactly what I, as a scholar, want to say that he says? How do we judge this match? Am I doing more than just quoting? The question is just as valid when we are quoting Mr X, agricultural labourer. We are faced with the alternatives of double contextualization or kleptomania, which is not a bad term: quotation is a form of appropriation, especially when undeclared, which is frequent when it is a case of plagiarism. On this topic we should analyse non-quotations, false quotations, or overt quotations that hide covert non-quotations. This work by the sociologist of science escapes the analyses which have become more numerous in recent years, since there is a 'citations index'[1] which shows how many times X or Y is quoted, and forms the basis of our scientific success ratings. Through a combination of automatic notation and computer programming, these analyses produce results that look scientific, but they take no account of [the problem of] the status of the quotation. There are a thousand ways of quoting: you can quote positively or negatively, but the non-quotations are often the most important. I shall not take this further, but I think that for those of you who are interested in the problems of the sociology of intellectual life, this can lead you to reflect.[2]

The effect of the social sciences on the social world

The second question is as follows: 'Should we take the expressions "a sense of practice" or "ordinary sense of practice" as being ideal-typical? Once activity reflecting on the social world has come into existence, above all now that the social sciences have become established and popularized, what has become of social innocence, of our unquestioning relation to the everyday world, and what has become of the feel for the game in the various fields?' This is also a question that I find important, and there is much I could say on the subject, but I will just indicate some paths to follow. I do indeed think that the existence at the heart of the social world of professionals of the science of the social world introduces a very important social change. I am not saying this to make myself as a sociologist seem important: the most significant effects are unfortunately not effected by sociologists but rather by people who claim and usurp this title, like the opinion poll pedlars or the public relations advisers who attract so much attention these days. These people, whom sociologists tend not to take seriously because they are not scientific opponents, should be taken seriously not as rivals but as objects of scientific study,[3] insofar as we can no longer think of the social world today without taking into account the people who make thinking of it their profession, who lead people (like politicians, for instance) to believe that they are able to think it, with significant social effects. Through their very existence, they change the way that the social world functions.

Since I cannot take too long over replying to this question, I refer you to the latest issue of the review *Actes de la recherche en sciences sociales* (which I am responsible for; I must reveal my hand, this is an advert, but I believe that it is legitimate), which is devoted to the political world and the sociology of the political world.[4] At least one of the articles, written by Patrick Champagne,[5] is concerned with an analysis of the social effects of opinion polls, and more generally the whole space of the agents whose profession is to analyse or manipulate opinion and whose existence profoundly changes the way the political field functions (the other articles also touch on this question indirectly). The political world as we observe it on television or elsewhere is profoundly transformed by the existence of people who, in the name of 'science' (I use [the word] between inverted commas, pointedly), intervene actively in the social world.

From interesting conditions to disinterestedness

Now I intend to pick up the thread of my argument and try to finish today what I had started saying about the juridical field, which I saw as an introduction to the first session. If you remember, my intention was to draw up a sort of balance sheet of the seminars during which a certain number of the issues that I want to broach are discussed; in particular, the problem of the relations between the juridical professions and the world of business. Last time, I had made a start on identifying the social foundations of the strategies that went towards instituting in the eighteenth century an autonomous and disinterested universe that I am calling the juridical field. I sketched the beginnings of an analysis of the position of d'Aguesseau, who is a sort of eponymous hero of the juridical profession: through his writings, through what Weber might call his exemplary prophecy, through his virtue, and through his exemplary manner of embodying the profession of the magistrate, he made a powerful contribution to the creation of a juridical field. I would be tempted to say more about d'Aguesseau (as always when you are plunged in a piece of research, it becomes an addictive hobby) and tell you what I have learnt since, that is, only just recently, in particular the sequence of events which, via the Girondins (who were advocates) and then all the advocates of the Third Republic who were among the founders of the republican order, contributed to this struggle of the magistrates against both the Church and the State to constitute an autonomous juridical order and led to things like the separation of the Church from the State and the existence of a secular juridical-political ethic, etc. But I must not go on; I have said enough for those of you who are interested to know in which direction this could be taken.

What I believe is worth noting in what I have been saying is the idea that in certain circumstances there are people who, while pursuing their own individual and collective interests (those of a corporation in this particular case), can promote something that we might call universal. In the present case, we have an answer to the very naive question that certain sociologists raise: Is there such a thing as disinterested behaviour? Is disinterested behaviour possible? Describing the debate in the terms of today, people tend to start with the emergence among economists, in particular with the Chicago School, of people who projected the economists' mode of thinking onto terrains which were not traditionally treated by economists. For instance, the American economist Gary Becker has analysed matrimonial exchanges with striking ignorance (of Lévi-Strauss and the anthropologists, for example), as if they were economic exchanges.[6] He has constructed mathematical models which enable us to account for matrimonial exchanges – not so badly, in fact, after all (models are always interesting when they are slightly crude and uncivilized because at least they clarify the problems). Others in his wake have tried to analyse very different things like charitable funds or blood donations. This invasion by mathematical models and above all by the philosophy that goes with it (briefly, a philosophy of rational calculation and of the social agent as calculator, as *homo economicus*) has provoked reactions, one of the arguments against it being that this philosophy cannot account for disinterested behaviour. How can disinterested behaviour be possible if all behaviour is motivated by interest?

Some rather naive critics obstinately ignore all the evidence and classify my work under the heading of sociologies of interest,[7] but it does not fit into that logic at all (I spend all my time saying the opposite). My analysis of d'Aguesseau, which could just as well be applied to Flaubert or Mallarmé,[8] to a mathematician or a philosopher, shows that, for representations, discourses and suggestions promoting disinterestedness to emerge, and *a fortiori* for explicit rules with the duty of disinterestedness as their principle (like the rules governing the profession of advocate that I shall remind you of in a moment) to emerge, it takes two sets of conditions. It needs ethical dispositions of a certain type, produced socially, and most often through family education. At the same time, with the two processes generally being in a dialectical, mutually supportive relationship, you need the social universes to be produced where (if I dare say – I am going to seem brutally materialist and I shall seem to be reintroducing the philosophy of interest by the back door having thrown it out of the front door) disinterestedness pays and is rewarded. I could generalize the proposition: for behaviour with claims to be universal and therefore tendentially universal, rational and disinterested, these two conditions need to be fulfilled. Consequently it requires the development not only of an ethical disposition, a moral rule, for instance a pure Kantian rule, confronting the individual subject in the solitude of their conscience, but also at the same time a public space in which these dispositions are rewarded, it being understood that they may be rewarded in non-economic ways. They can be rewarded in symbolic ways, for instance by purely psychological gratification.

The nobleman for instance is *nobilis*, that is, recognized and acknowledged, and his reward consists in the acknowledgement accorded to his nobility. Nobility is one of the most effective models to help us understand universes of the type that I am describing today, because it constitutes one of the accomplished forms of these universes of reward

where action finds its reward in the act of its accomplishment, by the
fact that its accomplishment is socially recognized and acknowledged.
In pre-capitalist societies of honour it is extremely important because it
is one of the foundations of honour: standing on your dignity to defend
your honour finds its reward in its own action because the other social
agents acknowledge it. Societies with honoraria (it is the same word
[as the word honour]) are societies where you are not paid with money
alone (the word 'honorarium' is interesting, it is a euphemism and
euphemisms often name the unspeakable); the fact of receiving, not
a salary, but an honorarium, is one of the gratifications of those who
are honourable enough to be honoured by means of honoraria (I shall
return to this point), of those who are honourable enough to be paid
in a euphemistic currency. For instance, a tacit law of exchange among
members of the bourgeoisie is that you do not pay each other with
money. Thus, when we ask a medical friend for a consultation (based
not on common sense but on scientific enquiry), an almost explicit rule
obliges one not to pay him a salary, but to make him a gift. This transmutation is important because it is part of an alternative economy, one
based on a denial of economics. As these are things that I have often
developed elsewhere, I shall leave it at that.[9]

The principle of sufficient reason and its suspension

I should remind anyone who does not see what I am getting at, however,
that for me the task of sociology is obviously not to reduce all social
behaviour to fundamentally economic foundations (in the sense that
our present-day science understands economics). The ambition of sociology is to propose a sort of general economy of practices by accepting
the equivalent of what Leibniz and the classic philosophers called the
principle of sufficient reason:[10] there is no social act without reason.
That is the only thing that we are obliged to agree about, for it seems to
me that there cannot be a science of an absurd act . . . More precisely,
we can undertake a science of the absurd act on condition that we see
it as an exception to the general law, leading us to suspend the general
principles of science in order to make ourselves understood. It seems to
me for instance that to understand certain phenomena of delinquency
in modern society, we have to abdicate that scientific temptation inherent in scientific thought.[11] I could draw up a very fine bibliography
of all the explanations (in terms of frustration, etc.) of the forms of
delinquency that exist in all modern societies, but I think that a lesson
that we can learn from this ambition to create a general science is

that sometimes science must be prepared to suspend its explanations: there are cases that are themselves explicable from a general theory of economic behaviour where the social agents can act with no reason, like heroes in a play by Beckett. This is not a denial of the principle of sufficient reason but a suspension of it, which is itself a response to very specific historical reasons. What I have just said is rather complicated and I am aware that I have not developed it sufficiently, but I did not want to ignore this important argument, which might have been lodged in your heads as an objection.

Logical logic and practical logics

To return to my argument. The anthropological enterprise of the social sciences relies on the postulate (which sociologists often accept unconsciously, but in this particular case, consciously) that nothing happens without a reason. 'Reason' is a complex word here. It does not imply 'rational reason', 'reasonable reason' or 'calculation' (*ratio*). It means that there is nothing that does not have an intelligible principle. Science postulates this, even though it must also accept the idea of a limit, as I have just done in my parenthesis. There are cases where this principle is suspended and all we can do is to ask why it is suspended in such cases. The principle of sufficient reason that I have mentioned finds its embodiment in practical logics, and social science has the function of describing universes that have their logics. The word 'logic' can also cause problems (I am trying to explain these words because each one of them may provoke misunderstanding). Saying that universes have logics does not mean that they are logical. A postulate that logic is not the source of practices (which does not mean that they have no logic) is another fundamental postulate of social science. You will find it in Freud, in Durkheim and in all those who wanted to understand human behaviour. Like the psychoanalyst, the sociologist accepts the idea that his work consists in reconstructing logics which are not logic itself, without forasmuch being illogical. Practical logics form a large class of logics which are the baggage, so to speak, of the social sciences. This is more or less what I was saying last time: the principle of practical logics is precisely that they don't have logic as their first principle. They do not have a logical intention.

A ritual consisting, for example, in twirling a toad seven times round your head anti-clockwise in order to gain sterility (the example is imaginary, but only just) may appear absurd at first glance (this is a trivial remark, but there are such theoretical regressions in some debates today that we are obliged to repeat things that we would prefer never to have to say again – it is the metaphor of the montgolfière that I used last time: we would like never to have to repeat them because there are so many other more useful things to say to make science advance, but we are sometimes obliged to repeat things that for complex reasons have become problematic again). We then postulate that these apparently incomprehensible practices, which a prescientific or a racist anthropology would call primitive, archaic or savage, do have their coherence and do have a logic for us to discover.

The danger of this postulate is that it leads us to seek out in practices a logic that is one of logic, partly because the scientific field calls for a logical logic, a mathematical model. For instance, we will formalize and make amateur analogies with modern algebra or construct more or less coherent mathematical models. The social sciences then are in a predicament. You can see this, I hope, from the way I am speaking; if at least I am communicating this, I will have communicated something that I find essential. I never launch a proposition without immediately making a correction, because one mistake hides another. If I tell you that 'there is a logic', you will assume that we are going to be able to model and formalize things, that 'at last the human sciences are going to become a science', and a host of people will latch onto this. No, the human sciences are scientific insofar as they know that there are logics which are not logical. That said, the scientific field, since it has been (largely) constructed in opposition to common sense, by formalizing and mathematizing, agreeing with Galileo that 'The grand book of the world is written in mathematics',[12] demands formalization and what we call hard logic. Since this hard logic has been constructed in opposition to practical logic, the anthropologist finds himself in a position of experimental neurosis: the social demands that he suffers oblige him to use a language destructive of the logics that he discovers [*Bourdieu hesitates to continue*]. (Since I have gone so far down this route, I had better go all the way, what the hell! [*laughter*].) Let us say that it is easy for him to obtain the most eminent symbolic gratification by doing things that are socially expected in the name of a local and regional definition of science, but at the risk of destroying his specific object. With a little mathematics and a lot of brazen cheek, you can practise a kind of anthropology that will be very well rewarded socially. We spend our time saying that there are obstacles to the scientific progress of the social sciences, but one obstacle which is far from minor is the fact that it is a false currency that is socially rewarded, for the reasons that I have just analysed (I could develop these arguments but I don't want to take up too much time).

The social sciences take their project to be to grasp universes like the juridical field or the scientific field, postulating that they nurture their reasons: they have their immanent reasons, what happens in these fields is not any old thing and it doesn't happen in any old way, there is a logic, things are not random. This enrages some Marxists who talk of 'contradiction' and point out that speaking of 'logic' is a kind of political postulate. Their reaction is legitimate and defensible, but it is extremely naive, since the logic of a practical field, for instance, may be a logic of contradiction and conflict, and this conflict may be a generator of logic.

One of the paradoxes that I am describing is how this conflict generates rivalry, competition and interest in logics which to some extent spill out beyond the conflict, rivalry and competition, and may transcend individual interests. How does it happen that social universes obey the general laws of the social world, where nothing is done without a reason, where people are not mad, where they tend to act, even without knowing it, from reasons that seem good to them, since they are guided by their habitus and positions? I believe that the agents' positions and posts, and their habitus, which are generally suited to the posts, are often more intelligent than the agents themselves; the positions and the habitus 'calculate' (in inverted commas) better than the rationally calculating agent. I always take this striking example: if you asked all the technocrats who are alumni of the Polytechnique and the ENA to meet to calculate a system of reproduction as rational and perfect as the extremely complex system of the *grandes écoles*, they would never manage, even if only because they would immediately try to make economies – if you only ever get the sons of magistrates and ENA alumni succeeding in the entrance competition, why not select them at outset and avoid wasting the State's time and money, leaving all the others in the *lycée* until their final year? [*laughter*] I am not making this up (I never make this kind of thing up), you can find it in a book (written by a polytechnician, but there you are . . . [*laughter*] . . .). This example is typical of the rational unconscious, which forgets that although it is true that there is a price to pay if you let students hang on until they finish their secondary studies, when it would be much cheaper to push them towards their natural fate, which is an apprenticeship, nonetheless, the considerable cost of deferring their elimination comes with fantastic gains in unconsciousness, misrecognition and acknowledgement for those who do succeed (those who fail say: 'They were brilliant, I was not very gifted . . .'). These things are part of the tacit conditions that make the system work. I have just said a lot in a short time, proceeding in an elliptical and confused manner, but these detours seem to me to be useful to flesh out the overall shape of my analysis.

Conditions creating interest in disinterestedness

Practical logics are so difficult to understand not only for the reasons I have given, but also because their principles are not rational in the traditional sense of the term: they are neither explicit nor methodical. The most effective principles of action in the practical universes are in a way the most unconscious. The social agents in a universe like d'Aguesseau's are all the more amenable and well-adjusted for having no idea what they are doing, and thus acting in the dark, totally ignorant of what is determining them and what their interests are. A sociological analysis is often shocking because it reminds us of things that nobody wants to know. As I said in my first lecture, the pleasure of demystification, which (we have to admit) is augmented by the indignation that its explication provokes, lays a trap for us, since it prevents us from fully understanding that, in acting from interest without being aware of it, and seeing disinterested reasons as the conscious motivation of their interested behaviour, social agents do nonetheless advance the cause. This is, I believe, the complete truth of this extremely complicated kind of process.

It is true that there are admirably devoted people without whom life might perhaps not be worth living. The sociologist knows this, but he cannot be satisfied with merely admiring them. The most admirable people do not admire themselves (we always forget that there is an ethical advantage in finding ourselves admirable), they are admirable naturally, or they refuse [to admire themselves]. Medieval treatises on charity reflect on these problems: people who are absolutely admirable know that they must not even allow themselves the form of concupiscence that is knowing that they are very good . . . which is statistically very, very rare! [*laughter*] (These extreme cases are interesting because they call into question all the other cases.) Today, then, I shall speak of people who do admirable things without even taking pride in doing them. D'Aguesseau is amazing: the biography by Monsieur Frêche[13] which I have been reading this week is extraordinarily eulogistic. Biographies are often like this, but this particular case is convincing: he was an absolutely astonishing man. That said, I think that a true analysis would argue that this man had specific interests which he embodied in such an accomplished manner that he could be the leading light of his group, that he could remind others of the rule of the group;

he was in a way a living norm and it is no accident if he is constantly cited. Weber spoke of exemplary prophecy, taking the example of Socrates:[14] these social agents teach us through what they are much more than through what they say. But they have a double virtue: d'Aguesseau is capable of theorizing, explicating, formulating, setting rules, constructing a disinterested discourse in terms that are approved and admired, using the oppositions of the time (reason *versus* passion, etc.), citing his sources, referring to the Latin; and at the same time, unlike those who are said not to put their preaching into practice, he practises what he preaches, and he expresses it even better in his practice than in his discourse. Cases of this type present a particularly interesting challenge to the sociologist; it requires, without being reductive and without acting the clever-clever bubble-burster, understanding that these cases are not without their reasons; we cannot see them as a sort of social miracle descended from heaven. A different reformulation of the principle of sufficient reason would be to say that there are no social miracles: if miracles exist, does science? For me it is the same problem: if there were social miracles, if there really were somebody who descended from heaven (I imagine that this would raise some theological issues . . . [*laughter*]) and were able to do things with absolutely no reason, this would be a failure of social science. Perhaps such cases do exist, but science can have nothing to do with them. If I have a theory of interest, it lies in this direction (but I don't think that it is a theory of interest).

Spontaneous submission to the rules of the field

To return to my particular case. For a disinterested universe to function, it needs people to be interested in disinterestedness, but it also needs that disinterestedness to be rewarded. More precisely, it needs the invention on the one hand of a spirit of public service (or a spirit of service of the State, a spirit of service of the public cause – you will remember how often the word 'public' occurred in d'Aguesseau's discourse) and, on the other hand, a public service, that is, a universe in which you can pursue a career when you are sufficiently motivated by the spirit of public service (or at least the appearance of the spirit of public service) to be publicly recognized as having it, with honours awarded, etc. (We could consider such decorations as constituting one of the interesting rewards allocated to disinterestedness.) In the words of d'Aguesseau, this is all about 'the love of virtue'. There you see the difficulty for sociology: you have to accept that virtue, like love in general, is something real, that it is a social force, without forasmuch taking it literally in the naive form that people experience it.

The argument that I advanced and that I have just recalled was part of a global approach whose aim was to describe the genesis of a juridical field. I said that I would try to describe the process of autonomization through which a microcosm is constituted in the social cosmos within which a special kind of game that follows the rules of disinterestedness is played. I indicated that I would trace this genesis on the level of the production of discourse and then on the level of the production of practices, with their practical rules. Having described the genesis of the discourse, I come now to the level of the genesis of the rules governing these practices and their systems of sanctions.

I am obviously going to deal mainly with the negative sanctions, for a game always involves inbuilt sanctions: if you do something that you are not supposed to do according to the rules of the game, you are automatically sanctioned. Inbuilt sanctions and regular rules rap your knuckles. Just as when you flout the laws of physics you receive a shock, so when you flout the rules of social physics, the rules of a field, you receive automatic shocks, since the sanction is written into the field. As Weber says when speaking of the economic cosmos, somebody who, like a pre-capitalist man thrust into a capitalist economy, flouts the rules of economics is thrown out onto the street; he loses his job or goes bankrupt, depending on whether he is a wage earner or a businessman.[15] In the juridical cosmos, somebody who ignores the regulations, the immanent laws or (to return to the word used just now) the logic of the field, receives automatic sanctions. In a learned field such as this, in addition to failing and being excluded from the field, he can be subjected to explicit sanctions of a juridical type. The distinction seems important to me: you are not only punished by falling arse over tip, you incur specific penalties that result from the application of the rules.

What I am going to describe superficially (although I have read a lot on the subject – and it does not make light reading) is the process which led to the founding of an Order of Advocates. The word 'order' is fascinating, and, if I had to choose, I might be tempted to say 'order' – in the Pascalian sense[16] – rather than 'field'. An order, like the Order of Advocates, is a corps that identifies with a Council of the Order: a fraction of this corps nominates the delegates, who have full power to act and speak on behalf of the corps, and who, among other things, promulgate the rules that the whole corps must respect, and apply these rules through negative sanctions and penalties and the positive sanctions that are essentially a career. One tacit law of the corps is that you can only progress within the corps insofar as you respect its rules and conventions.

What a field requires, to borrow a term from Spinoza, is *obsequium*[17] ['submission' for Bourdieu; 'obedience' in English translations of Spinoza], respect for the fundamental law of the corps and the field, that is, things that are very often insignificant. A field requires respect for the insignificant things through which the group expresses its most fundamental values, and the most insignificant things often express respect for the corps, that is, respect for those who dominate the field or for forms of politeness, which are extremely important. For it is indeed politeness that holds a corps together, and politeness is political. It is a permanent submission at every moment. Adapting a quotation from Malraux, we could say that it is 'the small change of the absolute'. These little acts of daily politeness are acts acknowledging the very fundamentals of the order and the corps. This permanent submission, which is channelled through apparently insignificant rituals (inaugural rites, ceremonies, posture and clothing, etc.) that seem unimportant, is all the more important because, precisely, it asks you to bow down for nothing, that is, for sweet nothings. Moreover, to those who do not bow down, they remark: 'You know, that would cost you nothing.' In the eyes of those who do want to bow down, it does 'cost nothing', but, precisely, in the eyes of those who do not want to agree to these sweet nothings, it does cost, because when you bow down for nothing, you bow down for the sake of bowing down. And fundamentally this is what social groups are asking for. You can find some very interesting things in Matheron's excellent book on Spinoza's philosophy, if you look up '*obsequium*' in the index. The word *obsequium* is very rich, because it says so much.

A corps requires this kind of fundamental submission, which is basically a corporal submission. It is no accident if the principal manifestations of *obsequium* are manifestations of politeness, that is, bodily gestures: bowing and scraping, etc. The gestures of submission are profoundly bodily. We see this clearly in societies where you prostrate yourself. In our societies it is less visible, but it is perhaps even more subtle, because when the movement of the body is reduced to its inception, when it is purely inchoate, it becomes mental. Perhaps when you prostrate yourself you are freer within than when you merely bow . . . [. . .]

In the social genesis of a corps, there is a whole process of creation of automatic procedures: how to recruit, how to co-opt, how to nominate, how to have a career, how not to have a career, what to be and what not to be, etc. All of that is codified. At the same time there is what is not codified, and that is obviously what is most important. (This is why outsiders generally fail to understand the procedures. The son of a non-magistrate who finds himself thrust into this universe has relatively little chance of success because it takes time to learn all these sweet nothings. He is in danger of overlooking them, or, if he does notice them, of thinking that they are of no importance. He will assume that what is essential is to know the Code Civil [statute book], whereas everyone knows that what is essential is not the Code, but the manner of quoting it properly, etc.) At the same time the corps invents the rules of the game. The conventions are set in place, as are the dispositions adjusted to these conventions which lead us to perceive these conventions as self-evident, and natural. The people who have assimilated these conventions are naturally obsequious without even being aware of it. They are freely obsequious. Here we could find the alternatives of disinterestedness and cynicism (this topic has been much discussed in recent years; it is presently at the centre of debates in the social sciences – it is not something that I have dreamed up on my own). People are naturally obsequious, whereas cynicism is not really very effective. Julien Sorel is a very good example: cynicism can lead you to the guillotine.[18] Or simply to exclusion or demotion, for all the reasons that I have just given. If things happened on the level of consciousness and calculation, cynicism could be profitable, but the nature of these universes is such that they are profitable for those who don't try to profit from them but who are paid at every moment to know what you have to do to be rewarded, who have been suckled at the breast of the fundamental principles of the logic of the field.

Genesis of the rules of the juridical field

How would these rules be enunciated, and in what contexts? As far as I know, it was around the 1830s that the great period of constitution of a corps of advocates started, that is, at the moment when the juridical field which functioned on the basis of principles in a practical state started to elaborate explicit rules. The Order of Advocates that had been dissolved under the Revolution was reconstituted under Napoleon. In 1812 the monopoly of pleading at the bar was restored. Once the basic foundations of an autonomous Order of Advocates had been re-elaborated, the corps felt the need to make explicit rules, to assert the rights of those who pronounced and practised the law. Thus they constituted a juridical code for the juridical field. One important difference between different fields lies in the fact that some are equipped with explicit codes and others with none (or hardly any). In the artistic field, for instance, there are conventions, there are things you should do and things you should not, galleries where you shouldn't exhibit, people you shouldn't exhibit with, unacceptable ways of being paid. There are then exactly the same types of rules as there are in the juridical field, but they are not made explicit, they are tacit, which makes them even more fearsome, for the more a field remains in an implicit state, the more difficult it is for outsiders and late-comers to enter. Indeed, the codification of the rules of the profession, which may appear to be a straitjacket, has a virtue (as in the paradoxical case of the law) that you might call democratic (if the word had any sense): it gives a chance to those who would not know instinctively (obviously this 'instinct' is socially constituted) that, for instance, you should not ask a client for a down payment.

The code of the guardians of the code, then, was elaborated in the 1830s and 1840s, and we will find in this process of constitution the fundamental principle of sufficient reason: in the particular historical circumstances where they were situated, the corps of the advocates had a collective 'interest' (in inverted commas, don't forget) in imposing rules to affirm their autonomy, essentially from the magistrates. It seems to me that we cannot entertain a hypothesis of [absolute] disinterestedness, which would imply that these people refused to receive payment and set rules for no reason. This would mean thinking that they were collectively masochistic, which moreover seems contradicted by the fact that, fifty years later, they fought to throw off the rules that they had imposed upon themselves. My opinion is that they imposed a set of rules upon themselves in order to avoid leaving any leeway for those who might want to impose their rules upon them. In fact, one way of freeing yourself from people who want to impose their rules upon you is to impose your own upon yourself: autonomy is a way of transforming heteronomy into voluntary submission to a rule that you have chosen for yourself; this is Kant's definition of autonomy, and a corps can find its interest in autonomy.

To give a precise example: the judge could check the honoraria charged and sanction advocates who asked for more, according to the task performed or the revenue of the client, but the corps preferred to impose a fair rate for the honorarium as a rule, and even rethought the honoraria completely. Firstly, they used the word 'honoraria', which, as Mollot explains, 'is derived from the fact that advocates in Rome in former times were paid for their services, not with money but with *honours*'.[19] The formula is very interesting. If you have a little ethnological culture, you will immediately see that it concerns transforming a tit-for-tat exchange, an explicit monetary exchange. In a tit-for-tat exchange ('I give to you and you give to me') we are telescoping into one moment two acts that are separated in an exchange of gifts. In the case of the gift, I make you a disinterested gift, as if you were never going to repay me, and, two years later, when I have forgotten all about it, you give me something in return: the gift and the counter-gift are separate. The tit-for-tat is rather brutal because it synchronizes things that the exchange of gifts dissociates (here I am summarizing a very long argument that I developed in a more elaborate form in *The Logic of Practice*, which spelled out its relation to analyses by Lévi-Strauss and Marcel Mauss).[20] The transformation of a salary into honoraria is a banal alchemical operation in pre-capitalist societies which have non-economic economies based on a denial of economics in the narrower sense. This action consists in transforming two simultaneous, interested actions into two disinterested actions totally separate in time. The rules announced by Mollot, then, contain an explicit rejection of anything that could transform the advocate–client relationship into a commercial relationship. A jurist who is often cited, [Armand-Gaston] Camus, says for instance that 'honoraria are a voluntary gift of gratitude by the client'. This formula, which transforms honoraria into gifts, is the motive underlying a series of rules that I shall discuss later. But for the moment what is important is that by imposing on themselves this ethical economics the judges free themselves from the control that their emoluments or salaries might attract from the magistrates charged with ensuring respect for the rules of probity, disinterestedness and moderation required by the codes.

Lest I forget, I would like make a point about the comparison I have drawn between this type of economy and pre-capitalist economies, regarding the exchange of gifts. The analogy seems evident, but it is only true to a limited extent, because, in differentiated societies, as I said last time, nothing functions in the same way as it did in the undifferentiated, pre-capitalist societies. The comparison may even be treacherous, for these honoraria are situated in a universe where there are other forms of payment, and where we know that honoraria are also salaries. In other words, they are situated in a universe where the economic field is constituted as such (based on the *Grundnorm*[21] that 'business is business' and 'there is no place for feelings in business'). Introducing a sub-universe obeying only the rules of gift exchange into a pre-existing economic field takes on a special meaning, and this sub-universe is permanently distorted by the existence of an established economic field. Among other things, the universe of gift exchanges clashes with the universe of business affairs.

Business law and pure law

This means that a great problem arises (which is one of the topics that I have been driving towards), a thorn in the disinterested conscience of the juridical world; namely, business law. This is in fact the starting point for the reflections that I have been developing here, as it was for Monsieur Dezalay's exposé[22] on the contradictions encountered today by certain arms of the law in confronting the world of business. [. . .] An advocate, for instance, cannot be the executor of a business affair. I shall read out a splendid quotation, an edict of the Council of the Paris branch of the Order for 27 May 1828: 'The advocate must carefully avoid anything that might compromise his dignity or the delicacy of his feelings [*what a lovely term!*], in particular anything that might lead him to overstep the limits of his profession and turn him into an agent or pimp for business affairs.' This is the very period when the artists too were coming together to compose a field, and we see writers such as Flaubert and Baudelaire evoke the theme of identification with prostitutes; their revolt is articulated around the slogan: 'We are treated like prostitutes by the law of the market.' I could develop this further, but I shall refrain.[23] They signal their distance from money and from all kinds of corruption: ultimately it all boils down to sex and money (I shall not give details, but you can find in the books that I have cited numerous examples of advocates struck off for sexual misdemeanours that today we would find venial).

Having drawn your attention to the code of the jurists, I shall move straight on to make comparisons, because there is always a danger in sticking to one particular national case, especially if it happens to concern your own native country. It is obviously the comparison with the United States, where the genesis of the juridical field took a very different form, that I find compelling. Moreover, Monsieur Dezalay was kind enough to tell me about an article that analyses discourse on business affairs in America at the end of the nineteenth century. It is really a very different national tradition. At a time when the French jurists retreated within their autonomous ivory towers and reaffirmed the autonomy of the rules they had prescribed for themselves in order to gain their independence from supervision by the magistrates, the jurists in the United States entered more or less completely into the world of business and the market. A classic book by Hurst on the development of the law in the United States shows in a way how the juridical world entered into the world of business, while still retaining a certain autonomy.[24] This last rider is important, for the jurist would not be an interesting economic agent if he were an economic agent like any other. He is an interesting economic agent insofar as he remains a juridical agent, and this is what enables his autonomy to last. In short, at the end of the nineteenth century, the great advocates, especially in New York, had become important collaborators in the capitalist world, amassing fortunes from the sale of their juridical services. In the hearts of the minority that dominated the profession (a puritan petite bourgeoisie consecrated by their cultural and juridical capital) a sort of ideology arose, a collective discourse through which the corps defended what Marx would have called its 'spiritual *point d'honneur*'.[25] These people, who had plenty of money, and sometimes plenty of honour too, wanted to affirm themselves as servants of the juridical ideal. You might say that they were inventing ideal interests which meant that they were interested in the ideal.

The critical sociologists who have sprung up (very recently in fact) in the United States in the area of the law have operated the first reduction that I mentioned last time, the one that considers that these people wanted to appropriate symbolic profits to add to their economic profits. In this light, their claim to purify the law is perceived as a fiction that disguises their interested motivation. The model frequently used is that of Victorian hypocrisy, a sort of double game constitutive of bourgeois ideology, where those who demand juridical competence are seeking to eliminate (what they call) the 'rabble' of petty advocates; it is a way of affirming the symbolic distinction of the jurists and, much more practically, the gap between the great and the small. This critical vision is not wrong, and we could link it with what happened in the composition of the great [art?] collections (the Americans sometimes speak of 'guilt money'): this ideology has a blindingly obvious aspect of 'compensating for guilt'. But it remains the case that when the collective imagination gets to work to assuage this guilt and idealize this spiritual point of honour, it has a real social impact. It produces a collective, and collectively approved, representation, which comes to constitute a universalist definition of the profession and exerts real effects on the agents who produce this body of doctrine. I have in front of me a quotation from a critic who says that this ideology is ultimately an advocate's self-indulgent hobby, like a collection of Japanese prints or a box at the opera.

That said, these people wanted to be worthy of the self-image that they had created, and to affirm themselves as a superior caste, which led them, through a kind of cunning of ideological reason, to start to finance schools of law, for example. They became in a way the supporters of a pure and disinterested juridical training, and they helped to form little backwaters, alongside the business advocates and other

legal sharks, where the pure jurists could survive, preparing their pupils
– very badly – for the ocean of business but still teaching them pure,
disinterested law, and the values of disinterestedness that go with it.
The dichotomy between the practical users of the law and the teaching
of law is to some extent, in this particular case of a liberal system, the
product of their guilt mixed with the defence of their honour by the
major advocates caught in their own trap of disinterestedness. So we
see clearly in this case how representations which are rather hastily
labelled as ideological may be efficient and could even be counter-
productive: these advocates, through their descendants, could become
victims of the disinterested politics that they themselves had initiated
and, as you know, there would be critical jurists who might perhaps
not have existed without this kind of mechanism. These people forged
a kind of fantasy image of the law as a pure, coherent, rational and
almost sacred science, into which you enter as into a vocation, a sort
of calling, and which was perpetuated in a state of insular isolation
outside the social field. This confers on them the status of a secular
nobility, which is not unconnected with the fact that, like d'Aguesseau,
they were part of the rising petite bourgeoisie. They did not really
belong to the upper Bostonian aristocracy, and, as a general rule, they
found in the universal a way of affirming their moral superiority over
the titular, hereditary nobility.

I think that we may take as a general rule the fact that the rising
classes are interested in ethics. I said this rather cruelly in *Distinction*,[26]
but it is true. I had in the past been inspired by a very fine book by
Svend Ranulf, *L'Indignation morale*,[27] which presents a history of the
theme of moral indignation from Greek antiquity up until the present
day. The notion of moral indignation is very interesting and, if you
are involved in sociology, moral indignation appears to be a petit
bourgeois speciality. I am speaking crudely, and since saying such
things is part of the class struggle, I always hesitate to make this kind
of summary, simplistic remark in public, for fear that what I am saying
might be reinterpreted along the lines of 'you are just a petit bourgeois,
therefore you feel moral indignation' [*laughter*]. But it is an observation that is important for understanding certain specific benefits.
Moral indignation brings its own satisfaction, and we should certainly
view such moral indignation with a Nietzschean suspicion. We can
always suspect the excessively strict (there is a famous analysis of this
kind in Sartre's *Anti-Semite and Jew*),[28] but the morally indignant may
nonetheless be agents of historical progress. Although my reading is
not at all Hegelian, if I were nonetheless to describe the genesis of
a field in a Hegelian logic, I would say that there is not a universal

class,[29] but there are fields which tend towards universality, where each class sings (more or less well) from its own song sheet, and where the petit bourgeois song sheet is indignation. In this guise, the petit bourgeois unmasks and unveils (think of *Le Canard enchaîné*, if you like [*laughter*]), he looks under the carpet, he sniffs out scandals, etc. The rising classes are often tempted by this disenchanted or demystified vision, and since there are universal rules in democratic societies, they can increase the force of their indignation by justifying it through an appeal to universal rules. They do not simply say: 'It's disgusting', but 'It is all the more disgusting because they say you shouldn't do it.' Or they argue that 'on the pediments of our public temples the words "liberty, equality, fraternity" are written'. This is the typical strategy for advancing the universal: you do not write 'liberty, equality, fraternity' with impunity, because, once it has been written, people who are morally indignant can use this somewhat verbose slogan in favour of specific interests, to make it more than just a form of words.

The New York advocates were in the same position. They were not quite equal to the Boston nobility; they had plenty of money, they had culture, but they had morality as well, which, especially in a country with a Puritan tradition, helped them make great strides towards nobility. For this reason, they are historically important agents. That said, during this period, the weight of these lonely, freelance individuals decreased in favour of the corporations and the collective cabinets of advocates. Within the profession itself, the relative influence of the advocates in court or in a tribunal lost ground to the business advocates. Increasingly the profession of advocate became a business profession. But however forceful this progress towards an apparent loss of autonomy, subordinating the juridical field to the economic field, the advocate only remains an advocate (as I suggested just now) if he is not entirely a businessman. He would lose his value for his clients, and would disqualify himself as an advocate, if he were completely at their service. This still obeys a logic of pious hypocrisy, or hypocrisy as the tribute that vice pays to virtue. Once a juridical field exists, an advocate is only useful if he serves as an advocate and if he employs the specific competence that distinguishes him from any old legal tough guy. To take an extreme case, he can only be respected by the *mafioso* who finances him if he still manages to assert his independence and retain a minimal value in the juridical field. What can hold him in check is not only the concern to defend his honour; it is also the fact that if he 'goes too far', as they say, he loses all efficacity in the juridical field. This is the kind of mechanism that you need to bear in mind in order to understand.

Cross-checking

I am approaching what will summarize everything that I have been saying so far. The subject of juridical disinterestedness (a formula that would encapsulate everything I have been saying) is not one individual, it is the juridical field – the whole set of interactions between the agents placed in positions of rivalry, themselves determined by specific relations of force. The determinants of a behaviour of universal style, and the gratifications it attracts, are constituted within this space. To give a small example: 'Unless I want to discredit myself (the word "credit" is important) and therefore lose my specific efficacy, which is based on belief (my client believes that I am effective, and I must not let colleagues remove me from the list of advocates), I must do what forms the basis of my credit, that is, respect the letter of the law and the unwritten laws of the corps.'

In France there was a fairly similar process, with the difference that, according to the sources that I have consulted, the move towards business happened later. The gap between ideal and reality grew wider at the end of the nineteenth century: the famous rules that I drew your attention to remained in force, but, for instance, where honoraria were concerned, the practice of accepting down payments, which was formally prohibited, became more and more frequent. Likewise, the idea that a salary should take the form of a gift came to appear increasingly obsolete, in particular in the eyes of the young advocates, who were more sensitive to realities and less socially attuned to the old system . . . (It is in a way a phenomenon opposite to the one that I always call the 'hysteresis of the habitus': as we grow old we continue to function in terms of the world in which we have been socialized, even when this world no longer exists. Whereas in societies that do not change, the old are king, in societies that do change, ageing means nursing within us the phantasm of a social world that no longer exists, leaving our habitus conditioned by the state of a world now extinct. The old are as deluded as Don Quixote: they expect the world to answer their expectations but it does not respond.)[30] In the case in point the young say: 'This cannot go on, there are some things that they must let us do.' The ban on delegation, for instance, gradually disappeared and the advocates tended more and more to represent their clients before the specialist tribunals. This process was a source of conflict between the upholders of rules and traditions and the proponents of change – who can appeal, as always in such cases, to the same rules that justify the elders in resisting change, to call on them to change.

These complex strategies do not deceive anyone, for another property of the fields is that in practice people do know the secret and make use of it (for instance to express their indignation); they practise an amateur, albeit partial, sociology. The difference between what I see as scientific sociology and this amateur sociology is that, in a given field, the latter has only one viewpoint, whereas the act of constituting a field makes you see all the viewpoints simultaneously. The young advocates, for instance, see the limits of their elders very clearly: they see that the old timers transgress the ethical code every day, and they propose to 'make the rules match the morals'. They see their adversaries' vision, as well as the viewpoint from which this vision is perceived, but they do not see the viewpoint from which they perceive their view of this vision and viewpoint, that is, their own viewpoint. They don't see that it is in their interest to see what the others don't see, and they don't see that it is in the interest of the others to see what they do see, and that they only see what they do see because it is in their interest to see it [*laughter*]. This is a very important law. You can apply it to our political life today: Monsieur X can easily see what Monsieur Y is doing, why he is declaring his candidature late in the day [*laughter*],[31] but that is not the same thing as constituting the space as such and seeing that everyone is an amateur sociologist apt to study everyone else, but very bad at studying himself. The sociologist is someone who uses the notion of the field to draw that kind of invisible line within whose boundary what was an absolute viewpoint becomes a particular viewpoint. I shall not take this point further.

In France, then, the new young entrants, although dominated in the juridical field, challenged the dominant, and, strangely, they tried to undo what the profession had done to establish its autonomy. Their predecessors had struggled to ban delegation; the new intake tried to make it possible once again, because, as the saying goes, 'times have changed'. In fact what had changed was the objective system of interests. Different times, different collective morals . . . As in the United States, what was called the 'justice of the law courts', or sometimes 'the judiciary', lost ground to the juridical, that is, commercial justice. The advocates increasingly turned to handling the signing of contracts, the drafting of company statutes, inter-group negotiations and consumer law; in short, they entered more and more into the economic life of the country.

Thus we arrive at the very interesting state of the juridical field which Monsieur Dezalay discussed in the seminar. I shall summarize this briefly because he showed very clearly how a field functions. I think that the Anglicism 'cross-checks' expresses this well: everyone watches everyone else, and everyone watches. . . . Polanyi, who is among other things a good historian of science, says in one very fine article that in the scientific field nobody can check the whole of science any longer.[32] Science has become a kind of unmanned aircraft; nobody is able to see the field as a whole (especially not the philosophers, even if they would like to! [*some laughter*]). That said, each scientist looks around him, so that there is a kind of checking of everyone in immediate proximity, which means that, in spite of everything, everything is more or less checked. This is Polanyi's thesis. We also find cross-checks in fields like the juridical field: the agents closest to the business world exert pressure in the direction of acceptable compromise, transformation of the law and adaptation to reality, but without ceasing to be submitted to the control of the upholders of pure law, who are often professors, and who constantly remind them of the limits imposed by juridical practice.

So we get a chiastic structure which I believe we can find in all the fields of cultural production. [*Bourdieu draws a diagram on the board*] At the first pole, we have the people who are close to the world of business. They earn a lot of money and have ethical standards that you could call loose from the viewpoint of the norms that I signalled just now. They are the business advocates, whom we may note as (+) in economic terms and (-) in terms of independence. At the other pole, pure law will be economically (-) and ethically pure (+). So *a priori* (I say this tentatively because I haven't backed this up with a survey) we have a chiastic structure. In many fields this chiastic structure underpins the cross-checking, because the bridges between the two poles are never burnt. In the juridical field, those who make the money are obliged, in the very interest of their logic of profit, to make concessions to those who practise the law: writing articles in scholarly journals, clothing in juridical considerations decisions whose principle was not the law, etc. It seems to me that it is the chiasmus which is the source of the pious hypocrisy which, as I said at the beginning, is not reducible to hypocrisy alone: the specific hypocrisy is all the more effective as it is the more sincere.

The force of the ideal

That was by way of summing up what I wanted to say. I now want to come immediately to my conclusion, which I have already announced several times. What seems to me to be typical of this kind of universe (although in fact the juridical field is one of the fields least independent

 Lecture of 24 March 1988

from the political and economic powers) is the fact that, because of their relative independence from the State and from business, they tend to function as competitive spaces within which reference to the ideal and its norms is relatively efficient and relatively profitable. Even in circumstances where, as in America in the 1980s, the autonomy of the juridical field seems reduced almost to nil, and the cynical, disenchanted vision of the reductionist sociologists seems absolutely true, the autonomy affirmed by means of the simple 'point of honour' still retains its efficacy, and the rights claimed by the universe of law serve as a weapon in the struggles within the universe of the law. For this reason there may be some progress towards the universal under quite unexpected conditions. In other words, the norms of the law become imposed on the makers of the norms, not through the simple force of sanctions (the Council of the Order itself does in fact conform to the general state of the field: its rules become obsolete without any need for this to be said, because nobody would think of applying them), not through the simple effect of being represented in people's consciences, but on the basis of the relation between the dispositions socially constituted to recognize the norms and a universe in which these norms remain at least verbally respected. This relation is itself the basis of reciprocal relations between the agents who are in the field.

For the norms governing juridical practice to be applied at least to some extent, firstly, each social agent engaged in the game must have been socialized enough to recognize these norms, at least verbally, or more profoundly, with their body and habitus (in the shape of things that must not be done, that are scandalous, etc.). They must recognize them in a practical mode; the Hegelian connotations of the word 'recognition' as I use it are pertinent, even if I think that the fields are based on very corporeal forms of practical recognition. This is why earlier I used the notion of *obsequium* when discussing etiquette: recognition is not necessarily a conscious act; belief is the extreme form of recognition. Here we should follow Pascal. He who kneels down experiences recognition because his body is bent down. Now, what the fields do is make men bend down. As we say, they 'develop a bent' (somebody asked me whether there was a personality to match each field . . . what I am saying is an answer to that question). In the juridical field, the people must have adopted the juridical bent. It is what we call the juridical spirit or the spirit of public service, which is a spirit of the corps that has become corporeal. (A few years ago I referred to Kantorowicz and the body, in the sense of a corporation that becomes a body, in terms of corporeal dispositions.)[33] Secondly there has to be a minimum number of rules of the game, through learned societies for instance, whose members have nothing in common but nonetheless go to listen to a professor of private law, while knowing that nothing he has to say has any relevance to anything . . . But they go there to defend the honour of their profession. They listen to his quotations in Latin and they pay homage to him, for it is indeed he, in the official hierarchy, who is their superior. This is important: this pole remains spiritually dominant, even if it is not comparable in terms of earnings; he is even all the more dominant, the poorer he is. The virtue of disinterestedness allows situations to be overturned. In the normal world, a man's value is measured by his salary. The values of disinterestedness allow hierarchies to be overturned, to transform destiny into choice and to make of poverty a virtue. In the artistic field, this is a fundamental mechanism.[34]

These two conditions are necessary, but not sufficient. My definition just now, arguing that a field supposes disinterested dispositions and a universe that rewards this disinterestedness, was rather simple. In fact, more is needed. As my analysis suggested, this universe also needs to function as a field of competition, and between the most distant poles a minimum of communication must subsist, at least enough to convey an insult. It is for this reason that it is not contradictory to speak of a 'logical conflict' (this could give us another classic examination topic: consensus/conflict): in my opinion, the essence of the social fields is to be united by conflict. For one property of the social fields lies in the fact that they agree on the terms of their disagreement. In fact belonging to a field is to agree sufficiently with the others to be able to reproach them with not being in agreement with what we are saying, while one way of excluding someone from a field is by refusing to discuss with them, refusing to recognize them as a legitimate interlocutor. Between the most distant positions in the juridical fields, there remains nonetheless a consensus on the legitimacy and the necessity of conflict, as well as on the ultimate values in the name of which to do battle. I mentioned just now the petits bourgeois who appeal to universal norms in order to challenge the dominant who appeal to those norms in order to dominate. Likewise, in a field, a classic strategy of the newcomers is to appeal to universal norms in order to combat the dominant, arguing that the latter preach the norms but do not practise what they preach.

If we have these three things (the dispositions, a field that rewards them, and reciprocal struggles in the name of the rules), we have a field in which something like the universal is produced. To triumph in such a universe, the social agents must at least universalize their particular interests. They must at least give them a universal clothing, because this universal clothing contributes to the force of the universal.

Escaping historicism

I shall finish in five minutes, and if I go too quickly, you can let me know in your questions. I want to raise a question that is currently the subject of much debate among philosophers. It was Habermas who made this problem a fashionable topic, but it is a serious matter: briefly, can we escape historicism? The social sciences develop demystifying enterprises that apply to all things and all people, including themselves. (On this subject, the philosophers are simply stupid when they say to the sociologists: 'You historicize everything, but how about yourselves?' If there is somebody who cannot forget this for a second, it's the sociologist ... I get annoyed when I hear the philosophers trying to teach us lessons as if we were schoolchildren ... well, that is just my personal feeling [*laughter*].) Sociologists and historians, then, destroy a certain number of universal discourses, and I think this is why the upholders of the universal find my analysis so aggressive, perverse and upsetting. By constituting the notion of the field, I do in fact show that the universes which produce the universal, or at least the claim to be universal, are themselves subject to laws and conflicts. Because I remind them that these are in a way universes like any other, the upholders of the universal find me particularly obnoxious. That said, you should not forget that all my work aims not to save the universal but to try to understand how under certain circumstances universes [do produce the universal, although] they are basically like the others: we are not dealing with saints or communists, as Merton says[35] (which is very funny for those who know who he is[36] [*some laughter*]), but with people who have specific interests, who mount operations, who have strategies, who establish monopolies, who oppress and dominate, etc. These universes are like the others in these aspects, but under certain conditions they do things that the other universes, such as the economic universe, do not do: they create the conditions for the production of something universal. Consequently it seems to me that the fact that reason has its history, the fact that it is born in historical conditions as repugnant as any other (the sociology of science is as sinister as the sociology of power), the fact that things which we consider to be rational or universal (universal religion, law or science, etc.) are produced in universes obeying the laws of interest, does not imply renouncing the idea of universal reason.

I would like rapidly to demonstrate that there is no need to invoke any transcendence of reason in order to save reason. Habermas faces more or less the same problem.[37] Those who have read a little will know that the Durkheim school formulated the problem quite naturally (whereas in France today people use Habermas to destroy what the Durkheimians constructed fifty or a hundred years ago). Lévy-Bruhl, for instance, spoke of a 'theoretical ethic' and a 'science of morality'[38] (which was even taught for the baccalaureate), asking whether, starting out from the laws that govern the functioning of the social world and normality, we can move on to establish the norms. At the time, right-thinking philosophers all said: we cannot go from 'this is how things are' to 'this is how things must be/what we should do'.[39] This is exactly the same enterprise that interests Habermas: he wants to try to show that, through purely anthropological, positive analysis of communication, using no metaphysical, ontological or transcendental jiggery-pokery, we can produce a must-be.

Since I am running out of time, I shall put things simply and crudely. The philosophers, at least the German ones, often use a philosophical envelope to package, as a sales manager would say, things which have been established by the social sciences. In the event it is Habermas who seems to me to recycle a certain number of principles that the philosopher and linguist Grice calls 'conversational implications'.[40] The term designates the universal presumptions implied in the fact of addressing somebody: when I speak to somebody, I presume that they will treat a rational argument as a rational argument and not as an act of violence, etc. In my opinion it is this kind of Gricean analysis, which consists in decanting the universal implications of any act of communication between men, that Habermas exploits when he says: 'I have at last found the Archimedean point, I escape the historicism in which we are plunged (he is thinking of Foucault, etc.), and I can give you a non-theological, non-transcendental principle to found reason itself; this principle is in communication, from the moment you start to speak.' Thus he will say to Bourdieu: 'From the moment that you argue with me to try to convince me, you are accepting reason, which contradicts your radical historicism.'

Without going into more detail, I reply that the conditions for validating this conversational principle are rarely fulfilled. It takes very special conditions for a conversation between Habermas and Bourdieu to take place. There mustn't be some soldier waiting to cut off your speech with his sword. I am answering in a ridiculously provocative manner, but in fact the conditions required include everything that I previously mentioned: it is a social game in which reason has to be paid for, in which you cannot refute a theorem with another theorem, in which 'none but geometers may enter'. Now all these things take centuries to come to pass: they are a historical production, and I think that we may say that there are very specific historical conditions presiding over the birth of historical universes in which something like universal reason may provisionally come into being, reproduce itself and furnish the social agents who live off it with sufficient specific gratifications for them to continue the process. I'll explain that more clearly next time.

Lecture of 14 April 1988[1]

The claim to be universal – Does a space beyond positions exist? – Two canonical positions – The organicist metaphor – A quasi-divine viewpoint – Durkheim's lapses – The reinvention of Hegel's theory – The State, a movement towards unity – Bureaucracy – Durkheim, State sociologist

[. . .] The first indispensable phase [of a reflection on the State is] a sort of extremely radical questioning of all the presumptions that assail us when we think of the State. To announce my main concern straight away, I think that a whole tradition of thinking about the State has considered it as a thinking social entity. The great representative of this tradition is Hegel, but we could find exactly the same theory in a semi-explicit state in someone like Durkheim. I think that in the unconscious of many thinkers of the social world, there is State thinking. It seems to me that we need to take Durkheim seriously when he says: the State is a social entity that haunts those who think about the social world, and perhaps all the more so when they are linked to the State as its civil servants. The State thinks within us, and there is some already-thought State-thought in our thinking. [. . .] The State can be considered as a thinking entity, and that is why we need to be especially suspicious of State thoughts, especially when we want to think of the State. This is the central [point] of what I shall propose. Formulated like this, it might seem rather rhetorical, but what I have done in the previous lectures is nonetheless an introduction to what I am going to do with the State.

Before launching into my argument, I shall devote a few words to one of the questions that have been put to me. In general I have the impression that I go too slowly, but it is true that sometimes I go much too quickly, and some of your questions confirm that the time I have spent commenting on certain topics was not entirely wasted. There are questions that I won't answer in detail, because they have already received a reply in what I have already said, or because they are going to receive one in what I am going to say. The question that I am going to answer is the following: 'Does preferring one pole of the contradiction that forms the axis of the field constitute a militant act, and does taking account of both poles constitute a scientific act?' This question suggests that I have not explained things too carefully myself. I shall say briefly what this means for me. One difficulty in thinking about the social world, as I said just now, is that our heads are crammed full of ready-made thoughts: we are inhabited by habitual thinking or pre-thought preoccupations. Thus it seems to me that the question is quite typical in its focus on habitual political thinking. We think of the social world in terms of a very common pattern – you only have to think of what is happening at the moment[2] – which is the pattern of right and left, the opposition between right thinking (or right-wing thinking) and gauche thinking (or left-wing thinking), orthodoxy and heterodoxy, heresy, and so on. This structure of thought runs very deep. You can throw it out of the window, but it comes back through the door (or vice versa). The question challenges my argument – which I may have presented too rapidly and superficially – that the people who strive to think of the relatively autonomous social universes that I call fields (such as the juridical field or the scientific field) usually do so only partially. I like to take the example of the sociology of intellectuals because it is the most typical. The sociology of intellectuals, which is obviously practised by intellectuals (there are of course some minor attempts at anti-intellectual Poujadism disguised as sociology, but they are produced by intellectuals), adopts certain viewpoints over the intellectual world and, since these analyses of the intellectual world are produced by intellectuals, these viewpoints are adopted from a point in the intellectual field. In my opinion, you need to bear in mind this notion of the intellectual field in order to confront any standpoint adopted towards the intellectual field, and question the position from which it has been taken.

I think of a series of articles from *L'Événement du jeudi* on the Heidegger affair that I was reading on the train a few days ago.[3] You saw side by side a series of judgements made by Emmanuel Levinas, Michel Polac, Luc Ferry and others. They each gave their view of the Heidegger affair, adopting a stance towards the intellectual field. Most often, when social agents take up a position on a problem, they treat the problem in fact as a pretext to discuss the intellectual field, their position in the field or the position they think they hold, and the positions that they want to assign to others, etc. It would be very instructive to make a sociological study of this set of articles on the Heidegger affair. In themselves, they are not of great interest, but as an object of research they are very interesting: a group of people have adopted positions that we might relate to the positions from which they have adopted these positions, suggesting an explicative relation between their positions and the standpoints they have adopted. When Michel Polac says that the Heidegger affair is ridiculous and that nobody has properly understood it, his interest in saying this is so obvious that the sociological analysis is self-evident. In the framework of a polemic, it is only too easy to relate the standpoints adopted to the positions of those adopting them, especially when somebody in a dominant position is looking at somebody in a dominated position: it is very easy to sociologize other people, especially when you are looking down on them from above.

It was in opposition to this that I launched the idea that the notion of the field demands a 'de-centring'. The notion has two immediate functions: it obliges us to refer any standpoint adopted to a position held in a field, but it simultaneously obliges us to retrieve the standpoint of the person adopting this spontaneous standpoint (when I say that we spontaneously sociologize other people, I mean that we spontaneously establish a relation between the interests associated with a position and the standpoint adopted). The notion of the field obliges us to refer this interested adoption of a standpoint towards a standpoint adopted ('I argue that Michel Polac is expressing the resentment felt by a marginal intellectual') to the position held by the person adopting this standpoint towards the standpoint adopted. The notion of the field imposes this reflexive distance ('you speak of a field, but you yourself are placed somewhere in that field'), which does not necessarily imply a devaluation or a relativization. We could say that what you have to say about the field will be all the less relativizable the more you have relativized it yourself by consciously referring to the position from which you are adopting this standpoint. Why does the question put to me imply in my eyes a regression from what I am arguing? It seems to me (correct me if I am wrong) that the question contains a surreptitious overtone: 'You hold a scientistic, positivist position, and yet you are implicitly or explicitly denouncing as naive the positions invested in any point in the field.' If, after my long commentary, we reread the question ('Does preferring one pole of the contradiction that forms the axis of the field constitute a militant act, and taking account of both poles constitute a scientific act?'), we can easily see that ultimately it is assimilating sociology to a third way: there is a right and a left, and we know the political position of those who claim to situate themselves elsewhere – it is the third way. Now I am trying to produce a different way of thinking, arguing that any standpoint adopted is situated, dated and located. The process of constructing these positions does not necessarily lead to some neutralism or objectivism far from the madding crowd, some 'third way', for it can lead to further militant commitment, perhaps of a different kind. I should develop this point.

I have made rather a lot of this question, because, as I often say without really managing to be understood, sociology is a science which seems exoteric, but is in fact esoteric. Behind its simple appearance, it is an extremely difficult science. There is no doubt that it is more easily available to the general public than other sciences, but at the same time it is extremely difficult, for the reasons that I gave at the beginning; since we think of the social world with thought processes that are products of this social world, we can never escape our social presumptions. It is a fundamental contradiction, we are always caught in a sort of 'double bind'. As soon as we start thinking, we make use of these thought processes (whether common and shared with the public, or learned, or even semi-educated) and are exposed to being thought by our own thought processes. One way out is to make a clean sweep: 'I don't want to know anything, I abandon it all', but then there is the danger of becoming an autodidact, naive and grotesque, and if there is one arena where the autodidact is unforgivable, it is the social sciences. It is possibly worse than in physics or chemistry. How can we escape the alternative of the pathetic, pretentious autodidact and the pre-packaged thinking that we adopt unwittingly? The example that I have chosen shows clearly how things that seem fairly obvious (such as 'You can only think from a position, you need to think of this position, and then think of the position from which you are thinking of that position') can be swept aside by a return of pre-packaged thought. In other words, everything that I am going to say is in danger of being refracted through the lens of the glasses that we all wear, which are linked to our position and therefore our social class, our education, our assumptions and the authors that we have assimilated, etc. People say that sociology is difficult because it trespasses on the ground of politics (with the right and the left, for instance), but the bias that we call 'political' is in the end the least dangerous. If that were the only problem, everything would be much simpler, because things affected by politics have been partially constructed and objectified into a state of discourse with a given structure, whereas in my opinion the most difficult problem is the instinctive, automatic thinking that inhabits us all.

Whence the difficulty in teaching sociology. The teaching would be facile if it were just a question of transmitting the facts established by the professional thinkers, but there is a supplementary problem: we need to transform the way people think. This is why I say that sociology is an esoteric science, and even, in some respects, initiatory: it aims to transform our manner of seeing the world. In my opinion, if I may use the language of initiatory philosophy, thinking of the State means giving you new eyes with which to view the State, or, to use an old metaphor, saying: 'You have motes in your eyes, so many beams that cloud your vision.'[4] Before casting your eyes on the State, which will dazzle you, you need to reflect for days on end, so as to remove your pre-packaged thoughts and knowledge, largely inculcated by the State, which is thinking through you when you think you are thinking of the State. When I say 'thinking through you', I am speaking of Hegel and Durkheim (who are hardly part-time, amateur thinkers . . .). I don't know if I have the right to put things this way, but this is more or less the drift of what I am trying to say, and if I didn't say it, the core of my teaching method might appear to be mere eccentricity. [You might wonder] why I don't run through the theories of the State with you. I would say that this would be almost too easy. There are lectures like that elsewhere, and they all tend to put thinking on hold: in that kind of lecture on the State, everybody, whether speaker or listener, thinks that they are thinking but in fact nothing is happening, we just learn that Mr X says one thing and Mr Y something else.

The claim to be universal

I return now very briefly to the principal conclusions of my argument, which can serve as an introduction to the analysis of the State that I intend to sketch. At the end of the last lecture, I noted (in a rather rapid formula, because I wanted to conclude certain aspects of the discussion) that we often discover a chiastic structure in the juridical field. I drew a little diagram on the board showing the opposition between business law and pure law. I said that, in a field like the juridical field, the checks that can be applied from the rationalist and universal viewpoints seemed to me often to be themselves cross-checked, in a conflict zone. This for me is the important point, suggesting that the universal – or the social process from which something like the universal or something claiming to be universal may emerge – often comes to fruition in regulated zones of conflict. The rationality or the normativity that claims to be universal is often born of a conflict fought in the name of the universal. A second conclusion follows on from what I have just said: contrary to what people claim, there is no antinomy between historicity and rationality.

We may argue that there is a social history of reason, without being accused of relativism, nihilism or irrationalism. I referred in passing to the Habermas thesis which, in deliberate contrast to philosophers of the recent French tradition like Foucault, claims to rescue reason from history without any metaphysical jiggery-pokery, without invoking anything other than history itself. Habermas bases his argument, without admitting it (like so many philosophers), on Grice's linguistics, which attempted to show that any conversational exchange was pregnant with 'conversational implications', that is, logical principles tacitly implicating any speaker: as soon as I address somebody, I obey some very general principles which, as a speaker, I presume that my interlocutor will respect in turn. Grice's 'conversational implications' are tacit assumptions, because there is no social contract for conversation (we don't say, for instance, before we start to converse: 'We agree on the fact that we will not assume that what we are saying is incoherent'). We accept these 'conversational implications' outside of any explicit contract; they are not spelled out as explicit conditions of linguistic usage, but are written into the situation of linguistic exchange itself.

Habermas has taken these analyses – which I shall not pursue further – and given them a more general application, making these conversational implications the basis of a general theory of rationality. Rationality is not given by the gods; it is engaged, to put it very simply, whenever two human beings come together to talk. It is therefore immanent in communication, insofar as all language entails a claim to validity. The minute I start to speak, I tacitly lay claim to the immanent validity of my expressive intent, which is recognized by my interlocutor in granting me his attention. Ultimately this double recognition of our rational assumptions forms the foundation of rationality. I am having some trouble reconstructing this analysis because I can't quite bring myself to believe in it . . . Habermas wants to escape from historicism, and the force of his thinking deserves our respect (I wanted at least to make that clear, despite my awkwardness explaining it). His attempt to escape from historicism without fudging the issue is a procedure analogous to Descartes' attempt to escape radical doubt without letting a *deus absconditus* [hidden God] that he had kicked out through the door come back in through the window. Habermas's attempt to use immanence to solve a problem posed by immanence seems interesting to me because he grounds his argument in the social sciences, which present philosophers with this problem. It is the social sciences, and sociology and history in particular, that have historicized the categories of thought, saying what I said to start with ('your minds are full of historical thinking, which you are using when you try to think of historical thinking'), and highlighting this as a dramatic problem, not least for the social sciences themselves. Habermas tries to find the solution to the problem in what causes the problem in the first place. He asks the human sciences to provide him with a solution to the problem of the foundation of reason that avoids all transcendence, and thus he finds this Archimedean point from which he will be able to construct the whole chain of reasoning. Whence the analogy with Descartes: once we have found a fixed point, we will be safe, we can hang everything on it. For Habermas, the Archimedean point is these conversational implications without which discourse and exchange, the *logos*, would make no sense. Even the historicist discourse that aims to demolish reason would be itself demolished as a discourse with rational claims, since it mobilizes the rational affirmation that it denies. This, roughly, is his argument.

My solution responds to exactly the same problem, but is opposed to this analysis. The formulation is the same but I believe that the solution is very different. We cannot escape historicity through a singular act, through a form of exchange, or by positing an implicit dimension to social exchange. We escape historicity provisionally and at the end of a historical process which is a series of imperceptible steps towards social spaces within which something like what we call 'reason' assumes a social validity at a certain moment. In other words, I admit that I am reviving a tradition of the philosophy of science (Koyré for instance) according to which the principles of reason can be historical (thus the forms of measure or the criteria – in particular the criteria on which we are able to agree that we are in agreement – are historical, and liable to be disqualified by the progress of reason, of science) while defining, at a certain moment, the conditions of validity of the thought that we call scientific. There would be more to say about this procedure of historicist rationalism or rationalist historicism. Where the empiricists would say that we can only ever pass by means of a 'leap' from 'being' to 'ought to be', from 'this is' to 'this must be',[5] I would say that we can only pass from being to ought to be, from historicist description to normative aspirations, as and when there emerges a language game, as Wittgenstein would call it, which is valid within a field; that is, a social space regulated and capable of imposing on anything entering this social space a rule transcending individual intentions.

Does a space beyond positions exist?

At this point I would like to sum up, because we are going to find exactly the same problem in the State that we found in the juridical universe. Does a universal class exist, as Hegel argues? Does there exist in the social world a point that is somehow outside the game? Is there in the social world a free port, a neutral zone, a place outside all positions? Are there people who hold a position whose property is to have no position and to transcend all conflict? The problem concerns the State but also those who think about the State, and who always postulate implicitly – which would justify Habermas – that they are situated in a place from where they can think the world independently of the social and historical constraints that affect the other positions (and sometimes they claim [explicitly] to be situated there). This is the problem of the scientificity of sociology and history: a sociologist who claims to be a scientist postulates that there is a point in social space where the social constraints that affect all the other positions and all the other manners of holding these positions are suspended. This fundamental question gives rise to the unavoidable question facing us: the truth of the social sciences – is there a social place from which it is possible to contemplate the social world without that thought being localized and located?

The problem concerns the State, and it seems to me that there is a professional ideology of the senior civil servant, an ideology of the universal that is manifest in the writings of all bureaucrats in all countries (from tenth-century China to the federal State of the USA, not forgetting the French State), according to which the State administrator is in a way outside the game and its stakes: he has no personal interest, he is above and beyond all interest. I shall give you some exemplary formulations of this professional ideology – those of Hegel are relatively well known, but Durkheim's are more surprising – which raise the problem underlying all the queries that I have raised over the course of these lectures concerning the problem of disinterestedness. Is there a place in the social world whose incumbents can claim disinterestedness? Is the State bureaucracy the universal class that, being a disinterested class, is somehow capable of seeing the interests of those governed better than those concerned themselves?[26] Would they be capable of seeing further and higher – since the metaphor nearly always used in bureaucratic discourse is that of the overview: the senior administrator and the higher civil service are *above* all conflicts, partisan divisions, personal and local interests, and they are able to see the wider picture and its future implications? On this subject I could quote texts and reports published by the [French State] planning commissions. For the [State] planning commission is a typical bureaucratic agency. It is invested with a mission of general interest, therefore a universal mission, and it is composed of people perceived by those who appoint them as more universal than the average, and who are supposed by their community, that is, by the mutual checks that they will impose on one another, to become even more universal, so that a report by a commission will be treated as a kind of universal discourse giving us the last word on, say, the housing problem or the problem of immigration.[7] This is what happens in a commission of sages[8] (an interesting word): the members of this type of committee are rendered universal by their mission. Moreover, it is for this reason that they accept [to be members of it], for one of the great benefits of belonging to a commission is to be rendered universal by the nomination, and everybody loves being universal. This is another topos from Habermas: the aspiration to universality is universal, and we can see an argument in favour of universality in the fact that every man has at least a claim to universality.

But bureaucracy's claim to universality can be challenged, and it is possible to elaborate two exemplary, ideal-typical positions on the problem of the State, analogous to those that I have formulated on the problem of interest and disinterestedness: to those who profess the existence, availability or possibility of disinterestedness we can oppose the reductive, disenchanted, demystifying vision according to which disinterestedness hides particular interests. The more subtle position that I shall develop is to say that there is an interest in disinterestedness, which creates a difficulty: to link what I am going to say to what I said previously, I think that saying there is an interest in disinterestedness means saying that there is a social basis to the universal. If there were not an interest in disinterestedness, if, to put it crudely, disinterestedness did not pay, if there were not the universal recognition of the universal that I have just evoked, there would be no place for the slow progress towards the universal that philosophers of a Hegelian persuasion have naively canonized.

Two canonical positions

Having said that, I shall proceed in a way that is unusual for me, but is useful, I believe, given the subject. I shall rapidly mention two canonical positions on the State which seem to me to cover the space that we are able to consider: the Hegelian position and the Marxist position. I shall be engaging in a history of thought, although I had said at the outset that it is ridiculous to repeat what other people have said, but my perspective is not the one that Nietzsche would have called antiquarian history.[9] In fact I think it is important (and I take this as a general principle for all practising social scientists) to attempt to objectify the exemplary forms of the object that we are confronting, as a way of exorcizing the pre-packaged thought which lurks in a confused state in the thinking of the thinker. The great philosophers allow us to objectify thoughts that exist, albeit in a less radical and methodical way, in a pre-conceptual state in the thoughts of ordinary men (or at least I feel able to make use of their procedures in this way). For instance, in my opinion, Hegel totalizes in quite an extraordinary, systematic and methodical way (I could give you chapter and verse, but it would take too long) a process of Renaissance thinking that had been developing over 300 years since the sixteenth century on the representation of the State, which is part of the genesis of the State itself. (This is a fascinating aspect of his thought, which impressed even someone like Durkheim.) The State is born in part from thought on the universal. D'Aguesseau is thus a small link in the long chain of people who, as higher civil servants, were in a universal position and who made their contribution to the construction of the State by conceiving a notion such as that of the public good and by saying that the interest of the public is not a private interest. This hill of thought has been built by thousands of historical ants, with the civil servants playing a very special part (which it would be easy to show statistically). The great contributions to thinking on the State, which often emanated from civil servants, have been summarized quite magnificently by Hegel. But if Hegel saw his theory of the State as the end of a process of construction of the State, he did not see that his thought was the culmination of a historical labour of construction which was part of the construction of the State. There I am being a super-Hegelian, I'm not sure if you noticed my move (I am tempted to repeat myself, but you would think I was losing my marbles) – but I am not saying the same thing at all.

I intend therefore to evoke rapidly these two great forms of thinking on the State. I ask those of you who might find these things trivial to excuse me, but in the first place I think that not everyone will find them so. And then, since I cannot explain the whole process of the historical genesis of the notion of the disinterested State, I find it more practical to consider the culmination of this historical genesis in the systematic form provided by Hegel. Hegel and Marx seem to me to represent two poles of a space of positions, and one of the questions I shall ask is whether we really have to choose between these two polar concepts and if it is not rather through the very antagonism between them that we might see the lineaments of the fundamentally ambiguous 'truth' of the State. You might remember what I said about the law, distinguishing the naive, the semi-skilled and the skilled: the reductionist vision of the claim to the universal is at once a necessary stage and a moment to overcome, insofar as the claim to the universal that the reductionist vision destroys has to be included in a complete definition of universality. In other words, the three phases need to be integrated. That is what I had in mind in contrasting the Hegelian and the Marxist concepts, not only as polar positions, but as views of the State that are not exclusive. To put it in a single sentence: if the State were what Marx said it is, it would not fulfil the functions that Marx attributes to it; it is because the State is both what Marx says it is but also what Hegel claims it is, that it does fulfil the functions attributed to it by Marx. If you have followed what I was saying earlier, you will recognize my model of thinking (I am embarrassed because I must be giving some of you the feeling that I keep saying the same thing, and yet at the same time I must be confusing others . . .).

The organicist metaphor

Hegel interests me for the way he gives a systematic, almost extremist expression to this idea that the bureaucracy is a universal group. For Hegel the State functions as an organism composed of interdependent parts which are united by exchanges of information and regulation. Behind the Hegelian idea of the State, then, there is an organicist metaphor which in reality has been constantly present throughout the process of construction of the State at work since the sixteenth century: the State is thought of as an organism. We still speak today of the *corps* of the engineers of the mines or the roads and bridges, referring to the idea of a social body whose genesis goes back to the Renaissance. The author of a very fine article that I read recently[10] shows that the pattern of thought at work in three quarters of writings on politics is an organicist pattern, which is an illustration of Bachelard's argument that scholars and intellectuals mobilize unconscious patterns of thought in their thinking.[11] One of the lessons that we can already draw from what I have just said is that whenever we think of the State we must constantly be on guard against falling back on the organicist model which, when applied to the political world, as Canguilhem has shown in various writings,[12] is laden with political imports. You cannot think the social world as an organism without introducing an ensemble of fundamental presumptions, such as the primacy of the whole over the parts, the fact that the totality is an organic therefore coherent totality, or the fact that consensus is a fundamental and integrating factor.

But I need to qualify this already: the organicist concept can be more or less subtle. For instance, the theory of systems that is making a strong comeback in sociology with Luhmann[13] in Germany is a more noble form of elementary conservative thinking insofar as it sees the internal connections of the social body as performing integration through communication. Reinforcing the organicist metaphor with a cybernetic metaphor (the two fit easily together) is one of the simplest ways of founding conservative thinking; this is why it is constantly born again . . . We need to separate such primary organicisms from a more subtle organicism, one which considers that the parts of the body are integrated through conflict and checks and balances (the notion of checks and balances, or homeostasis, underpins many theories of the social world): the return to equilibrium may be an equilibrium between tensions. So we need to avoid excessive simplification: there are different organicisms and I could fit everything that I have been saying on the notion of the field into a theory like Montesquieu's. Montesquieu's intuition was that the social world is in fact an organism, but one whose different parts are integrated; he uses an image [. . .] In a metaphor he uses in his *Notebooks*,[14] I think, he sees the State as the fulcral point of a set of scales, a sort of mobile fulcrum: if it tips too much to one side, I must quickly push to the other side of the arm to rebalance it.

These metaphors are very important and, given the kind of brain cleaning that needs to precede any adequate thinking on the social world, it is vital to remind ourselves, as I have just done, of the major metaphors that underpin our thinking on the State and the social world. We should identify all the metaphors which we have at the back of our minds and which we mobilize simply by falling back on our everyday vocabulary ('balance', for instance: the idea of 'the balance of powers' – taught at Sciences Po – implies a theory of the State which supposes, as in Montesquieu's metaphor, that there is someone whose job it is to provide the counter-weight).

To close this parenthesis and return to organicism: it argues that the parts are united by exchanges of information and checks and balances. Durkheim picks this up almost literally: he insists strongly on the role of the exchange of information at the heart of the social body and considers that one of the roles of the State is to encourage these exchanges of communication. For Hegel, the parts of the State are harmonious elements of an individual totality (in passing, we must mention a difficulty which is faced by any reflection on the State: the ambiguity of the word 'State', which designates not only one part of the social body among others – the government, the site where decisions which we might in a Hegelian perspective call 'conscious' or 'voluntary' are taken – but also the totality of the social body. There are moments, for instance in the *Elements of the Philosophy of Right*, where Hegel does make this distinction). The State fulfils a certain number of functions: it draws on taxes and personnel for its resources; it organizes exchanges within civil society, which is at once regulated by the State and a regulator of the State, because it exercises checks and balances of different sorts on the State that regulates it. Marx challenged this postulate, saying that the bureaucracy is deaf. He did not say it in so many words but he did consider the State to be hard of hearing – except in one very interesting chapter in *Capital* where, discussing the Factory Act, he nonetheless remarks that the State does listen;[15] I shall return to this point. But for Hegel the bureaucracy entertains a cybernetic relationship with the different elements: it checks and controls and it is checked and controlled. It plays a determining role in the sense that it provides the different parties with their general orientations.

A quasi-divine viewpoint

In the Statist tradition that Hegel's thought exemplifies, the State is always credited with a kind of viewpoint that is irreducible to a single viewpoint. This is the Leibnizian metaphor of the geometric locus of all viewpoints:[16] the State occupies a position in relation to the social world that is God's position in certain seventeenth-century theories, which is the geometric locus of all viewpoints, that is, a neutral place where all viewpoints negate and compensate each other, or again, an enlightened place from which there is an unreciprocated view over all viewpoints.

This quasi-divine, Hegelian position is obviously tempting for thinkers in the social sciences. Driving the ambition to pursue a sociological career, there is often the unconscious urge to attain this viewpoint over which there is no other viewpoint, that is, to be God. Here again, I may be giving the impression of enunciating rather careless propositions that have neither rhyme nor reason, but I could show that a considerable number of *technical* errors in the construction of a questionnaire or the elaboration of a research project are motivated by what you might call a nostalgia for being God. The illusion of being God is betrayed for example in the fact of not objectifying the viewpoint of the person doing the objectifying. As I shall try to show, one of the great differences between the sociology that I attempt to practise and the sociology practised in the days of the great classics, of which Durkheim was the most exemplary, is the desire to include the viewpoint over the objectifying viewpoint. Thus I think that Durkheim's theory of the State is a fascinating case of a projective test of Durkheim's scientific unconscious. When he speaks of the State, Durkheim reveals his lapsus: 'I am a State official, therefore I am a universal thinker' (here I am anticipating on my argument).

What I have just been saying is that, for these theories of the State whose paradigm is Hegel's theory, the bureaucratic, Statist viewpoint is a quasi-divine viewpoint that is oriented from above, from [on high?] (these spatial metaphors and notions of perspective are important), it is a global overview. As I shall perhaps show even more clearly in the case of Durkheim, the State thinkers, who are thinking via the State when they think the universal thoughts that lead them to identify with the universal State, do in fact have a philosophy of individual error, of spontaneous sociology (Durkheim did not speak of 'spontaneous sociology' but of 'pre-notions'), which is the Spinozist philosophy of error. On this subject I could quote texts such as the introduction to Samuelson's book on economics,[17] or texts by Durkheim, among others. The unconscious of these thinkers on the social world harbours this idea that the error is a problem of deprivation, since singular individuals (you and I . . .) have in their everyday existence points of view that are partial, therefore partisan and biased.[18] Consequently, for them, the universal thinker (that is, the State, but also the State thinker in the case of Durkheim or the State philosopher in the case of Hegel) escapes the error because he is able to adopt the viewpoint of the Whole instead of having these partial or mutilated visions that are the lot of ordinary social agents. The problem of totalization and specialization in the social sciences is at the heart of this. Indeed, specialization may be seen as an abdication of the ambition to be universal and achieve totality; the practical choice in the scientific life of a sociologist or a historian to become a specialist of the particular or a specialist in the universal is not unrelated to the strength of the unconscious drive behind the scientific project and ambition to be God the Father (what I am saying may not be crystal clear but I do think that it makes sense).

I find Hegel's theory resembles a case for the psychoanalyst; it is the exemplary expression of a form of State neurosis. I think we should realize that the Hegelian vision is present in our minds. Yet as a sociologist I must immediately correct this statement: the Hegelian vision is present to differing degrees according to our position in the social space and the intellectual field. All through my exposé I have given you to understand that it was particularly present in sociologists, and in the sociologist who is addressing you now. The temptation of the Hegelian State is so strong because it is almost a sort of professional secret. I think that the Hegelian State and what it implies, that is, the role of a quasi-divine thinker, is part and parcel of the social drives and fantasies that help to explain how and why someone becomes a sociologist.

Durkheim's lapses

I can find proof that sociologists are particularly prone to this vision, in the theory of the State as expressed by Durkheim. In saying this, I immediately run the risk of upsetting the order that I had planned for my exposition, but I think at the same time that it can help illuminate those aspects of my argument concerning comprehension that I mentioned at the outset. Durkheim is very interesting because on the one hand he said things about the State which I find most profound, in particular, that we know nothing about it. I shall quote two passages that everyone has read, but that are extraordinary. At the start of *On the Division of Labour in Society*, Durkheim makes distinctions between public and private law, repressive and restitutive law, and observes that we cannot base a fundamental classification on a notion like the State: 'What, moreover, is the State? Where does it begin and where does it end? We know how controversial the question is; it is not scientific to make a fundamental classification repose on a notion so obscure and so badly analysed.'[19] When we read that, we recognize the great sociologist that we are familiar with. In *The Rules of Sociological Method*, he says: 'In our present state of knowledge, we do not know exactly what the state is, nor sovereignty, political freedom, democracy, socialism, communism, etc. Thus our method should make us forswear any use of these concepts so long as they have not been scientifically worked out.'[20] Here again this is excellent Durkheim: he knows how to handle language and is suspicious of its pre-notions; he doesn't want to fall into its traps.

On the other hand, Durkheim does develop between the lines a theory which is in fact his unconscious view of the State. This clearly illustrates what I wanted to say at the beginning: sociology is a very difficult science. The greatest sociologists have their lapses, and Durkheim's theory of the State is an enormous lapsus. There are moments when he shows himself to be very vigilant ('take care, I know that I don't know what the State is') and yet there are occasions when he gives his opinion on, for instance, a strike by civil servants (this is one of the great temptations for sociologists: they are asked for their opinion on a public issue because they are scholars, and since they want to appear learned, they respond), saying that 'civil servants should not go on strike' (he said this).[21] On another occasion, questioned on the ethics of civil servants, he says that the duty of discretion should be observed by even the village schoolteacher and that civil servants should make a clear division between the civil servant and the private citizen.[22] All this is punctuated by explicit declarations on the State as the 'brain' of the social body (he says it for instance in *On the Division of Social Labour*),[23] that is, the organ which controls the rest of the social body and which possesses knowledge; he says that the State *thinks*. In fact he subscribed to the Hegelian theory of the State as rational agent.

The reinvention of Hegel's theory

One question that I pondered when I read these texts was whether Durkheim had read Hegel. If the historians of thought had done their homework, they would be able to answer, but it is so much easier for them to simply comment on the text. I am sure that Durkheim had read Spinoza, and I even think that Spinoza's schema of error as deprivation, which I mentioned just now, helped him formulate his definition of the role of the State sociologist as the person who thinks the Whole, who escapes partial viewpoints. As for Hegel, I don't know. Durkheim could not have been ignorant of Hegel, but I am not sure whether he knew the *Elements of the Philosophy of Right*, which may not have been translated. In fact this is a purely historical question. That said, I would actually prefer him not to have read Hegel. It would back up my claim to treat a certain number of philosophies more as documents than as theses. In many cases we resort to a logic of influence to interpret things that have in fact been invented anew. Although it is true that the Hegelian vision of the State is the systematic and methodical expression by a professional philosopher of a sort of fantasy that is relatively universal but particularly strong in certain thinkers in certain situations, we may still entertain the hypothesis of simultaneous inventions: different people can reinvent the same theory. Just as in May 1968 all students were Marcusian without having read Marcuse (it was sufficient to take a poll: the question 'Have you read Marcuse?' received 80 per cent negative responses). Some simultaneous inventions are merely the product of a process of explication of the thoughts that impact on certain positions at certain moments in history. So I would rather like to think that Durkheim rewrote Hegel without realizing it. I tell myself that, being as honest as he was, he would have put 'cf. Hegel'; but he never did this. I prefer to think that he was not a Hegelian, and that if he was Hegelian, it was beyond his control. Here I am saying one of those things that are very naive and should not be written down; but a lecture is not a written text: it allows us to communicate things that we would never want to write but which are I believe ultimately more important [than the things that we do write]; if you have been following me, you will automatically read a certain number of my texts. In my case it took me quite a few years to manage to liberate myself from philosophical authority and read Hegel in the way I would read a text by a senior civil servant or a book on the State. They don't teach Hegel at Sciences Po, for sociological reasons that I understand all too well, but they should, because they do Hegel there all day long. If the Sciences Po people knew this, they would teach Hegel [*some laughter*] . . . A whole shelf of literature by senior civil servants on public service and the State, which I tried to analyse at one moment in my career,²⁴ is Hegelistic and Durkheimian through and through. And yet I am certain that those people have never read Hegel. In fact they completely reinvent him, except for the professional parts, which the philosophers appropriate as their privilege and which I have obviously glossed over.

To explain, briefly: one obstacle to reading philosophical texts as documents is the art that philosophers have as professionals in fore-grounding an overt architecture to their argument (this art is part of their expertise). For example, Guillermit showed in a very fine article that the plan of Kant's *Critique of Judgement* is a product of the trans-position of the structure of the *Critique of Pure Reason*.²⁵ A formal and visible structure is reproduced in the form of titles, chapters and paragraphs, and the professional commentator, who feels the need to perform at the same level as the text that he is studying, and therefore to take it as exemplary, is not going to track down its unconscious drives; he will accept its overt architecture and say: 'In bourgeois society, the Idea has not yet acceded to the for-itself, to the idea of itself, the State is the access of bourgeois society to self-awareness, etc.' This rhetoric is very significant, it is the transposition of the Hegelian logic onto the terrain of politics . . . I think that this set of mechanisms enabled Hegel to couch his fantasies of the State in an exemplary form. That said, if we limit ourselves to the overt phenomenal structure, we become blind to the latent structure which uses the overt mechanisms of the structure to find its exemplary expression. One of the func-tions of the canonical mechanisms of thought is to enable the thinker to risk spelling out everything that he has in mind, which if spoken bluntly would be slightly ridiculous and impossible to say. What I am saying must appear monstrous to some of you, but if I do shock you it is not for the fun of it: twenty years ago I myself would have been revolted if I had heard all this. The formal, scholarly structures allow the return of the repressed. They enable us to give it a form, to say it more systematically instead of harbouring a naive bureaucratic vision of the State. For instance Poniatowski[26] (you have certainly not read him, but I have . . .) has a philosophy of the State that philosophers should read, for they would realize that he is saying the same things as they are, which is a problem [*laughter*] that creates a mental block. A professional philosopher *per definitionem* cannot speak as Poniatowski does, even to a class of baccalaureate candidates [*laughter*], it would be suicidal . . . The form, the professional apparatus, the mechanisms of thought then have a dual function: they are what enable us to say what we really think (for, as you all know, when you can't find the words, you can't find the corresponding thoughts), but they are also what enable us to say it in an acceptable, permissible form. (I imagine that a lot of people give lectures on Hegel without realizing what they are saying and they would be revolted if they heard it said in the basic language used by Mr Poniatowski. I have just indulged in a rather indecent parenthesis, but it has enabled me to explain what I am doing, since I am speaking of Hegel in a way that is not orthodox.)

The State, a movement towards unity

I shall now attempt to sum up Hegel's thought on the State as I myself read it in the *Elements of the Philosophy of Right*: the State is an organism which thinks, and which conceives itself, which thinks because it conceives itself. To use a more orthodox formula, we might say that in bourgeois society the Idea does not yet exist for itself, it does not possess any conscious unity of itself; it is an unconscious unity, which comes to fruition through a sort of cunning in the interaction between individuals. My analysis is based on the use by Hegel of Mandeville's metaphor of the invisible hand (highlighted by the historians of thought): in relying on a form of equilibrium through rivalry, competition and the cunning of reason, bourgeois society is an expression of Mandeville's idea of the invisible hand.[27] Reason comes to fruition through individual interests, which are seeking something quite different from the universal interest. This progress towards unity and reason is not conscious of itself. The individual interests produce reason, but without knowing it; they know not what they do. This struggle of each against all, which finds transcendence and reconciliation as it moves towards unity, accedes to self-consciousness through the State; it is the State that sets itself the explicit project of unification and communication. The individual struggles then to find their true *raison d'être* in the unity of the State. The cunning of reason finds its *raison d'être* in the self-consciousness proposed by the State.

Another (Hegelian) development in what we might call an orthodox exposé (which you can find in all the critics): unlike the States of classical antiquity, the modern State is powerful enough to be able to take the risk of letting individuals' egoism produce reason unwittingly, it is powerful enough to let the principles of subjectivity and egoism run their course. It can let the egoistic drives off the leash, whereas in the States of classical antiquity, according to Hegel, people identified directly with the established order (there was no need to say 'liberty, equality, fraternity' since everyone felt free, equal and fraternal: the order was given in advance). The modern State can allow itself to give free rein to individualism because it is capable of orchestrating these individualisms[28] (this Hegelian compromise is one solution to the problem that I raised on the subject of disinterestedness and finding how to fashion general interest out of particular interests). Hegel's idea is very modern (when I say that it is important to bring this kind of approach to our reading of the great authors, it is to avoid wasting time: the problem is much more clearly stated in Hegel than in the contemporary debates on the alternative 'more State'/'less State', since that is what it comes down to): he says that there is no difference between liberalism and socialism, since the modern State can take liberalism to its extreme because it has the resources to orchestrate individual drives and act in such a way as to make antagonistic interests become reconciled in the unity of the Whole. In passing, an important idea that we should no doubt keep in mind is that the unity does not exclude antagonism; there is a unity that can be born of conflict.

So much for what we might call the philosophical part of Hegel's theory of the State. We could sum up this philosophical construction by saying that the State is a self-thinking organism. It is a sort of unity that is not aware of this unity as such, but which does accede to self-awareness. It is a movement towards unity which accedes to the idea of itself. But what is the concrete, empirical description of the State underlying this projection of theoretical schemas that Hegel has applied to other objects? Marx, who develops a reading of Hegel fairly close to mine, considers that Hegel confuses two levels. This is in the passage where he writes his famous phrase on the confusion between the things of logic and the logic of things, which I often quote:[29] Hegel is pulling the wool over our eyes, mystifying us by combining philosophical logic with an empirical description of the historical State. Marx suggests that Hegel has in mind the Prussian State (the prince, the State, the representative bodies, etc.) and that he pretends to deduce from his general theory of the relation between the in-itself and the for-itself an empirical justification of a state of things that has always been at the back of his mind. If you remember, we had already found this jiggery-pokery in the jurists who legitimate a verdict after the event by presenting an observation as if it were a deduction.

Bureaucracy

For Hegel, the key to this reconciliation is the corps of the bureaucrats, which is characterized by the fact that it intuits and desires the universal interest. I told you at the outset that Hegel is the culmination of a whole historical process, and it is obvious that he has read Rousseau. Here he has in mind the opposition between the general will and the will of all, and his bureaucrat is the heir of Rousseau's legislator: the bureaucrat avoids being the aggregate of the individual wills and accedes to an immediate vision of the general will, which, unlike a vote, is irreducible to the aggregate or the statistical sum of the individual wills.[30] The bureaucracy is a universal class because it has this vision of the universal. This vision of the universal is not a negative vision of the universal in the sense of the slave in the *Phenomenology of Mind* or the proletariat in Marx. It is a positive vision, insofar as the State is itself universal. When it perceives the universal, it is because it is seeing itself. Here philosophy comes into its own again ... (I don't want to give the impression of awarding bonus points, but here Hegel reverts to becoming a sociologist). The intuition and the universal will are not the products of the bureaucrats as individual persons but of the bureaucracy as a system of relations[31] defined by two essential properties: hierarchy and specialization. Durkheim will use exactly the same words and will also say that the characteristics of the bureaucracy are hierarchy and specialization, which he is very pleased with, since the division of labour thus appeared to be an index of rationality.

For Hegel, the bureaucracy, as well as being hierarchical and specialized, also coordinates. Marx demolished that idea too (I should have presented you with the two positions together from the start instead of presenting them successively, but it's too late now ...), arguing that we should distinguish among the bureaucrats between the senior administrators, who occupy a dominant position and who are the thinkers, and the lower civil servants who carry out orders (so that nobody actually ever does anything: the petty bureaucrat executes the task without understanding the Whole, and the higher bureaucracy thinks, without being aware of the actual consequences [*laughter*] . . .). Hegel doesn't see things like that: in his eyes, insofar as the senior bureaucracy is both hierarchical and specialized, it is capable of coordinating, it is able to conceive both unity and difference. It is at once unified (since it is hierarchical – for if there is a hierarchy there is a centre) and diversified (since it is specialized). It is therefore both one and multiple. Being both the one and the multiple, it produces unification and coordination, and it solves the problem of the conflict between private interests and the general interest. Here again I could cite texts: for example in the *Encyclopaedia* Hegel calls the bureaucracy 'the class that thinks' (*der denkende Stand*), and says that it takes a particular interest in the universal interests of society.[32] Elsewhere, and despite Marx's reproaches, he says that the bureaucracy does not advance blindly: while it is at work, it is constantly subject to external controls. In addition to having the sort of reflexivity that I mentioned earlier, it avoids all solipsism, maintaining a constant dialogue with the outside world. The bureaucracy is constantly learning, through being the object of controls by the prince, the corporations, the press, public opinion, requests and petitions (there would be more to say about this . . .).

In addition the bureaucracy is subject to internal constraints. Here we broach the idea that it could have its own interests, these interests, however, being characterized as universal. It develops a bureaucratic ethos (which is equivalent to saying 'a bureaucratic habitus'), resulting from bureaucratic habits. I refer you to the *Elements of the Philosophy of Right* again.[33] This habitus is linked with the tendency of the bureaucracy to persevere in its being. The usual criticism of bureaucracy emphasizes the negative consequences of this tendency to perpetuate itself. The inertia of bureaucracy is a commonplace complaint . . . But, if it is true that the bureaucracy thinks of itself as the universal class, the tendency to perpetuate its being can have positive effects: the concern to live up to their own definition can lead the individual bureaucrats to transcend the historical circumstances of a particular case and do things that go above and beyond what is required by their immediate interest.

I am insisting on the ambiguity because I am convinced that, if at this stage (when I am only just starting my enquiry) I have an opinion on the law to express, it is the idea of its ambiguity. If I had to say it in one word: on the subject of law, I would speak of rights, and exemptions from the law.[34] For there to be exemptions, the law must exist;

there cannot be exemptions from the law if there is no law. I think that the exemption is written into the law and that there is a specific form of capitalist accumulation where the person possessing a right can profit from exercising that right, but also from the suspension of that law, that is, exemption from it. If you think about it, whole universes are going to open up for you . . . An enormous part of bureaucratic power is the power to give authorizations (for instance building permits) which are paid for partly in backhanders (to mention the most evident form) but also in gratitude for your bureaucratic generosity or intelligence. The right/exemption formula encapsulates this ambiguity which I find inherent in the law and the State. What makes the State open to rationality, and all the qualities that Hegel ascribes to it, is also what leaves it open to attack. It is the recto and the verso of the same piece of paper, you cannot have one without the other. If these naive Hegelian-type visions pose a problem, it is because each step towards a greater degree of law is also progress towards more exemptions. If you bear this pattern in mind, the reflections on 'too much State' or 'not enough State' should become clear in your eyes: you can't have one without the other. I am expressing myself rather badly because I intend to develop this at greater length in the lectures to come, and I prefer to leave it here in axiomatic form. I would happily say simply: 'There is no right without exemption' . . . signed La Rochefoucauld [*laughter*]. But the sociologist owes it to you to be explicit, which is both simpler and more complicated.

To return to the main menu. The bureaucracy is subject to regulations. It is the place par excellence of a rational division of labour: it is rational in its structure, and its structure produces things rational. I would like to make a brief remark in passing on the historically crucial opposition between the bureaucrat and the noble that informed the whole eighteenth-century struggle over the State. The *philosophes*[35] were very good sociologists, they said very interesting things, but indirectly (the architecture of their discourse disguises the essential . . .). The bureaucrat overcame the conflict between private interest and general interest (or public service) whereas the noble wanted to sacrifice himself and yet remain the same self. He too wanted to sacrifice to the State his individuality and his glory (as d'Aguesseau puts it), his person, his unique being, but without abdicating his independence in the face of the State. This opposition is very illuminating. From the sixteenth century until Rousseau, theories of the State constantly mobilize this opposition. The bourgeois who wrote on the State and who were often civil servants, Jansenists or Protestants, cooked up theories of public service as the sacrifice of the individual to the universal. D'Aguesseau is a typical representative of this category. I forgot to tell you the first time round, but d'Aguesseau was one of the first to use statistics, and the word 'statistic' derives from the State.[36] Statistics are an instrument of knowledge that arms the modern State. Vauban, whom we know from the fortifications he built, but who was also a great theoretician of the modern State, said: 'The Chinese have been using statistics for a very long time: we need to do the same, we cannot govern a State without statistics.'[37] When they say, 'the State thinks', it signifies something serious.

One thing I want to make clear in passing, because it is at the back of my mind all the time: the first developments of the notion of individual interest were made in relation to the State. Scholars nowadays who are tracing the genealogy of modern notions of 'interest' are discovering the links between the first uses of the notion of private interest and the questioning of private interest (do governments have a private interest that coincides with the universal interest?). For instance, one of the theoreticians of the absolute State considers that the king has no private interest, his interest is in the universal and his private interest is the interest of his subjects. There is nothing left for him to gain, and the only thing that can happen to him is to lose, if he makes his subjects lose. It is in this context that many of the developments of the notion of interest have arisen. The author of a recent work distinguishes different currents. One current that I shall call individualist passes through Montaigne, and Charron. Then there is the current of pessimism on the State: 'Withdraw inside your tent and leave the public world as it is.' We would situate d'Aguesseau in the humanist political current, which is composed of civil servants believing that the high-born man must sacrifice himself to the State and identify with it. He must serve himself in serving the State and must not withdraw from politics. D'Aguesseau thus criticized the philosophers of the individualist persuasion, who withdraw from the world. The idea that the true philosopher must live in the City is a vision held by the servant of the State. There remains the bizarre category of the great aristocratic pessimists who, from Saint-Simon to the Cardinal de Retz (including some less well-known people), speak a language very close to that of the Jansenists. It seems to me that they illustrate Hegel's statement: 'They are willing to lend their voice to the State but only if they can retain their singularity.' They do not accept the total oblation that the petit bourgeois, Jansenist civil servant lauds and attempts to universalize. (What I am saying is very confused, but it is to help you situate the debate a little better . . .). The ideal civil servant is the petit bourgeois who owes everything to the State. He is what I call the 'oblate', who, according to one of the great principles driving any organization, gives his all to the State, the Church or the [Communist] Party because he owes everything to the State, the Church or the Party.[38] You can only obtain absolute devotion from those who owe you absolutely everything. This helps us understand what I am going to say next about Durkheim, who was a typical oblate: he owed everything to the Republic, and he gave it everything. There I am decidedly mixing it all up! [*laughter*].

So the bureaucrats no longer signal a distance between their private interest and the general interest; but what exactly is this private interest, since it does nonetheless exist, and somehow coincides automatically with the general interest? It is inevitably linked to the perpetuation of the bureaucracy. It is Spinoza's famous *conatus*. There is a bureaucratic *conatus*, that is, a tendency for one's being to persist. For his being to persist, the bureaucrat must make the bureaucracy persist, along with his own position in it. This point is very important. At the moment, I am researching into the struggles that accompanied the reforms introduced in the years around 1975 in housing policy in France.[39] This research is miles away from Hegel's concerns. It deals with things that seem trivial and disconnected from what I have been talking about. Nonetheless, it shows that we can't understand these struggles, the forms that they take, and their outcome if we don't formulate the hypothesis that, beyond their more evident interests, civil servants in some cases engage the vital interest that consists, to put it rather crudely, in preserving their function: if such and such a benefit is suppressed, the service that handles it will disappear. I am of course expressing myself in rather crude terms (a service doesn't disappear overnight), but the bureaucratic interest works on two levels (and Hegel sees this): there is a general interest in perpetuating the bureaucracy (if there is no more bureaucracy, there are no more bureaucrats), then a general interest in perpetuating one or other branch of the bureaucracy. For instance, when considering the means of constructing roads in France, the engineers are likely to oppose any reforms that risk making them disappear as a corps. When the reproduction of a body is threatened, its defence mechanisms reappear (note the organicist analogy). Take what happens in the French university sector: when the existence of a discipline is threatened, those who teach it are themselves threatened (if you abolish Latin, you abolish the Latinists) and we find what we call 'corporatist' reactions. The word 'corporatism' is outmoded, but it is interesting if applied to the Hegelian scenario: in defending their corps, the agents are defending their bureaucratic existence, their existence as bureaucrats. The bureaucratic interest, then, is an interest specifically linked to the existence of the bureaucracy.

Hegel's argument is very similar to a spontaneous sociology, and sees only the negative side to this bureaucracy (it preserves itself for the sake of preserving itself), but, if you pause to think, you could credit Hegel with the idea (or make him say) that, when the corps to be preserved is one that defines itself by its claims to be universal, it is possible that in preserving itself it does preserve the universal. The struggles between those corps whose stake is the preservation of the corps are indeed carried out in the name of the universal – one bureaucratic body cannot kill another citing only their bonuses as a pretext (they never mention their bonuses; when you conduct an enquiry, it is difficult to know what bonuses the senior civil servants enjoy . . .). The fact that in order to emerge from these struggles triumphant you need to have the universal on your side is important for the future of the universal. It is exactly the same for the jurists: a bureaucrat can only win using the weapons of the bureaucracy, even if everyone, not least those within the bureaucracy, knows that the bureaucratic weapons most often dissimulate non-bureaucratic interests, as well as their bureaucratic interests; and Marx brutally confronted Hegel with the existence of non-bureaucratic interests – you will remember that Hegel posits the autonomy of the bureaucracy. When Weber speaks of the 'innate tendencies of the sacerdotal body', he is partly Hegelian:[40] to understand the evolution of the Church, to understand the priest (who is the bureaucrat of religion), you need to understand that there are tendencies specific to the sacerdotal body, not least the tendency of the Church to reproduce itself. But in order to reproduce itself, the Church produces people who want to reproduce it, that is, oblates. It will recruit its bishops from the simple people rather than the aristocracy because, as Hegel says, the aristocrats will never want to sacrifice their glory entirely. A petit bourgeois bishop is much more reliable than an aristocratic bishop, who may perhaps be a bishop of Saint-Denis, a *gauchiste*, or lean towards Rome when the official tendency is to be Gallican. Those who do not owe their all to an institution can take liberties with it (I keep drifting away from Hegel's bureaucrat, but he is so difficult to concentrate on . . . I feel sorry for anyone who has to discuss the Hegelian bureaucrat! [*laughter*]).

Ultimately, for Hegel, the function of the bureaucracy is to control, censor and organize civil society from above – especially, it is important to note, in wartime, when society becomes particularly organized and coordinated.[41] According to Hegel, bureaucracy comes alive in wartime, that is, when its functions, its hierarchical structures and its specialization are revealed. Even if I have already said it, I would like finally to emphasize what we should retain of this Hegelian fantasy.

I said just now that the sociologist should objectify fantasies in order to exorcize them, but although these fantasies are biased viewpoints, they may contain some reality. Hegel's critique of Kantian ethics (Hegel arguing that you cannot ask an individual will guided by ethics alone to become the permanent defender of the universal) has the advantage of stressing the fact that the source of access to universal interest is not rooted in individual morality but in an organizational structure. Hegel's argument (which was shocking enough) is that the subject of the universal is not an individual will but the bureaucratic organizational structure, with its hierarchization. In this sense it is very close in political philosophy to the realist tradition, that is, the quasi-sociological tradition of Machiavelli, for whom it is not virtue that founds the Republic but the Republic that founds virtue. It is a certain organizational order that more or less compels individuals, whatever their drives or private interests, to universalize their actions.

Durkheim, State sociologist

So as not to finish abruptly on that note, I shall say a last word about Durkheim. Since I have already said what is essential, this will not take long. I think that you will be as astonished as I was, since I had long nurtured the idea that, as I said just now, Durkheim had the splendid discretion to say that he did not know what the State was. I found Durkheim all the more intelligent and satisfying because, for years, I repeated: 'I never speak of the State, because I don't know what it is, and in this sense I am much more scientific than the others, who don't even know this.'

Thus I found Durkheim so good because he was saying what I thought I believed, until I discovered that there did exist nonetheless dispersed among his writings a surreptitious theory of the State. For instance, in an extraordinary passage in the *Lessons of Sociology*, he says that the State is 'the organ of social thought',[42] before developing an argument about the masses, whose thoughts are confused. He establishes an opposition between the masses, who have a knowledge of the first type, and the bureaucracy which has knowledge of the third type.[43] The masses have 'confused' thoughts and collective beliefs which are 'diffuse', dispersed and contradictory. The language he uses to speak of the masses is that of spontaneity, the primitive, lack of reflection (the word 'prejudice', as well as the very interesting term 'subconscious', are used). The model underlying all this is the same as that used by thinkers like Le Bon: the vision of the masses reproduces socially constituted stereotypes of the way masculinity posits femininity; the masses are feminine, that is, emotive, 'unreflecting' and spontaneous. Durkheim does not say it in so many words, but the State is the opposite, it is masculine. It is the place of deliberation and reflection ('it is truly an organ of reflection'). It is the clear consciousness that frees itself from belief and prejudice and it is assured of a freedom from the masses that is the foundation of its rationality.

In other texts he says that 'the people' are those in a State who do not participate in its government. Those who direct it do not possess a power, but the instruments of reason. In *On the Division of Social Labour*[44] he says that the State is the 'brain' that controls and thinks the social body. He says in *Lessons on Sociology* that 'the essential function [of the State] is to think'.[45] In other words, the State is an autonomous rational instrument charged with accomplishing the general interest. Here, although there are differences, he comes fairly close to Weber, for whom the establishment of the State marks a progress in rationality (I shall not develop this further; since it is already difficult enough to refer to Marx, Hegel or Durkheim, I don't want to add Weber, who is a sociologist more difficult to manipulate, more complex and subtle). In a text entitled 'The State', published in a volume edited by Victor Karady under the title *Fonctions sociales et institutions*, Weber places the State above diverse other forces; it is a 'higher force'.[46] This is what I was saying just now on the idea of a spatial vision, of a viewpoint over all other viewpoints, of a viewpoint from no viewpoint.

I have selected some disparate elements, but the overall idea given by these texts is ultimately something that is at the heart of Hegel's vision of the State; namely, that the State is a group of civil servants *sui generis* (to use one of Durkheim's expressions), and is in a sense unclassifiable. If we were to define him in a word, we could say that the civil servant is unclassifiable. He is above the class struggle, he is outside the social space, he has no specific social interests. Unlike Hegel, Durkheim does not even mention the existence of an internal interest in reproduction. And of course he says nothing about the external interests which Marx will remind us of . . . At the extreme limit the State becomes a kind of absolute object that the sociologist has no need to deal with: in saying that the State is off limits, beyond the social space, they mean to say that it conceives the social world, without being an object of thought itself.

I imputed the absence of a sociology of the State in Durkheim to the legitimate prudence of a radical sceptic, but, to be entirely logical, we must envisage an alternative explanation. There cannot be in Durkheim a sociology of a corporation thinking the social world, a sociology of the civil servant. When we know that our sociological author is a servant of the State (he is a State civil servant), we may suppose that the principle motivating the exemption from, or bypassing of, the law that he accords the State is his status as State civil servant. I think that, for Durkheim, there is no more a sociology of the civil servant than there is a sociology of the sociologist, and my idea is that he unconsciously exempts the State from sociology so as to exempt himself from sociology. Durkheim is the embodiment of the oblate of the republican State. For a thousand reasons (his Jewish, petit bourgeois, provincial origins) he is the ideal-typical representative of the school oblate, the scholarship boy made by the State, the public man. The scholarship boy owes everything to the State: right from the start he has a kind of consciousness identified with the State and he grants the State what he grants himself and asks of the State to grant him; that is, autonomy from politics, classes and interests. It seems to me that if the State is unthinkable for Durkheim, it is because to reflect on the State would oblige him to reflect on and consider what there is of State thinking in his own thoughts. Moreover, he does make the university professor play an extraordinary role as a State civil servant . . . If for Hegel himself the exemplary senior civil servant was the Prussian senior civil servant, for Durkheim it is the pro-Dreyfus university professor. This is a very classic situation: people universalize not their private interests (these things are much more subtle . . .), but their fantasies, their situations. Durkheim proposes a philosophy of a university civil servant under the Third Republic, this philosophy having every likelihood of passing for universal for those who wish to universalize the same situation. I have written, wickedly, that Kant's aesthetics are a professor's aesthetics and that, being read only by professors, they are always perceived as universal.[47] This is very unkind, but . . . it is true! [*laughter*] In the same way, Hegel's theory of the State is basically the theory the philosophers would have formulated if they had dared. But they don't dare because they know that Marx exists . . . I will say more about this next time. Marx remains most useful, but I don't want to simplify or be simplistic. It is not enough to say that 'these people universalize their private interests', which is something that people understand all too easily, without going any further . . . What I would like to do (and I have done very badly today) is to try to create a wounded consciousness of the State. It would at least be an achievement to manage to stop people giving in to their unilateral reflexes or churning out thoughts fit for the third part of a dissertation. I would like to leave you in a state of wretched consciousness of the State [*laughter*] . . .

Lecture of 21 April 1988

A charitable reading of Marx's theory of the State – An enchanted vision and a disenchanted vision of the State – The unconscious corporatism of the sociologists – A sociological critique of the social sciences – First false problem: does sociology liberate or manipulate? Second false problem: continuity or break? – Towards a social history of the social sciences – The 'prehistory of the social sciences' – The birth of the social sciences in an awkward position – Scientific sociology and France as a special case – The separation of national traditions during the interwar period – The triumphant postwar development

A charitable reading of Marx's theory of the State

[. . .] The critique of Hegel [by Marx] is an almost line-by-line critique, which makes me think of Leibniz's critique of Descartes, in a kind of marginal note that he called *in Cartesium*.[1] We find Marx's theory of the State embarrassing because its most systematic formulation is to be found in the text where Marx [is subordinate to Hegel?], since he situates his commentary largely on Hegel's terrain.[2] It is in arguing against Hegel that he is led to say things about the State that he did not arrange into a systematic theory. For instance, he attacks the Hegelian bureaucrat's claim to universality, but says only in passing that there are corporate interests. Rejecting Hegel's representation of the bureaucracy united in its consciousness of itself, the State and society, he also says that there are internal conflicts, and that these conflicts between rival fractions are conflicts for the appropriation of administrative resources. This is not the central idea [of his critique] but these secondary ideas interest me because they avoid reducing Marx to slogans. (It is unfortunate how political and academic usages in general conspire to reduce authors to slogans, to 'sloganize' them. Since I am a victim of this myself, I have a particular interest in defending authors against 'sloganization'.) The simplistic vision, where Marx sees the State as an instrument of domination in the service of the interests of the dominant, although not entirely false, should be nuanced in the light of what I have been saying. Marx does not dispute the autonomy of the bureaucracy but he insists on the fact that the bureaucrats, despite what Hegel says, operate a sort of private appropriation of the public. I think that at the peak of his powers Marx could have done better. In particular he could have said that this private appropriation of the public has a political impact, which is important. The private appropriation of the public is one of the foundations of what I call 'symbolic violence', the violence exerted with the consent or the complicity of the dominated, who would not accept such domination in the same way if it displayed the true arbitrariness of its appropriation of the private, its privatization of the public, or, as it is sometimes called, the patrimonialization of the State. If power were purely private, some of the effects of domination, misrecognition and recognition could not be exercised. The State, then, does serve the interests of the dominant, but it manages rather well to conceal the fact. (At the risk of being the devil's advocate, I am applying to Marx what English language philosophers call 'the charity principle',[3] which consists in treating an author as kindly as possible, granting them as much coherence as possible. It is an elementary principle of game theory: in order to win, you must not treat your opponent like an idiot. And yet very often in scientific struggles we reduce our opponent to a state of total stupidity, making it easy enough to triumph. When our only judges are thirty rather inhibited students, we get away with it [*laughter*], but it does not make for scientific progress.) It seems to me that by using the 'charity principle' we could fill in the gaps between the lines in Marx's thought and construct a fairly subtle theory, which would come close to reconciling Hegel's theory with the traditional, reductive Marxist theory. This theory would be close to the provisional solution that I intend to propose. In fact I think that in our research we are constantly led to lend authors ideas that we have given them (in my case, at all events, it is something that I very willingly do). In reading them in a charitable manner, we see things in them (that afterwards we will appear to have taken from them . . .).

The privatization of the State is one way for the bureaucracy to make use of it while serving it and its dominant interests. Without offering a long commentary on this, I refer you to a very interesting chapter in *Capital*, chapter X of Book 1, which seems to me to be mostly ignored when people discuss the problem of the State in Marx.[4] In this chapter, Marx discusses the industrial legislation of the 'factory laws', and on the subject of the 'factory inspectors'[5] he develops a very interesting argument about the neutrality of the State (although the argument is not overtly concerned with the State). He says that in the long term the factory inspectors play a major role in favour of the dominant since they ensure the establishment of a minimum of humanist morality. In a way they protect capitalism from being tempted by the excesses of uncontrolled capitalism (here I am extrapolating a little, according to the 'charity principle' . . .). But their work is very ambiguous, for at the same time as they protect capitalism from itself by leading it to make minimal concessions to the demands of the workers, they help (with the philanthropists in particular – whom Marx criticizes most violently, by the way) to render the State a little less deaf to the demands of the workers outside it.[6] Marx also alludes to the press[7] and attributes an analogous role to it: he doesn't fail to say that the press acts in the service of capital, but since [in this chapter] he is studying the real world, he treats reality in all its complexity and shows that the bureaucracy remains relatively open to pressure. These people [the factory inspectors, the press] are in fact structurally ambiguous: they serve the bourgeoisie by helping to curb their worst idiocies and the backlash they provoke, but they help at the same time to reinforce the image of the State bureaucracy as being neutral, sensitive to moral imperatives, and situated above class differences. Here Marx is touching on something very important, with particular relevance to the reflection on the relations between social science and the State that I am going to try to offer you today.

Those who insist on treating social problems practically, and whom we might call, to use a general term, the 'social workers', can be described in two absolutely contradictory fashions. In a Marxist logic (the logic of the 'final struggle'), they are the accomplices of capital and their humanism is a subtle and perverse manner of serving the interests of the dominant. But they do enable the workers to obtain a minimum of dignity and they contribute thereby to giving them a minimal awareness that can encourage them to revolt against their condition (Marx does note this; if you read the text you will find it all there). It is then something very ambiguous.

I am insisting on this point because it seems to me that the social worker and the sociologist are brothers. In the beginning, especially, the sociologists were basically perceived as collaborating with the philanthropists, and entered the scientific field with an extremely ambiguous objective identity. This objective identity would suffice to elicit an ambiguous image of their vocation, but it was compounded by the fact that, for subjective reasons due in particular to his social trajectory, the sociologist often entered [sociology] with the ambiguous image of a philanthropist: he wanted to be useful, in particular to help the dominated in periods of crisis. This disparity between the objective definition and the subjective vocation, then, underpins the identity of the sociologist; it is intimately connected with the problem of the ambiguity of the State, and its agents. To see this link better, you should recall what I was saying about Durkheim and his relation to the State.[8]

To return to Marx for a moment: you could reduce his theory [of the State] to a simple antithesis of Hegel's theory, but it seems to me more interesting to say that, without having clearly formulated the theory, Marx did touch on the idea of the relative autonomy of the State and the idea of its neutrality. In a way, he could have integrated into his theory of the State the Hegelian vision, which does not contradict his own. We might say that the bureaucrat as Marx would have imagined him is inserted within an organized and organic corps (Marx grants Hegel his organicist vision of the State), endowed with the specific interests of the corps and divided by struggles, tensions and conflicts that are subordinated in the last resort to the collective interests of the corporation. Here we find an implicit axiom of the social sciences, arguing that a corps or a group does not commit suicide. Without it being explicitly stated, a corps is always credited with the will to survive as a being, to lick its wounds and heal its scars, like a body. This tendency of the bureaucratic body to survive does limit the attacks on the corps that its internal struggles might engender. Far from excluding the existence of struggles within the corps, Marx describes them in extraordinary fashion. Since he was very irritated by Hegel (criticism sharpens the intelligence), he says for instance that withholding information is one instrument used in the bureaucratic struggle.[9] As I said, Hegel's theory allocates a major role to the circulation of information,[10] and Marx understood that the common currency of the bureaucratic struggle included leaving files unopened, refusing to give information, etc. He indicates in passing that the manipulation of information and other stratagems are exploited in the service of careerism and the competition between rival bureaucratic cliques (as if the engineers from the école des Mines were undermining the foundations of the corps of the inspectors of finance).

So Marx had noted the existence of these internal struggles and understood that they were circumscribed within the collective interest of the bureaucracy: in the last resort, in moments of crisis, the bureaucrats know how to [stay in control of themselves]. As I have suggested, we can also refer to what he said on the social workers in order to grant him the intuition that disinterestedness and submission to the universal, which form the bureaucracy's ideological representation of itself, are one of the conditions of the successful functioning of the bureaucracy. The bureaucracy, believing itself to be universal, manages to get others to believe it, and this image of universality contributes to the symbolic efficacy of the representation, if you accept my definition of symbolic violence as violence which is not recognized as being arbitrarily linked to the particular interests that determine it, and which is thereby recognized as legitimate (without even needing the act of recognition there would be in a Hegelian logic). The misrecognition of this arbitrariness founds the recognition. Using a wider Marxist logic, in a charitable spirit, we could then grant Marx a theory of the neutrality of the State and find him showing how representing the bureaucracy as disinterested and universal contributes to the successful functioning of the bureaucracy, one of these functions being to pronounce universal verdicts.

For indeed (to sum up in a single sentence a whole argument on the power of nomination that I have developed at great length in previous years),[11] the verdicts of the bureaucracy are in our world the equivalent of divine verdicts; the bureaucracy is the last resort, the agency which has the last word in the final appeal and which holds the monopoly of the definition of identity. I have devoted a long analysis to certification as the bureaucratic act par excellence[12] (the disabled badge, the sick note, the veteran's service record, the teaching certificate, the academic diploma, etc.). When we speak of 'to certify', we never know who is the subject of the Latin verb.[13] In a sense it's the State (that last resort beyond which there is only God . . .) which certifies that you are worthy of teaching (or that you are really ill and that you are entitled to a pension) and it is impossible to object; the State certifies in the name of us all. The bureaucratic act of certifying grants the sanction of the universal to a particular act of categorization and it is nearly always accompanied either by the attribution of a stigma (in the case of a criminal record) or symbolic or material profit (pensions or benefits). These acts of attribution, of legitimate distribution, are universal and cannot be challenged. Nobody can oppose them (unless they want to sue, which implies relying on the State – to challenge the verdict of the State). The certificate as a bureaucratic act tacitly supposes the misrecognition and recognition of the arbitrary.

If we suppose that the State is at the service of the dominant, as Marx said it is, it is not perceived as such in the real practice of its functioning, and it would not function properly if it were perceived as such.

Indeed, what we can often reproach Marx with is the fact that, if the social world were what he says it is, neither the State nor labour would function properly (this reading of Marx is much less charitable, but it does nonetheless reflect the thoughts that he expressed). (To make a brief parenthesis: if labour were really constant alienation at every moment,[14] it would not work – no need to evoke the Japanese model.)[15] I am putting things very schematically and I am contradicting myself. I simply want to make you realize that behind this specific analysis of Marx's thought there is something much more general. I can make the connection with a subject that I mentioned last time: Marx's thought owes its popular and popularized diffusion to the fact that it delights the semi-educated, who, with their first-degree reductive vision ('disinterestedness does not exist, it hides interest'), fail to see that if interest were the real and exclusive model of any behaviour claiming to be disinterested, the effect of disinterestedness would not exist.

An enchanted vision and a disenchanted vision of the State

To close this series of reflections, I want to come to the relations between social science and the State and put to social science the questions that it puts to the State. I shall state things very simply. I first outlined a critical questioning of the State's representation of itself, through the theory of disinterestedness and public service proposed by d'Aguesseau, one of the first great ideologues of the State. D'Aguesseau elaborates a humanist ethic which comes to fruition, not in the retreat and the private life, as in Montaigne, Charron and the libertines, but in the sacrifice of the private individual to the public, in serving the public. This representation was constructed during the same period that the State was being constructed. Then I set out the critical visions that oppose these representations. Through the opposition between Hegel and Marx, I reformulated the opposition between disinterestedness and interest, between the enchanted (or rather, mystified) vision of the State that accepts as common currency the representation that the State gives of itself (the word 'representation' to be understood in its various senses, and especially in its theatrical dimension), and the disenchanted vision of a Pascal, for example, who said that ermine and the gown are theatre.[16] In a way, the disenchanted, critical, reductive vision, usually incarnated by Marx, denounces dramatization. It reveals the 'backshop', as Montaigne would say,[17] or takes us into the 'back regions' or the 'wings', in the words of Goffman[18] (who is very typical of this tradition . . . the fact that Goffman was the son of a grocer[19] is not irrelevant: he knew that behind the splendid displays in these shops there is what is said in the store room ('this is what we need to off-load . . .' [*laughter*]. I'm not joking, he describes very well in his book the head waiter who arrives at full speed but assumes a different posture the moment he emerges from behind the swing doors [*laughter*][20] . . . The vision of the State is there too . . .). At the other extreme [from this tradition], there are those who accept the dramatics and the ceremonies of what is called a 'civic religion' by Bellah,[21] who has no hesitation in accepting this State theatre. The 'civic religion' is important in the United States: it's the State making a spectacle of itself, the great civic ceremonies, politics as theatre.

The unconscious corporatism of the sociologists

The spontaneous vision of the sociologist ('all this is a theatrical display') is that of an adolescent who wants to appear to be clever, saying: 'You can't fool me, I know it's only theatre, it's all for show.' This vision forgets that representation may be effective and that we wouldn't be so annoyed by representation if we didn't have so much of it in our own minds. It also forgets that the question put to the State ('In whose name, with what right, do you claim to be universal? Your claim to the universal can be reduced to the specific interests that you universalize by identifying them with the universal') is reversible and that it should be put straight away to the sociologist. The elementary weapon of defence of the non-sociologist consists in turning the question back against the sociologist: 'You relativize everything, but the viewpoint from which you relativize is relativizable.' This very low-flying riposte is the usual reaction to the social scientist. Most often, the sociologist protects himself against this relativization by donning his armour, by inoculating himself like Mithridates,[22] by accustoming himself to this objection, saying that it is ridiculous or that it is unfounded.

Sometimes, he may be tempted simply to forget it. Thus, for Durkheim – as we have seen – the State enjoys autonomy, and the State's public servants, who include the sociologist, share in this autonomy. I am not exaggerating, I think that Durkheim's solution was this: the Republic (of the professors) is universal because it conforms to the professorial vision of the universal. The New Sorbonne[23] was at once an attempt to constitute an autonomous social science through a break with pre-notions or common sense, and a contribution to the construction of a neutral, universal State, illuminated by science and capable, thanks to the reflexive faculty borrowed from science – that is, the professors – to make society accede to self-consciousness and guide it rationally. Durkheim does not offer a methodically explicit solution but it seems to me to be latent in all his work: there is no need to question his universality or his disinterestedness or the interest that he might have in the interest of others (I think moreover that Nietzsche is much more sophisticated),[24] or the particular interest of reductive sociologists in operating this reduction. For Durkheim sociology is justified in existing; he is the official sociologist, the sociologist as public servant.

This raises the question of the history of the relations between the social sciences and the State, which I shall answer with a kind of sweeping overview (I don't know if we can get an overview to sweep [*laughter*], but no matter). Can the social sciences avoid the question of disinterestedness? Do the sociologists who don't speak of the problem not lag behind Chancellor d'Aguesseau? We should not forget that d'Aguesseau was one of the first enlightened technocrats who tried to use statistics, among other things, especially to understand famines, and failures of the wheat harvest. He had at least the merit of formulating an explicit discourse to try to justify his disinterestedness, which is better than nothing. Durkheim and most sociologists draw a veil over the whole problem. Historically, very few sociologists have really faced the problem that I am raising today.

To my mind, the only way for the social sciences to escape at least some of their particularity, singularity and social determinism – that is, to become ever so slightly, if not disinterested, at least liberated from private interest, selective bias and partisan choice – is to try to take this question seriously, to try to understand their own particularities. Some of these particularities depend on the historical genesis of the position of the sociologist, and, to put it briefly, on the fact that the position of the sociologist originated as the position of a social worker. The sociologist runs a serious risk of becoming one of the objects, or to put it more crudely, of becoming grist to the mill, when he studies his colleagues or the social workers. He may believe that he is objectifying by being clever. He is also in danger when he studies the State, which is often the source of his capacity (it is important to remember that he owes his regular salary to the State) and his tendency to show how clever he is. (I won't take this self-reflection any further, because people are not used to this sort of public socio-analysis,[25] so it might be perceived as a kind of narcissism. Because of the social expectations that they arouse, certain things cannot be said, since they would be perceived, at any rate subjectively, as the exact opposite of what they are. I make this clear in order to explain why I am reluctant to say some of the things that I believe to be important, or why I sometimes decide to couch them in euphemized form. When the conditions of reception are not fulfilled, we need to censor ourselves at least partially, because we might appear to say, or be heard to say, the opposite of what we might want to say. This parenthesis is important for me to be able to say what I am going to say.)

Having given you the context that I am going to situate myself in, I shall try to recapitulate. Why, in my opinion, are we unable to approach the problem of the State in an innocent manner? Why does this problem oblige the sociologist more than other men to reflect on himself? Sociology is so vulnerable to the boomerang effect, it can so rarely ask a question without making someone feel the need to ask it back, that I find it difficult to understand why sociologists are not always self-reflexive. They should always be on the alert, but their theoretical and methodological armour, their collective ethic and morale, are so strong that they protect themselves from attack. Moreover, we could show that the hostile expectations aroused even here [among the audience at the Collège de France] contribute to this. On the one hand, people deify the sociologists, they seek their opinions on everything (I can bear witness to this: I have made a list of all the subjects that I'm constantly asked about).[26] Today the sociologist, even more than the philosopher and the psychologist, is one of the people expected to have an answer to everything, from the 'Hole in the ground at les Halles'[27] to the question of 'public opinion'. On the other hand, quite rightly, they are given no credit: 'Sociologists know nothing, it's not a science.' This twofold expectation, which is tuned in to the broadcasting wavelength of sociological discourse, helps to encourage the sociologists to withdraw and refuse to be self-reflexive: so much is demanded of them and so little is accorded them that they think that, if they start to admit the fantastic difficulties that assail them as specialists in the pursuit of that strange object, the social world, they will be granted even less. There is a sort of unconscious corporatism, and I am no doubt in great danger of disappointing people when I spill the beans by saying that only the radical doubt which I practise can offer the slightest chance of opening up a scientific discourse on the social world. Many people are likely to say: 'Bourdieu, whose statutory post is at the top of the social sciences, has said that sociology . . .'. This discipline which is constantly starting, constantly threatened, has always got a political revolver held to its head . . . we know all these things, but since we forget to say them, we end up forgetting them, and the sociologists cling to a kind of provisional ethic,[28] a provisional epistemology, a weak consensus of scholars: 'We exist, therefore we deserve to exist.' I think that things

are not so simple . . . Pardon [my way of expressing it], but that is what
I really wanted to say.

I shall repeat this in more academic terms. If we are unable to
approach the problem of the State as a sociologist, a historian or an
economist without suffering the boomerang effect, it is because we
cannot follow the normal procedure of the sociologist and call into
question the official representation that the State institution gives of
itself without feeling the repercussions, leading us to call into question
the official representation that the discipline of sociology gives of itself,
grounded partly in a mandate or a delegation from the State, in the fact
that there are academic chairs, that certified professors use these chairs
to certify, that sociology has the *licentia docendi*.[29] I think this is a risk
that we must take, which implies questioning the foundation of Kant's
extraordinary text, *The Conflict of the Faculties*.[30] Kant distinguishes
between two main types of faculty: on the one hand, the temporal
faculties (theology, medicine and law) which receive their mandate
from the State and have no need to question their basis, because the
State tells them that their existence is founded in order to fulfil a social
mission, that they have a function to perform; and on the other hand
there are the sciences which we might call pure and which do not
receive a delegation from the State. These latter sciences question the
temporal faculties on their scientific foundation: 'You jurists, doctors
and theologians are founded temporally, but we question your foundation nonetheless, we put to you the question of religion within the
boundaries of mere reason,[31] we question you, not on your social foundation (we are not revolutionaries), but on your scientific foundation.'
Faculties that are not socially founded are led to consider the question
of their scientific foundation, and I think that the question of foundation that haunts philosophers is a knock-on effect [. . .]. Is sociology on
the side of the temporal faculties, or the pure faculties? Historically,
the sociology faculty (if it existed . . .) is on the temporal side. It was
born, like a faculty of theology, medicine or law, from a need and a
demand, from a social mandate to provide theoretical assistance to
the social reformers. You need to know this to avoid playing a double
game. In fact, when sociology avoids the question of its foundation
and sends the philosophers packing, it is because it is worried about
being socially founded or being founded in theories that, like Marxism,
are themselves a social foundation (but there is not even a need for
that: you can be a Durkheimian reformer – when people say they are
'Durkheimians', this is often what they unconsciously have in mind).

A sociological critique of the social sciences

I shall now put the question of the status of the social sciences and attempt to set the agenda for a sociological critique of the social sciences (the work to be done is enormous). The word 'critique' is to be understood in the Kantian sense: what are the social conditions rendering social science, as it exists today in the various countries where sociology is spoken, possible?[32] I raise the classic Kantian question, specifying it sociologically: what are the social conditions of this possibility, and thereby the limits inherent in these social conditions? We need to ask how these sciences are able to exist, how it is possible for their existence to be legitimized. The question as to whether there is a demand for the social sciences is periodically raised, and sociologists immediately reject it as naive: 'We exist as a science, we are justified by the pure drive for knowledge.' The central idea which I am going to develop is that ultimately this pure drive for knowledge is only an afterthought, a marginal development obtained by a sort of misappropriation. To put this in cruder terms, the social demand is not a demand based on pure scientificity, but a demand for *service*, and it is thanks [to some specific conjunctures and] in the light of particular logics, which I hope to define briefly, that a fraction of the people socially mandated to study the social world are able to misappropriate the social mandate that is granted them and divert it towards pure and purely internal ends, or at any rate to ends that they believe to be pure and purely internal. It is by a sort of ruse and misappropriation of social energies that this pure logic is able to develop. This applies to all the sciences but particularly to the social sciences, and I would be quite ready to defend the thesis that in fact nobody wants an authentic social science. There is no social demand for an authentic social science because social science unmasks things that we do not wish to know. I shall not develop this . . .[33]

First false problem: does sociology liberate or manipulate?

The problem that I have just raised, concerning the social genesis of the social sciences or the social foundations of their existence, seems to me to be generally posed in rather superficial terms. I would like to spell out two or three questions that the debates appear to turn on.

I shall formulate the first question in the light of an article by Daniel Lerner[34] which is an exemplary text. Firstly, it dates from a period when the social sciences were triumphant (whereas at the moment we are in a period of recession – I shall return to this in a moment – when they are under attack and their funding is being cut). Social science was literally borne on the wings of a demand and a sort of all-pervading neo-Keynesianism.[35] Next, the text was published in the United States, where Lerner is a fairly good incarnation of the *establishment* of the times. In this perspective, the social sciences are essentially an instrument of enlightened transformation, of rational government, intended to form the basis of a rational organization of social affairs. On this subject Lerner has some extraordinary formulae: the progression of the social sciences [. . .] is the march of reason through history, it is the salt of the earth,[36] it is absolutely what Durkheim called it, 'self-observation under democratic government'[37] (you couldn't make it up . . .). It is the idea of self-awareness: the sociologists receive from a democratic government a mandate to make a scientific study of the social world, and help to enlighten the democratic government to encourage more democracy. The sociologist is absolutely not a critical sociologist in rebellion. He has an attaché case and a computer, he goes into the office every day, he is well dressed, well groomed and well integrated, he takes part in national and international colloquia, gives papers, and so on. He is characterized by a certain style of being. He knows how to draft reports, he can immediately tell the difference between a good and a bad article because there is a scientific consensus ('No, it [this article] isn't right, it is critical, but where are the data?'). And there is a confident collective community that judges.

To take one example: Lerner wrote a book entitled *The Passing of Traditional Society*,[38] which was closely linked to the classic *pons asinorum*, the benchmark of American sociology, which is the idea of modernization; here we see progress from the traditional to the modern, a one-way traffic, and we know how to help societies with this process. I shall say a few words on this extraordinary book which must have been published in the same period and gives an idea of the context. It is based on a questionnaire that had been circulated in five Middle Eastern countries (including Egypt, for instance), and which comprised about eighty questions, of which sixty-five, I think, related to the media, television and radio [*some laughter*], etc. Among many questions of the type 'when you see a film, do you identify [with the characters]?', there were, quite by chance, one question on people's level of education and another on their level of income (I hardly exaggerate). On this basis the civilizations concerned were classified along a slope of progress towards modernity, one of the criteria being their capacity to project into other conditions. Reacting to this enchanted vision, I remember having cited in my criticism of the book[39] a terrible sentence from Nietzsche on English happiness: finally happiness in England is a seat in parliament! [*some laughter*]. Lerner constructed a barometer of the degree of development from barbarism to civilization in the name of the idea that our democratic, developed society has the most advanced instruments of knowledge, such as questionnaires and computers, and can instruct us in absolutely anything. This vision was not even seen as racist or ethnocentric, but as humanist. I am caricaturing it, but this tendency is still rampant in the social world. In fact, these people are Durkheim's children. They reconcile everything: academic scientificity, internal consecration by a university recognized by the State, and political consecration. They very often enjoy important scientific careers and receive considerable economic benefits. Those whom we called the 'jet sociologists'[40] often belonged to this category (there is a whole list of American *and even French* sociologists [*laughter*] . . .).

The opposite position consists in seeing sociology as an instrument of manipulation in the service of the dominant. You can see that we are faced with the same two alternatives that we had in the case of the State (is the bureaucrat the servant of the universal, leading to progress, or an instrument of manipulation in the service of the dominant?). And what I was saying just now on the ambiguity of social workers, as Marx saw them in his chapter in *Capital*, takes on its full force here. To sum up, is the sociologist an instrument of liberation or manipulation? In 1968 there were debates on repression, and seeing the sociologist as the long arm of the law. Depending on their position in the economic field, sociologists obviously have very unequal interests in signing up to one or other alternative. We could say that the less professional they are, the more they have an interest in saying that the sociologist is an instrument of repression. I am simply saying this to make any sociologists who might be listening to me reflect, to invite them to ask themselves: 'Where do I fit into in the space of the profession, where is the space of the profession in the State, where is the State? How far does my position explain my propensity to be more on one side than the other?' In my opinion, the alternative opposing 'instrument of liberation' to 'instrument of manipulation' is a very false question, but it is socially very persistent. We are typically confronted with a social question that has been converted into a sociological problem, and it is tragic when a science uses the crude questions that people put to it in order to question itself. I said at the beginning that sociology should not be deaf to questions concerning its existence, but it has the right to choose to submit its own questions, which supposes first of all that it is aware of them and then that it filters them, examines them and carries out the procedures that I have mentioned in full. We cannot answer the question unless we have formulated it completely, we cannot accept it in the form delivered by a journalist (if tomorrow a Parisian weekly asks: 'does sociology liberate or manipulate?', all the sociologists will reply – there will be some exceptions, I can assure you, I can guarantee it [*laughter*] – but many will reply). We should not avoid the questioning, but we need systems of defence against these questions.

Second false problem: continuity or break?

The second problem is rather more sophisticated (every time I raise one of these issues, I could cite an immense bibliography): is there continuity or a break? Briefly, we may wonder whether social science emerged in the second half of the nineteenth century in connection with the great social and political struggles of the time, or whether it has always existed, in which case we could take its origins back to Plato, Machiavelli and Condorcet, etc. It is not just an academic question. It is academic, because it allows us to write theses, and many sociological problems exist only because people write theses and the thesis exists as an institution. Many sociological problems exist only because sociological journals agree to publish articles on them. As I was saying just now, the sociologist is protected from radical attack by the fact that he is not in danger of losing his salary (or at least, only his symbolic salary). There are places of publication where we don't have to ask whether it is worth the trouble to write the 405th article on the State in Durkheim: if there is a social demand, I am justified [in doing what I am doing]. If this kind of social demand disappeared, many sociologists would have to ask themselves all sorts of questions . . .

On the question 'continuity or break?', there is an interesting book by Hans Maier[41] (I know that there are people in the room who are interested in this sort of problem). It deals with the genesis of the *Politische Wissenschaft* (the science of politics) in the German principalities in the seventeenth and eighteenth centuries. Maier analyses those counsellors of the little German princes (Leibniz is a famous case) who produced for the government authorities a sort of political counsel, but who are often referred to without people knowing much about what they said. In this category there are what we might call 'institutional characters', ambiguous figures who it would be interesting to study (in fact some of you here [in the audience] are studying them):[42] Vauban, for instance, was a theoretician of the State, but a statistician at the same time – at all events, he set out an agenda. D'Aguesseau, and, later, Condorcet are interesting too. I shall speak of 'the prehistory of social science' to designate these people situated half-way between the traditional political or social philosophy incarnated by the great tradition of Plato or Aristotle on the one hand, and modern social science on the other. They are half-way between the normative political philosophy of the prince's counsellor, and a theoretical and empirical science of the mechanisms of society and the State. And in fact these transitional theories are often concerned more with the problem of managing society than with those who manage it. There is little reflexive science on the subject of government agencies.

On this issue there is once more a clear-cut divide. The dominant and most common thesis, which we find everywhere, is that social science is connected with modern life, modernity and the transformation of society, and is an integral part of the process of social transformation and the construction of a State that assumes functions of welfare and the management of social problems. (The three alternatives that I raise are not completely independent – when we answer 'yes' to the first, we are more likely to answer 'yes' to the second. If I am setting them out independently, it is because most critics confuse them.) The argument, then, implies that there is a break: the new situation in the nineteenth century, with the emergence of a modern society characterized by social change and social struggles, corresponds to a modern science. The social sciences, which are an integral part of the process of transformation, are in a way a public service and a part of the State apparatus.

The opposing thesis is a reactive one, and is rather conservative. (It is often an amusing exercise to see how political stances in the social field as a whole are reformulated in a more limited space, in the guise of an academic problem such as the continuity/break debate. There is a right and a left in both cases, but they are not exactly the same; when you are on the left in the global space, you are likely to take up a position on the left in the more limited space, but there is a transformation. I don't know if I am making sense, I can't explain all that in a few words, but I hope that those of you who are keeping the idea of the field in mind can understand what I am trying to say. End of parenthesis.) The reactive position, according to which the social sciences are not so new, is more a position of the philosophers or historians of philosophy, and it is no accident that I have cited a German [Hans Maier], at the farthest extreme from Lerner. This tradition says: 'We are educated, we can't be fooled, these things were not born in Chicago in the 1930s, it all existed in the German principalities in the seventeenth century.' (Here we have an example of 'specific interest', the notion that I mentioned the other day:[43] the historian has a specific interest in always finding a precedent. I like to cite the example of the argument that Montaigne invented the 'Memoirs', as opposed to the argument that they were already known to one or other of the ancient Greeks. With the historians we can launch into an infinite regression towards the past – with others it is towards the future, the avant-garde. This specific interest may seem insignificant but it is vital: there are those prepared to die to prove that Grotius preceded. . . .) According to the reactive thesis, a political science oriented towards the interests of the prince has existed since the end of the seventeenth or the beginning of the eighteenth centuries. Traditional Marxists look down on this and speak of the idiocies that were peddled to the little German princes. They see in them a typical sign of German backwardness, with people still preoccupied with the petty problems of the German courts and provincial sub-prefectures, whereas in the West people were already concerned with social issues. This is traditional Marxist reductiveness, but it is not wrong.

In fact it is the opposition that is artificial. If I have time I shall give you the details in a moment: the partisans of continuity exhume a political philosophy centred around the prince and his government and call it political science ([Shils?][44] has developed this topic in a book). I shall move on quickly: we pass from a social philosophy to the social sciences, but, in spite of everything, there is continuity insofar as in any case we are looking at problems facing a State bureaucracy, and the theories proposed are responses that owe their particularity to the nature of the State considered and to the position of the people being considered in relation to this State. So we are still in the presence of these things but the conditions have changed. In which case, the diagnosis of continuity or break depends on the definition adopted. If we adopt a definition in strict conformity with a state of the State and with the relation between the State and those who comment on it, we will say that there is a break and that the empirical social sciences, founded on statistics, emerged in the nineteenth century, along with social work. If on the other hand we take a wider view, [we will say there is continuity]. (The problems of continuity and break are periodically brought back into fashion because they enable us to introduce effects of break and distinction, but I think that in many cases they can be solved as simply as I have just demonstrated.)

The third problem: is social science pure or applied? And should it be pure or applied? The problems are constantly overdetermined: factual problems take on a normative appearance and vice versa (this is also valid for the question of knowing whether social science is 'service or manipulation', 'contemplative or active'). On each of these three problems, I could lay out a whole bibliography, but I shall refrain.

Towards a social history of the social sciences

These problems are socially dominant, but they hide a problematic, which I shall attempt to formulate as rapidly as possible, for it enables us to make a genuine social history of the genesis of social science. The first question is to investigate the relation between the social sciences and the State. We need to enquire into the greater or lesser independence of the State in the face of the dominant forces, such as the economic powers. There is no universal answer: the degree of autonomy of the State is a fundamental source of variation. You will be able to verify this when I come to use this problematic to propose a sort of overview of the social history of the social sciences. A second point, which is related to what I have just said, is connected to the global philosophy of 'the State', how it is represented, its function, its mission and its action. Roughly speaking, we could oppose interventionism and liberalism. The more a State is inclined towards liberalism, the more it is suspicious of interventionism, and, by the same token, of the sociology that is meant to explain it. Interventionism, Keynesianism and the 'welfare state', on the contrary, are characterized by a very strong demand for aid on behalf of the State.

The second set of questions that we need to ask relates to the tradition of the educational system. How independent is the educational system from external forces and pressures? This question, which we addressed in the first instance to the State, must be put to the educational system, since this will be one of the possible bases for our science. As regards the autonomy of the educational system, there are once again two poles: is the system autonomous, capable of defining its own aims, or does it occupy a purely subservient position dependent on the social demands of the dominant? The autonomy of the educational system can be defined in two respects: either in relation to the demands of the dominant, or in relation to the State. These are not exactly the same, if you accept the idea that the State enjoys a relative autonomy.

This brings us to consider what I shall call the antinomy of the social sciences. I am anticipating a little on what I am going to say in a moment and there is a danger that I may not express myself clearly (since it is a difficult point, I had written it out in advance, but I am having trouble deciphering my notes . . .). For a social science that is seeking autonomy from the dominant forces, salvation is to be found in the State to a certain extent. For instance (as I have already argued), the fact of being a guaranteed wage earner, protected by the rules and regulations of public service, gives the sociologist a considerable freedom, even against the State and *a fortiori* against external pressure. The State is one of the fundamental sources of scientific autonomy, the guarantor and ground of this autonomy. However, this autonomy from external pressure has to be paid for by dependence on constraints of a State type. These are not necessarily economic constraints. For example, as I was suggesting just now, they may be connected with the fact that there are State journals, official journals with a national title (*Revue française* . . ., *American Journal* . . .), which are certainly not marginal or underground.[45] This is the autonomy of the State sociologist: the price to pay for this autonomy from external forces is dependency on the State. I shall return to this.

Up until now I have spoken of 'the State' and 'the educational system', but to be true to my terminology I should say 'the bureaucratic field' and 'the academic field', to remind us that 'the State' or 'the educational system' are not unequivocal universes oriented towards a single aim and function, but sites of conflict, competition and struggle (which is the problem that I raised [at the start of the lecture] in relation to Marx). For instance, we should make a concrete study of the relations between the sociologists and the State, using very simple examples: Who has received subsidies over the last thirty years, and from which agencies? How do the labs operate? Which labs are funded and which ones aren't? Which ones work with pencil and paper and which have technical tools or computers?[46] To study all this, we cannot just label people as 'State sociologists'; we should appropriate the means necessary to make a concrete study of the relations between two fields that are themselves fields of struggle and internal competition. In the field of the senior civil service, there are the dominant and the dominated, conservatives and progressives, liberals and interventionists. The field of sociology is also differentiated, which gives rise to all sorts of alliances. (Sociological analysis is not clockwork. People who think of the State often have in mind Althusser's metaphor of the State as apparatus:[47] they see the State as a kind of machine to be seized and commanded like a ship; you press the button, and with a 'click' the action is performed. In fact nothing in the social field – and certainly not the State or the university – is an 'apparatus' [. . .], everything is a 'field', and it is only in very abnormal contexts such as totalitarian regimes that the fields are reduced to the state of apparatuses. Let us be clear: an apparatus is easy to control – if you have the right button in the right place and the apparatus is in good running order; and still supposing, against the odds, that there is no piece of grit in the works – whereas a field is practically uncontrollable. In the modern universes, which are differentiated and complicated, there is always someone who has an interest in doing something other than what they are supposed to do. All this is important for what I am trying to say.) If you have to make a concrete study of the relations between sociology and the State, then, you must think of a bureaucratic field (with inspectors of finance and inspectors of roads and bridges – who will be at daggers drawn with the inspectors of the mines, etc.) and, on the other hand, a field of sociology (with its dominant and its dominated, etc.). We could sum up the relation between the two fields, whose consequences are extremely complex, by speaking of 'State sociologists', but this is a very simplistic shorthand.

Behind all this I find the antinomy that I mentioned just now: everything happens as if the social sciences are unable to win their autonomy against the external social forces unless they rely on the State, that is, lose their independence from the State. This has nothing to do with the left/right opposition, and, to 'perplexify' things, I could say that a left-wing State favourable to the social sciences is in a way more dangerous for the autonomy of the social sciences . . . if only to make you stop and think [*laughter*]. The exercise of reflection is dangerous but, to a certain extent, a left-wing State that demands and expects everything from the social sciences, which wants expertise and is apparently ready to listen, is much more dangerous for the autonomy of the social sciences than a State which leaves them in a state of undernourishment and contempt.

To recapitulate: I first recalled the questions that we usually ask about the social sciences ('do they serve a useful purpose or do they manipulate?', etc.). Then I stated how the question ought to be phrased. Now, bearing this problem in mind, I would like to sketch a comparative history of the relations between the field of the social sciences and the bureaucratic field from their origins. You see that this is very ambitious, and I have only half an hour . . . (With luck I can hope to cover up the inevitable gaps in my analysis. . . .)

The 'prehistory of the social sciences'

I mentioned just now how the prehistory of these relations arose, in the guise of the learned counsellor of the prince. This prehistory was the work of the bureaucrats. D'Aguesseau, whom I have copiously discussed this year, is typical of this category, whose vision of the social world and usage of analysis of the social world have as their aim to justify and guide the policies of the prince. This is a princely vision, and basically during this period of prehistory (I think that this was valid until the time of Condorcet . . . to a certain extent, it was valid until Lenin, but that is yet another thing that I am saying on purpose to annoy you! [*laughter*]), this science was made by people who wanted to use it in order to govern. It is a science of government for men who want to govern either personally or by proxy [. . .] It is a science of conservation. It may be defined as an aid to reproduction. Machiavelli, the only one of them to whom I would grant the title of pre-sociologist, had the merit of giving himself this explicit aim as such, and thus the goal of creating an almost scientific act of foundation.

I am speaking in very general terms. To make myself clear, I ought to give historical examples and examine them in detail. I can suggest one (for those of you in the know, it will be enlightening, the others will just have to trust me): the birth of German conservatism.[48] I can develop this example because a lot of historians, in particular American ones, have worked on it.[49] For historical reasons, after the Second World War, people wondered what were the particular factors that impelled those godforsaken Germans to develop the extraordinary ideology of Nazism. They looked through the sources (this is an example of a social problem becoming a scientific problem) and they discovered a category of people in the 1815–1830 period, whose ideal representative was Adam Müller. It seems to me that this intellectual was one of the first right-wing ideologists. He theorized the conservative discourses that others at the same time, the Junkers, were delivering in the first degree. There is in fact a difference among the conservatives. Hegel characterized Thucydides as an 'original historian'.[50] The 'original historians' are interesting because, since they lived in the period they were recording, they convey to us what they found self-evident, what went without saying. They are first-degree historians. There are even original State ideologists, for example the duc de Rohan. These men of power, reflecting through and for power, were what you might call 'primary' conservatives.

After the shocks of the Revolution and the Napoleonic wars, the second-degree conservatives emerged (Adam Müller is one of the most typical). Their situation relates not only to the order of the State but also to a nascent scientific field. These are people who 'are facing two ways at once'.[51] Whereas the aristocrats, the ordinary Junkers, made first-degree statements – 'we must conserve', 'The State is the State' or 'Discipline is the foundation of the State' (we still have such original philosophers; Poniatowski, for example, whom I mentioned the other day,[52] is an original State philosopher) – our Adam Müller has a dual connection. He is connected with the State but also with the scientific and academic fields. In relation to the democrats, on the left, he says: 'We must justify the State and democracy.' His discourse marks the beginning of a lineage of ideologists whom we might call 'right-wing intellectuals' (Schumpeter, etc.) and who have a kind of dual vision: they are not content to say, 'This is how things are, and that is fine'; they say, 'This is how things are, and that is fine, *although others may disagree.*' They laud modernity, for instance, while they value tradition. When you are within a tradition, you do not say that there is a tradition. Thus, in the words of an Arab proverb, 'they are fighting for the survival of a traditionalism that does not see itself as such'.[53] As soon as a tradition perceives itself as a tradition, it knows that there are other traditions and that it has had its day. The traditionalist says, 'This is how things are, and that is fine', whereas our good man [Müller] is starting to say: 'A tradition enshrined in discourse is worthy of establishment, it is worth defending.' The movement passes from intellectual to intellectual, down to Heidegger or Gadamer, who sings the praises of tradition.[54] Enough of that example (I'm afraid I've said too much or too little . . .). In this prehistory, the political philosophers then are the first degree. The beginnings of professionalization start with the professional conservatives or the professionals of conservatism who have provided the nascent social sciences with substantial subterranean and surreptitious nourishment.

The birth of the social sciences in an awkward position

I now come to the philanthropists who were most concerned with social problems, and to the type of social enquiry typified by Le Play. An enlightened right wing (I use this vocabulary with hesitation, I don't want to over-simplify), a conservative aristocracy, used the denunciation of pauperism to attack the bourgeoisie, and this made them attentive to social problems that the bourgeoisie refused to admit. Adam Müller and the people I referred to were clearly the inventors of a pair of oppositions that laid the foundations of the unconscious of German sociology: they established the good opposition between the aristocrat and the peasant (as countrymen living in an enchanted paternalistic harmony), and the bad one between the bourgeois and the worker (with the bourgeois becoming the Jew for Heidegger and the pre-Nazis). This opposition allows us to understand how a form of right-wing populism can today be seen to be a precursor of sociology.

Those who study Le Play[55] today saying, 'Look, he wrote monographs on the family, etc.', should recognize this (but this does not detract from his monographs – Le Play is the only person who ever enquired into Béarnais peasants and I am very grateful to him for this[56] – but I think that he had interested motives relating to his position in the dominant space, the internal struggles of the bourgeoisie, and the field of power).

In this conjuncture riven by social problems, the social scientists, then, appear to be a reformist, left-wing bourgeoisie, very often connected with the State (I can't argue this through, I just haven't got time . . . – but it is no accident if the Protestants and the Jews, who are typical oblates owing their salvation to the State and who are awkwardly placed in the dominant class, are in this position of enlightened, reformist right-wingers). We might note in passing that sociology is historically linked to socialism in its origins, by a very bizarre link which brings to mind the film *The Defiant Ones*,[57] where a black man and a white man are chained together. The link between sociology and socialism seems to me to be of this order: it is a kind of historical chain, a forced and conflictual solidarity that is very complicated.

The workers' movement and the trade union movement present or provide problems for the philanthropists, who ask the sociologist to deal with them. The sociologists in their turn, in treating these problems, elevate them to the status of scientific problems but dissolve them as political problems. They therefore play a distinctly ambiguous role and are perceived as reformist. This is why, for instance, the question whether Durkheim was a conservative or not has caused so much ink to flow. If you bear in mind what I have just been saying, you will see that the question does not make sense. Durkheim is in fact structurally ambiguous. He is a progressive insofar as he elevates social problems to the scientific universe, which would never have bothered with them (it was only concerned with Babylon, or Greek manuscripts, or the like). But at the same time he dissolves these social problems by establishing them as scientific problems and providing the tools for handling them to his colleagues and professors, who are in power.[58] This is a fundamental ambiguity of the State.

The impetus of social science is nearly always linked to the modernizing, reformist group. I refer you to an article published in *Actes de la recherche [en sciences sociales]* under the signature of M. Damamme on the birth of Sciences Po,[59] which is typically an institution of enlightened conservatism. It makes no sense to say that Sciences Po is 'the right wing of the left' or 'the left wing of the right'. We are not surprised to find among its founders a very high proportion of people, like

Jews or Protestants, who held marginal positions in the bourgeoisie. In a simplistic logic of denunciation people might see the hand of capital, a diabolical ruse, in this. But we might also say that it is an opening through which an enlightened bourgeoisie can nonetheless listen to the world. It is in fact a structurally awkward position.

This is what I wanted to say: social science was born in an awkward position, which derives from an extremely ambiguous social vision. It responded to a demand emanating from the bourgeoisie, but from a subordinate fraction. This fraction of the dominant wanted to modernize society, it wanted to modernize the dominant class and it wanted sociology to help with the modernization of society.[60] That is what Sciences Po is all about. The idea was that if a dominant class is to manage to conserve itself, it must be able to jettison ballast in order to conserve itself by transforming itself. The sociologist is a sort of transformation assistant. It may sound as if I am making this up, but you can verify what I have been saying, in a few sentences that may seem somewhat harsh and political, if you analyse the role of the sociologists in the commissions of the Plan[61] (on what occasions are the sociologists consulted, which sociologists are consulted, on which problems, and what are their replies?). This enlightened avant-garde is closely committed to a rational representation of its role, and of the State. The notion of the Plan is vital, and it is no accident if after the Second World War sociology experienced its maximum development during the times of the great periods of the Plan.[62]

Scientific sociology and France as a special case

What I have been saying in general terms, I shall now apply to some brief historical examples from different countries. In Great Britain, social science emerged among small private societies that were the equivalent of our clubs for reflection (such as the Jean Moulin club).[63] In the Victorian period, there was an atmosphere of concern favourable to considering the great social problems, with people like Dickens, Ruskin, [William] Morris or even Carlyle. There were the workers' movements and the elite clubs, which debated avant-garde problems. The Fabian Society was extremely important. It was at the origin for example of the London School [of Economics], one of the most scientifically respected social science institutions, whose origins lay in a enlightened militant reformist society. In Germany there was the group that Weber joined, the Verein für Sozialpolitik.[64] The word *Sozialpolitik* ('social politics') is interesting. The founders of the group were economists like Gustav von Schmoller, attracted by history and empiricism. They were concerned with empiricism insofar as their concerns were practical. The link between empiricism and practice is very important: you cannot be satisfied with a vague social philosophy when you are trying to frame rational political action. In the United States (I am going rapidly because I am pressed for time) the first professional association, the American Social Science Association, was created in 1865. Then, nearly every five years, a new association was created, in economics, in demography, etc. The model that emerged from the statutes of these associations was always the civic one, in the lineage of d'Aguesseau's civic humanism: it was the model not of the neutral academic, but of the committed citizen who wants to place science at the service of the State.

The case of France is extremely bizarre, and this is not an illusion created by a product of our national imagination: to draw up this rapid sketch I have read a lot of research into the social history of the social sciences, and practically all the researchers who have any regard for comparative studies have noted the singularity of France, and the fact that it was in France that scientific sociology was affirmed for the first time. It is no accident if Durkheim is considered to be its founding father. This is no doubt because of historical characteristics that I shall very briefly and concisely mention. We could say roughly that of all the modern countries France is the country where social problems (in the sense of problems involving social groups) have been most violently expressed; as in the case of the Commune. Because of this, the field of power was haunted in a particularly acute manner by anxiety about the masses, pauperism, etc. In parallel, the French university system offered possibilities for the construction of a more autonomous science on the basis of the State university, the State civil servant, the Republic of the professors. The 'Nouvelle Sorbonne', in which the sociologists played a decisive part and from which the university as we know it arose, accumulates all these ambiguities in a way. Very schematically, it cannot be separated from a concern to restore republican order, after the Commune (see the problems of *anomie* that Durkheim raises). It was established against the Commune but also in tune with the Commune. It was in sharing the energy of social anxiety that haunted the population of the dominant that the Durkheimians were able to found a discipline like others (which was Durkheim's anxious concern). They were able to use the autonomy of the university – with the freedoms that the university had acquired and that the reformists of the New Sorbonne defended even more strongly – to found a science not only scientific but able to resolve social problems because it was scientific (Durkheim provides the ideology for this State science when he says that the State is our conscience).[65] It is important to note that in this university it was the philosophers who dominated. If we had to choose an indicator of university autonomy [. . .], the status of philosophy would be key. In the struggle by the social sciences for their independence from social forces on the one hand and the State on the other, the existence of a strong philosophy faculty nourished strong pure theoretical ambitions (for good or for ill, this philosophy itself being very subservient, both to external forces and to the internal forces of the academy). This would merit a year of lectures but I find that people talk too much about Durkheim already (although not in this way, of course . . .).

The separation of national traditions during the interwar period

A third phase would be the period of development from 1920 to 1940. It is very confused and rather badly researched, but the major tendency seems to me a kind of continental shift: America drifts away from Europe and the two traditions of the social sciences become very divergent. Those of you who are in the know must think that in expressing myself like this I am going too far, but I think that I could substantiate my argument by constructing hypotheses that would be verifiable or falsifiable on the basis of empirical studies or even secondary analyses of existing empirical studies. For me the icon of this period is the Chicago School, which became firmly established in the 1920s, and perhaps understood the Durkheimian project most completely, that is, the affirmation of specific methods (statistics, observation, enquiry, etc.). This school reinforced its specifically scientific nature with a capital of specific techniques borrowed from the dominant sciences like geology or physics. At the same time the Chicago School incarnated a form of insubordinate interaction with the powers of government. But with an ambiguous aspect: it countered its submission with the rigours of its methodology, but even this may be a superior, euphemistic subservience, if the methods that were the emblem of its autonomous honour were to be bent to the service of non-autonomous problems. For indeed it is possible to autonomize your methods and apply autonomized methods to problems which are not themselves autonomous, and this would fulfil to the highest degree the service of rational legitimization of the demands of the State. There would be more to say about this (the emergence of associations, etc.), but briefly, I think that to understand the comparative development of the European and American systems, you need to take very seriously the difference between the university traditions. That may seem to be self-evident, but social historians very rarely situate their research in the perspective of the three factors that I identified at the start: the externalists who take into account the intensity of the social problems forget the university problems, and the internalists who acknowledge the university problems forget the social problems. With Roosevelt in particular the social sciences were in a way in power, and at the same time, the particular structure of the American system – with its autonomous, competitive universities, combined with the existence of very special institutions like the foundations and a certain number of very powerful professional associations – assured the social sciences of a particular independence.

I ought to give more detail, but it seems to me that in Europe, between the two wars, the social sciences remained more confined within a theoretical framework, and more subservient to philosophy. They devoted their reflections to sociological problems, such as axiological neutrality. For instance, it is very significant that the traditions encountered by a French sociologist entering sociology in the 1950s[66] would be shared between a post-Kantian epistemological reflection (Gurvitch, Weber and Raymond Aron), the empirical sociology coming from the United States, and the Durkheimian legacy. We should also note the differences in Europe. The situation of Sweden for example would be very interesting to study, because the State there is oriented towards social problems (this is one of the variables that I studied).

The triumphant postwar development

I shall now very rapidly move on to the fourth phase, the Keynesian period after the war, with its very strong demand for contracts by State and politicians.[67] The considerable increase in social demand and in the dependence of the social sciences on bureaucratic and State demand can be seen in practically all countries. We could analyse an enterprise as typical as the observation of social change. The French sociologists invented the OCS[68] (it is no accident that it has a bureaucratic acronym): it answers their dream of having points of observation, thermometers of social conflict, observatories of social change (the word 'observation' is interesting: as if detecting seismic tremors, we can find out if Toulouse is likely to erupt). This kind of process can be seen everywhere. We see an increasingly strong demand. To put it rapidly, the sociologists had never had their existence so justified as then, even if at the same time they had never been so dependent on demand.

Here again we need to look at the particular case of France (I had intended to reveal the elements that would help you understand the sociology of sociology, but I don't have time . . .), with the creation of specialized institutions like the CNRS or the École des hautes études [en sciences sociales], which was a very strange attempt to reconcile two commands in order to create something free of both.[69] To put it briefly, what Braudel and his team attempted to do with the École des hautes études was to use academic authority (the Durkheim tradition, etc.) on the one hand, and American foundations on the other, to make a science both critical and academic. I had prepared a splendid virtuoso piece [*laughter*] where I compared Horkheimer's experiment in Frankfurt[70] to Braudel's experiment in Paris. If you look at the detail you will see that they had practically the same project. Horkheimer wanted to create something interdisciplinary and politically committed, whereas Braudel did not say as much (he did not want to say it), but all his choices (the first teachers, etc.) show that he had a committed vision (and not in the naive sense of the word). He also sought autonomy and universality for his science (*Aufklärung*, etc.). I think that these people set themselves an explicit project which was as near as you can get to what a social science of the social sciences could designate as a project, for anyone who wanted to found an autonomous social science (speaking in these terms I seem to be making an *ex post* celebration . . .). As for the difference between Horkheimer and Braudel, it depended on the people they worked with, and the context (said like this, it sounds ridiculous, I shall probably be obliged to look at all this again next year).

Afterwards, we should mention the post-1980 period (Thatcher, Reagan): sociology had its funding cut and lost the justification for its existence; it had to justify its right to exist anew. At least in France, this was to a certain extent a blessing in disguise: it forced some agonizing revision of presumptions that the automatic renewal of contracts had allowed sociologists to postpone to an ever-vanishing future horizon.

To sum up in a few words, so that you can see what I am driving at: the social history of the social sciences is a game with three players – the bureaucratic field, the academic field and the field within which the field of the social sciences itself and the field of sociology are situated. These fields have different structures and balances of power that depend on their national traditions, and I think that this is the way to understand the differences in sociological production. We should proceed like this, in my opinion, because, as I said the other day in perhaps rather too enigmatic a set of formulae, the problems that sociologists and historians have to study (I took the example of conservatism just now) are produced in this arena. The essential problems that sociologists deal with are produced in the bureaucratic fields in reaction to groups that cause problems. They are social problems that become translated into academic problems, subjects for theses and research, research that is then translated into subjects for dissertations. In other words, there is a whole collective enterprise establishing problems without a subject. I think that the only way to establish a scientific subject is to objectify this collective enterprise of producing subjects of research, so as to prevent social problems being smuggled in under the guise of sociological problems.[71] We can show this for social problems, but also for the categories of analysis, that is, the systems of classification, the categories of INSEE, and, if I had had time, I would have made an analysis of the relation between a sociologist who is independent, believing in his independence, and a bureaucratic State sociology like INSEE.[72] In other words, I have today sketched (rather clumsily, but you can fill in the gaps for yourselves) what constitutes in my opinion the only manner of not being the object [of problems?] that we believe we are freely choosing.

Lecture of 19 January 1989

The essays on the State – Disinterestedness is suspect – An inverted world and its genesis – The ghost of economic reality – Understanding the oblates – Two universal observations

I wish to announce my programme of lectures. This year I intend to devote the five lectures that I shall deliver in Paris (I have already delivered a first part of my course at the University of Lyon)[1] to the problem of State bureaucracy, and more precisely to what is specific to the bureaucratic space when you compare it to other social fields.

But in the first instance I would like to follow on from my argument last year here in the Collège de France, and remind you very briefly of where we had got to. I had pointed out that, before launching into any sort of reflection on the supremely difficult problem of the State, it was important to make as radical a critique as possible of State thinking on the State. In the light of this logic I examined two things: first a certain number of major theories of the State (those of Hegel, Marx and Durkheim – I left Weber out for the time being, but this will be one of the objects of this year's analyses). I examined these theories taking them as anthropological documents rather than philosophical constructions, but obviously without totally ignoring that aspect of specifically philosophical construction. From there I tried to set out a number of stances adopted towards the State that seemed to me to cover the range of possible standpoints. On the one hand the Hegelian and Durkheimian position characterizes bureaucracy as a universal group endowed with insight into and knowledge of the universal, as well as the will to organize it. At the other extreme the Marxist position characterizes the bureaucrats as usurpers of the universal, that is, social agents who in a way usurp the universal and appropriate public resources for individual, private ends. More precisely, they act as the private owners of public resources; which is what we sometimes call 'patrimonialism'.

Meanwhile, I had also sketched out a social history of the relations between the State and the social sciences – although it would take several volumes to deal with the question adequately – with the idea that this kind of historical genealogy of social thinking on the State is one way of clearing the minds of those sociologists who want to undertake this task. In a kind of grand historical panorama (rather clumsily put together, I have to admit – but in these cases I tend to think that it is better to do what you can, rather than nothing at all, and that what I was indicating could be thought of as a project for the future), I had for instance observed that social science often finds its defenders in the avant-garde of the dominant, that is, in the categories who work on the construction of the State. I concentrated on just one particular case, but I believe that it was particularly significant (the more I learn about d'Aguesseau, the more I bless the chance that led me to find him). D'Aguesseau is one of those historical characters who, in satisfying their particular interests (while meaning to serve the corps claiming to be the legitimate power), have helped to produce that particular reality which we call the State.

Now that I have very briefly brought us up to date, it seems to me that two key questions arise, which I now propose to deal with. The first is the neutrality of the State, or, in other words, the disinterestedness of the bureaucrat. This question, raised by Hegel as well as Marx and reiterated, in a different language, by Durkheim, seems in its turn to raise a much more general question, a fundamental anthropological question, that I shall sketch rapidly, referring to things I said some time ago in the first lectures that I gave here.

I shall try straight away to discuss the problem of knowing how a disinterested act may be possible. This question may appear to be philosophical, in the worst sense of the term, but it is extremely important. It underlies and informs most of our reflections on the State, whether these have theoretical ambitions or are merely reflections expressed in everyday life in casual discussions of the State.

The essays on the State

In passing: I had intended to present you with an overview of the fashionable theories of the State [although I am giving you the elements of this], to explain why I did not get to the end of the task that I had set myself, I have to admit that my scientific courage failed me because this literature, as they call it, sent me to sleep. Yet there is important work that remains to be done here. This preliminary work of radical criticism would provide a way of turning sociology against itself, of using it as an instrument to construct the instruments of knowledge, and above all the instruments of unconscious knowledge, for instance, to understand the problems that seem to be self-evident: 'the big State/the small State', 'all power to the State/no power to the State', all those debates that preoccupy the daily press. One manner of objectifying those structures which we use, most often unconsciously, to construct our objects of study would have been to take this problem as a major object of study. I shall probably allude to it. Another reason that stopped me was the idea that you would have thought that I was yielding too easily to the pleasures of polemics. In fact, what Bachelard called 'the polemics of scientific reason', that is, the legitimate criticism of the instruments of knowledge, takes a polemical turn in the social sciences. Often the scholar who wants to make progress in his work starts by demolishing his colleagues, and himself, insofar as he participates in the confused consensus of collegial thought that they all agree on – you are supposed to know what a State is; there is a sociology of labour, so you are supposed to know what labour is, etc.

This kind of radical questioning is in my opinion something absolutely fundamental and indispensable to scientific research. But this criticism is also what is most difficult, and often most painful, because it appears to be directed at external opponents, but in fact these opponents are only interesting because you are one of them. These polemics are often very badly accepted, and they show up their author as a kind of troublemaker or a wet blanket, a slightly diabolical person playing at last man standing. This is one of the reasons why I called a halt, but you can work out the issue for yourselves.

There's a whole library of books on the subject, ranging from Pierre Rosenvallon to Alain Minc,[2] with many in between, which are often produced by servants of the State, and it is one of the interesting properties of modern bureaucracy that it increasingly feeds into the production of discourse on itself and on the social world (I may return to this point). Where the principal opponents of sociologists like Durkheim, for example, were the jurists, ours today are the graduates of the ENA, that is, people who see it as a constituent part of their professional enterprise to make normative and positivist definitions of their profession and the social world. This is the context within which many of these books were written. They are often the work of technocrats, journalists or techno-journalists, whose sociological status would be quite difficult to define: their books are often libellous attacks on other scholars, or essays with scientific ambitions whose superficial scientific appearance disguises a rhetorical discourse that is impossible to verify or falsify. They make reference to scientific research and statistics – always second-hand, of course – and to scientific authorities. To describe them we would need to resort to the language that Plato used to describe the Sophists. These are people who are difficult to pin down, and, to a certain extent, to refute scientifically, because they have the whole social order on their side. I often find myself falling into the kind of despair that Socrates felt in the presence of the Sophists: scientific research is difficult enough already without the exhausting effort of having to face up to this kind of semi-learned *doxa*, which is all the more threatening because it has both the social order and scientific appearances on its side. To give you just one example: the unsinkable, armour-plated debate on the innate versus the acquired. Why is this debate so buoyant? It succeeds because it has no real existence. But to be able to appreciate the fact that it doesn't exist, you already need a degree of initiation that is beyond the reach of most of the people who engage in the debate.

That is more or less what I would have liked to do. This was the programme that I intended to pursue. Now I want to explain something of the method that I would have used to carry it out, and the method that I am using at the moment to study the critics of Manet in his time:[3] I posit a discursive space, where the people who produce these various discourses on the State today are not placed at random. We need first to situate them in the bureaucratic, intellectual and journalistic spaces, or at their intersections. Once we have situated these people, we need to find the relation between the position they hold in these spaces and the stances they adopt, since the spaces can refer very roughly to the opposition between right and left, and we can often classify them in general terms on an axis running from the far right to the far left. But the political characteristics that we start with are often of very minor importance. What is far more important is their classification according to their positions and trajectories in the specific spaces (such as the bureaucratic space, and so on). This is the programme of work to be accomplished. We shouldn't study one essay writer in isolation, but rather take them as an ensemble, bringing to the forefront the objective relations that link them with one another and are at the root of their existence, with their differences and identities. I have not done this, but having said what should be done I feel greatly relieved [*some laughter*].

Disinterestedness is suspect

I come now to the problem I want to debate – the question of the neutrality of the State and of bureaucratic disinterestedness. Is bureaucratic disinterestedness purely ideological, a sort of 'spiritual point of honour' (as Marx would have said)[4] for this category of bureaucrats, or, bluntly speaking, a kind of mystification? Or does it on the other hand have a foundation in social reality, at least as a normative goal for the behaviour of people who hold positions in the bureaucratic field? More generally, as I was saying a moment ago, does disinterested behaviour exist and how should we interpret it? This problem, which I find crucial, is sometimes discussed in a manner that I do not much appreciate, since it seems to me too much like a scholarly dissertation. The subject that I am formulating is often a pretext for examination questions: 'interest and disinterestedness', 'the disinterested gift', 'is a moral action possible?', and the like. I shall try to show that, when we are confronted with these acid tests, [we should] demolish received wisdom and reformulate the question from scratch.

To show how difficult the problem is and how deeply it is involved in reflections on bureaucracy and on the State, I am going to refer to an article by a professor of law, Laurent Richer, 'L'action administrative bénévole'. It is to be found in a collection of papers which were given at a colloquium and which, as is often the case, are of very uneven quality, though some of the articles are interesting (the collection is edited by Laurent Richer under the title *L'Activité désintéressée, réalité ou fiction juridique?*, published by Economica in 1983).[5] The whole article is interesting, but I shall discuss only the first few pages (because I think that they set up the problem very well), which are towards the end of the book that he edited (pp. 123ff.):[6]

In the classic conception of liberal theory the public service assumes a disinterested character, in hypothesis and in essence. Maurice Hauriou has insisted that we should not forget this 'fixed point that the State should always be a disinterested enterprise' [*this is in Hauriou's* Traité de droit administratif[7]]. Achille Mestre reminded us that 'between the two points of view – lucre and public service – [there is] an irreducible difference'.

In the terms strictly formulated here, the opposition between public service and the lucrative has long ceased to correspond to positive Law [*in the reality of the law, it no longer exists*]. The pursuit of a financial interest by the administration is accepted in numerous domains [*the author is referring to Teitgen-Colley*[8]].

However, it is still possible to consider that the administration never seeks profit for profit's sake. For this reason, the disinterested character of administrative activity is not diminished if we define disinterested activity as the opposite of the pursuit of profit [*this gives us a clear definition of interest: 'disinterested' means 'not in pursuit of economic profit'*].

[*But here things become more complicated:*] Yet in fact administrative Law shows that disinterestedness is not necessarily defined by the absence of lucrative intent. For in fact within the general category of 'administrative activity', itself considered as a subset of the category 'disinterested activity', we find 'disinterested activity' as a category [*this is very interesting, because very important*]. What makes this category singular is not its relation to the notion of the lucrative, but its relation to the notion of the general interest.

In fact in certain cases – which are marginal, we must admit – administrative action may benefit a private individual in such a personal manner that it may appear to be serving the aims of a private interest. If this aim is really predominant, then the administrative action is of course illicit.

What does the author mean? What he means is that, in this particular universe that is the administrative world, disinterestedness runs the risk of being interested [*some laughter*], and becomes suspect. If you have the pavement repaired in front of the house of a departmental councillor, who happens also to be a member of the prime minister's cabinet office, there is every likelihood that the dice are loaded and that this disinterested action which could be thought to be in the general interest does in fact hide a personal interest. I shall return to this point, I just wanted to give you a foretaste. There is this fantastic formula declaring that 'the administration does not seek its own benefit': the benefit has all the appearances of circumvention of the law, of favouritism. I shall return to this notion of favouritism, which strangely had never been studied before I came to look at it[9] (I am amazed to think that nobody had thought to study the relation between the law and favouritism). Drawing benefit is a suspect action. We should contrast it with benevolence: benefit is a benevolent action which affects individuals, whereas the act of benevolence should be universal.

If administrative law – that is, the law of this particular universe, of this field that I call the bureaucratic field – is suspicious of individual benefit, it is because its rules are universal. If we make it particular, the particular interests that inspire it must immediately enter into contradiction with the universal ruling. I find this article very interesting and very amusing, and indeed still very topical. I think that it helps us to understand what we might call the theoretical or philosophical foundations of what happens in the political and administrative world.

From the legal point of view – which is what I want to concentrate on at this stage of my argument – disinterestedness, then, is something abnormal. I may be exaggerating slightly, but in this universe whose law is one of disinterestedness, a certain type of private disinterested action, concerning benefits, gifts or donations, is suspect. In other words, the administrative universe is a special universe, at least in legal terms, an autonomous space that is the site of a legal exception – which is an important phenomenon.

An inverted world and its genesis

Here the discussion is situated practically on the level of the field: a field is a universe that is subject to laws of functional practice, often allied to functional norms, which are different from the laws of functional practice and the ideal functional norms of our universe. The world of the administration is one of those microcosms which I call 'fields', where things happen differently from elsewhere. Things that are good elsewhere, are bad here. What elsewhere is disinterestedness becomes interest here. It is the world inverted.

This is my starting point for a sociological analysis of the problem raised. Is not the bureaucratic world and what happens in it ultimately an inverted world? Is it not an inverted world in the sense that it is not a world ruled by the ordinary laws of ordinary life in societies like our own – although we should take great care to avoid universalizing too hastily – not a world whose economy as such is constituted, as I have told you so many times, on the basis of the tautology 'business is business'? Is the administrative world not founded on an exception to the general laws of the economy, on a bracketing out of the 'business is business' rule? That is the first question. And is this *nomos*, this fundamental law, an ideal law with no basis in positive reality – to use the distinction made by the jurists – or is it a law with some basis in reality, however tenuous, at least enough to oblige people who play this game to pay verbal homage to the ideal law? This is the fundamental question that I wish to raise. It will lead me back to the more general question of the possibility of disinterested behaviour.

There is a second question, which is extremely difficult and would merit much historical research (but obviously, as always, people make a virtue out of necessity. In such cases people say that it is quite something to raise the question, even if they can't fully respond to the research programme that they have outlined in putting the question. I even have doubts about my own . . .). The question that I want to put is the following: if it is true that there exist social universes such as the administrative field, that is, universes which are, in Hegel's terms, somewhat 'inverted worlds',[10] inverting the economic world, if such universes do exist, how did they come into existence, how did they become possible? What I suggest is a shift in theory. We normally question whether a disinterested action is possible. This is Kant's question: 'Has a moral action ever existed?'[11] We are looking for specific cases: has a genuinely virtuous action ever existed, an act that cannot be reduced to some suspect form or other, as enumerated by Kant himself (he was well enough acquainted with a whole range of Puritan possibilities)? But instead of putting the question in these terms, might we not put it in sociological terms, that is, in the realist mode? My hypothesis is that, if a moral action has existed in some place at some time, it would have been in a universe where there was an interest in moral action [*some laughter*]. Whence the question: can we write a historical genealogy, that is, the genesis of a specific universe (there are also the worlds of science, art or literature: they are based on different fundamental laws, but they have in common with the administrative world the fact that they are inversions of the economic world)? How can we describe the genesis of these universes? And before we describe their genesis, we have to ask whether they are possible universes, or pure fictions, kinds of mystification, as Marxist theory in its strictest form would say. Are they mere mystifications, throwing dust in the eyes of the poor dominated, who are taken in by this staging of disinterestedness, this theatre of public service, this dramatization of civic virtue? Are they mere mystification or are they social universes whose fundamental law is disinterestedness, where public service may possibly exist? And if so, how and why have they existed? It is not enough simply to say that, as soon as something exists, we have to find a *raison d'être* for it; we need to ask what social mechanisms might have lain behind the creation of this very special game where you have to be disinterested. This is the question that I shall raise, and this year I want pick up the threads of what I sketched out in previous years, and start weaving an analysis. [*Because of an interruption to the recording, the end of this discussion and the start of the following, are missing.*]

The ghost of economic reality

In all societies there is an inevitable ground of materialism, and the societies that repress interest and the principles of the world of common sense have problems. How to do things that you can't do? How can a Brahmin receive his food without betraying his faith? To seal a contract of honour, a Kabyle man says: 'You will repay me later', but he leaves the deadline open, in an economy which does have deadlines, which does count and calculate. This economy has a name, they call it the 'women's economy'. It is opposed to the official economy: here we find the absolutely crucial opposition between the official and the unofficial; it is one of the most central anthropological oppositions that concern what I am studying today. The official economy rejects calculation and accountability, interest and deadlines, taxes and trade-offs, the 'I gave you that much, you will repay me by this date', the tit-for-tat.

As I explained a long time ago, the tit-for-tat is the negation of the gift and the counter-gift, it undermines the truth of the gift and the counter-gift.[12] I shall present the argument in a few words because it is central to understanding this issue – the exchange of gifts is a denial of the tit-for-tat. In the tit-for-tat, you give me this and I give you that, and we can accomplish our transaction in an instant. In the exchange of gifts, on the other hand (and this rule has been noted by all the anthropologists in all societies), the golden rule is to return something different from what you received. If you return the same thing and/or you give it at the wrong time, you are relapsing into the tit-for-tat. Because to return a gift immediately is to reject it: 'you gave me it, I'm returning it', meaning I'm rejecting it. Consequently, there needs to be a time-lag. I have shown the importance of something that people had not noticed: time is extremely important, it changes everything. It is true that we can turn up as sociologists after the event and practise our double-entry bookkeeping, drawing up two columns for the two families involved (which is what I did as an ethnologist, and it is what others do, that is, founding the economics of non-economic, disinterested practices): 'the X family, on the occasion of the marriage of their daughter, gave this much to the Y family: 40 litres of honey, 25 sheep, etc., and the Y family responded . . .', and we check to see whether it all adds up. In fact these exchanges, which we show patently and visibly written down on paper in black and white, are hidden from the eyes of the very people who deal in them, even if, confusedly, in a repressed fashion, they do count, in periods of crisis, even in the domestic economy, which is where this economy is located, which

Aristotle called the *philia* [and which is characterized by] the refusal to count (in the family, you don't count).

In a period of crisis, or, without going so far, in periods when things are not going well, they start to count what they had refused to count (this would be worth analysing in depth). The universe of the *philia*, of the exchange of gifts, is based on an economy that is not negated, but denied: it does exist, but they act as if it didn't, which supposes a collective effort . . . for individual denial is always very difficult. If you are the only person to say 'That doesn't exist', it is hard, it is very difficult. But if the denial is a collective effort, if there is a whole group saying 'That doesn't exist', the thing may finally cease to exist. However, this supposes permanent vigilance by the group, which must constantly impose its order on the misfits who are not properly socially trained and who launch into tit-for-tat, the rebels who consciously flout the rules, or the cynics who consciously transgress.

To finish with this argument: for a universe of disinterestedness to work, you need your delegates to behave in a state of denial. [In a traditional economy?], this would be your domestic servants . . . It would be worth analysing the term 'domestic servant'. The sociology of domestic servants is one of the most difficult to study . . . We encourage domestic servants (and younger siblings, it's the same thing . . .) to honour the family, to have children; we treat them as members of the family so that they will treat our family as their family and comply with the *philia* and not ask for a rise in their wages, etc. In fact, this is all part of the same logic. I'm not sure that all this is clear, but I need to move on. What is important in the analysis that I am trying to establish is the fact that the economic reality of the practices is always there, like a ghost in the social machine. It is always lurking there, it looms, it wants to return like the repressed, like the *libido*. In fact, we need to manage this repressed reality. Often enough the division of labour between the sexes, for example, or the division of labour in politics, are there to solve this contradiction, to enable the social order to deceive itself. In such cases, I quote Mauss's splendid words: 'Society always pays itself in the false coinage of its dreams.'[13] What I am arguing is an illustration of this dictum.

We have the younger siblings, the women, the domestic servants, and in our societies those whom I often call the oblates. The oblates, in the religious tradition, were people given by their families to the Church. These children became in a way the sons not of their families but of the Church, and they often enjoyed illustrious careers within it: owing everything to the Church, they gave everything to the Church. I think that in a very general fashion, the corps, in the sense of the established corporations, are very fond of their oblates. It is the same for the political corps: the political parties are very fond of their oblates, those people who are nothing outside the party and who because of this give their all to the party.[14] We see cases of devotion to the party which cannot be otherwise understood.

Understanding the oblates

To return to the bureaucracy. Will the bureaucracy find its oblates? To make a realistic sociological study of a bureaucratic universe whose fundamental law is disinterestedness, which makes a profession of disinterestedness, which inscribes disinterestedness on the pediment of its temple, we need to ask ourselves what resources it can draw on to make this succeed. In this case, we cannot appeal to the wives, the younger siblings or the domestic servants. I think that there are two categories.

It seems to me that if we start out from an anthropological type of analysis we could almost deduce *a priori* things that statistics will afterwards confirm, to wit, the properties of the people who make good civil servants. I may be exaggerating, but I do so to show the interest of this type of analysis: it may appear to be gratuitous and arbitrary, but it does allow us to understand in retrospect things that we have found obvious. For instance, we find it obvious that the minor civil servants are petit bourgeois, and that the senior civil servants are higher bourgeois and the sons of senior civil servants. When you read this in my books you say: 'Really, did he need to use statistics to discover that? We could have guessed all that . . .'. That said, if you want to understand what I am driving at – why, for example, the son of a managing director tends to study at HEC [Hautes études commerciales (business management institute)], whereas the son of a magistrate tends to study at ENA [École nationale d'administration (senior civil service training college)] – you need to keep in mind the sort of things that I have been saying. To understand that a certain proportion of the population of senior civil servants seems to accomplish the ideal of the universal class, which is an exception to all the fundamental social laws that I have been trying to review, we need to follow my analyses through in the way that I made them.

To return to the oblates. The concept is illustrated in the most striking way in the case of the educational system, with its 'hussars of the Republic' and their reputation for pedagogical devotion.[15] The republican schoolteacher did in fact work overtime (at least statistically; we must not be too idealistic after the event); he often did everything that was detailed in the bureaucratic definition of the post and often a bit more, in fact, much more than a cynic might believe. Should we consider in this case that these were really disinterested people? We would face the same problem if we wanted to understand hospital nurses (where in addition there is the gender variable). To understand the devotion of the minor civil servant who is not rewarded for their devotion, who is in general very poorly paid and does not enjoy much social esteem, we need very subtle explanatory systems. The model I have offered consists in saying that there will be behaviour perceived as disinterested, that is, not reducible to the strictly economic determinants of the practices, every time we find a match between a system that formally rewards the respect of formal rules of disinterestedness, and social agents socially disposed to be sensitive to those formal rewards. The oblates – that is, the socially mobile petit bourgeois who becomes a devoted minor civil servant or an incorruptible tax inspector (this virtuous character does exist, no need to say more) – are only possible, I think, through the occasional encounter of a man of '*ressentiment*' [. . .] with a post where you have to say 'The rules are the rules', 'After the deadline is after the deadline'. In other words, it needs people who take a spontaneous interest in following and imposing bureaucratic regulations.

I think that if we obey this logic we ought to be able to explain things without being reductive. In fact it is important to remember that sociological analysis easily takes on a cynical colouring. It seems reductive or . . . how shall I put it? It seems to invoke determining social factors which, while not economic motivations, are just as inadmissible – and sometimes more ridiculous. All the types of oblate, whether religious or charitable, all those that Goffman calls the 'do-gooders',[16] all their actions have . . . For instance, in the idea of the do-gooder, there is the idea that somebody is doing good in order to be seen to be doing good. There is then a symbolic profit in the act of doing good, and they are self-rewarding actions. From a Kantian viewpoint this is quite wrong, they are not pure actions at all, they are not respecting the rules for their own sake, but seeking the symbolic profit of morality. I think that there are social categories who accumulate 'morality capital'. This capital, 'morality capital',[17] is an important aspect of symbolic capital. We might say for example that the sacrificial disinterestedness of the oblates is experienced as pure respect for the rules while being surreptitiously haunted by a search for moral profit: 'I want to be able to look at myself in the mirror', 'I want to be proud of myself', etc. There are social categories whose speciality is morality. This is true of the petite bourgeoisie: they are ethical classes because that is the only form of capital that they can accumulate.[18] Are these analyses disenchanted and reductive? This question is always very embarrassing and I am embarrassed [because people will say:] 'This is frightful, it's pure Machiavelli, you leave nothing standing, it is absolutely terrifying.' This is in fact because it is such a difficult analysis to achieve. You are supposed to find a discourse that would include all the previous analyses. As I was saying just now (I didn't intend to develop this theme, but I shall do), the *illusio* is born of an immediate relation and attraction of the habitus to the field. In fact the person who does what they are supposed to do experiences what has to be done as the only thing to do. I return to the nobility, but we can also do it for the petit bourgeois (for the simple reason that the nobility is the easiest example, and for good reason: it is easier to speak nobly of the nobility . . .).

We say, 'noblesse oblige', but things are more complicated than that. It took me years to understand it. What is a nobleman? How does the nobility work? What is it that makes a nobleman feel obliged to act nobly? It is very complicated. We need to take the expression 'noblesse oblige' literally. It connects nobility in the sense of being noble ('he acts nobly', 'his behaviour is an expression of nobility') with nobility in the sense of a noble manner of existing that has become embodied as an unconscious reflex. Nobility in this sense obliges and constrains the nobleman. It is stronger than he is, there is no need to tell him to empty his purse,[19] he cannot do otherwise. Even at the risk of his life. Here we can clearly see that his body refuses to obey him. He wants to escape, but he can't, he is made of such stuff that he must stay put and risk his life, 'you are trembling, Carcasse',[20] etc. He has incorporated what we call the values of nobility, which have become in practice the principles of his practices, ignoring all calculation. We can rework the analysis for the petit bourgeois. The republican oblate is one of these admirable people (I think that my analysis does not detract in any way from the admiration that we feel for them), but he cannot do otherwise, there is a mightier force at work. Just as he once learned to pen his [well-formed?] letters, he imposed on the whole universe of the school and the village a norm that had been imposed upon him, a norm stronger than he, which was inscribed in his habitus and in a relation between him and the liberating school, the extraordinary thing that appeared to him as a sort of absolute ideal because it had liberated him. We should not forget this: the republican oblate is somebody the liberating school has liberated. By the same token, he devotes himself totally to the liberating school and he wants to universalize his own liberation.

I can take my analysis a little further to show that we can defend the undefendable petit bourgeois.[21] The republican schoolteacher, especially in small rural communities, or perhaps the foreman, such as Paul Nizan's father,[22] the small-town engineer, or the lowly office worker, is a migrant. He is cut out for culture and cut off by culture, he acts in the name of culture. What else could he do, what could he do better to reconcile himself with himself, to assuage his guilt, his wretchedness, his misfortune of being expelled (I ought to develop this, for he is in fact not simply someone who escaped and is admired, but also someone who was expelled, someone who was betrayed and who is rejected)? To soothe the pain, the only salvation is to universalize his proselytism. And – according to the many studies I have devoted to this question, to the frequentation of museums, etc.[23] – the cultural proselytism of the first-generation petite bourgeoisie, which only recently won access to culture, culminates in the museum. This is where we find the greatest number of proselytes and cultural fanatics who want everyone to visit museums. It is not a question of intent or of planning, but something written into a relation between a habitus – which subsumes a lot of things: a career, a relation to their parents, etc. – and a position. When this miraculous encounter occurs (I am using the word 'miraculous' in the statistical sense, meaning 'improbable', 'uncommon') people do extraordinary things, but without positing them consciously as extraordinary. A famous title by Kantorowicz, *Pro Patria Mori*,[24] examines the question of how to get someone to die for their country. In fact we don't know how to obtain this because we never know if those who die for their country really did die for their country, but no matter . . . It happens [that people do die for their country], and I think it is analyses of this kind, which go beyond ethics, that are the type of thing that we should do.

Ultimately, we would prefer good deeds always to be motivated by good will. Whether we have read Kant or not, we all share a kind of Kantian ethic, and we apply to actions the Kantian maxim: 'Was this action really intended to be moral?' In other words, we see action in rational terms: to consider any action as moral, we want it to have been the object of an ethical project posing this action as an explicit, conscious end, etc. In fact (Hegel said it long ago,[25] but it is worth repeating), if a moral action is really of this type, there has never been a moral action (moreover, Kant himself said as much).[26] In other words, for actions that might be considered as moral and disinterested (devotion to public service, to culture and values . . .) to be possible, there need to be mechanisms of the type I am describing. Finally, what Hegel said about Kant – not to mention what Nietzsche said, which went further in the same direction[27] – applies completely to the ordinary theories of rational action: there is a sort of fanatical definition of . . . Hegel spoke of the fanaticism of the Jacobins,[28] of the purity of their rules, and there is something fanatical in people's reactions to socio-logical analysis when they perceive it as disenchanted, determinist and designed to drive not only the factory workers of Boulogne-Billancourt but even more the clientele of Sartre's favourite café, *La Coupole*[29] in Montparnasse, to despair – whereas in fact the problem is knowing whether it is truly possible to find an action that may be sanctioned as universal. In fact my whole analysis is designed to say that, in order to attain the universal, you need to have an interest in the universal.

Two universal observations

I shall continue this argument for a moment, because there are two things I wanted to say that I haven't yet said, and that I will discuss more fully next time. On the subject of the anthropology of universal behaviour that I have been trying to sketch today, I think that we can posit two universal observations. The first proposition is very risky, but I think that with a minimum of anthropological foundation it can be sustained – it is that there is no society that doesn't look suspiciously on disinterested conduct. In every society in fact we find a philosophy of suspicion of behaviour that claims to be disinterested and ethi-cally pure. Ultimately, La Rochefoucauld's Jansenist vision of human action is fairly universal. The principle of universal suspicion of behav-iour claiming to be universal is the suspicion that it is the universaliza-tion of an individual interest: we always suspect someone who is acting the universal to be universalizing their individual interests. He says 'we' ('we think that . . .'), whereas it is 'I'. In other words, he moves from 'to be' to 'ought to be' through a manipulative slippage from 'I' to 'we', from the individual interest to the general interest. I think that this logic of universalization is almost universally perceived and denounced. I shall leave it there.

The second universal observation is, I believe, that we can say that there is a universal recognition of the universal in all societies (I keep saying 'all societies' . . . but at all events it is valid for most of the societies that I have been able to study or read research on), there is a universal recognition of our submission to the universal: what a social universe always demands, even from those who transgress its rules, is to do the right thing. I thought long and hard about the expression 'do the right thing' when I was working on the Kabyle, and I shall imme-diately take an example from there. In the Kabyle tradition, marriage with a parallel cousin, that is, with the daughter of the father's brother, is lauded as the ideal marriage. But when you look at the statistics, you note that this ideal marriage concerns 3 per cent of the normal population and 5 per cent of the Marabout families, who are the best upholders of official tradition because they are its guardians.[30] So we can easily see that there is a gap between the publicized rule or ideal and people's practice. That said, somebody (I nearly said 'somebody smart enough', but it's not about being smart) with a habitus attuned to honour well enough to transform a potentially catastrophic, forced marriage with his parallel cousin (an ugly girl whom nobody fancied, and somebody did his duty and took her on . . . I am giving a single example, but it did really happen . . .) into an ideal marriage enjoys symbolic profits of a universal nature. His family would say that he married a girl who had been seduced and abandoned, that he took her to save her honour and the honour of the family, that he is the 'veil for their shame', because you can't leave a girl all on her own.

There are symbolic profits of a universal nature, so that a whole part of human behaviour is motivated not by obedience to the rule, as a naive ethnologist in a hurry might think (you have to be quite smart to observe this in a society, rather than simply listening to what people tell you, you need to think about it . . .), but by formal respect for the rule, that is, the concern to do the right thing. Most often groups demand no more. They say: 'At least, he did that.' But if somebody doesn't do it, it's terrible. The real transgression is in ostentatiously defying the rule. This formal respect is what Spinoza – who comes to mind – called *obsequium*, that is, the sort of fundamental respect we pay to the group as group.[31] Groups demand this, and this demand for universalization, even in public service, even if only lip-service, is a form of recognition of the universal. Another example: the English and the Americans call the great private art collections 'guilt money': this is the same idea, which we need to develop.

There is, then, universal recognition of the facts of the universal and at the same time a permanent temptation to denigrate artificial submission to the universal. You could even say that there are benefits to be gained from this denigration. Furthermore, one of the temptations that the sociologist has to resist is the temptation to derive benefit from denigration, and to see this benefit as scientific gain. I shall give you one very brief example, then I shall finish. Someone ought to use this logic to make an analysis of gossip, hearsay, slander and rumour, all those strategies of everyday existence that are the synthesis of everything that I was saying just now. For instance, someone who denigrates the easy virtue of another person has two benefits. He has the benefit of denigration, defamation and disqualification, of making himself at least equal to his object ('he's no better than me'), which is an important subjective benefit. And in addition there is the moral benefit. This is well known. Here too, common sense will tell you that there is nobody fiercer at becoming a paragon of virtue than a woman of easy virtue when she no longer has the means to transgress. It is common sense that says that; I am not [endorsing] the proposal, I am expressing it as an example of this universal insight into the universal strategies of universalization. That said, these universal strategies of universalization (that is, the fact that social agents are always summoned to encourage and pay homage . . .) are still something very important. [*The recording stops here, no doubt a little before the end of the lecture.*]

Lecture of 26 January 1989

A plan for an enquiry into the Pechiney affair – A transhistorical sociology of ethical dispositions – The habitus and the Kantian ethic

I shall today make a very direct reference to the most urgent current affair, because it happens that the social world, or living history, is our laboratory material. We have before our eyes social procedures which so perfectly illustrate the argument that I was developing last week – which alluded to this reality, but without being inspired by it at all – that I cannot help taking advantage of the occasion, not at all for the sake of effect (one that I wouldn't know how to categorize . . .), but to show how the most theoretical analyses are often those closest to practice, and how, in order to understand with a certain distance and what we call a certain objectivity what is most urgent in the social world, we often have to have models that may seem very abstract and slightly unreal. It is then a way of showing that sociological analysis can claim, with some chance of success, as Weber would say, the right to a form of objectivity which is not at all what it is usually thought to be. This objectivity has nothing to do with what Weber for instance called ethical neutrality;[1] it has nothing to do with indifference or an alleged distance from the events taking place. It is a neutrality that is born of the very construction of social reality. It is obvious that, in an audience like ours [in the Collège de France], there are people 'of every opinion', as they say, and I think that we may speak of the most urgent matters, precisely those that divide opinion most strongly, without offending any of these opinions, by paying due respect to the lay spirit – we are still talking about disinterestedness – which is the norm in public education.

So I shall attempt to analyse what has been called the Pechiney affair.[2] I won't enter into detail. I may work on this more in the future

– at the moment I am still collecting documents – to try to make a more serious study, but I wanted simply to show you that the procedures and the affairs that you read about in dribs and drabs every day in the papers can be subjected to a rigorous analysis.

If you remember, to sum things up very simply, I said that virtue could spring as it were from a relation between, on the one hand, ethical dispositions that might seem immoral, and, on the other hand, the logic of certain fields or social places. In other words, I was suggesting that, if there is in the social world something like disinterestedness, virtue or the universal, and if the universal may happen to make progress, it is not because the moral prophets are obeying some absolute internal laws or pure rules, but because there are historical conjunctions of dispositions and social mechanisms which mean that even directly interested dispositions may engender practices that transcend this disinterestedness.

A plan for an enquiry into the Pechiney affair

I shall now very briefly recall the chief figures in this affair. There are to begin with the two agencies that control banking operations: firstly, the American agency, the SEC [Securities and Exchange Commission], which seems to have triggered what is now called The Affair.[3] This agency is obviously linked to political organizations and we might suppose – I am of course only voicing hypotheses, a historian of the present or the future will need to do the research – that this agency is not indifferent to the fact that the government which is open to criticism is a socialist government.[4] I shall not develop this point, I have no proof, but we can suppose that this action is not entirely without what we call ulterior motives, or interested considerations. There are, for instance, benefits at stake which are linked to the development of Paris as an important financial hub. Such a marketplace is situated in a field of financial centres which are in competition with Paris and which could have an interest in weakening it. I realize that I am going out on a limb here. This is the boldest part of my analysis, but it is a plausible hypothesis.

Secondly, there is the corresponding French agency, called the COB [Commission des opérations de la Bourse/Commission for Stock Exchange Operations], which shares the same footing as those various bureaucratic agencies that they established in the hope of introducing morality into the world of television.[5] They are very vulnerable agencies, whose weakness stems partly from the fact that we can always suspect that their apparently universal verdicts are inspired by interest (there have been all sorts of specific scandals connected with this). These agencies, then, are very fragile and they are much more liable than the juridical agencies (which are in fact in the same situation, but as we are more used to them, we are less aware of the fact) to have their universality questioned.

It is interesting to note that the social world very often makes efforts to understand itself, and sometimes the field of the producers of discourse on the social world generates analyses that are almost scientific. Obviously nobody sums up this research, but I think that after the analysis has been done, we could reread the different standpoints of the different journalists *ex post*, and in recomposing them, say, through a system of citations, treat the analysis as if it had been made in the field. Of course this has not been done, nobody has done the summing up, but it is the nature of scientific work to create the possibility of a summing up, using for example a notion like that of the field.

(To open a parenthesis. The analysis that I have to offer raises the question of the place of the sociologist in the social space. Where does he stand? So I shall indulge in a play on words straight away, because I am sure that someone in the room will do it: we could say that the sociologist is 'meta' [outside, beyond] and I could say, 'I am Meta, too!' [*laughter*]. There you are, someone was going to crack that one, so it was just as well it was me! Otherwise my remarks will be polemical and someone will say: 'But who does he think he is? He adopts a sovereign position, a divine position, and he establishes the whole set of social fields as games that he observes and he's the one who sets their rules and fixes their stakes. What right has he to say what he has just said, which is that Mr X, Y or Z, Mr André Fontaine or Mr Jean Daniel,[6] are moving their pawns laboriously about on the board, elaborating as best they can without being aware of it a truth that he alone knows how to interpret?' Since it has often happened historically that people in a theoretical position – from Hegel to Marx, via so many others – have done what I am in the process of doing, it is important for me to say 'Meta is me too!' so that you know that I am conscious of what I am in the process of doing, which can enable me to control the effects of this temptation to take the divine viewpoint that is inherent in the scientific enterprise in the social sciences, which is no doubt one of the most profound motivations of the sociologist's vocation[7] [*some laughter*].

I am saying this because I feel particularly targeted by the accusation. I ought to expand on what I have just said, but I shall refrain, otherwise, as I metamorphose, I shall lose you along the way [*some laughter*]. I simply want to say that I am aware of this position and its temptations that leave us open to a certain number of theoretical and empirical errors. If you are interested I can refer you to the introduction to *Homo Academicus*,[8] where I have tried to set out the problem at length as a preliminary to the analysis of the academic world that I belong to – which I think however that I can analyse as if I didn't belong to it, while still enjoying all the benefits, and knowledge, that belonging bestows.)

Having admitted this peculiar position, I return to the space of the SEC and the COB. Yesterday, or the day before, I read in *Le Monde*[9] that the COB is poised as a young challenger, a newcomer attempting to accept the odds and rise to the challenge. This is an absolutely classic law in a field: the little newcomer, the challenger, must play the game. In a social field, the latecomer, the young pretender, must in general make a display of virtue and conformity to the official norms of the field, in order to beat the dominant player on his own ground, as it were. Here we are on the ground of ethics and, if the COB were a totally free player (if it enjoyed absolute autonomy . . . that said, autonomy also has to be fought for, this is a very classic problem), we might expect it to exaggerate its ethical stand to affirm its autonomy, in particular in relation to power. This 'challenge effect' operates in a space that is subjected to the existence of a norm. In a field like the economic field or the field of television, the neutral agencies of control are instituted as guarantors of a universal norm, the universal norm of the field. And to affirm themselves, to exist and give themselves some importance (often in a field to exist means to give yourself some importance), to be interesting, to have the rewards associated with existence in a field, these agencies must defend the norm, for they are the guarantors of this norm. In the case in point, among the profits and losses to which the agents in question are exposed, there is on the one hand the danger of discredit, of loss of credit or symbolic capital (which is often one of the prizes fought for in the struggles in the fields of cultural production), and on the other hand the hope of credit: to be worthy of the institution, and by the same token to elevate your stature and reap the profits associated with moral superiority. I think there are ethical profits that can translate into the *légion d'honneur* or career advancement or simply an honourable reputation. All these things are to be played for . . . I ought to develop this, but I don't have enough information. What I am giving you are the overall patterns. Then there ought to be interviews. I am giving you a plan for an enquiry rather than a true analysis.

To continue. There are obviously politicians in the right-wing opposition[10] who have a definite interest in handling the affair and using it to accuse the government. They are tempted by the benefits that I mentioned last time (I referred to the benefit of gossip). As I showed last time, these accusatory benefits are twofold. There is a first benefit in proclaiming the rule and recognition of the rule ('I am good because I say that we must act for the good'): the accusation brings credit to the person who makes it. At the same time it brings a supplementary benefit, which is the discredit done to the people accused and with whom they are in competition. They [the political opposition] therefore have a direct interest in accusing, but everybody knows this, since they are part of a political game which is quite open (we should reflect on the difference between the political field and the bureaucratic field). The rules of the political game are those of victory or defeat, and its principle, its fundamental *nomos*, is that of friend against enemy. To a certain extent there is a logic of total war (even if one question that arises is whether in the political field the war is really total – I think not, for otherwise it would not be a field). The political adversaries then have an obvious interest in denouncing, but run the risk of appearing interested in their professions of disinterestedness and being caught in the act of transgressing the very norms that they are in the process of promoting: they are exposed to the 'feedback' or 'boomerang' effect. By increasing the intensity of their demand, they may transgress the law of the middle way, which requires them to avoid demanding every-thing, and exacting too heavy penalties, for fear of seeing themselves exposed to reparations. Once again, this partakes of a very subtle logic. [*The conclusion to this section of the argument is unfortunately missing from the recording used.*]

A transhistorical sociology of ethical dispositions

I have forgotten this year to make the appeal for questions that I make every year: you are invited to hand in either during the break or at the end of the session any questions, objections or remarks that you wish, for me to answer either straight away or soon after. This is particularly important on occasions like today, when I am trying, without overstepping the bounds of academic propriety, to go as far as possible towards satisfying sociological thinking. Basically I am trying to do something that all educators should do, which is to neutralize what I call the *scholè* effect as far as possible. We have never taken the etymology of the word 'school' seriously enough: it comes from the word *scholè*, which means 'leisure',[11] and the world of the school is a derealized world, so that everything that is said and done there loses any structure of reality. Ever since schools have existed, people have argued that they should be brought closer to life. There is a structural divide, and in the case of sociology this divide is particularly sinister, because as long as we are satisfied with a formal understanding of sociology, we can understand everything and nothing and be unable to do anything with what we do understand. I think that an important part of sociological teaching is unconsciously designed to transmit things that we can really do nothing about in the social world. I shall not develop this point. It would be important enough, but if I did I would probably be abusing the pedagogical authority conferred on me by this chair.

So I return to what I was saying before. I want to try to show the structure of my argument and sum up what I have just been saying so that you may at least retain a certain number of clear principles. I wanted to show through this rather sketchy analysis that in certain historical situations actions that are universalized, universalizing, becoming universal or contributing to the advance of the universal can be generated when socially composed individual drives (as we find in the word *libido*)[12] come into contact with the states of certain fields. In other words, there are states of the field that give positive ethical drives the opportunity to express themselves, or states of the field that give ethically negative drives the opportunity to express themselves in such a way that they benefit from the ethical. That is what I really wanted to say.

Although things are much more mixed in reality, we can very schematically oppose two classes of disposition in any given field. There are firstly the dispositions that are ethically positive in relation to interest (taking economic interest as a universal reference, returning to what I said last time); for instance, the inclination to generosity that may be an aristocratic disposition. If I had the time and if it were central to my argument, I could for example rework the analysis by Bénichou, a major author rather diminished by terribly anti-sociological teaching in the preparatory classes.[13] A somewhat revitalized Bénichou would be a great help towards understanding what I am saying. For instance the socially composed aristocratic dispositions towards generosity, lauded in Corneille's theatre . . . There are for instance some very fine pages on *La Princesse de Clèves*, on the rejection of jealousy, on generosity in the relation between the sexes. These ethical dispositions are socially composed through a process of socialization of which the parable of the purse gives an idea.[14] These socially composed dispositions can, when circumstances allow them to reveal themselves, lead to heroic acts of sacrifice. [They can also reveal themselves] in our everyday lives.

To persuade you that a transhistorical sociology of ethical dispositions is possible: I think that even today aristocratic dispositions are established in opposition to bourgeois dispositions, such as submission to money, and to good manners. Aristocratic dispositions may be expressed in journalism in the guise of leftist anarchism . . . They may also be expressed in the dispositions of eminent dignitaries of the Church, who, being unwilling to succumb to the petit bourgeois tendencies of the Church today will become bishops of Saint-Denis and offer assistance to immigrants.[15] My analysis is very summary; we should [in order to be more profound] analyse these aristocratic dispositions and study their genesis, both autonomous and relational. This last point is very important: in a differentiated society ethical dispositions are always both substantive and relational. An aristocrat is also shaped by his aristocratic dispositions, independently of other factors, and also by dispositions that are not bourgeois and which, if you had to choose, you would call more popular than bourgeois. Well . . . Do I make myself understood? I have been going too fast because this is not central to my argument, and since I need to move on, I would hope that you might understand all this before I have even explained it [*laughter*] . . .

The duo, as described by Bénichou, of the Cornelian aristocrat and the Jansenist, Racinian, Pascalian, La Rochefoucauldian bourgeois, seems to me to be a relatively transhistorical opposition in terms of ethical dispositions. You can see it operating in diverse contexts. In my analysis these ethical dispositions lie behind the ethical drive, the *libido ethica* (the disposition towards moral indignation of the rising petit bourgeois,[16] the generosity disposition . . .), which may come to fruition and fulfilment if the opportunity is given (the field is in fact the source of such opportunity).

So we will find disinterested actions, some of which are the product of a socially composed disposition to disinterestedness, and others the product of dispositions that are interested in terms of their relation to interest (economic for instance) but obliged by the law of the field to transmute themselves. In other words, we find two principles engendering actions perceived as disinterested: some simple and direct, the others, the opposite. Well, I'm afraid that I am not being at all clear . . .

I shall rapidly give the description of a case where the ethical dispositions are more or less in phase with a field that requires disinterestedness . . . I need to find an example to make myself understood . . . Take the aristocrat raised in the [*word inaudible*], who risks his life on the battlefield for no reason, and gets killed by the English archers. A historical search would enable me to give precise backing to what I have just said.

This kind of disposition generates ethical behaviour which, as I said very rapidly just now, is not open to judgement in terms of its merit. In the last analysis, the person who commits a virtuous act in this logic has no merit in doing so, because in a sense he could not act otherwise without negating himself. It is in such cases that people say: 'Rather die than do the opposite.' In other words, these dispositions are beyond interest.

I shall pause here for a moment, before taking this theme further, to say that in fact my whole analysis of the habitus and the relation between the habitus and the field[17] gives us the basis for a description of ethical conduct that takes its place in a very old philosophical tradition, running from Aristotle to Hegel, according to which moral behaviour is not motivated by a conscious intention to submit to a rule, but by what Aristotle called a *hexis* (which is the same word as *habitus*)[18] and Hegel an *ethos*, that is, permanently incorporated dispositions which generate actions that objectively conform to the rules, but are not actually driven by them. In other words, virtue for Aristotle or Hegel is a virtue that does not take virtue as its goal. It is a virtuous action whose virtue is an extra. There is a classic philosophical *pons asinorum*, the commentary on Plato's *eu prattein*.[19] Since every philosophy teacher has practised this exercise, I hesitate to do so, but I may be able to give it a new twist. The Greek phrase *eu prattein* – I hesitate to say this because it is so well known . . . – means both 'to succeed' and 'to act well', which leads us to say: 'What an extraordinary connection: a person who acts well (*eu prattein*) is happy and at the same time he is successful.' In fact the theory of the habitus that I am promoting enables us to describe virtuous or generous acts, which appear superficially to be the product of a conscious will, oriented towards a goal, motivated by obedience or conformity to a rule, but which do in fact belong to the order that I have described: they are such that the person performing them has no merit, because in performing them, given his constitution, he cannot do otherwise than be generous. Let me think. . . . [*Bourdieu hunts for an example*] . . . it's like the person who knows that someone has to pay for the next round of drinks. Obviously, if he is a social climber [*Bourdieu smiles, thinking of what is to follow*], in a petit bourgeois universe where everyone mimes the gesture of reaching for his wallet for as long as possible in the hope that someone else will beat them to it [*laughter*], he appears to be extremely generous. That said, he didn't make a conscious choice. I am simplifying, that was rather a caricature, but you can find examples like that out there in the real social world.

The habitus and the Kantian ethic

To make it clear why this ethic founded on a theory of the habitus has nothing to do with the Kantian ethic which, as I said just now, we all have at the back of our minds, we need to refer to a text by Kant that some of you may perhaps know. The exact title is more complicated but I refer to it as the 'Essay on Negative Magnitudes'.[20] It is a text where Kant raises a certain number of typically philosophical ethical questions.

A central debate in the social sciences today[21] is the debate over what American students wittily call the RATs and the CATs. The RATs defend the 'rational action theory' and the CATs the 'collective action theory'. The first have as their philosophy of action the idea that all actions are based on positing an intentional, conscious, deliberate and calculated principle, directed towards an end. Following this logic, Olson[22] and this whole tradition thus pose the question of collective action: how is collective action possible? How is it that, when I can listen to the 'Radio Music' channel for free, I am prepared to send them 500 Francs? I have no reason to do this . . . How is it that, when one can benefit from the services of a trade union without joining the union, there are people stupid enough to pay their union subscription? [*some laughter*] This kind of problem is a consequence of considering the exclusive principle of human action to be the rational calculation of profits and costs. This tradition is just what founded Kant's theory. It is the tradition according to which an action can only have been motivated by the positing of an end, which may be respect for the rule. In the 'Essay on Negative Magnitudes' Kant raises a certain number of questions that Elster sees as obvious paradoxes.[23] In general Elster uses even more simplistic examples: 'How can I stop smoking?' There is another great example, which I always quote for a laugh. It is the kind of question debated at length in exclusive philosophical circles, with the required Oxford accent: 'I am a major landowner and I have liberal political ideas, but I'm afraid I might regret my action. So I declare in front of my wife: "I donate my lands to my slaves", so that I cannot renege on my promise, because that would dishonour me in the eyes of my wife.' This is the kind of abstract question that is posed: 'How can I decide to stop smoking?' 'Who is this "I" who gives "me" an order?' 'Take two misers, one at grade 10 and the other at grade 5. They both undertake a grade 5 moral act – which has the greater merit?[24] It is obviously the grade 10 miser, because he scores 15, in algebra. [*Reacting to some laughter in the audience:*] No, really, this is important because this theory of virtue, morality and merit is based on the idea that virtue can only be a vice consciously overcome. We suppose that there are wicked impulses and that these wicked impulses can be overcome at the expense of a pure reference to the rule by a pure intention. I mention these examples for those of you who are interested in these problems: the whole theory that I am trying to establish is a totally different response to these questions. I am opening up a lot of horizons . . . In fact I was wondering whether I should make this reference because in fact I could do without it, but I think that there may be those among you who are interested in these problems and who – depending on educational circumstances – may not know that I am replying to these questions, and who might continue to be 'rational action theorists' while still thinking that 'Bourdieu says some very good things' [. . .]

Against the people who promote theories of rational action – which I have defined – others oppose the 'collective action theory'. They say that there are collective actions: 'There are collectives, there are groups, there are the masses, the political parties – there are subjects of collective action, collective action is possible', etc. For me these debates are metaphysical and derisory. That is why I mention them in passing. I would find it very tedious to do more than mention them in passing. So there are people who say, 'Yes, there are collectives, classes do exist, you can have nations', and the others say, 'But no, it isn't true, they don't exist, there are only individual subjects.' You can find contributors to this debate all around [us?]. I shall leave it at that.

In my opinion this alternative is completely unreal, and my whole theory of the habitus is based on the idea that there are actions which are reasonable, but not rational, which are spontaneously collective, without ever having been intended as such. An action may be collective in the sense that it is objectively attuned to others; or, under certain circumstances, if someone issues an order, it can become really collective and mobilize people through their objectively orchestrated dispositions. By this I mean (if you follow the argument) that, if you take people who have roughly the same disposition, the theory of the habitus leads us to hypothesize that they are going to have roughly the same reaction to the same stimulus. Looking at the same painting, they will have roughly the same reaction. They may differ (one will say, 'It's fantastic', the other, 'It's not bad'), but in the first place they will both have come to look at the painting whereas others will not, and then they will both have a largely favourable opinion. The habitus forms a basis for reasonable action without having reason as its principle (as opposed to rational action theory), and it founds collective actions without a collective being the subject (as opposed to collective action theory). In my opinion these two theories form a ridiculously false alternative which can only exist and persist in the scientific field because they find multiple external echoes in the form of oppositions like individualism v. socialism, right v. left, etc. It is no accident if the theory of rational action – which I had thought dead and buried several times in the course of my not so long life – returns at certain moments in History. If the theory of *homo economicus* can recur,[25] it is because behind it there are social forces, interests and drives which have nothing to do with scientific knowledge. That parenthesis was very rapid and rather clumsy, and I run the risk of seeming to force the issue, but I don't want to take this further, and I wanted you at least to know that this is what I am referring to indirectly.

Unlike Kant's miser's merit, which is proportional to his effort, an ethical action of the first type (that is, an ethical action having for its principle dispositions spontaneously perceived as disinterested in a certain state of a field) implies neither effort nor merit. If merit is measured according to the importance of the vice overcome, if the virtue of generosity is measured according to the scale of the avarice and the effort it took to overcome the impulse to withhold payment, these people have no merit, because, to a certain extent they could not do anything other than pay. They would have found doing the opposite unthinkable and unbearable. Disinterestedness as an ethical drive linked to a positive disposition, which may be accompanied by the pleasure of accomplishing it . . . Here we find Aristotle and his magnificent text on the noble animal accomplishing its innate function,[26] happy to find fulfilment in doing its best. On this subject I have come up with a moralist's formula that I want to share with you. It is destined for those who, confounding sociology with the discourse of those we call moralists (La Rochefoucauld, Montaigne, etc.), may have come here to hear some moralizing formula. This is one I have devised in order to analyse it in sociological terms: 'Good deeds do good to those who do them.' That could be signed by a moralist. In other words, there are cases where the good deed does good to the person who does it, but without the person doing the good deed even finding any benefit from being perceived as doing good. There is a degree zero of ethics where the person doing good cannot do otherwise than do good, because he is accomplishing his innate function, he is fulfilling himself. He is like Aristotle's galloping horse. He is fulfilling what we call his nature, that is, his habitus. There is one form of generosity [of this type], which happens to be full of charm. For instance, if pre-capitalist societies have such incredible charm, at any rate for people who share my values[27] (which are connected with the habitus and socialization, etc.), it is because these people are still spontaneously, naturally and splendidly guided by dispositions that are disinterested, virtuous and generous, enjoying a type of enchanted relation that our societies of calculating, timing and clock-watching no longer know. There are for instance societies in which people take something which we know to be extremely rare, their time. A reductive analysis would argue that, if people can take their time in these societies, it is because their time has no value, it is not convertible into money, etc. That said, even when they are transported into a universe where time is money, the people who have been raised in these societies where time has no value keep the dispositions that cause them not to count their time, and they retain a tremendous presence. This is an example of the sort of analysis that we can do.

Action, then, is driven by dispositions, and to a certain extent the person who does good, who acts well, is pleasing himself. These are in a way actions of self-fulfilment that are self-motivating, that are their own end. This is the absolute opposite of what I would call pharisaism, that is, action which consists in doing good for the benefit that it will bring, in the logic of an interested and calculated investment. Seen from the viewpoint of rational action there is clearly no alternative to cynicism or virtue, it is Kant or cynicism. Which is why these theories are unable to cope with practical reason. Whereas my argument today is based on a valid theory of action, which I have developed in *The Logic of Practice* [*The recording stops here*].

Lecture of 2 February 1989

The regulated transgression of the bureaucratic rule – The political field and the bureaucratic field – The categories of technocratic understanding – The notion of profession, a scholarly myth – Defining the concept

I keep feeling that I am wandering off the beaten track . . . I am going to try to tie up the loose ends, and fill in the gaps. [But] I also want to tell you about two things that I had forgotten: among the offences committed against the duty of disinterestedness which are mentioned in the research, we find something called *'pantouflage'* [leaving public administration for a job in the private sector]. I think that I shall have to return to this, because this institution – there is no other word for it – does I think [raise a much more interesting question?] than the traditional question that the politicologists put, regarding the relation between the ministerial cabinets and the senior civil service. The politicologists adore this problem: 'Does the politician wield power over the administrator? Is the administration infiltrated by the political? Does the fact that many administrators become politicians – and vice versa – affect the autonomy of the bureaucratic bureaucrat?' I think this is one of those typical false problems that divert our attention away from a genuine [problem]. Which is that we accept too easily the idea of the autonomy of the bureaucratic order. This is an internal question: it only arises if you place yourself at the point of view of the people who subscribe to the bureaucratic representation.

Another remark: [. . .] the sociologist is attacked when he says certain things that the jurist can say without attracting opprobrium. You are obviously going to ask me why. No doubt the sociologist says it differently from the jurist, but what does this difference consist of? It is connected with *obsequium*.[1] One of the things that I believe the sociologist should query, in order to be able to really call the social world into question, is *obsequium*. Which sometimes causes problems when the sociologist takes as his practical principle the practical principle of his scientific activity. It is an almost existential problem, a difficult problem – although it lacks pathos – that any sociologist worthy of the name knows: the approach and the reaction to the social world required for sociological work create difficulties because they must deny the social world what it most requires, which is not a big deal, but is something major . . . To someone who offends against *obsequium*, people say: 'Why don't you do it, it would cost you nothing.' But something that costs you nothing may be very costly, otherwise they wouldn't ask you to do it. They say, 'Why don't you say "Monsieur le president" when you are addressing a president?' There are people who don't find this a problem: that is what *obsequium* is all about. I think that if the question is put, it must be something that hurts, because it costs you nothing yet it is still being demanded of you . . . I'll leave it at that [*some laughter*] because I may say too much . . . But I think that this is what we need to feel very strongly: the sociologist places himself in the situation of radicalism and makes the radical break that the philosophers very often claim for themselves, although I find that they hardly ever put this into practice: a fundamental philosophical *obsequium* enables them precisely to avoid the transgression that the sociologist is obliged to accomplish, which incidentally earns him the fury of the philosophers – and also of some sociologists.

The regulated transgression of the bureaucratic rule

'Feathering one's nest' raises one very urgent question: is this not one of those transgressions of the bureaucratic norm which are organized bureaucratically, which are a condition of the functioning of the bureaucracy? I can but [ask]. For the moment, these are just questions. For the moment I am not sure I have an answer, but I have my doubts. It is too easy to say 'I denounce *pantouflage*', my description is not an accusation. It is astonishment: why is this thing, which is nonetheless an extraordinary lapse from the official deontology of the bureaucracy and its duty to be disinterested, so natural? [. . .] Why, for example, does administrative law sanction certain kinds of lapse so strongly? There are cases of very gross lapses but you will see that they present only a difference in degree from *pantouflage* in due form (the 'in due form' is very important, it is linked to *obsequium*: social groups demand essentially that things be done according to due form, because following due form is paying your formal respects to the formal rules).

What is the difference between *pantouflage*, in socially respectable, approved, and even sometimes recommended form, and, for example, the (compulsory) resignation of the inspector of Dassault's taxes who becomes an employee of Dassault? Tell me what the difference is, think carefully . . . Studies on cases of sanction draw attention to the problem: the path to resignation was driven by the desire to abusively exploit, I quote, 'the knowledge, experience and even the authority acquired in public administration'.[2] This is a definition of *pantouflage* . . . in the case of the tax inspector who, six months after checking the accounts of company X, with too short a break (time is always the problem),[3] becomes an employee of the company, there is a sanction. But when Mr X moves from the Tax Inspectorate, where in fact he checked the bank accounts of the banking company, there is no sanction. This raises problems which I find interesting.

I shall take another example of regulated transgression of the rules. Which is another way of saying *obsequium*: the height of *obsequium* is a regulated transgression of the rules. The greatest art in a social universe is to so master the rules of the game that you become capable of playing with the rules while observing them. If the highest posts are so often hereditary, it is not because the sons are brought up to follow in their fathers' footsteps, as in the nineteenth century, it is because it takes generations to acquire this art of *obsequium*. You have to be born into the universe to become a virtuoso in the regulated transgression of the rules, to know how to do these things without overstepping the mark. One of the most frequent sanctions in a field is the one that strikes the man who is following the rules at precisely the moment when he should be more flexible . . . a well-born man knows that you cannot blindly apply the rules when you are dealing with an infraction by the prime minister [*inaudible phrase*]. (I am taking a ridiculous example, but I could take a less ridiculous one [*some laughter*]. You see, I am often obliged to play for laughs, otherwise you would no longer grant me the distance that I grant myself.) All these regulated distortions of the rules seem extremely important to me. They should be taken into account in a general theory of the bureaucratic order in the light of what I was saying just now: would things function without them? You might see them as mistakes needing to be denounced, etc.; but I myself think that they are structurally necessary.

I can give you another example by quoting an article by Jacques-Sylvain Klein entitled 'Processing competition funds or the art of manipulating budgetary rules'[4] (we note immediately that he speaks of an 'art'). This author is critical, and normally he should not have written this article. He explains what competition funds are. I am not sure that I have completely understood, but I suspect that it matters very little whether I have understood what I am conveying to you. These funds generally come from local government and other sources. They have the property of being available to be attributed, received and spent outside of any parliamentary control. They are an income that eludes parliamentary control. As the author says, by means of these competition funds – which are entirely legal and official – 'considerable sums of credit [are] left to the discretion of the administration'.[5] They were evaluated at 1,700 million francs in 1981.[6] I have no idea what that means, but what we can see is that this is a kind of bureaucratic slush fund. It is also interesting to see the autonomy of the administration, something that you need to write down in your memory for when we come to reflect on the bureaucratic.

How are these credits allocated? Their distribution immediately gives us some information on the normal function of these funds: 3.2 per cent is spent on the remuneration of permanent civil servants; 7.4 per cent on the remuneration of assistant staff (the author does not say as much, but their functions are probably cited when there is a need for a legal justification of these competition funds); and 90 per cent is spent on bonus payments and indemnities. These bonuses and indemnities obviously do not benefit the cleaning staff. The supplementary remuneration is mainly paid to the fiscal civic servants. They represent on average 34 per cent of the basic salary of these administrators (34 per cent is an average, but this can rise as high as 54.8 per cent for the central administration – one is always best served by oneself – and at the margins it can be 11 per cent for the central management of competitivity and prices).[7] Sixty-two per cent of the bonuses are financed from the competition funds, and one of the major functions of the competition funds is to finance these bonuses. After side-stepping, then, this is another example of the 'transgression' of the norm of bureaucratic disinterestedness which is defended by the people I am speaking of. I am [just now] starting to analyse the discourse of the president of the Council of State,[8] who every year celebrates disinterestedness (as at the Academy they celebrate virtue). These people are among the beneficiaries of this privilege, and perhaps the most privileged among them, which raises the same old question, all over again . . . I shall leave it there.

The political field and the bureaucratic field

I shall move on. I have started to sketch out the lineaments of a portrait of this bureaucratic field: we have on the one hand the virtues of disinterestedness, an ideal of disinterestedness and an advertised norm of disinterestedness; on the other hand, we have practices that contradict those norms, and even – as I have just explained in detail – official and officially recognized practices that contradict the official rules. This all functions perfectly well without contradiction. It is this uncontradictory contradiction that we need to keep in mind, and that I believe any model of bureaucracy needs to account for. You may remember that last year I drew on Hegel and Marx[9] to stake out the two poles of the space of theoretical possibilities for the bureaucratic universe, while telling you: 'I have simplified the two authors in question but their vision is nonetheless rather simplistic.' [We can tell this] when we look at examples like the one I have just given you. Moreover, if ever I publish something on these topics I shall give much more detail, because we need to see the details of these contradictions and procedures, measures, half-measures and counter-measures in order to seize the full bureaucratic reality in all its complexity, and not gloss over the problems, as theoreticians unfortunately so often do; it is on this condition that we may perhaps go on to develop very simple but realistic models, which is my aim. I can admit to you that one of the causes of my confusion, and perhaps what leads me unconsciously to defer the moment when I tell you what I really think of the State, is the fact that I am not yet able to say in a completely coherent fashion what I think should be said about the State. This is why I am inviting you to join me in my own approach to research, where I say: 'Look, this is how I work, I have identified various different things and I am going to look for connections, I am going to look for the reasons for things being what they are and not otherwise, to see whether things that look contradictory really are so, and if they are to a certain extent contradictory, whether they might not be understandable from a higher principle, etc.' [I am not saying this] to make excuses, this is the way we should work, I believe . . . Unfortunately, as I often say, the teaching situation does not authorize me to say this kind of thing. In a teaching situation we are supposed to say things that are established and officially transmissible, that go without saying, at least for the time being. But this is not at all [how it really happens] . . .

Now I would like to go a little further and try to say in general terms how sociologists approach the problem that I have tried, with my analyses and examples, to set out, albeit in a slightly muddled manner. Among the most common themes there is one that consists of the opposition between what I call 'the political field' and 'the bureaucratic field'. They say that the bureaucratic field has properties which distinguish it from the political field; for instance, the bureaucratic field – as I have briefly indicated – is distinguished by its claim to neutrality, by its rejection of everything that pollutes politics. English and American writers, for example, often cite a phrase by someone (I don't know who, I think that it was a Labour member of parliament, a minister)[10] who said: 'Only a civil servant can engage in politics and deny it absolutely.' This is a pretty good formula which does in fact correspond to what I intended to say in my argument about denial: the bureaucratic universe handles the same matters as the political field, but the issues that are overt in politics become [in the bureaucratic world], not negated as you might say, but denied, that is, people say they are not doing what they are in fact doing.

There is then a sort of double game of bureaucratic bad faith. On this, you can refer to an article that I wrote a few years ago in number 36–37 of *Actes de la recherche en sciences sociales*.[11] The issue is dated February–March 1981 (so the article must have been written in January 1981) and, if you reread it now, you will see that sociology sometimes has the power of foresight:[12] you will see the cover[13] and the contents, I would like to see you look at them . . . In this article, which predates May 1981, I insisted on the fact that political struggles were struggles for the monopoly of the legitimate use of objectified political and public resources, and I also insisted on the fact that these political struggles were struggles for the monopoly of the resources controlled by the State bureaucracies, and thereby for the monopoly of control of the State bureaucracies themselves; and these goals were openly admitted, even if the politicians . . . I illustrated the article with a photograph showing Pierre Mauroy in the act of making a speech at a lectern which bore the inscription 'He is fighting for you.'[14] This was, I repeat, just before May 1981. Political action has interested aims ('I am fighting in order to seize power'), which are denied, but so flimsily that we could say that, of all the fields, the political field is the one whose public image comes closest to the image recorded by the scholar. It is a case where the degree of credence given by the public at large to the denial voiced by the monopolistic holders of the specific capital needed to play in the field is particularly weak. It doesn't hold water. The political field is particularity susceptible to a transparent, reductive or shall we say cynical reading. It allows itself a small margin of error in its denial, with 'in the public service' being replaced by 'at the service of the people' or 'at the service of the interests of France'. But if we look at the opinion polls, it seems likely that, in the case of politics, there is less of a gap between the representation offered by the agents and the representation acknowledged by the outside world than there is in the case of the administration.

The political field, then, obeys the logic of interest almost openly and it aims for the goal of power. The bureaucracy, on the contrary, denies its interests. A series of studies has raised the question of the difference between administration and government. These are the studies that I was alluding to just now. They analyse in detail the opposition between the ministerial cabinets and the administration. To summarize these rather unexciting things: we might say that on the side of the administration, we have management, that is, a manner of treating politics which makes the conflictual problems disappear and reduces problems of antagonism and conflicts of interest to elements of a rational choice that can be settled by competence. The key word is 'competence': where you have two social groups (for instance, in a study of housing that I conducted, local councils who are in conflict with the residents), the role of the civil servant, of the technocrat, is in a way to rationalize choices in order to find a rational solution that will satisfy both parties at the least cost, with the technical solution supposedly best suited to the collective interest. Such management is based on consensus, on this union given by knowledge of the general interest, and the technocrat could echo Descartes: 'It is enough to judge well to do well.'[15] Political choices are in fact of the order of judgement and not of the will (the will is in a way no more than the result of a rational calculation). 'I am a manager', means: 'I am with the civil servants.'

The categories of technocratic understanding

There is, then, on the one side management and union, on the other side division, prejudice, party, constituency and the local. There is an opposition between the central and the local. The civil servant and the senior civil servant are on the side of the central and the interest of the centre; that is, the point from which we survey all points. This is the viewpoint over all viewpoints. Leibniz's famous metaphor for God (as the 'geometral' of all perspectives,[16] the geometric locus uniting all points of view, the viewpoint over the points of view) is a metaphor for the senior civil servant, who sees himself as a viewpoint over the points of view that are necessarily local and partial. As taught at Sciences Po (this will bring back memories to those of you who have been there), the local is always blind, closed in upon itself, interested, restricted, petty and mean. It is the Poujadist small farmer who clashes with the enlightened comprehension of the bureaucratic *Aufklärer* capable of seeing the point of view of the ensemble.

Once in an American university I heard a commentary on an extraordinary text by Durkheim (I never managed to find the title,[17] so if anyone can find it . . .). Durkheim, who was a reader of Kant and Spinoza and had in mind Spinoza's analogy of error as privation, defines the function of the sociologist in contrast to simple individuals who have particular, interested views (the interest in a particular case lies in being particular, in seeing only what hits you in the face, only what happens on your doorstep . . . these are the typical Sciences Po topics of corporatism and lobbies, of a France which would be no more than a cluster of lobbies if the bureaucracy were not there, fortunately, to make the best choices, etc.). The individuals have an individual, private and local point of view, the word 'private' being taken in the Spinozist sense of the term,[18] meaning [that it is a point of view] deprived of the vision of the ensemble. This vision of the ensemble is restored by the Durkheimian technocrat or sociologist, who submits these viewpoints to an overview that shows them up as individual points of view. Then, to convince [the individuals] that they are really individual – which the Greeks called *idios* (which is 'idiotic', of course[19] . . .) – you need an ideological process.

I have looked hard at the ideological process used by the senior civil service to justify its monopoly of management. In an issue of *Actes de la recherche* [*en sciences sociales*], I even drew up a dictionary of the themes of bureaucratic ideology.[20] You will see [if you read it] that this is not idle chatter: I have worked hard on these texts which are very hard work to read, but someone has to do it [*some laughter*] . . . This opposition between the particular point of view and the total point of view, the individual point of view and the overview of the points of view, is one of the fundamental structures of French bureaucratic understanding today. Durkheim's text is fascinating because he theorizes this. Likewise, in Paul Samuelson's treatise on *Economics*[21] there is a development of this sort of fallacy of the . . . I shall not take this further, but those of you who are working in this area will know what I mean.

On the one side we have politics, represented by members of parliament, local representatives and the mayors of small communes. This will give, for instance, things that I have studied concretely, like the famous Raymond Barre commissions and the Nora commissions[22] dealing with housing policy. In the commissions what I have described in the abstract is embodied in agents. A commission comprises inspectors of finance, roads and bridges engineers, mining engineers, local councillors and members of parliament, etc., and one of the sources of conflict is the opposition between the local and the central. The local man will say, 'You are central, which means you are out of touch, you don't understand anything here, you're from another planet', etc., and the other man will reply, 'But you are too closely involved, you have a finger in the pie [. . .]'.[23]

Here we touch upon oppositions that are, let us say, very strong. I had told you that I was going to talk to you about sociologists, but I am talking about the real world. This is because a whole section of sociology is no more than a surreptitious import of categories of thought which we find in their practical state in the real world. I said just now that one problem for jurists is that, in order to consider reality, they constitute as concepts notions like sovereignty which are part of the conditions that constitute the reality they want to consider. This is also true of sociologists: the sociologists spend their time making surreptitious borrowings, for instance of the opposition between local and central. I won't quote the authors [. . .]. There are entire sociologies constructed on the uncritical introduction of this opposition, which is one of the issues at stake in the real-world conflict in the first place. Which does not mean that this opposition does not exist in the real world (it would be too simple if performing the exact opposite of the spontaneous error were enough to enable good sociology). In fact we need to start by suspending these oppositions to see how far they are well-founded illusions. They do not lack solid foundations. The opposition between the Parisian technocrat or inspector of finance and the member of parliament for Bourges, whether RPR or socialist,[24] is not without foundation, even if, in becoming a mental structure and also an instrument of struggle in the conflicts opposing the two categories, it tends to confuse our thinking about the opposition.

One last question: on union, consensus, competence and intelligence . . . These belong to the system of categories of thought of the technocracy. I refer you to the issue [of *Actes de la recherche en sciences sociales*] on the ideology of the technocracy, I forget the title ['La production de l'idéologie dominante', 1976] . . . When Lévi-Strauss applies this kind of analysis to myth,[25] everyone finds that it is scientific, but if the study concerns the mythology of the graduates of the ENA, they treat it as a polemic. And yet it is exactly the same thing. It is even more difficult I think [in the second case] – having done both,[26] I think that I can say this. Competence and intelligence are to be found, then, in the camp [of the technocrats]. I conducted my study under Giscard's presidency: Giscard's intelligence[27] was celebrated in page after page by the technocrats who, with their tendency to universalize their definition of intelligence, considered men to be intelligent whose intelligence resembled their definition [*laughter*].

Another interesting proposition: full time. The bureaucrats are full-time professionals, whereas the locals are small-time people, partial and partisan, living with the party and in their constituency, liable to absenteeism,[28] etc. Obviously I'm giving you the central version, because the local version is much less articulate than the central version.

This opposition comes fully into play when we think of the opposition between senior civil servants and ministerial cabinets. Which leads us to wonder whether the opposition between the two is increasing or disappearing, if it is stronger under the Fifth rather than the Fourth [Republic]. At Sciences Po they are working away at this: was the number of civil servants greater under Pompidou or under de Gaulle? It depends on what you are comparing . . . there are many studies, I've read a lot of them, but I can't make you . . . Sometimes a professor is someone who forces people to share his suffering [*Bourdieu and the audience laugh*]. But I don't have sadistic tendencies, I shall spare you! However, there is a whole literature on the evolution of the technocrats in the cabinets, for instance. They say that under Pompidou there were slightly fewer – as we might have suspected – than under de Gaulle, who had his ideal of public service, etc., and rather more than under Giscard . . . in short, I shall spare you all that. But the problem [in the texts] is finding out how these two categories, the political and the bureaucratic, are ultimately articulated. Yet I think that this is a false point of interest.

(Here I must reveal a professional reflex: the old soldier of research ends up seeing things that are often not analysed; he feels that if so many people show so much superficial interest in such a superficially important problem, there must be a trap there. I may be wrong, but I want to reveal my secret: you need what we might call a kind of paradoxical disposition, because the *doxa* tells you that this is what you should be working on. Among the traps that the scientific field tempts you with, there is this one: you want to show that it isn't 12 per cent under Pompidou and 14 per cent under Giscard, but 12.5 per cent and 14.8 per cent. You could spend your life on such things . . . The scientific field lays traps and it censors; it's one of the ways in which, as Plato said, they file the nails of the lion cubs:[29] the lion cubs want to have a scientific revolution, and they are told: 'Beware, we have 12 per cent, [your percentage] needs revising' [*laughter*].)

Here I am obviously thinking of French research, and it is not surprising (with French research being the bureaucracy it is, so I shall leave it at that . . .). In the United States the problem that I have raised [is rather different] . . . If I return to the literature (very superficially) it is also to help you appreciate a little better the drive to demolish received wisdom that is implied in what I have been saying so far and what I shall be saying later. Otherwise, you may not be aware of it, you may find things natural that in fact aren't so natural at all.

The notion of profession, a scholarly myth

I shall now make a rapid sketch of what is a vast section of American sociology, which is the sociology of the professions – I am using the English pronunciation of the word 'professions', because it is an English-language word. Through some unfortunate historical accident, the English and Americans have acquired this concept of 'professions', which designates an ensemble of not very well-defined occupations – this is one of the problems facing researchers (more than they realize). From the 1960s until our own times, an enormous literature (I haven't read a tenth of it and yet I've read a good hundred or so articles . . .) discusses what a 'profession' is, what its boundaries are, its primary and secondary characteristics . . . I mention this because, among the characteristics of these 'professions', one of the most commonly stressed is disinterestedness. In its widest definition, such as that given by Talcott Parsons, for instance, the notion of professions includes scientists, researchers and sociologists. Dare I say that this shows an obscure interest on behalf of the researchers . . .?

I'll tell you about Parsons' article . . . As a loyal teacher, I ought to read you almost all of it line by line, because this man has dominated the world of sociology for the last twenty years.[30] It is a text that is mind-bogglingly unreal. I shall just reveal the substance, but I'll give you the reference so that you can check it out for yourselves, because otherwise I would be foisting an authoritarian value judgement upon you . . . It is the article 'Professions' – in no less than the *International Encyclopaedia of the Social Sciences*.[31] So read the article for next time, okay! . . . [*laughter*] This is really something that you absolutely must do, but I don't want to discuss it right away. This literature is interesting for two reasons. Otherwise I would not be telling you about it. Unfortunately it is a professional obligation for a sociologist to know about this literature. It is a sinister fact that one of the obstacles to the progress of the social sciences – I am saying this to advise the younger generation – is that, to be a professional in the social sciences, you have to read masses and masses of rubbish. If you have not read it all, you are not a professional. This is something very complicated, and I think it is true for all the sciences. Because [if you have not read all this literature] you can't even understand what the problem is, you can't even understand why certain objections are being raised, you can't even understand what the people who don't understand you are saying . . . so it is extremely important.

What I have told you can be very helpful in understanding how to use a bibliography. Obviously in the bibliographies this odious literature is promoted, because it is easy to sum up, because it has behind it all the logic of the social forces, etc. For those among you who are starting out on a career in research, it is perhaps the most important thing that I can tell you: faced with a sociological text you should always ask, 'What kind of a thing is this? Might it be some counterfeit discourse smuggled in under plain covers . . . Couldn't I read the same thing in the *New York Times*? Is it only a pedantic, sinister, tedious retranscription of something that the authors read in the *New York Times* – or *Le Monde* – three days ago . . .?' But, having done that, you shouldn't go to the other extreme and say, 'I shan't read any of that, it's all American ideology', for this would be one way of missing the 10 per cent of extraordinary studies which are one of the conditions of progress in the profession. Pardon me for saying all that, I shall regret it enormously, it's the kind of thing that makes me feel really bad after [the lectures].

To return to the [studies on the] professions, which are interesting because they are the archetype of the learned myth: Canguilhem has often analysed these kinds of construction elaborated by sciences in the making.[32] They have all the outward signs of scientificity, and all the more so the less scientific they are. I wrote a paper on this question that I called 'The Montesquieu effect'.[33] I'll just give you the outline of the argument: although Montesquieu's famous text on the North and the South has often been taken to be the first expression of geographic determinism, a scientific anticipation, I showed – clearly enough, I think – that it is in fact a mythical representation of the type that ethnologists describe, with North/South, hot/cold, dry/wet, etc., but cloaked in all the scientific regalia of the time, that is, the 'fibre theory' elaborated by English scientists. We have then a myth, but a myth disguised as science. The social sciences are full of scholarly myths, which may be disguised as mathematical formalism, or a number of other things.

Here lies the first point of interest [of this discussion of the sociology of the 'professions']: to show how an ideological space functions. In the case in point, the principle behind this ideology is in fact meritocracy.

This theory of the professions is a sort of immense hymn to meritocracy, that is, to the dominant ideology of those who dominate in the name of knowledge, including all the scholars and scientists of the social world. The second point of interest: it is a contribution to the sociology of sociology and it helps to some extent to underpin the somewhat prophetic statements that I have just made, it puts you on your guard in practice. To put it in a few words, the notion of profession seems to me to be a dangerous notion, and I say so even more today because [its revival?] is also one of the effects of symbolic domination: today the notion of profession, thanks be to God, is moribund in the United States, but there are people reintroducing it in France in order to play games in the French fields,[34] under the pretext that modernity is *a priori* attributed to the United States. In the sociology of sociology, the central idea is that the notion of profession is the very type of the native concept smuggled into science; that is, without examination, without control.

Defining the concept

Having said that, I shall try to tell you about it, then I shall return to its uses, because I tend to blurt out my theoretical intentions before I have set out the . . . Well, I'll tell you afterwards what we can infer from it.

There is then an enormous bibliography arranged around what is primarily a vast exercise in definition. No author starts without a definition. In the name of a positivist definition of the definition that Durkheim had[35] but that he constantly transgressed: since 'one cannot think scientifically without well-defined concepts', they start by defining, forgetting that what is at stake is precisely the definition (who is involved in the game and who is not involved?). Too often sociologists define their object *a priori* ('I call an "artist". . .') for functional purposes, for instance, forgetting that the definition of their object is contentious in the real world. In saying, 'I call an "artist" such and such a category', I destroy the very object that I want to study, before I have started to study it, because in reality one of the major issues in the artistic world is knowing who is a genuine artist, who is a 'true' artist. There are some very fine reflections by the philosopher, Austin, on what it is to say of somebody that he is a *true* philosopher.[36] If you have been following my argument, the truth may progress through the struggle for the truth, and the fact of saying, 'He is a "true" philosopher', is in fact a homage to the truth. The struggles to be a true philosopher or to denounce somebody else as not being one, can make truth progress.

To return to the definition of the professions. To put it very briefly, we take a list of attributes that seem to be characteristic of the professions. What is the irreducible core of the professions, what we call their crucial 'main characteristics'? There is a whole literature of 'trend reports' on this subject. For those who don't know, a 'trend report' is a very interesting, sociologically created genre, which is designed to draw up a picture of recent developments in the science. This literature is very typical of the English-language countries, at least in sociology, because there are social conditions of production that encourage it: professors pay students to read the books and make filing cards, and then they give lectures based on a stack of these filing cards. They call that a 'trend report'. Today they would call it 'theory'. These cards, with their summaries of the books, and their bibliographies, can be very useful placed end to end, but only if you are aware of the social conditions of their production and therefore of their usage. A great number of 'trend reports' say: 'Mr X has written on the professions and has discovered fourteen characteristics, Mr Y has discovered eighteen characteristics, Mr Z has found twenty-five, and I personally say that the "main characteristics" are in fact the following four.' I'll give you the reference immediately, so that you know I am not making this up [*Bourdieu writes the reference on the board.*[37]]. This semi-vulgarizing article notes twenty-three elements that have been recorded in different definitions of a profession. I have noted some of them: for instance, there is competence or 'skill' based on theoretical knowledge, there are education, training, competence testing, [. . .] (a) professional code of conduct and the fact that these are occupations serving altruistic functions.[38] The idea of altruism, of disinterestedness, occurs nearly all the time.

Here we see various interpretations of the concept: what are the characteristics that we retain as constituents of the concept? In a critical phase of this literature, other [authors] vary its extensions. They ask whether by chance the variations observed in defining and interpreting the concept might not depend on the fact that people have in mind different extensions of the notion. For instance, some are thinking of doctors, barristers and accountants, while others are thinking of professors and scientists, etc. It is astonishing, but when you look at the articles (as I have) you notice that the categories are in general derived from a very small number of occupations which are not the same from one article to another . . . (I repeat that this is one of the great scientific debates: the *American Journal* [*of Sociology*] in certain periods had to publish at least one paper on the subject every year.)

Firstly then, the categories are taken from a small number of professional bodies. Secondly, these professional bodies are not always the same. Thirdly, the list of the professions concerned is not always explicitly noted. Fourthly, as is common in taxonomies, they are always tied to the Anglo-American context, yet nobody admits it . . . There is a paper that says: 'In Europe, they don't have this concept, they have things like "executives" . . . Is our concept universal?' But nobody raises the following question: 'Might we not have this question on the universality of the concept only because we have this concept?' This is a question that I honestly have not found anywhere in the literature.

Funnily enough, I was saying just now that the truth of the political field is more transparent than the truth of the other fields, such as the religious field . . . And I was thinking that just now, but I was censoring it, which is quite funny, in fact. When there is a *Streit*, a strong theme in a discipline, you need to discuss it at all costs, which is also interesting for the sociology of science: the people farthest apart in the space, that is the upper bourgeois from Boston and the humble Jews from Chicago (who do nonetheless create subversion in American sociology), all speak of profession. Those from Chicago do indeed study the professions in detail,[39] enough to be subversive at all events. But they still retain [the notion of] 'profession', which means that what is good in what they are doing is tainted, at least in my eyes, by the fact that they have been infected by the dominant problematic, which they have not analysed as such because they have not done much socioanalysis.

I am running out [of time], I shall finish, but I shall take one more moment. So people count and enumerate the professions. Then come the people who measure (I shall write the reference on the board next time); this is the positivist phase where they look for measurable indicators of the degree of professionalism.[40] I forgot today to say that 'profession' generates 'professionalism' and 'professionalization'. 'Professionalization' is a research project: Are there stages in the process of professionalization? Do all the professions – which we are not sure how to identify – pass through the same stages? In this positivist phase people measure, and in order to do this they create criteria, measurable indicators of the degree of professionalism. They draw on Millerson and use a Guttman 'scalogram'.[41] Between 1960 and 1970, this technique was state of the art. But it is very rigorous (I for one have never come across anything as ['scalogrammable' as] that in the social world . . .), it is a technological Procrustean bed, which leads them to lose four of Millerson's fundamental criteria. I quote: 'Unfortunately, we need to eliminate some characteristics considered important such as the degree of autonomy of the profession (which is not insignificant), the degree to which the practice is based on a theory and its degree of conformity to the altruistic ideal.'[42] So they drop the third criterion, but they measure! And they are happy with the results – I shall stop here – because this shows what they were looking for, which is a very strong correlation between the degree of professionalization and the age of the profession. In conclusion they say – I hesitate to pronounce it in English, but . . . 'Professionalization is a long drawn out process'[43] [*laughter*]. That is the conclusion, on pages 48–49 of an article whose reference I shall give you next time. I shall start with that, and then I shall tell you how the problem concerning the stages of professionalization has evolved. And I shall show you how we return to our own concerns afterwards [*applause*].

Lecture of 9 February 1989

A sociodicy behind the description of a historical process – The profession, a scholarly myth – Profession, corps and field – The theory of the professions as a negative theory of the State – The school as liberator – Continuity and genesis of the great corps

I shall pick up my argument where I left it, that is, at the description of the professions proposed by the Anglo-American tradition. If you remember, I first recalled that an important proportion of the studies devoted to this notion offered definitions, and I showed how these definitions were often inadequate because the ramifications of the concept were never spelt out and their interpretation varied quite a lot. The question that I raised was whether these descriptions concerned an ideal type in the Weberian sense of the term (that is, a definition obtained by accumulating particular cases in order to reach a conclusion, but I don't want to reduce a long discourse on the notion of the ideal type to a throwaway comment),[1] or an ideal. Another question that I raised: measuring the profession. I said that in the Anglo-American tradition, when a concept becomes a subject of debate, there comes a moment when you ask how you set about measuring it.

I had reached the point where I was telling you how Hickson and Thomas described in their article the study they had conducted to try to measure the degree of professionalization by constructing measurable indicators for professionalism.[2] I showed you what absurdities they ended up with, following a logic very common in the social sciences, and unfortunately in the sciences in general (the concern for measurement, which is an essential element of the scientific ambition, can lead to measuring the measurable instead of trying to measure what should be measured:[3] you end up reducing the object that you can grasp to what is measurable in it, instead of asking yourself what the object is, and then trying to measure as best you can what you have constructed as a real scientific object).

So I reminded you that these authors had eliminated from the definition borrowed from Millerson a certain number of properties that he had found fundamental, finally concluding with a sort of correlation between the degree of professionalization and the age of a profession, a result that could have been guessed in advance. All too often these exercises in measurement terminate in rather pompous tautologies, which does not mean that I condemn the intention to measure itself: it is a reaction against the positivism which nourished a certain theoreticism which is as stupid as what it is fighting against . . . I am just [for my part] expressing some reservations about one form of the ambition to measure.

A sociodicy behind the description of a historical process

After the debates on definition, and the attempts at measuring which deliver their pompous and ridiculous results, a third aspect of this immense debate – which I am schematizing and simplifying – is a philosophy of history constructed around the notion of 'professionalization'. These critics take an ill-defined notion, the profession, make it implicitly represent the end of history, and say that the profession is characteristic of modern society (there you see one of the reasons why I wanted to speak of this: you may perceive my argument on the professions as a digression, but I believe that you will come to see it as central to my research into the State). So they take an ill-defined notion, they try to measure, then with no further form of analysis, they ask how they got there, their assumption being that the process which led to this point is progress. In this way they obtain a purposive and ethnocentric evolutionism, which happens very often in sociology and especially in American sociology. A lot of North American sociologists, forgetting to study the sociology of their relation to society, have a tendency to make of America the end of history and to see their description of American reality as depicting the end product of history. Most of the great theories of the processes of modernism – another *pons asinorum* that was the object of many debates in the 1970s[4] – of responsibilization, professionalization, etc., see these processes as evolutions towards a state they consider to be final and tacitly ideal.

The criticism that I would address in passing at this evolutionist theory would I think be valid for all the grand discourses or concepts applied to ongoing processes. If you have read my work, you will have noticed that I hardly ever formulate general propositions on the evolution of societies,[5] for example on the processes of confinement,[6] rationalization, professionalization, bureaucraticization. In fact I think that in the present state of social science these stances are in general very obscure professions of faith even for their author. They hide an ill-mastered philosophy of history and an ill-analysed vision of the present world in which the author of such theses lives. In other words, these concepts give much more information about the person using them than about the realities which they are supposed to represent. Which is why I abstain from them fairly systematically.

The authors who want to describe the processes of professionalization strive to establish the stable sequences and series through which all the occupations and vocations in the process of becoming professions would pass. How does an occupation become a profession? There are certainly some very fine studies along these lines, in general written by historians (they are the least pretentious and the least ambitious, which means that they are often the best theoretically); there are for instance some quite remarkable studies of the history of the professions of pharmacist or psychiatrist . . . I don't include these in my present criticism; on the contrary, they are genuinely reliable contributions to the history of the genesis of the cases that I want to study. My criticism is not aimed at them but at the studies by sociologists which are based in general on second-hand knowledge and which claim to describe the main laws regulating the tendencies and thereby the stages of the process followed by the professions.

There is for instance a book by Caplow, *The Sociology of Work*.[7] I shall refer to an article by Wilensky[8] which I find typical, but I could have chosen many another. Wilensky says that the process of professionalization passes through the following phases:

- First, the emergence of a 'full-time' occupation or vocation.
- Second, the creation of a school and therefore the professionalization of the transmission of the skill in question, with its competence, capacity, aptitude and techniques, etc.
- Third, the constitution of a permanent professional association, endowed with statutes.
- Fourth, a drive to protect the association through the law. This is in fact an effort to legalize the profession, which is what happened for example with the creation of the Order of Doctors. One problem for the professional association is having the capacity to be able to sanction its members and to define the boundaries of membership of the profession (who counts as a member?). For this, the profession

needs the help of the law. It needs to be recognized juridically and to have its juridical right of decision recognized thereby.
– Last phase: the codification of the profession, with the adoption of an official, formal code.

So what does this all mean? You are going to think that I am contradicting myself . . . you might say – as one of my old philosophy teachers used to say: 'It's not even wrong!'[9] It is not even wrong, which means that, by and large, things do happen like that, but not necessarily in that order, and does it really matter? . . . What is important in these cases is the fact that basically we are accepting the end of the process as an accomplishment, and that under the appearance of a positivist historical description we are creating a kind of sociodicy. Let me explain the term 'sociodicy'. The word is fashioned on the model of 'theodicy'. For those who don't know it, I recall the excellent formula of Max Weber, who, to define the discourse of the dominant regarding themselves, said that the dominant always formulate a 'theodicy of their own privileges'.[10] Theodicy is a word coined by Leibniz. It is the justification for God:[11] showing how God is justified, how the world is as it should be, and how God is neither mistaken nor wicked, etc. To say that the dominant derive a theodicy from their own privileges is therefore to say that they produce a discourse designed to show that the world is what it should be, that it cannot be otherwise, thus justifying their privilege. The notion of sociodicy summarizes all this and says that these are justificatory discourses, justifying the social order. In the present case, the sociodic ambition is expressed in an evolutionist schema with a positivist appearance: the sociodic ambition is disguised as the description of a historical process.

The profession, a scholarly myth

Another way of treating the problem (which I shan't spend too long discussing, because I would like to spend most of my time this week and next on tying up the schema that I intended to expose): the functionalist variant, that is, the functionalist theory of the professions. This theory is illustrated primarily by the work of Parsons, but it did in fact guide the whole discourse of the sociological 'establishment' in the 1960s, and it is still rampant today in the minds of most sociologists.[12] This functionalist theory declares openly and naively what the evolutionist theory I have just mentioned had disguised under the appearance of a positive description of historical evolution. I am going to refer to a text by Barber.[13] [*Bourdieu writes the reference on the board and takes the opportunity to indicate the other 'major references' used in these arguments on the sociology of the professions: the articles by Parsons and Wilensky.*]

This functionalist tradition reformulates the essential attributes that the different positivist descriptions included, while in a sense declaring openly the intention that confusedly lurked behind the superficially positive definitions that I was telling you about. The first property of the professions according to Barber is a high degree of generalized and systematic knowledge. The professions concerned (we think of doctors and barristers, etc.) suppose a high degree of knowledge or, in the untranslatable [. . .] jargon of the American sociologists, a 'high degree of generalized and systematic knowledge' (there you are, that is what they say . . .).[14] Second property: – *I translate word for word* – 'primary orientation to the community interest rather than to individual self-interest'. Others call it 'altruism'. Third property: 'a high degree of self-control of behaviour, by means of moral codes internalized through socialization and through voluntary associations'. This brings us back to the previous definition but it is [slightly more?] normative. 'A high degree of self-control of behaviour' means that people are morally controlled and suggests in particular that they are disinterested, and the voluntary associations that were implicitly described in the previous definitions as pressure groups or lobbies aiming to obtain the recognition of the corps, to obtain advantages, to control its members, are described here rather as associations of collective control of individual behaviour. Fourth property [. . .]: a system of rewards in a very wide sense which is above all a set of symbols of work achievement.

Behind all this, then, there is a functionalist thesis, which consists roughly speaking in saying that if professionals are so well paid (especially in symbolic recognition – there is no reference to the fact that they also receive material benefit), if the social world grants them so much, it is because they are the elect, it is because they are worth it. That is the fundamental functionalist thesis in terms of stratification (from one parenthesis to another I am in danger of losing the thread. . . .): the division of labour and the division of the produce of labour are what they should be. 'To each according to his worth' . . . It is a meritocratic ideology translated into a theory of stratification. The description of these professions, of these occupations which are distinguished from the majority of occupations by their superior material and especially symbolic profits, amounts to saying that things are fine as they are, that the professions are – a second very surprising Anglo-American concept – 'service or community oriented'. They are, then, altruistic professions which apply a body of systematic knowledge (theories and bodies of knowledge) to problems that are vital for society. This idea does not figure in the Parsons article, but in other texts (because there are variants, which I have not quoted, so as to avoid burdening you with too much bibliography) we find the idea that, if they are so well paid (think of what a doctor earns) or so strongly recognized (for example, doctors are often ranked in first place in enquiries into the hierarchy of the professions), it is because they fulfil functions that are vital for society. Consequently, they receive a remuneration that legitimately corresponds to the scarcity and value of their services. By the way, these functionalists include their own profession in their proposals, that is important [*laughter*]. [. . .] To put it simply (I am schematizing, but I can assure you that if you read the texts you will see that I am not exaggerating anything. [. . .] I refer you to Parsons' article, which is stunningly boring, and worth reading for that reason): they are basically saying that these professions are greatly rewarded because they are altruistic professions. The more altruistic, the better rewarded.

To sum up the central thesis of Parsons' article: there are differences in the rewards, whether material or above all symbolic (prestige, esteem, etc.), and their functions are linked to the hierarchy of talents . . . Merit, talent: it is interesting to see how these lie at the heart of a sociodicy that must account for a privilege based, ultimately, on educational qualifications. We gravitate naturally towards a sociodicy based on two concepts, merit and giftedness. I shall return to this. Having 'talent' is the equivalent of being 'gifted'. There are, then, differences in rewards which are linked to the hierarchy of talents, and this hierarchy of rewards means that the talents are applied to the service of the needs of society. We should analyse these ideologies – but I don't like using that word, I prefer 'sociodicy' . . . Sociodicies are always very difficult to analyse, because there are connections which we sense but which we destroy as soon as we formalize them. For example, there are two propositions: (1) there are differences in rewards and talents; (2) this difference in talents leads to (they say 'leads to' instead of 'causes' because they know that you shouldn't be naively purposive) these talents being applied to serve the needs of society. So it all happens as if this admirable distribution of rewards was designed to ensure the devotion of the best to doing good deeds, for the welfare of the public. There you have by and large the two theses. How are they articulated? They are articulated as in a system . . . (often philosophical systems, especially in political philosophy, are of this type; it is just that the philosophers are much smarter and articulate the connections better).

Having stated what seems to me to be the central tenet of these theories, I shall now state briefly something that was already implicit in the way that I presented them. Ultimately – as is often the case in sociology – these theoreticians turn their sociology of the professions into a professional ideology or a sociodicy of the professions. This is a sociodicy of a very particular type. It would take a long time to demonstrate it, but I think that there are invariants of sociodicies, whether it is the sociodicy of a warrior aristocracy, a mandarinate, a technocracy or a priestly power ... One invariant of all the theodicies of privilege is the fact that they transform historical properties into something natural. All the sociodicies amount to saying that things are what they are, and are fine as they are, because they are part of the nature of the natural world (cosmologies serve as theodicies) or, more especially, the nature of the dominant (if the dominant dominate, it is because it is in their nature to dominate, because they have in their nature the properties that in fact and in the law found the right to dominate). That is my first proposition.

Second proposition, which obviously proceeds from the first: the sociodicies vary according to the privilege that needs to be legitimized. If it is to legitimize a warrior aristocracy, the sociodicy draws on the philosophy of blood and earth, biological heredity, etc. If it is to legitimize a bureaucratic technocracy, whose power and legitimacy are grounded in diplomas, the legitimization draws essentially, as in Parsons, on the natural gift, which is supposed to be the condition of educational success, and on merit and disinterestedness. This combination leads into a sort of charismatic-meritocratic ideology. *Charisma* – the Greek word means 'grace', and charisma, in the educational system, is giftedness. When someone says, 'This pupil has a gift for mathematics', they are saying that he has charisma. If the sociodicy is to justify the technocracies, that will generate charismatic-meritocratic sociodicies, of which the functionalist theories on the professions are an example.

Here we see that sociology is not a simple science, because you find your object of study in the writings of your colleagues. And often the most eminent. Parsons' vision is widely shared. In his time there were three big names in world sociology. I mean the 'Capitoline triad': Parsons, Merton and Lazarsfeld.[15] At the same time, Merton was developing a sociology of science, that is, the sociology of another profession – the profession that, like Parsons, he belonged to – according to which the scientific world obeyed the values of disinterestedness. Merton characterized the scientific community as a communist community, for instance, sharing possessions and knowledge, etc. I am simplifying, but, in his book on the sociology of science, Merton gives a description of the scientific profession which harbours the same presumptions as Parsons'. Merton's aim is not to say, 'That is why they are well paid', but his description does the same job.[16]

To sum up their vision: the professions are very efficient groups which are characterized by an intellectual training that confers on them an authority founded on expertise rather than power. In a way their power is an extension of their expertise. These people act as independent experts, independently of the State, and are free of all compromise with the government bureaucracies. The thesis of these sociologists also includes the idea that these professions are guided by a vision of the 'common good', the welfare of the public (for those of you who heard me speak of d'Aguesseau,[17] the d'Aguesseaus are people tending towards public welfare), what these sociologists call 'collectivity orientation'.

Profession, corps and field

Now I shall take this criticism a little further. We see that the professions are a typical example of a scholarly myth which is enhanced with theoretical or empirical elaboration, and which has the merit of revealing everything that I have just said, that is, how a scholarly myth can dress up in scientific or theoretical costume something that is a sociodicy, an interested view of the social world. That said, the notion of profession can be criticized on a more positive plane, on the very terrain where those who present [the characteristics of the professions?] in simple terms are situated. To clarify things and pin down the notion of the profession succinctly, I would like to show very briefly that, as is often the case with common-sense notions crudely imported into science, it is a mongrel, unthought notion. I would like to show you that 'profession' obscures the construction of two notions that in my opinion are more adequate: on the one hand the notion of field, on the other the notion of corps.[18] In fact to speak of profession is to fail to identify these two objects. Depending on their state, on the stage of their evolution and on all the variables that can affect them – in particular the historical variables – occupations can approximate more to a field or more to a corps. Let me explain.

In what ways are many occupations fields? Here I refer you to an article by William Goode,[19] which is interesting for several reasons [*Bourdieu writes the reference on the board*]. I shall not give you a full summary but I would be tempted to enter into the details because it is really exciting for two reasons.

I maintain that with the notion of profession we miss out on two concepts, field and corps, whereas in fact every professional group is potentially a field and potentially a corps. Every professional group is disparate, sometimes more, sometimes less. Think of teachers: they are disparate in their titles, their functions, their disciplines, their salaries and their incomes, etc. Every occupation is disparate, yet at the same time, in support of their struggles against other professions, among other things, they would prefer to be integrated and homogeneous. In other words, every profession is a field which would like to become a corps and which, under certain conditions and at certain times, could be a corps. If you think of the teachers, there are situations where they couldn't be any more disparate – they can be divided into pass, fail and re-sit[20] in a competitive exam – but if you start to challenge them, as is happening today,[21] they will immediately club together to create one single body. This corps-creation is extremely important; the corps is something that groups *create*. Groups create a corps on occasions, among others, when they are in conflict with other groups, for instance in cases of rivalry for advantages distributed by the State. But this does not prevent them from existing as fields. When you think with concepts as I handle them, you are not in a realist universe: you can be both field and corps at the same time. This means that there are problems of identity, because if you take your object as a field, the teachers are extremely disparate: how can you put nursery school teachers and professors of mathematics at Orsay [University] in the same bag? That said, under certain conditions, this field can organize itself as a corps: either the corps divide up the field, or the whole set of people who have it in common to be in the field constitute themselves as a corps. This depends on the action of the agents, which itself depends on the position the agents occupy in the field and the position the field occupies in the space of the fields. We find ourselves then in a much more complicated but much more real universe; I think that what I am saying is much closer to reality than what these . . .

Goode's article is interesting because he refers to the struggles that arise when a field is established. There are in particular struggles over the abuse of titles (illegal wearing of a uniform, illegal use of titles . . .) or, in the field of medicine for instance, over the illegal exercise of an activity that a corps wants to preserve as its monopoly. A corps is nearly always organized around winning and holding the monopoly of a service. For instance, if sociology is not a corps, it is because no sociologist can say: 'Here there is an illegal exercise of sociology.' Well, I am often tempted to regret it [*some laughter*] . . . So the article is interesting, in that it shows the disparity of the professions, and the fact that they function as fields to a greater or lesser degree.

The second aspect (which is the second part of his article), is that he shows sociology itself to be particularly concerned with this kind of problem. But I think that the sociologists' slightly pathetic interest in the professions comes from the fact that they would dearly love to be a profession themselves [*laughter*].[22] On this point I could even say more, on vocations, for example: for some sociologists, studying the professions is a way of entering the professions by the back door (people who should have studied at the ENA find a way back to the high ground by making the ENA their object of study). I may seem to be exaggerating, but I could cite cases that are more solidly based. It was simply to show you that when somebody is studying an object you should always consider their relation to that object of study. In this particular case, I think that there is a vast social unconscious, not only the unconscious of the dominant who want to utilize their domination, but also a more specific unconscious of the dominant holding a certain position in the field of power and anxious to legitimize their profession by using their specific resource, which is a discourse on the professions. What I am saying here is quite peremptory and arbitrary, but I assure you that it does have a solid basis. You could use it to construct a well-founded thesis if you illustrated it with specific data.

The article does analyse the relations between psychiatrists and psychologists very well. Those of you who are familiar with this domain will know that in this arena people who actually have the same clientele confront each other with two different training routines (more medical for some, more traditionally academic for others). Their professional ideologies, their 'systems of knowledge' as Parsons calls them – are different, contradictory and conflictual. Goode also takes the example of the relations between psychosociologists and sociologists: can the sociologists be treated as psychologists when they practise their social psychology? There are conflicts at the national level between the societies of sociology and psychology. All this is interesting and is one of the reasons for reading this article.

What is important for my present argument is the fact that occupations in the process of becoming established as a corps need to define the boundaries of membership of the corps which are at the same time . . . How shall we say . . . Let us say that the people who want to establish themselves as a corps are always fighting on two fronts. They are fighting against the outside, but it is simultaneously a fight against the inside: to give value to the corps and to authorize the corps to hold a monopoly over the services it wants to sell, to make it competitive with other corps that would like to hold the same monopoly, the – shall we say – aspiring dominant must cut out their universe decisively. They must in particular promulgate deontological rules, rules for conditions of access, and say, for example, 'Let none but mathematicians enter here', or 'Let none but graduates of the ENA enter here', etc. In other words, the struggle to establish a corps is above all a struggle among claimants to membership of the corps. Basically, it is never so obvious that the professions are fields as when they are struggling to become a corps. Because, to put it crudely, there are sacrificial victims or people who, if the corps exists, will no longer exist as members of the corps. For instance, if you want my opinion, it is one of the reasons why we can't professionalize sociology: if sociology were a corps with a deontology and definitions, too many people would fall by the wayside. This is why so many people have a vital interest in a pluralist, tolerant and eclectic definition [*Bourdieu smiles*] of sociology . . . but this is a problem for all the professions . . . I shall not take this further, I think I have said enough for you to understand me. Too much, even . . .

The notion of profession glosses over everything that I have just been saying, which is that in a professional field there are tensions, contradictions and moments when something like a corps becomes established. Efforts have to be made to limit conflict, preserve unity and find ways to promote the general interests of the occupation over the particular interests of those who harbour contradictory definitions of the occupation. In other words, there is something exciting in creating a corps and becoming constructors. This is where we see things very differently [from the everyday vision]: those who construct a professional association, who work to create unity, and oblige people from antagonistic training backgrounds to confront one another in dialogue, are in general those who, even unwittingly, are most interested in its potential function as a corps. Those who resist are those who feel confusedly that they are going to be excluded: 'Of course it would be fine if sociology were to be established as a corps, but would I be a member?' Obviously, these things do not surface at a conscious level. Otherwise, it would be easy to practise sociology (besides, the article in question does not say everything that I am saying, it simply describes and provides the elements needed to understand . . .).

In order to exist as such, and to present a united front in general, a corps needs to be a well-integrated whole. This means that the members of the corps must construct their unity, for instance through an order, like the Order of Doctors, and, to construct that unity, they must also keep the competition under control. They need to draw a line round the people who are authorized to participate in the competition and exclude people who represent disloyal competition . . . [*Here a passage of the lecture is missing from the recording used, but it is probably fairly short.*] The idea that disloyal competition should be excluded is a tautology . . . But it is important to take our time to see what is hidden beneath such popular knowledge. For disloyal competition to exist, there need to be clearly defined limits of the people who have the right to take part in the game. You need to define the limits and the conditions of membership of the field. The higher you set the bar, as they say, the more the competitors find themselves in the same boat, so to speak, among people who accept the same rules of combat, people who accept what are the legitimate instruments to be used in the struggle, and also people who refrain from attacking each other. For instance, the conventions through which the doctors set limits to competition merit a study: we have all had the experience of noticing that a doctor never speaks ill of another doctor, except perhaps among friends and family, because transgressing this precept would affect the very foundation of loyal competition, that is, belief in the legitimacy of the medical act. I am putting things simply and rather crudely, but it is merely to make you feel . . . Assigning limits to the competition in such a way that within those limits the competition is loyal is in fact a way of imposing a *numerus clausus*. We see in fact that the constitution of a corps is inseparable from [the operation consisting in limiting the number] of people placed in a situation of legitimate competition for a benefit of which the corps as such, and not the individuals, holds the monopoly.

Here I link up with the arguments on the process of profession-alization, but in a way, I think, that is very different, even if it is very schematic. I was wondering before I came here if I was going to say all this, but I felt that I could not leave you on a purely negative note with a criticism of the notion of profession that might seem purely ideological. I also wanted to offer some technical criticism, but I am doing it badly because it is taking me away from the main thread of my argument, which lies in a different direction. One condition of this con-trived production of unity is the production of a consensus (however artificial) among the doctors – what in medieval Latin was called the *communis doctorum opinio*.[23] This production of a consensus of the doctors, to be maintained through a process of avoidance or rejection of difficulty, leads or may lead to something that characterizes the false sciences, that is, a logic of orthodoxy, which is very similar to the logic of science. In fact Merton, Lazarsfeld and Parsons (the 'Capitoline triad' that I told you about) typically constituted a profession, in a sense that they themselves admitted: from a concern to give sociology a legitimacy and make it appear respectable, they produced an ortho-doxy, with a rather skilful division of labour (one defending empirical sociology, one grand theory, and the other medium-range theory); they produced a sort of *communis doctorum opinio*, with some major jour-nals which shared the same common criteria for access. Strangely, they produced exactly what they were describing on the terrain of science, a terrain where you can produce what you might call a simulation of the logic of science; that is, not a consensus on the disagreements and the conditions of resolution of disagreements, but a consensus on the very foundation of theoretical agreement, a kind of simulated consensus. I must not develop this further, it would take me too far . . . but what we call deontology in describing the American sociologists is in fact this *communis doctorum opinio*, and the system of rules of decorum that allows it to be perpetuated: it is the avoidance of all the actions that would lead belief in the corps to collapse, if the consensus of the corps, which is needed to obtain belief, were to collapse. I shall say no more about this. I have already said too much given the time allocated to me.

One important thing is the link between the corps and the notion of *numerus clausus*. From the moment a corps is constituted, it aims to define the conditions of its membership. Here I return to my general line and one of the central points of my argument: when it is a ques-tion of installing a *numerus clausus* that enables a corps to function as a corps, the aid of the State is nearly always indispensable. In other words, it is through the State that the professions manage to secure their monopoly of a clientele and also, closely connected, their monop-oly of access to the profession. I shall expand on that straight away.

The theory of the professions as a negative theory of the State

If I have made this detour through the professions, it was rather by chance, but now I am pleased to have done so, and I hope to be able to tell you why. I was thinking in the French tradition, where the notion of the corps is strongly linked to a historical definition (the defini-tion of what we call the *grands corps*: la Cour des comptes (Financial Court), le Conseil d'État (State Council, etc.). Although in my work I have spontaneously expanded [the definition of the corps] for theoreti-cal reasons, I remained attached to the historical definition. The fact of having reintroduced the notion of professions obliged me to rethink the problem in all its detail and to see for instance how foolish it is for historians to say: 'The *grands corps* is a French national tradition.' In other societies there are equivalents, such as the 'professions'. I felt it was legitimate for me to have taken this roundabout path but you may not understand why I did so. The main reason I did it was because those who defend the professions have a further aim – in addition to the ideological operation of sociodicy that I mentioned – one that you might call liberal: to show that in the ultimate state of the State that is the United States, there is basically no State and that, in societies of this type, it is the professions that stand in for what we traditionally call the State. I have expressed this badly but that is roughly my thesis. In other words, in modern, democratic, liberal States, like the United States, the dominant social force is the professions. In which case, justifying the professions is obviously justifying a whole state of affairs. But another of their implicit aims is to say that the professions are free universes, independent of the central power, they are self-governing and obey their own norms, norms which are those of science and the expert. It is a sort of theodicy of expertise. We are dealing with a State of experts, and if the State withers away (if the United States does not have a State, or only a weak State or a central federal State, etc.), it is because they don't feel the need: those who govern are self-governing. So that is my thesis. I am sorry to have to go so fast . . .

For instance, the aim of seeing whether these professions can function as corps without the aid of the State is crucial. And that is where I shall refute the argument. These critics see in the professions the final state of the State, or – to express it in terms that are alien to theirs – the withering away of the State; but it is only through the State that these professions can exist as they claim to do, and through that fundamental State agency, the educational system – even if the educational apparatus is not itself an agency of the State (and we may say that it is even less so in the United States than elsewhere). I don't know if you see what is at stake, I have not been very clear, but this is because the truth is complicated. So, to continue [*Bourdieu seems to realize that since he has been speaking for an hour, it would normally be time to stop*], I shall not stop here, because I want to conclude my argument. Yes, if you want to, do please leave! [*laughter*] . . .

I am going to consult my notes more closely in order to rephrase what I have just been improvizing: the theoreticians I mentioned, Parsons, Barber and some others, see a sort of structural opposition between the State and what they call the 'professions'. They contrast governmental control with the free exercise of professional authority, an exercise incumbent on autonomous individuals, whose trajectories have led to membership of very clearly defined communities of trained experts. A book by Magali Sarfatti Larson[24] expresses plainly enough [*Bourdieu writes the reference on the board*] this thesis of an opposition between the central State and the . . . It includes a reminder of the theory of the professions but, among other things, it expresses the thesis of the independence of the professions from the State and offers, you might say, a description of the functioning of a society almost lacking a State. The issues in this debate on the professions cover the ideological arguments that we encounter today: 'more State or less State?'; 'does the bureaucratic world place intolerable constraints, in particular on the liberal professions, on medicine for instance?' (a question frequently raised in England);[25] 'should we liberate the professions from State intervention?'; 'are they sufficiently self-governing to be able to do without government intervention?' These are debates that we all recognize. In Parsons we find a coherent version of the myth of the free professional expert who operates independently from the State and the State bureaucracy.

Ultimately this theory of the professions serves as a manner of founding an ultra-liberal vision where the State in the 'modern' sense of the term is replaced by what Parsons calls the 'professional complex', which supplants all the State's models of centralized organization, not only in capitalist societies but also in socialist societies (another of these evolutionist theories at one moment was the theory of convergence: things are the same in the East as in the West). Today this 'professional complex', I quote, 'is the most important component of the structure of modern societies'.[26] To note in passing: there is currently a return to the State [in sociological studies], a generation of young sociologists in the United States has risen up against the 'triad', and it is no accident if this generation, for example Skocpol,[27] who is one of the best-known names, has placed the State at the forefront of social studies. These are precisely things that we don't understand if we fail to see that the aim of these arguments on the professions was in fact a discourse on the State. The dominant tradition in American sociology had made the State disappear, but today there is an ambition to reintroduce the State as an autonomous agent possessing its own logic, irreducible to the 'professional complex'. I think that this is important for understanding the recent evolution of so-called theoretical debates in the United States.

In this theory of the professions we find a negative theory of the State. There you are, I have managed to say it . . .: this discourse on the professions is interesting as a negative theory of the State, as a liberal theory of the superfluity of the State. In fact these theoreticians would say that the State is good for rather underdeveloped countries. In countries where the professions have not achieved a high degree of intellectual accomplishment and ethical autonomy, a State is needed, because only the State is capable of imposing the public interest, and even if it is slightly military, that does no harm . . . But the United States supposedly has no need of a State because it has finally acquired a regime of self-governing experts on whom there is no question of imposing an external authority. We can counter this discourse with various arguments, but we can also counter it with facts. These professional groups are, even in the United States – you might say 'especially in the United States' – falsely independent. In fact they too depend on the authority delegated by the State. For instance, doctors receive a form of protection in the guise of titles which guarantee them the monopoly of certain services. Such protection exists also for architects or jurists (we discussed this last year). This protection appears when the *numerus clausus* weakens. A corps can in fact become a field again. I told you just now that we don't have to choose between corps and field: a corps can never be certain of not regressing back to the state of a field. In the 1970s in France, all the corps (the doctors, the barristers, etc.) were threatened. It is no accident if at this time some rather leftist journals such as *Actes* for the magistrates were launched,[28] and the Order of Doctors was challenged,[29] etc. The *numerus clausus* then found itself under attack (as was even more obvious in the case of the architects), since a proportion of the candidates for entry into the corps had interests that diverged from those that dominated the corps. They had no interest in seeing the dominant of the corps close the doors and maintain the *numerus clausus*. The dominated in a corps where there are candidates attempting to enter it have an interest in the corps reverting to its function as a field. I shall not take this further.

The link between the State and a corps can be seen when the corps is threatened by the weakening of the *numerus clausus*. For instance, in the case of the 'lawyers' – who were protected by a *numerus clausus* and restricted entrance conditions, etc. – we saw avant-garde, leftist 'lawyers' emerge who were critical, who started to sell their services and create new markets. As I explained last year, they started, for instance, to practise things that were scandalous from the point of view of the deontological norms of the corps – advertising, for instance. Can you imagine a corps worthy of the name (a medical or pharmaceutical or juridical corps . . .) advertising its wares? And yet in certain states of the development of the corps it may happen that agents on the margins could have an interest in advertising, at the risk of bringing discredit on the corps, as they say, by affecting people's trust in the corps. Do the people who care for me *ex officio*, with authority, retain their strict legitimacy when others are offering the same services with the same definition, but advertised on the open market, thereby situating the service in an alternative reality, establishing it as a service like any other?

Bearing these ideas in mind, we could relaunch a number of debates. If you reread the collection of *Actes*, the magistrates' journal, you will see that what I am saying is not theoretical at all (well, it is theoretical, but not in the pejorative sense of the term). Thus we see in periods of crisis, when the *numerus clausus* is threatened, that the professional groups depend enormously on the authority delegated to them by the State and the security accorded by the State through the existence of the protected market that it guarantees. I should note one of the properties of the professions straight away, for fear of forgetting it: the 'professions' have extraordinarily ambiguous and contradictory strategies. This arises from what I was saying just now – rather clumsily – about 'the field and the corps'. The professions always want two contradictory things: on the one hand the protection against disloyal competition (that they can only obtain from the State) which leads them to be exclusive, and on the other hand independence from the State (they don't want the State to meddle with their affairs). When they take to the street, the professions are always very ambiguous and contradictory: they ask the State to protect them as a corps while simultaneously preventing the State from intervening in the management of the corps. I think that this is true in a much wider context too. Think of the teachers . . .

I don't know if you realize, but I hope you do, that I am venturing onto an extremely difficult and risky terrain. I think that what I am saying here is, for once, extremely original [*laughter*] . . . No, really [if I say this], it is to beg your indulgence, because it is extremely difficult. I don't know if you realize that I am engaged in a very difficult intellectual combat, because I have to confront a reality that has already been thought, where everything is confused, where what needs to be thought is very intricately interconnected with the thinkers. I say this to crave indulgence for my rhetorical vaticination. To refute, or criticize as we usually say, these functionalist theories that are so powerful in the global intellectual field and in the minds of sociologists, I could have stuck with the criticism I have already made: they are an ideology, a sociodicy, etc. But the stakes are much too important. What is at stake, behind this theory of the State as superfluous, is also the very reality of modern societies, the specific logic of the functioning of modern societies, the role of the State in these societies and in particular the question of the relation between the occupations (as we would call the 'professions' in French) whose authority is based on educational qualifications, and the powers of the State. In other words, it is also a question of the boundaries of what we attribute to the State. This is why it is important to have reintroduced the professions. When teachers say, 'We are fighting the State', or when doctors say, 'We demand new benefits from the State', are they inviting us to forget that they are part of the State? And indeed, are they not themselves forgetting that they are part of the State? If you like, my thesis, which I believe to be empirically verifiable, is that these supposedly independent professions only exist as such through the State. They collaborate with the State, the State is a constituent of their existence. We see it in the corps of the mines, the roads and bridges, and now of the ENA: finding it exotic, the Americans who disembark in France immediately understand it. It strikes you immediately that they are corps in the sense that I have explained: they are established through diplomas and competitive examinations run by the State; they give access to the powers of the State, in the limited sense of the term, to powers of an administrative type. You see it straight away. But we shouldn't feel bound to accept preconstructed limits to reality and forget that the same is true of those famous liberal professions – once again I use the word 'liberal' on purpose, I have avoided this so far, but 'professions' can be roughly translated as 'liberal professions'. These liberal professions, which set themselves up against the State, and serve as the basis of a theory of the non-State, are in fact the State [*some laughter*]. This is why they are difficult to talk about. They are the State. They are the State because they have no existence as corps, unless they relapse back into the state of a field, as we see today with alternative medicine.[30] They have no existence as corps, just like the nobility in the eighteenth century (to take a long-term, historical view; on this subject there is a very fine article by an American sociologist, David D. Bien, which appeared in the March–April 1988 issue of *Annales*; I mention it in case you want to read it before the next lecture).[31] [*The end of this discussion and the start of the next are missing from the recording we used.*]

The school as liberator

These holders of a specialized technical knowledge [. . .] are at the same time holders of a universal knowledge, they are holders of an authority that is not only political but also moral. What I am trying to reveal here is the dark underside that nobody dares to express in these terms. On this point Parsons is very useful in saying what all the modern dominant think but do not dare to say. If this explanation is well founded, it leads me to believe that we can locate these social foundations in the emergence of technocratic powers, [. . .] which are powers of the State, over the State, and guaranteed by the State. In fact what I want to show you quite rapidly is the emergence of a form of domination whose keystone is a mode of reproduction of a completely new type, a mode of reproduction with an educational component ('component', for the school is not the only transmitter of capital), capable of founding the transmission of power and privilege from one generation to the next in a manner as sure (but at the same time infinitely better distributed and thereby infinitely more legitimate) as those of more primitive modes of reproduction, such as the transmission of power in direct line from the king to his son. This mode of reproduction came into place progressively over time, through the invention of an educational system, a State and a discourse on the State, which is not a discourse of legitimization of the State but a discourse on the constitution of the State, part of which is the whole discourse on disinterestedness that I discussed with you last year (including in particular the collection of d'Aguesseau's writings that I commented on).

That is more or less what I wanted to argue. I would like to show how the relation between the professions and the corps on the one hand and the State on the other hand is disguised through the very operation of the mechanisms that ensure reproduction as I describe it. Here too Parsons can come in useful. I was saying just now that I saw his texts as a kind of ideology, or charismatic-meritocratic sociodicy. In the French tradition this charismatic-meritocratic sociodicy has crystallized around the myth of the school as liberator. The school as liberator is one of those collective mythologies whose moment of birth, whose origins and whose productive groups, can be dated fairly precisely. This ideology of the school as liberator is based on the idea that the educational system, especially in its elementary stages, allocates educational qualifications in proportion to the talents or merits of individuals. On that score, the ideology of the school as liberator has been established in opposition to the traditional representation of the nobility.

I say 'ideology', but when we say 'ideology' we think of something discursive . . . I don't like the word 'ideology', firstly because it is so overused that it has become a cheap polemical insult, but also because, since we hear 'idea' in 'ideology', we think that it refers to subjects of discussion. On the contrary, a sociodicy, as I understand it, is an ensemble of mechanisms that justify society, beyond and beneath the discursive level. To see the myth of the school as liberator at work you should read an article by Yvette Delsaut in the last-but-one issue of *Actes de la recherche en sciences sociales*.[32] She offers a description of a '*cours complémentaire*' [post-primary class] in the 1950s, including its most elementary functions: cleaning the classroom in the evening, the fact that there is a pupil entrusted with wiping the blackboard, the fact that the pupils do PE and are asked to lie on their backs, etc. In all these trivial features of the ordinary school routine, this ideology was at work. It was omnipresent. Moreover, it was often connected, via a town council secretary for instance, to the town hall and the republican order, etc. The school as liberator was not a representation like the bust of Marianne, to which you paid homage, it was the reality of the most everyday activities, that network of the choices you make without even choosing, thus fostering the process of reproduction.

The first studies of the sociology of education called this image of the school as liberator into question.[33] They showed that, paradoxically, the school has had a conservative function. Faced with this kind of sociological challenge, the school as liberator has had to express itself – generally in indignant terms. But normally it didn't need to express itself. It was lodged in people's minds, in institutions, on the blackboard, in the grey overall of the republican schoolteacher, etc. It was embedded in material and mental structures. The form of mental structure where it was most present was the structural opposition between merit and privilege (or heritage), or to use republican language, between the elite and the nobility. The school as liberator was established, but there were forces at work trying to revert to the criteria of the transmission of *ancien régime*-style privileges. I shall try to show how they had erected something like a nobility, that is, a nobility of the school and the State, against the nobility of the blood. The nobility of talent and merit felt spontaneously opposed to the blatantly and naively hereditary nobility. [. . .] If the sociologist is unbearable, it is because he impinges on the deepest level of the republican's unconscious. He disturbs the left-wing republican unconscious as much as, if not more than, the right-wing republican unconscious, and this is important – because the left-wing republican unconscious took the form of a meritocratic sociodicy organized around the opposition between birth and merit, according to which the school, with its anonymous competitive examination (which, I have heard claimed a thousand times, is allegedly still fairer than nepotism and favouritism, and overt [recognition?] of the right of succession), enables us to finish with birth. The opposition between birth and merit, then, has become one of the oppositions that underpin the structure of modern man's unconscious, and it is exactly what Parsons reformulated as an opposition between 'ascription' and 'achievement'.[34] In my opinion, this category of Parsonian sociology has only been accepted so easily because it echoes an opposition that we all have at the back of our minds. The school as liberator, then, in which sociodicy has become both an object and a mental structure, was the major obstacle to rethinking the school, to thinking a common sense of the school.

I can make a confession, to show you the difficulty of the work that I am trying to do and also to crave your indulgence if I upset anyone's thinking (because it is true that I say things that I have found very difficult to think, partly because they shock me too). [*The following passage is difficult to understand and its transcription is sometimes uncertain*]. [They had to] render the myth of the school as liberator visible, but the enunciation (and not the 'denunciation', even if there was a slight denunciatory aspect) of the myth of the school as liberator had not got far. To take it to a successful conclusion,[35] you had to break through the sociodicic screen and discover that, behind the oppositions between birth and merit, nobility and elite, is hidden the fact that what we call the republican elite has all the properties of the nobility,[36] for the educational qualification functions like a noble title guaranteed by the State. There are obviously specific differences because of the fact that the transmission of the title of school nobility and the transmission of hereditary nobility obey slightly different laws: the transmission of the latter is purely genealogical and basically is limited only by genealogical rules ([only?] the men inherited, the elder son taking precedence over the second, etc.) whereas the transmission of the nobility of the school or the State is mediated by an apparently autonomous educational institution. The transmission between generations is no longer mechanical but statistical: in the medieval nobility, the eldest son was sure to inherit, whereas in the modern nobility, the son of a State Counsellor is not sure of going to the Conseil d'État (which is seen as an objection to the analyses that I have made). In any case, the simple transmission of a parchment is not sufficient, he has to make a detour through the educational system, through Sciences Po and the ENA. At the end of the day we will find a very high proportion of sons of State Counsellors in the Conseil d'État, but this transmission is accomplished through a statistical mechanism that makes it at once more risky and formidably more dissimulated. What I have shown is that the difference is much more one of degree than of nature.

To return to the ideology of the school as liberator: I think that it is the French – that is, the republican, 1789 petit bourgeois – version of what Parsons was describing in the United States. So that, when you smiled at the mention of Parsons, you were laughing at things which are still deep structures in your minds (I'm sure of this, because they are in mine too, despite my best efforts), and which will manifest themselves for instance in the form of the adjectives that you use to qualify an intellectual performance. This then is the central thesis that I wanted to propose: the opposition between the nobility and the elite at the heart of the republican ideology (in 'elite' there is the idea of election, selection, competitive examination, anonymous competition, fair competition which nonetheless rewards inborn talent . . .) has hidden from us the fact that our elite is a nobility with all the properties of the nobility.

Continuity and genesis of the great corps

Sometimes, historians encounter this problem, for instance when they consider whether they can write a history of these corps. They have well-trained professional reflexes and they say, rightly, that we should be suspicious of what I myself have baptized as 'the illusion of the constancy of the nominal'.[37] The historians and, even more, the sociologists are inclined to act as if an institution that has kept the same name has itself remained the same: they believe for instance that they can study the Conseil d'État as if it descended in a straight line from its origins in the seventeenth century. When you hear this example, you will say: 'What fools they must be.' But, for example, the historians often compare the bishops of the 1850s with the bishops of the 1950s,[38] because the word has stayed the same, whereas the object has changed enormously. Likewise, there are lots of studies where the historians flatly compare statistics for doctors in the 1850s with those for doctors today, even though everything, including the recruitment system, has changed. These anachronisms are a product of the illusion of the constancy of the nominal, the illusion that consists in thinking that, when the word stays the same, its object is identical. That said, for the *grands corps*, the historians do wonder whether the *grands corps* have always been the *grands corps*, and the best of them resist the temptation of the illusion of the constancy of the nominal and say: 'Beware, the *grands corps* of the *ancien régime* has nothing to do with the Napoleonic *grands corps*, which has nothing to do with the *grands corps* of the Third Republic; the continuity is only superficial and is moreover a purely national, French definition [of the corps].'

All that is fine, but so often in the social sciences one error hides another. In the event, the problem of the continuity of the *grands corps* hides the following problem, which is absolutely crucial. If we take the long-term view, we observe an imperceptible but progressive process. It starts in the twelfth century, has moments of acceleration, particularly in the seventeenth century, and announces the constitution of something that we could call the corps, if we give the concept a conceptual rather than a historical sense, by giving it, as I have done today, a wider sense which includes the professions. There emerged an ensemble of social groups whose titles function like a title of nobility, but are guaranteed by the State, and are complicit in State schooling because it is State schooling that guarantees the title, and with it, the technical and social competence that defines the modern [elites?].

The historians then are right to say: 'Take care not to confuse the corps reconstituted by Napoleon after the Revolution in a logic of restoration with the corps of the former monarchy!' But, as long as we observe this proviso, we do still have the right to speak of the corps and to say that there is a continuity between the parliamentarians of the sixteenth century studied by historians and the members of the Conseil d'État who have graduated from the ENA. And to write the history of the genesis of these corps is inevitably to write the history of the genesis of a certain type of educational and bureaucratic institution, the representations of that bureaucratic institution, and the functions of the holders of bureaucratic power that go to constitute the State. Basically, what I hope to tell you about next time is this kind of genesis of a State power exercised by social agents whose entitlement to exercise their State power is granted by the State, meaning that the powers of the State are not reducible to its central bureaucratic power. The senior administration is at the heart of the central bureaucratic power, but the powers of the State extend much further. They include the advocate, the doctor writing a certificate, the teacher awarded a diploma; in short, all these statutory holders of some power delegated by the State. To study their genesis you have to describe the genesis of the State, because in fact it is the same thing . . . What I am going to try to do is write the history of the people who are implicated in the State. If I have shown at length that the liberal professions, despite their libertarian airs, are involved in the State, it is because I am going to proceed to describe the genesis of the corps of people who, in order to establish their position as modern advocates or doctors, have had to invent the modern State which guarantees the status that they enjoy. Part of their effort to create this modern State was the work to produce representations of disinterestedness.

If I have insisted so much on disinterestedness, it is because this is perhaps the most difficult aspect of the work of creation of the State, and it has been constantly overlooked by the theoreticians of the State. The theoreticians of the State generally write the history of the administrative institutions. They do sometimes take parts of the educational system into account, but very rarely. The historians who study the history of the birth of the ideas of the State and the constitutionalists of the seventeenth century are not the same. I myself think that we cannot understand this phenomenon unless we look at the whole picture. It forms a single history, with the parliamentarians, the d'Aguesseaus and today the technocrats, who are often moreover the descendants of the parliamentarians. We can still today see visible genealogical links (d'Ormesson, Talon[39] . . . like so many others, are ancient names), but these genealogical names are not very important in the end, because there is a statistical logic: one family replaces another. That said, the structure remains the same.

To understand these modern forms of power that the American theoreticians naively describe in their most naively ideological aspect, we must therefore create a history uniting the genesis of the educational qualification and the colleges of the eighteenth century (why did colleges in that period experience such a 'boom', with a much greater number of people suddenly transiting through the educational system?[40]), the genesis of the bureaucratic system (with the invention of procedures irreducible to those that characterized the Church – although they borrowed heavily from it – or the juridical corps – although they still drew heavily upon it) and the genesis of representations of power and the means of managing men (with the creation of notions like those of the public, public welfare or the school as liberator). In other words, the obstacle that we encounter at the start of any sociology of the school is one of the products of the very social order in which the school plays such a decisive part. That is what I want to do next time, to try to give a retrospective coherence to things that may have seemed rather disparate to you.

Lecture of 16 February 1989

The medical profession and the State – Weber and the 'patent of education' – State magic, certification, magic and the educational universe – The confinement of the dominant – A programme for research

Since this is the last lecture, I would like today to try to tie up the bundle of conclusions that I have reached and at the same time define the guidelines for an essentially historical research into the genesis of the State, whose results I hope to present in the years to come.[1]

The interest of the analysis of the professions through which I have digressed during the last lecture is to show that the State is not reducible to the administrative field and that the categories of people involved in the State are in fact spread very broadly over the social space, so that to the corps of senior civil servants, whom we associate closely with the State, we should add all the specialist corps and even the liberal professions that we traditionally oppose to the State insofar as they are one of the elements of the opposition between liberalism and Statism. Consequently, the problem that arises when we proceed to this kind of clean sweep of conventional wisdom is that of the relations between the State, the school system and power. What I wanted to show was that in modern societies it is no longer possible to debate the issue of power independently of the educational problem. Power has been much discussed, particularly by philosophers, after the events of 1968,[2] yet for sociological reasons that you can think about for yourselves, the philosophers have situated power almost everywhere,[3] but almost never in what I think is the heart of modern society, that is, the educational system. What I would like to do, with the help of Max Weber – who of all traditional thinkers is the one who has come nearest to what I take to be a just theory of the relations between the school, the State and power – is try to raise the question of the fundamental relations between the educational system, with its institutions such as examinations and the rational control of knowledge, and the new forms of power, the technocratic type of power.

The medical profession and the State

Before starting on all that, let me give you a reference that I forgot to give you last week. Geison was the editor of an important book on the professions and the French State that includes an article by Jan Goldstein on the origins of the medical profession which seems to me to illustrate the analyses that I offered you last week.[4] I shall give you the substance of the article. In it, Goldstein shows that the medical profession, in particular the psychiatric profession, was established with the help of the State in an attempt to base a theory of moral contagion on the model of medical contagion – which is an analysis that I find very exciting. With reference to political disturbances, the medical profession founded a theory of moral contagion based on analogies between moral contagion – political contagion finally – and traditional medical contagion. According to this author, we see that underlying certain strategies through which the corps of doctors became established there is a sort of political theory. Goldstein shows that in the 1860s there was what was called at the time 'an epidemic of diabolical possession'. On the basis of this analogy between moral contagion and biological contagion, these diabolical possessions – which emerged as if by chance in Savoy, which had just been annexed by France – served as a basis for doctors to claim a sort of police power – at least symbolic and physical. The doctors did in fact on this occasion see themselves delegated a State authority implying the power to resort to the police. More generally the author shows how the medical monopoly relied on procedures and modes of thought of this type to extend or appropriate a delegated power which (unlike the power of the corporations in the time of the *ancien régime*) did not belong to the corps as an ensemble but to each doctor. This point would merit development in a separate analysis. I shall not return to this, but it is important not to consider the modern corps too simply on the model of the *ancien régime*. A major difference, especially after the French Revolution,[5] is that the modern corps receive individual delegation. It is each agent (each doctor or professor, etc.) who is mandated, and no longer only the corps. In other words, there is delegation at one single level and not at two levels. This is a considerable change, which also contributes to the liberal illusion, the illusion of the independence of the corps of the liberal professions from the State.

This article clearly shows how the State is implicated in the process through which each corps, and in particular the medical corps, is established and, through its monopolistic power, establishes its control of a market. Then it goes on to show how, for example, with the constitution of a welfare state, institutions such as health insurance – which I alluded to last time – create a kind of direct link between the doctor and the State through the intermediary of an indebted clientele assigned to the doctors through the existence of statutory guarantees accorded to the patient. To a certain extent – here things become most interesting – health insurance can lead to the ruin of the foundation of liberal ideology, that is, the principle of the practitioner's free choice, in the sense that the insurance is only accorded to those who choose the right doctors, those who are, in the official term, 'accredited',[6] that is, recognized by the State. Health insurance thus punishes medical bad taste. To visualize where this might lead [. . .] imagine if intervention by the State were to punish aesthetic bad taste, and say: 'Don't buy colour prints at a cut-price market stall . . .' – I have just been reading a very good book on colour prints by a Swedish sociologist.[7] You can perfectly well imagine a hyperactive minister of culture saying to us: 'Stop buying colour prints! If you want to be refunded by the aesthetic service, you must buy . . .' [*Bourdieu reacts to some laughter in the audience*]. You only have to follow that train of thought, to push things to their limit, and you see what is obvious [but goes unnoticed]: '. . . you must buy your paintings in accredited stores and only there, and from painters accredited by the State'. This is not cloud-cuckoo land, it is a situation fairly close to that of the nineteenth-century salons with their guarantee from the Academy.[8] So, in a way, without our noticing it, health insurance ruins the principle of free choice for the doctor. You are free to go to a complementary practitioner but you won't be refunded, which means [if you are a complementary practitioner?] that you will have to secure your market with the sword of Damocles of the illegal exercise of medicine hanging over your head. So much for the State, but imagine how it would be for religion . . . see the analogy: 'People going to Lourdes will not be refunded.' And yet the *aggiornamento* of the Church was something like that[9] . . . I shall not develop this further because I might shock you, but the analogy works almost perfectly.

Thus the State protects patients from their medical bad taste, by punishing any bad choices. We see in passing that this policy contradicts the fundamental presumptions of the liberal optimism that often

inspired the affirmation of human rights (the right to have education and instruction, and the like). This liberal optimism supposed
that each citizen was capable of choosing, [and choosing] well. This
revolutionary utopia, which lasted until the 1880s, with authors like
Jules Simon, consisted in saying that the citizens were masters of their
political choices, that they were capable of making political choices.
But since people were starting to doubt that capacity, political competence became very strongly allied with the existence of an educational
system able to nurture it, and one of the justifications of compulsory
education was this need to give everyone the means of attaining that
competence. If we extrapolate this a little to think of our own times
(you will see that things are not so simple): nowadays, opinion polls
suppose that people are competent, and there are awkward implications in the fact of reminding ourselves, as I did in an article written a
while back now (1970),[10] that the apparently democratic postulate of
political competence is in fact anti-democratic, because it consists in
attributing to people competences that they don't possess, and thereby,
drawing attention to answers which they might have produced without
competence, that is, often against their own interests. Behind apparently anodyne analyses there are formidable consequences.

Weber and the 'patent of education'

With the 'welfare state' and all the measures that are involved in it,
then, the State takes in hand, as it were, the medical choices of the
patients. It tacitly orients these choices through positive or negative
sanctions, contradicting the liberal optimism according to which the
citizens are able to recognize where their true interest lies, which is one
of the postulates of liberalism. I think that this is a fairly good place to
start studying the problems arising. What I would like to do today is
attempt to see how this alliance between the school, the State and the
power of those who dominate the State, or dominate with the guarantee of the State, functions. Before starting this analysis, I would like to
briefly mention something that we will encounter . . . So I shall perhaps
start by referring rapidly to the fundamental text by Max Weber that I
have long considered as expressing my own thought, even if – as I shall
explain today – I have been very surprised to discover that ultimately
Weber adopted a very naive position towards this problem. I take
this opportunity to make a remark. If I were to restrict myself to a
professorial commentary I would grant Weber what everything seems
to indicate: unlike Hegel or Marx, whom I have mentioned, it seems

to me that he had seen something very important, which is the link between the educational system and the State, between educational qualifications and the competence accorded to the holders of modern forms of power. But this partial insight had hidden from him something that I have tried to recall through a historical analysis, and whose consequences I would like to trace, in trying to show you what could be a more rigorous theory of the link between the school and the State.

Weber's text is to be found in *Economy and Society*, volume 2. (This volume is unfortunately not translated into French.[11] I don't know when we will finally get a [French] edition [worthy of the name] of Max Weber.[12] This is a shocking situation; for example, in meetings of historians, the German historians have a kind of statutory advantage in the fact that they can read Weber in the original, whereas the French historians don't have access to Weber's text and, in addition, they feel bound to look down on their colleagues' comparatist pretentiousness. That was a parenthesis designed to goad the historians, but I shall return to Weber's text.) This famous, classic text has often attracted commentary arguing that, according to Weber, the process of rationalization leading to the modern State is inseparable from a process of rationalization of the modes of recruitment of civil servants. Among the characteristics of this process of rationalization Weber insists on the existence of rational forms of training, that is, training oriented with explicit reference to the profession to be exercised and therefore explicitly oriented towards explicitly declared ends.

A second point is that Weber insists on the fact that these pedagogical structures are in a way subsumed by the modern examination or competitive examination, as a rational instrument for measuring rational competences. The examination differs from trial by ordeal, for instance, where to know who is right in a judicial debate the two [protagonists] are thrown into a fire and the survivor is declared innocent. Certain forms of educational test are of this type. For instance, [Clifford] Geertz tells us that in Bali the transmission of knowledge between masters and pupils is consummated in a kiss.[13] I imagine that these may be quite pleasing forms of training [*discreet laughter from the audience*] but whose technical efficiency we might question. We could draw up a history of the forms of charismatic training that linger on within allegedly rational systems. I think for instance that the system of the *grandes écoles* is ultimately more charismatic than rational, even if with the help of their exercises in charisma they smuggle in a smidgeon of rationality.

That said, Weber insists on the fact that the examination is rational and that, because of this, the processes of rationalization of the forms of government are accompanied by rationalization of the forms of measuring competence: we arrive thus at forms of government tending to exclude from public service 'love, hatred, and all purely personal, irrational, and emotional elements which escape calculation'.[14] That is Weber, sure enough: it is a system without passion or emotion, without anything connected to affectivity and thereby to anything personal. *Sine ira ac studio*.[15] This rational bureaucracy, then, excludes the passions, and everything that eludes calculation. If you remember, for Weber the definition of bureaucracy or the rational State is the fact that it obeys principles ensuring calculability and predictability:[16] it is organized according to rational laws; you know what you are dealing with, even if you transgress it. You can transgress it with eyes wide open, knowing the risk that you run, whereas in charismatic forms of justice things will depend on the humour of the prince or even, in traditional forms (like Sancho Panza on his island, or what I call *Kadijustiz*),[17] on the mood of the judge, for instance. With rational, ideally defined forms of the law and the State, you know where you are, you can predict and calculate. This is not wrong: every big American firm, as we all know, employs cohorts of lawyers to predict sanctions and choose the least costly one (sometimes, when the sanction is less costly, it is better to calculate and incur it [than to follow the law]).

This is how Weber sees rational law, and according to him the expert, who governs without passion, is the product of a division of labour. This is another property of the bureaucracy, whereas in the patrimonial system, and even more so in the charismatic system, everything is combined: the domestic, the political, the family, business affairs, etc. Where the charismatic system, if you like, mixes everything up together, a rational system divides up the functions, circumscribing competences and geographical responsibilities, but also the areas of power. The system of the rational model of bureaucracy is thus inseparable from the figure of the expert filed in his cubby-hole and able to apply to this cubby-hole the universal rules which, mediated by his competence, find their specific application there. Ultimately the expert proceeds by deduction – as I argued in relation to the law[18] – using the universal rules that apply mathematically to any given x factor. In fact the jurist for Weber is a kind of geometer who replaces the variable by a particular variant and, studying the equation set him by the law, finds the answer to the puzzle. This expert, says Weber, is indifferent to human considerations and because of this is 'strictly objective'.[19] We are fairly close to the Hegelian view of the bureaucrat as bearer of the universal. The reason why Weber's analysis is so plausible and so difficult to dismiss is that it gives a good account of a certain number of undeniable properties of the modern bureaucratic system, not only in their ideal organization but even in their concrete and practical identities.

That said, when we read the text in detail (if we look into Weber further now, moving on to 'Bureaucracy and Education', in *Economy and Society*, volume 2), we see that Weber proposes, somewhat between the lines in passing, analyses which contradict the central theme that his critics have focused on. This is something classic: the critics cleanse a thought of its doubts and its afterthoughts (we didn't need the deconstructors to tell us that),[20] which are often to be found in the notes or in the subtext lurking beneath the text. In fact I have done this kind of thing myself, because we often read the critics before we read the authors themselves ... and when we come to read the authors our minds are already quite settled. The impetus for my re-reading came from the moment when I opened Weber and saw that he called the educational diploma a *Bildungspatent* ('patent of education'),[21] which is quite astonishing ... Given the context I was working in, the word 'patent' jumped out and hit me, because it is the State that delivers a patent. So we see clearly that the diploma is something which, through a sort of guarantee, establishes its owner as a licensed patent holder, that is, for instance, someone authorized to write 'graduate of' on his visiting card or 'consultant of the hospitals of Paris' on his name plate. In so doing he affirms a technical competence which is at the same time a social competence giving guarantees to his clients, and these guarantees are themselves guaranteed by a sort of central credit bank which is none other than the State. Ultimately the diploma has properties absolutely analogous to those of a currency, another entity which has no existence beyond the central bank of economic credit. Just as the State functions as a central bank of economic and monetary credit, so it functions as a central bank of symbolic credit, the diploma being a form of guaranteed symbolic credit.

This is a very practical distinction, which we see at work the minute we conduct an enquiry. In order to understand it, you only have to think of the difference (if you have read *Distinction*) between the man we might call cultured, capable of showing off his culture in a social conversation, or, say, in the ordinary circumstances of life, and the holder of a diploma.[22] In extreme cases, you can be a cultured man with no guarantee or a guaranteed man with no culture. This is one of the reasons why professors don't want us to measure culture. The guarantees are statutory, universal guarantees, which in fact are precisely largely made in order to – in such cases we can say they are 'designed to' – provide a guarantee even in the absence of what is being guaranteed. This is very important. As I was saying the other day, you may not grasp the consequences of what I am saying. This is why teaching it is so difficult: when I say, as the canon lawyers say, '*dignitas non moritur*' ('The king is dead, long live the king'),[23] they say to me: 'Yes, how interesting, it's a historical topos, okay . . .'. That said, it is mildly astonishing to say, 'The king is dead, long live the king', meaning that the monarchy survives the king, which is difficult to swallow in terms of rationality. But if we say culture . . . Then the canon lawyers referred to by Kantorowicz[24] insist on the fact that the monarchy survives any kind of biological misfortune that can affect the king (he can die, in the most radical case). [*The end of this discussion is missing from the recording used*].

State magic, certification, magic and the educational universe

To resume my argument. I think I shall be obliged to limit it to its outline, but I hope to manage to give you at least the overall pattern, not of the demonstration, but of the programme of verification that I would like to propose. I was insisting just now on the fact that to properly understand the mechanisms on which power is founded in highly differentiated societies, like French society today, you need in a way to place yourself at the mercy of the sort of paradox involved in the notion of State magic. By 'State magic'[25] I mean those entirely paradoxical social acts that lead to the endowment of either a thing or a person with properties irreducible to what our ordinary reason [. . .] can grasp or measure.

Well, here I must speed up – I hope that those of you who have heard me before will remember what I was saying and that what I have to say will be sufficient for the others – although I ought now to repeat at length my analysis of the process of validation, homologation or certification.[26] I took the example of the certificate (the fact of awarding a sick note or a certificate of health or disability, etc.) as a typical act of bureaucracy: it is an act perfectly characteristic of rational bureaucracy, and yet at the same time it involves a formidable element of magic that draws on mechanisms analogous to those which motivate magic in archaic societies. I am thinking of the essay on magic by Mauss,[27] which is a text that is still very badly read, because it is read by professors who haven't the faintest idea what a magical rite is. They have never seen one and when they have one under their noses they don't see it, like those who speak of fetishism . . . Honestly, I know what I am talking about here. Those who speak of fetishism don't know what fetishism is even when it is there under their noses. I can help you understand what I mean by returning to the example of fashion[28] [. . .] The act by which a fashion designer signs his creation and multiplies its value thirty times over is a typically fetishist act. Yet I don't know of any dissertations on fetishism, and God knows there were enough people thinking of that sort of thing in the 1960s. [Usually, when people speak of fetishism,] it is either as a pure concept or it is all about primitive peoples [. . .]. In fact the magic is all around us. It is in the most unexpected places, at the very heart of the haven of rationality, the machinery of State.

The act of certification for instance is a very relevant example. Everything that I wanted to say is encapsulated in the formula we use when we say: 'They have put their house in order.'[29] I have analysed the process: to follow the rules, to be in order, to conform to the group. Another example is the different types of certificate that we may grant a person. What for instance is a certificate of compliance? Is it a simple technical act whereby we say that something is compliant with what it is supposed to be, or is it something more? Why is it, for example, that if I were to issue a sick note it would have no value, whereas if I issued a certificate of competence in sociology (I haven't been asked for one, but if it did happen . . .) it would have a certain value (that's why nobody asks me for one, by the way! [*some laughter*]). So the certificate is worth what the person certifying it is worth. But who certifies the worth of the person who certifies? This is pure Kafka, as I argued a year ago[30] – from one step to another we end up with God. Then we say 'God is the State', for the State is what in the last instance certifies all those who certify, whereas it is not itself certified by anyone. We therefore have a kind of negative theology and we can trace all sorts of ramifications that follow on from this state of affairs.

I shall leave it at that, but diplomas do certify. The word 'certification' makes it plain to see that we are in the world of belief: it [the State?] says that something is certain and it demands from those whom it addresses belief in the certitude of what is affirmed by the certifier. This sort of demand for belief is one element of the magic circle as Mauss described it, if you read his text carefully. (You have surely heard commentaries on the 'Essay on Magic'; like the 'Essay on the Gift',[31] it is one of the unavoidable texts that you absolutely must reread because, since they are truly compulsory reading, they are the most imperfectly read, being badly interpreted for the reasons I have given.) Mauss's 'Essay on Magic' is an extremely simple text. He says: 'When we, as modern men, ask about magic acts, we wonder: "Where does the magic come from. Wherein lies the magic? Is it in the instruments used?" No. "Is it in the agents?" No. "Is it in the place?" No.' In this way he enumerates all sorts of things and says that the magic lies more or less in the relations between all those things. It lies in the relations between all those things, and the relationship is one of belief. For magic to function, for the act which consists in adding a signature to a product to have the effect of multiplying its value, as I have argued, we need a universe of belief, we need other designers with whom the designer is in competition (they do battle in the name of a common faith in haute couture), we need fashion journalists, we need annual parades which generate a discourse on fashion, we need salesmen, etc. It is this extremely complex universe of belief that is the condition of the successful operation of the singular act which we call 'magic'. When we grasp this act in an isolated state or when we are outside the circle of belief we don't see it as 'magic'. We no longer interpret what we see as magic and we say: 'They must be mad.' Finally, in this particular case, madness for us is other people's magic, whose principles we don't understand because we are not in the circle of belief – which is also perfectly true of religious magic.

In the light of this analysis we can see that the educational universe, identified with rationality, science and progress, is a magical universe. Like the State, it is a magical universe . . . well, it is a partially magical universe with a technical dimension. It is unfortunate for me, but as so often when we want to make progress in our research, we are obliged, in the words of Mao Tse-Tung, to twist the bar in the other direction.[32] In this particular case, since we are dealing with belief, and a very strong representation that 'the State is rational', I shall accentuate the aspect that 'the State is magical'. But once I have said this very strongly, please don't forget that the two aspects are inseparable and what makes our modern forms of power extraordinarily original is the fact that it takes a lot of rationality to produce the particular magic that is State magic. So if I say, 'The school is a magical place', and you write it down in your notes, when you read them back [later you will say] 'But Bourdieu is mad'. There are people who don't hesitate to operate this kind of mutilation: as soon as you have a slightly complicated thought, it is so easy to divide it up into three parts and . . .

On the one hand, in one of its least-known aspects, the school is a magical universe of belief which nurtures phenomena of the type that Mauss describes: the person who delivers the diplomas is certified to do so, believes himself to be certified, and addresses people who have solicited the diploma only because they believed in its value, because they recognize the diploma from having worked to prepare for it, and if by chance they have not prepared, they will be subjected to tests which will prepare them. For instance, the school tests – the word 'trial' comes to mind – are obviously an opportunity to measure a technical competence, but also an occasion to reinforce in those who aspire to a diploma their belief in its value, in the value of the title awarded.

The confinement of the dominant

I shall not take this further, but it would be possible to show that the whole educational system, even in its dimensions which conform most closely to how we imagine rational schooling (the École Polytechnique, the École normale supérieure for the sciences, etc.), is a place where mechanisms are at work producing value and belief, using a whole panoply of techniques.

The most obvious technique, which we have all noted, is encapsulated in the title of a famous book about English public schools, *The Cloistered Elite*,[33] for it has ever been apparent that, in most societies, one way of establishing an elite *qua* elite is to confine it. We should not forget that the most confined in most societies are the dominant. But confining them is a way of setting them apart, and, if you have read Durkheim properly, as a good sociologist (that is, once again, not purely academically) you will know that the sacred is what is separate, what is confined.[34] Our famous secular school, which is often experienced as the opposite of the confessional school, is a religious place. It is a religious place in the Durkheimian sense of the term; it is dominated by people who come from places like the École normale, which are religious in that they are established on the basis of initiatory breaks, between those who belong and those who don't. For instance, the Weberian selective examination, which is – more or less obviously – a measure of competence, is at the same time an initiation trial, a rite of separation through which a barrier of birth and essence is erected – which makes us think of the nobility, which is defined by a barrier of birth and essence – between the last pupil accepted and the first one rejected, who, as we all know, are often separated by only a quarter of one percentage point. This technical difference is the equivalent of the designer's label. We wonder whether the signature on the label of a bottle of perfume changes the technical composition of the perfume, [we ought to wonder whether] the signature 'normalien' on a perfume of competence changes it nature . . . You see that these problems are real problems.

The initiation break, then, is marked by confinement, but the confinement is only the most visible, external sign. There are many other signs, such as what you might call mental separation. This is something most extraordinary. It is what I call a 'rite of institution' and what others call a 'rite of initiation':[35] the function of most rites is to have a frontier accepted. When we think [of the acceptance of a] frontier, we always think of the acceptance of a frontier by those who are on the wrong side of it. But in thinking, for instance, that we should get women to accept that they are inferior to men, we forget that we should also get men to accept that it is fine to be a man, and that this comes with a lot of duties, etc. There is a very fine phrase by a great specialist in the theory of boundaries, Owen Lattimore: 'We think that the great wall of China was built to protect the Chinese from the people outside, but we forget that it was built to prevent the Chinese from escaping.'[36] If you think of this in relation to the rites of initiation, it is not a detail, it is something important. If you reread Flaubert's *Sentimental Education*,[37] you will see that the inheritors don't want to say, 'The king is dead, long live the king!', they would prefer to do something different . . . It may happen that the inheritors of an educational system would prefer to play rock and roll . . .

One function of the educational rites of initiation, where the school functions as a rite of initiation organized by the great initiates who are themselves products of rites of initiation (the preparatory classes, to be precise),[38] is to make sure that these people, once isolated, separated and constituted as a clergy (this is Durkheim's definition: the clergy are those who are simply separated from the profane),[39] are perceived as different. People have to believe that they really are different, made of another essence – which, in a society where the technical dimension [is privileged], supposes some technical difference. I need to point out this precision, otherwise you are going to think that I am starting to . . . Well, at the same time the initiates themselves need to feel that they are of another essence. There we find one of the properties of the nobility: when we say 'noblesse oblige', it means that the nobleman is obliged to be noble. A true nobleman is someone so constituted and produced that the idea of not being noble does not cross his mind. A nobleman's habitus leads the nobleman to act nobly without effort, in a natural way. Likewise, the *normalien* acts in a *normalienish* way . . . No, really, this is very important, because this is no crude analogy: there is a general category of production of nobleness, of which the nobility, in the historical sense of the term, is a special case. By setting out the problem of nobleness as it arises in all societies, in its most general definition,[40] as the naturalization of the arbitrary for the purposes of power (which is what is at stake), we better understand the specific nature of a historical nobility, inherited through the blood.

A programme for research

Now I shall move on more quickly. This is one way of disguising the limitations of my historical culture, because it is a vast programme. You will immediately see that it would take several whole teams of historians to accomplish the project that I am going to elaborate. Unfortunately it often happens that very important projects are not studied by anyone at all, because neither the social conditions needed for studying them, nor the mental conditions implied, are fulfilled. We then conclude that these problems cannot be studied. But I personally think that it is sometimes better to raise the issues and sketch out the problems and their solutions, rather than gloss over them in the name of a positivist definition of research while in fact responding to the problems, using partial mini-monographs[41] to destroy them. That was a brief parenthesis addressed to the historians (whom I greatly appreciate, because they are practically the only colleagues that I can really base my work on in most of the things that I believe in).

The diploma, the educational qualification, is a title with a magical dimension, bearing the trace of the magical action of the State. More precisely, if we admit that it is a privilege magically constituted and guaranteed by the State, then this privilege corresponds to the definition given by David Bien in the *Annales* article I quoted last time, where he characterizes the privilege of the nobleman under the royalty as a 'right to the exclusive exercise of some function, and to the enjoyment of certain revenues'.[42] In other words, the privilege is a legitimate monopoly over a function, accompanied by the associated profits. If we accept this definition, and if we see that this privilege is guaranteed by the State, which in this case acts the part of a sort of public treasury of symbolic funds guaranteeing private appropriations, we are led in a way to revise the whole history of the relations between the school and the State that Weber did sketch, although he succumbed to a unilateral vision, envisaging this history as a process of rationalization and modernization. In fact it is an ambiguous, two-faced process, exactly like the title whose ambiguity I showed just now. I think I know enough about its history to be able to argue for a need to rewrite the whole history of the examination, the diploma, the State and the *grands corps*. We need to rewrite the history of this ensemble of institutions simultaneously. Only if we proceed to a simultaneous rewriting of the history of this process of constitution of the educational institutions, the State institutions and of what we call the corps (but giving this word a really broad sense, emptying it of its French historical connotations), which all owe their power to the State institution, can we really account for the ambiguous reality that a synchronic approach presents us with. Here I shall read my text, which, I think, sums up fairly well what I am trying to say. The birth of what I call the State nobility – that nobility whose title is guaranteed by the State on the grounds of its recognition of a technical competence inseparable from a social competence, and which in its first historical form in France was the nobility of the robe – is inseparable from the development of an ensemble of institutions among which figures the diploma. In other words, we need to reconstitute a whole series of correlative and complementary innovations.

[*The start of the following discussion is missing from the recording used.*] We need [. . .] to study the specific cases as specific cases and specific reactions, to see in which respects they follow the general rule and where they differ. In other words, in order to write history we need concepts, even though historians most often define their work in opposition to the concept. I allow myself to say this in peremptory, simplistic fashion, but I think it is important, if only to clarify the position of any historians among you in relation to my argument. The question, then, is not whether we are still talking about chivalry, when the pen [succeeds?] the sword as the horse succeeded the suit of armour; the question is whether we have passed from one nobility, socially recognized as a body worthy of governing, to another nobility, passing from one mode of reproduction to another.[43] The new nobility has found in the model of the ancient nobility, in opposition to which it was established, [the principle according to which] nobility is to be found in the service of the king. The process accomplished, since its mode of reproduction was the school, has led them to say that to be noble is to serve, not the king, but the State, the public (remember d'Aguesseau: 'to serve the public'). That changes everything. For indeed, I don't serve the king in the name of a hereditary mission, or, as Parsons would say, by *ascription*, having been mandated by heredity for that task, by a sort of fatal link or connection with the king that would be inscribed in my nature (a relation between my nature and the nature of the king); no, I serve the king by vocation, by choice, because I devote myself (this is the concept of *Beruf* (vocation), whose implications Weber developed at length),[44] I devote myself to the function of obedience to the king, and the service of the king then becomes the disinterested service of the State.

One last point that I need to evoke very quickly, at a gallop: the service of the king is no longer attributed to and inscribed within a social vision of the nobility, according to the equation 'to live the noble life is to serve the king'. It is no longer a destiny which is not chosen but which you are born into, and which you can only fulfil or betray. It is the deliberate choice of a vocation, an occupation knowingly assumed, for which you have to prepare yourself because it supposes special competences acquired through schooling. Thus we immediately discover that it is something which has to be earned, willed and merited. This means that these people are committed to competence and talent, and it is no accident if they elaborate pedagogical theories where the notion of merit appears immediately. That said, they will elaborate the relation between their corps and the educational system by elaborating the definition of their service. It is the idea of public service.

But this means that they must elaborate a theory of the State and the role of the servants of the State. We therefore need a third layer of historical studies, completely separate from the two preceding ones: studies that we might call a history of ideas or a social history of ideas, in particular in the Anglo-American tradition, to show how, from the jurists of the sixteenth century, through the Girondins and up to the reformists of the École nationale d'administration, a theory of public service as disinterested devotion to the general interest has progressively been constructed. In other words, there has been an extremely protracted process, which includes studies made by the philosophers. These people are not studied as part of the philosophical syllabus, because they are thought to belong to the history of ideas, except by a few critics who are somewhat isolated from the general world of professors of philosophy. I shall nonetheless quote a very interesting reference, Nannerl O. Keohane, *Philosophy and the State in France*. It is one book among many, but you will find in it a sort of rapid history of theories of the State, in particular all the *minores* that are always overlooked in the history of philosophy. In this book you will find a splendid description of what the author calls 'the civic humanism of the civil servants',[45] basing herself above all on thinkers called Louis Le Caron or Louis Le Roy, who as early as the sixteenth century were saying things very like d'Aguesseau. They insist on civic responsibility, in opposition to the individualists, whom we do know something of: people like Charron, the sceptics and above all Montaigne, who say, 'Let us distinguish between the private [and the public]', according to the famous axiom *intus ut libet, foris ut moris est*, which was Montaigne's solution ('on the inside, I think what I like, on the outside, I am a conformist'). The 'civic humanists' say: 'No, that is scandalous.' They are referring, if you remember,[46] to what d'Aguesseau called 'the philosopher', that is the sceptical philosopher who separates politics from . . . This is one of the reasons why these people do not figure in the philosophy syllabus. The philosophy of the professors is founded on the philosophy of philosophy, and politics is outside . . . (You may be thinking that this is untrue, but I could show you that it is still true, despite appearances, in the guise of the repression of the social sciences.) The inventors of civic virtue, those people who are called humanists ('the civic humanism of the civil servants'), want to write a political philosophy. They refuse to retreat into libraries, they want to establish a whole set of civic powers. Philosophy for them is a philosophy for the man of his world and time, who must establish a conduct for his world in his time. There we have the whole Jansenist current which, as I had rapidly explained,[47] I had sensed lying behind d'Aguesseau. These people helped to elaborate simultaneously a theory of schooling, a theory of competence grounded in the corps, and a theory of the State as the place where this universal, rational competence was exercised in the service of the universal, in the service of the public. A whole constitutionalist tradition has developed out of this. A word or two in conclusion: I think that where Weber saw a relatively stable and unilateral process of rationalization without political implications, we need to reconstruct, through a real genesis of the nobility of the State, a process in which the agents with an interest in the universal create a game in which the universal bears interest. There you have it, that is just about it, in very simplified terms [*applause from the audience*].

Pierre Bourdieu at the Gates of the State: Situating the Lectures of 1987–88 and 1988–89

Julien Duval

As professor at the Collège de France from 1982, Pierre Bourdieu devoted the first five years of his teaching to a course of lectures on 'General Sociology', focusing on a presentation of the theoretical foundations of his sociology.[1] He took a break from teaching in 1986–87. This volume collects the lectures that he gave in Paris in 1987–88 and 1988–89, which addressed the same audience and formed a homogeneous and continuous whole. Alongside these lectures, in the first year Bourdieu organized a seminar on the sociology of law (using the conclusions from this as the starting point for his lectures)[2] and in the second year he gave two of his lectures at the University of Lyon – publishing their transcription himself.[3]

The lectures collected here correspond to the start of a new cycle of teaching focusing on the State,[4] spread over five years.[5] These lectures are, however, also a prolongation of the preceding cycle: in them Bourdieu – who sometimes admitted to 'working in spirals' – develops and deepens the themes that he often broached, without making them the centre of his argument, in his lectures on general sociology between 1982 and 1986. At all events, as the title of the lectures, 'On the State' (perhaps chosen to avoid raising false expectations), suggests, Bourdieu does not deal with the State head on. If he does speak of it, it is after delaying the moment to do so, and he proceeds, as he says, 'in a negative manner' and 'tangentially'. He deals with the obstacles that a sociologist of the State encounters, and he considers at length the universes which participate in the State without becoming part of it: the juridical field, the bureaucratic field, the 'professions' and even sociology. Conversely, he constantly returns to problems linked to the State but which seem to transcend it: disinterestedness, and the universal.

The object of the following pages is to provide information enabling us to situate these lectures in the context of Bourdieu's teaching at the

Collège de France and his work and intellectual career more generally. These operations of contextualization lead us in passing to reflect on issues with a wider remit, in particular the place that enquiries into disinterestedness and the State hold in sociology, and the interest that Bourdieu brings to bear on law. The approach used sketches a genesis of his analysis of the State, including links with the historical and personal conditions in which the sociologist constructed his argument. This work of contextualization also sheds light on doubtless unfamiliar, but no less interesting, aspects of the articulation between Bourdieu's teaching and the partly novel forms of his engagement in French intellectual life in this period of the late 1980s.

Approaching the State

'I had long been aware that I would one day have to face the problem of the State. But I was wary of this immense object, entangled in endless theoretical discourses, and I wanted to approach it in my own way', said Bourdieu.[6] In the lectures themselves he explained that he said to himself: 'I never speak of the State, because I don't know what it is, and in this sense I am much more scientific than the others, who don't even know this.'[7]

In fact, 'if we consider the ensemble of his scientific works, the word ["State"] only makes an appearance in his work at the beginning of the 1980s, on the occasion of his inaugural lecture at the Collège de France',[8] and, astonishingly, the term hardly figures in his research into the production of the dominant ideology, political representation, modes of domination or political opinion. At most we note isolated interrogations, for instance during a talk on 'strikes' dealing with the power relations between workers and employers. Bourdieu wonders about the State, that 'possible third actor – which may not be one', which has the 'appearance of reality' but which does not exist as a 'real agent'.[9] In *Distinction* and *The Logic of Practice*, which in 1979 and 1980 were in many respects syntheses of the research Bourdieu had conducted up to that point, the term 'State' is barely used, and when it is, it is always in an anecdotal context.[10]

The word and the concept figure much more strongly in the lectures on general sociology that Bourdieu inaugurated in 1982. It was in the course of his work on language – which appeared in book form shortly after the start of these lectures[11] – that he first spoke of the State. This work projects onto the sociological terrain the analysis of the performative proposed by J. L. Austin: words can do things when certain social conditions are present. A sentence such as: 'I decree a general mobilization'[12] thus unleashes the general mobilization if it is pronounced by a head of State (in official circumstances), whereas spoken by someone anonymous it remains without effect.

Bourdieu proposes to see the social world as the site of a symbolic struggle between unequal social agents to impose their point of view. At the start of the lectures on general sociology, he confronts two diametrically opposed discourses: the insult, which displays the impotence of an individual agent trying to defend his honour; and public language, which, when emanating from a person mandated to act in the name of the State, tends to be heard and recognized by everyone (and therefore to 'exert action').[13] Under these conditions, the State appears to be 'prising social subjects away from their individual (Nietzschean) perspectivism'; it 'is a kind of neutral place that provides an authorized, socially recognized perspective on all social agents'.[14] As the lectures proceed, Bourdieu multiplies the variations and diversifies the formulations on this theme: 'The State has the means to make its truth come true';[15] it pronounces the 'verdict'; it is 'the last resort'[16] in the 'life and death' struggles for 'the construction of the identity of self and others';[17] 'this social agency' has the power 'to tell someone what they are with relatively uncontroversial authority',[18] that is, 'the power of nomination'.[19] The State produces 'a trans-subjective and objective signification'[20] to the point where it can be identified with 'common sense', etc.[21]

Holding 'the monopoly of the legitimate viewpoint over its social subjects', the State is the 'geometral of all perspectives'.[22] From the 1980s onwards, Bourdieu often uses this formula from Leibniz (initially relating to God). Similarly, he starts to appropriate Weber's definition of the State in terms of the 'monopoly of legitimate violence': the State, which 'has the power to tell you what you are', holds the 'monopoly of legitimate symbolic violence'.[23]

Educational qualifications are indeed guaranteed by the State, as are titles of nobility, deeds of property and the right to practise a number of 'technical and social skills'. In 1985 (Lecture of 9 May), Bourdieu develops a long argument – which he will refer to on several occasions in the following years – on the certificate, for instance the sick note signed by a doctor. This raises the question of who is the certifying authority: the doctor certifies the illness, but who certifies the doctor? And who certifies the Order that certifies the doctor? Bourdieu explains that, in our societies, this type of regression generally leads back to what we call the 'State',[24] the 'central bank' (and not only in monetary affairs) 'where all acts of guarantee would be guaranteed'.[25] If from one lecture to another he notes the diversity of what is guaranteed by the State (socio-professional categories, currency, words and things . . .),[26] he emphasizes above all the role of academic qualifications[27] and the decisive support that social categories, whose principal capital lies in the diploma, find in the State: through the educational system (for instance, by means of a *numerus clausus*), the State can maintain the scarcity and therefore the value of their capital. This observation tends to be valid, says Bourdieu, for all 'the producers of services with a cultural orientation'.[28] These analyses, such as the observation that the State decides the outcome of conflicts like those between anaesthetists and doctors,[29] prefigure the long development on the professions that he offered in 1989.

In the lectures on general sociology, the State even starts to intrude into the analyses of the fields, which had rarely, or never, been the case before. The lectures of March 1984 on Kafka were the occasion to describe an intellectual field which had become independent of the State and the site of a symbolic struggle of each against all, with no arbitration.[30] In 1985, dealing with 'the invention of the modern artist' and discussing the Academy system, Bourdieu describes a situation where the State guarantees the value and 'the exchange rates of the painter'.[31] He argues that the Impressionists aspired to replace the 'power of the State within the artistic field' with a form of anarchy.[32] By suggesting comparisons with science, he invites us to become aware of how much the scientific field owes to the State.

While we may note some remarks, initially linked to the reflections developed in *Ce que parler vent dire*, on the linguistic dimension of the construction of the State (the imposition in a country like France of a standard or official language involving disqualification of local dialects),[33] or on the 'historical process whereby the State concentrates [. . .] the power of nomination' in particular,[34] it was not until the start of the 1990s that Bourdieu came to truly analyse the birth of the State as a 'process of concentration of the different species of capital'.[35] In particular he studied the formation of the monopoly of the 'power of nomination', through the manner in which the king increasingly controlled the distribution of honours in different matters.[36] Bourdieu was attentive to the way in which the construction of the State was accompanied by the unification of social spaces, a process that attracted his interest again in the second half of the 1990s when he spoke of the constitution of transnational spaces in the context of 'globalization'.[37]

In the course of lectures given from 1982 to 1986, the State appears as an institution impossible for sociologists to ignore, but also as an extremely dubious and difficult object to analyse. In the passages devoted to the specific objects of sociology, Bourdieu returns to the debate over the names of collectives, something that the individualist tradition of the discipline wanted to ban, seeing it as purely meta-physical. Bourdieu, however, considered that we should investigate the mode of existence of the collectives.[38] Although the social classes hold a very important place in his declarations, he also illustrates his arguments with the cases of 'the Church' and 'the State', two words that are 'very difficult to define'.[39]

People speak of 'the State' without knowing what it is,[40] 'and we should much reflect on . . . what we understand by that'[41] rather than deduce from the existence of the word the existence of the thing.[42] The State is an abstraction particularly prone to the risk of reification. The word 'is a kind of shorthand, but using shorthand in such a case is fatal'.[43] Bourdieu multiplies examples of phrases which, in philosophical or political parlance, turn 'the State' into a subject endowed with a will and an ability to pursue rational actions and ends: 'When they say that "the State serves the dominant class", they are supposing an end, in the absence of a subject.'[44] At the same time, Bourdieu acknowledges that these phrases are inevitable, and he does not say that the State does not exist. He considers rather that the State does exist, but not in the way we generally suppose. For him the word designates 'a universe of extremely complex relations', 'the whole space of what I call the field of power'.[45] In other lectures he defines it as 'the structure at a given moment of the balance of symbolic power between agents claiming legitimate certification of advantages or disadvantages'.[46]

And finally the State is present in the lectures on general sociology through various references to a 'State science'.[47] In the first year, discussing social classification and categorization, Bourdieu questions the work done by the statisticians of INSEE. Along with the demographers, theorists and 'the majority of the economists', they are 'State scientists'. They declare publicly and officially what the social world is, without being challenged by anyone.[48] The science 'guaranteed by the State'[49] is performative in its way, but suffers from the 'inevitable fundamental antagonism between science and the State'.[50] It continually confuses the 'two ways of justifying a discourse on the social world', the one that finds 'its validation through facts and objects' and the one that draws its strength from the 'consensus of a group'.[51] Sociology is 'helpless' when confronted with this 'unanswerable' science. These analyses, sometimes presented as a turning point in Bourdieu's career (compared with the period in the 1960s when he worked with the administrators of INSEE),[52] went further in the lectures for 1987–88, taking a direction that questioned the ability of sociology to remain outside the 'State sciences' (see below).

The lectures published in this volume should also be situated in relation to two research projects that Bourdieu was involved in during the second half of the 1980s. The first was an enquiry into the private housing market, which he undertook with his team, and which was closely concerned with the way in which the State contributed to the structure of the market, for instance through changes in regulations or laws intended to influence consumer choice. This research, an important aspect of which was the analysis of a bureaucratic commission, is only occasionally referred to in the lectures in this volume (Lecture of 14 April 1988). It has to be said that the report had not yet been published.[53] On the other hand, Bourdieu refers to it often, and sometimes at length, in lectures between 1989 and 1992.

In the second half of the 1980s, he also finished a (weighty) volume, composed largely of a reworking of articles published during the previous fifteen years.[54] He doubtless concentrated his efforts on making it into a coherent whole. If the origin of the book is to be found in the enquiry into the *grandes écoles* that he initiated in the 1960s, at a time when education was a central focus of research at the Centre de sociologie européenne,[55] the volume – which is more than just a new sociological study of the school – included research into business management and an unpublished section entitled 'State Power and Power over the State', most probably written during the period when the lectures published here were being delivered. Some of the reflections and analyses of documents (in particular the texts written by Chancellor d'Aguesseau) presented in the lectures of 1987–88 appear here rewritten in condensed form, and seem sometimes to be the source of Bourdieu's notes for the lectures in the second year, 1988–89.[56] The book appeared in March 1989, just after the last lecture published here. In the lecture of 9 February 1989 Bourdieu offers an explanation (not explicitly presented as such) of the title he gave to the book, *The State Nobility: Elite Schools in the Field of Power*: as well as questioning the image of the 'school as liberator' that he had offered in the 1960s, he progressively came to show that the 'academic elite', the source of recruitment for most of the positions of economic and technocratic power, is a nobility that differs only in secondary aspects from the nobility of the *ancien régime* with which it is generally contrasted. Thus the subtitle of the book expresses in condensed form the need, exposed at length in the lectures of 9 and 16 February 1989, to study 'the progressive establishment of an educational system, a State and a discourse on the State', and 'the correlative invention of educational, technocratic and State institutions'.

The time for law

In the first three lectures of 1987–88 Bourdieu approached the State from the angle of the law. In the lectures on general sociology the link between the law and the State had already been underlined: the modern State – which Weber defined as 'rational law (justice) and the power to execute it (the police)'[57] – is the first place where the universal rules [of rational law] were put into practice;[58] it associates 'bureaucratic judgement' with this 'rational law';[59] it is accompanied by the appearance of characters such as the person on 'official welfare benefits', distinct from the traditional beggar because he is defined as having *rights*,[60] etc.

In retrospect, the second half of the 1980s appears to be the principal period when Bourdieu took an interest in law. He produced several talks and papers on this topic, which also inspired two issues of the journal he had been editing since 1975, *Actes de la recherche en sciences sociales*. Most of what we have just been saying about Bourdieu's interest in the State is also valid for the law. There is however a difference: unlike the State, the law had never been totally absent from his purview. His first research (into the Béarn) led him to take account of the law of succession, and to denounce legalism, or 'juridicism', as faults which, in the language of the 1980s, implied taking 'the law as an explicative principle of the practices'.[61] Whether as sociologist or ethnologist, Bourdieu placed the accent on practice, even if he was just as hostile to the reduction of law to a pure ideology,[62] and refused to exaggerate the opposition between law and custom: 'The legal discourse is verifiable insofar as it proclaims what will be proclaimed, insofar as it imposes something that is self-evident, insofar as it consecrates something that pre-exists it.'[63]

Actes de la recherche en sciences sociales published articles relating to the law, such as a text in 1976 in which the British historian Edward P. Thompson elaborates a thesis according to which 'The law is a specific means of mediation and site of confrontation between the classes, not a simple ideological instrument in the service of domination by the dominant class.'[64] In particular he points out that the law 'counters the advantages of the authorities with constraints on the actions of the directors'.[65] Two years later, a long article by a young sociologist called Pierre Cam, entitled 'Red Judges and Labour law',[66] was published. In 1986 an issue was published under the title 'By What Right?' It included texts by Jean-Pierre Mounier and Remi Lenoir.[67] In the opening article, 'The Force of the Law',[68] Bourdieu announces the intention of contributing to a 'rigorous sociology of law' through an analysis which counters the legal professionals who accord total autonomy to juridical form, but which also attacks the reduction of the law to an instrument of domination, in order to concentrate on the juridical field. The law is an affair for professionals endowed with a specific competence and thereby separated from the profane. The legal field is grounded in the 'reciprocal conflict' of these professionals. In particular, the jurists and theoreticians, who are tempted to angle the law in the direction of pure theory, are opposed to the ordinary judges and practitioners. The article sees in the law 'the form par excellence of an active discourse capable of producing effects through its own merits'. Bourdieu insists in particular on the *vis formae*, the force of form, the symbolic efficacy due to juridical formalism. He also refers to the question of the homology between juridical offer and demand, particularly the emergence of new types of law with the rise to power of the dominated in the social field in the nineteenth century.

This article has echoes in the lectures on general sociology. In particular Bourdieu refers to the *vis formae* on several occasions during the year 1983–84.[69] In a more general fashion, the law is a *leitmotif* in the lectures, admittedly more or less discreet or emphatic depending on the context. The reflections on the law seem to have been stimulated by research into language. In this respect they are comparable with those concerning the State – to which they are sometimes (but not always) linked. In fact, Bourdieu reminds us on three occasions of the proximity revealed by Émile Benveniste between the vocabulary linked to the act of speaking (*'Je dis'*) and the juridical vocabulary (*dikè* – 'justice') in the Indo-European languages: the judge is the person who speaks (*'qui dit'*).[70] A strong moment in the analyses connected with the law comes in 1983–84, when Bourdieu proposes detailed developments based on extracts from Weber's *Economy and Society* (in connection with the operation of codification, or taken from the section on the law).[71] In particular he looks in depth at the transition from a law symbolized by the *Kadijustiz* of Arab societies (or the judgements of Sancho Panza and Solomon) to a rational law, as well as at the universality of juridical ruling (he returns to this last analysis on several occasions, including in one of the lectures in this volume)[72] – this economy of intelligence, time and energy[73] realized by rational law, whereas customary law ignores the universal juridical formula and falls back on good sense and practical procedure.[74]

During the five years of the lectures on general sociology, Bourdieu insisted, more or less incidentally depending on the context, on the properties of the law. As was his habit, he diversified the expressions, to formulate things a little differently each time. The law transforms the discontinuous into the continuous, it 'slices through [. . .] the middle of the *continuum*,[75] it instils differences, 'it reifies perceptions',[76] it operates a 'theory effect',[77] it is an 'upright, straight and orthodox vision', an 'orthodoxy',[78] it represents 'the vision that a social universe has of itself',[79] that is, a masculine, dominant, legitimate vision.[80] The law – whose ideal-typical form is 'the verdict of the State in the struggle for identity'[81] – operates forms of 'objectification', 'publication',[82] 'codification'[83] and 'physicalization'.[84] We can also mention, without exhausting the references to law, the developments on the *numerus clausus*[85] or the lectures on Kafka's *Trial* which speak of an upside-down world (as opposed to Weber's vision of justice), since Kafka's tribunal is characterized by its unpredictability.[86]

The simple observation that 'the dominant representation of the social world [produced by the law] is part of reality'[87] obliges sociologists to take an interest in the law. But within the framework of this course of lectures on general sociology, almost the first of this genre to be given at the Collège de France,[88] Bourdieu also considers that 'the struggle between the sociologist and the jurist is absolutely fundamental to the existence of sociology'.[89] He reminds us of Durkheim's endless battles 'with the faculties of law',[90] and also draws attention to another phase, when, for Marx and Weber, 'confrontation with the law [was also] capital'.[91] He puts that down to the fact that 'the juridical discourse on the social world has a form of validity',[92] or that, in other terms, 'the law is a powerful sociology . . . that has the force of law'.[93]

The seminar on 'the sociology of law' organized in 1987–88 was probably some kind of substitute for the empirical research into law that Bourdieu did not undertake, for lack of time, but no doubt also because, having been trained as a philosopher, he was aware that he did not have a very good grasp of legal studies (which in addition he constantly described as highly formal, and where he knew that the specialists were not generally welcoming to outside interlopers).[94] 'I am not a great specialist in the history of law',[95] he admits in one of his lectures. In different circumstances he says that he regrets being able to offer young researchers on law only advice [. . .] 'limited to methodology', because of his 'very reduced knowledge of the juridical world'.[96] In his research centre, the Centre for European Sociology (CSE), the researchers too had mostly come from a literary background (or from the courses in sociology that had been launched in the arts faculties from the end of the 1950s). There were no more than two scholars who published articles on this topic in *Actes de la recherche en sciences sociales*: Remi Lenoir, who had studied law (but whose research, at least until the 1980s, had focused above all on old age and the family), and Yves Dezalay, who was a specialist collaborator with the CSE in the 1960s (for the enquiry into the *grandes écoles*), and then left the research centre, returning only at the start of the 1980s with the project of a State doctoral thesis on the jurists to be supervised by Bourdieu.[97] Finding that Bourdieu could offer only the basic elements of the subject, Dezalay looked into the ways in which the notion of field could be used in empirical research into law.[98] He gave two talks at the seminar on the sociology of law organized by Bourdieu in 1988. The other participants in this seminar were also forty-somethings (but did not belong to the CSE). Several of them had also attended the Centre for Interdisciplinary Research at Vaucresson, an institute attached to the ministry of justice and the CNRS, and started to take magistrates as the object of their research, something that was unusual for the time.[99]

Bourdieu drew on this seminar (which fed into number 76–77 of *Actes de la recherche en sciences sociales*, 'Droit et expertise' [Expertise and the Law]) at the start of his lecture course in 1988. If 'The Force of the Law' worked partly to project onto the juridical field observations that had initially been established for the religious field, in the lectures of 1987–88 the procedure became more genetically focused. It resembled the procedure used in the study of the literary field.[100] It undertook to sketch a 'social history of the genesis of the juridical field',[101] taking an interest in the production of new types of discourse, new 'practical rules' and new 'systems of sanctions'.[102] Bourdieu looks in detail at d'Aguesseau, whom he says he was delighted to have discovered by chance.[103] He tends to see in him the incarnation of an 'initiatory phase', a sort of 'nomothete', to use the word Bourdieu uses in analogous cases. He takes his research on d'Aguesseau as an opportunity to reflect on 'what we might call a professional spirit, a juridical spirit that seemed to be an important element in the genesis of a field'.[104]

This work was linked not only to Bourdieu's preoccupation with the State. It also related to the theory of fields he had been constructing since the 1970s through a continuing projection of his research and analysis onto new objects of study: starting out from a rereading of Max Weber's sociology of religion, he launched into in-depth research into the literary field of the nineteenth century, studies of the scientific and philosophical fields (Heidegger), and general analyses of the ensemble of the fields of cultural production, etc. In the 1980s he turned his attention to universes less linked to culture in the strict sense, such as economics, with his research into private housing, or the law. He thought that 'modes of thinking like those that are engaged in the notion of the field can be valid on terrains where they have not been applied before now'.[105] He sought each time to 'project' the analyses produced in other fields, by taking their specifications in order to explicate 'the general properties of the fields'.[106] The comparative dimension of his approach is easy to see in the lectures, as for instance when he compares the degree of denial in the political and the bureaucratic fields.[107]

In the case of the law, one of Bourdieu's manifest objectives is to establish the fact that the juridical universe presents a 'dualist' or 'chiasmatic' structure of the same type as the one that he has brought to light in the fields of cultural production. He regards the juridical field as 'one of the least autonomous in relation to the political and economic fields', but nonetheless grants it a 'relative independence from the State and from business', and notes its reference to ideal norms.[108] Drawing up 'a sort of balance sheet of the seminars' which were held in Autumn 1987, he mentions 'the problem of the relations between the juridical professions and the world of business'.[109] The summary of these seminars published in the *Annuaire du Collège de France* suggests that the different participants often revealed the influence of factors of the structuration of the juridical universe: oppositions between a technical justice and a 'transactional and paternalistic' justice (Yves Dezalay), between 'pure' jurists and other more 'political' ones (Alain Bancaud), between a juridical pole and a therapeutic pole within the family justice system (Jacques Commaille). Cautiously ('I don't have an enquiry to base this on'),[110] Bourdieu mentions the contrast between business lawyers who 'earn a lot of money and have ethical standards that you could call loose' and the representatives of 'pure law', who tend to have the inverse properties.

This analysis of the law is an opportunity for Bourdieu to highlight the cross-checking that generates the chiasmatic structure of a field ('the bridges between the two poles are never broken'): the temporally dominant pole is led, in its own interest, to respect at least to some extent, through a 'pious hypocrisy', the 'pure' values that the other pole imposes.[111] Taking the example of the situation of the law in the United States in the 1980s, Bourdieu goes so far as to develop an apparently paradoxical hypothesis: a movement towards 'mercantilism' in a field does not necessarily produce a loss of autonomy; competition and cross-checking continue to operate. He concludes that 'for this reason there may be some progress towards the universal under quite unexpected conditions'.[112]

As Bourdieu's work progressed, he returned to the law and the jurists in the context of his later teaching, focusing on the State and the genesis of the modern State and the bureaucratic field. He concentrates then on the nobility of the gown that gave a universal form to its particular interests and in so doing contributed to the birth of the modern State. He mentions the way in which the jurists accumulated and concentrated 'a capital of specific competence' and gradually obliged the king to come to terms with them in encouraging the transition from a dynastic principle to a bureaucratic principle, from the 'house of the king to the reason of State'.[113] Bourdieu returned to the law again, but more rapidly, in 1993, when he looked at the threat that the 'power of journalism' brings to bear on the autonomy of certain social universes.[114]

The origins of sociology

The lectures include many parentheses relating to the social sciences, for example on the particular difficulty these disciplines have in 'letting go of common sense',[115] or the risk of importing technocratic common knowledge into scientific analysis.[116] Although all of Bourdieu's teaching includes this sort of metadiscourse, the long preamble that opens the way for 'a sociological critique of the social sciences'[117] is specific to the lectures of 1988. Bourdieu had been talking of 'a sociology of sociology' since at least *Le Métier de sociologue*,[118] and at different moments in his work he repeated that in his eyes it was not a 'specialism' among others but one of the primary conditions of a scientific sociology:[119] sociologists need to know the determinations that weigh down on them if they are to have the slightest chance of escaping them. If none of his major empirical research projects was directly concerned with the study of sociology, he did work in particular in the 1970s on universes that had links with the academic world, philosophy (through Heidegger) and science.[120] In 1975, speaking of 'colonial science', he insisted on the importance of the historical dimension in the 'sociology of a sociologist',[121] because of the fact that 'the unconscious of a discipline' is its history.[122] As time went by, he tended to speak rather – or more generally – of a 'social history of the social sciences'.[123] The sketch that he offered in 1988 of a 'comparative history of the relations between the field of the social sciences and the bureaucratic field'[124] is perhaps one of his most substantial essays in this area.

In 1968 in *Le Métier de sociologue*, which affirmed the need to 'construct the object of study', Bourdieu had already insisted on the fact that sociologists are vulnerable to 'extrinsic [. . .] demands'[125] and that they should resist 'the claims of social problems to exist as sociological problems'. Ten years or so later he noted that 'no one – among those who are in position to command or commission it – [. . .] really asks for the truth about the social world', and he infers that 'a really scientific sociology is a social practice that, sociologically, should not exist', so that it has no option but to advance in disguise.[126] In a sense, he repeats this conclusion in the lectures for 1988 in noting that there is no 'social demand [. . .] for pure scientificity, but a demand for *service*', and that 'nobody wants a true social science', 'because social science reveals things they don't want to know'. But the argument is now backed up with elements relating to the genesis of the discipline. It was not born of the working-class movement, as is sometimes said, but from the 'enlightened reaction' of a fraction of the dominant class, which, being connected with the State, asked it for some kind of assistance. As a result, sociology can only hope to develop into a 'pure science' on the margins, and, to use a word applied sometimes by Bourdieu to the autonomy of fields,[127] through a kind of detour. From this past history, sociology has inherited a notoriously persistent ambiguity, a tendency to seek to 'do good', to be useful.[128]

These historical factors, considered in conjunction with the problematic relations with the State, enhance Bourdieu's reflections on sociology. In *Le Métier de sociologue*, he was simply concerned with the question of the bias caused by the 'class ethnocentrism and the intellectual or professional ethnocentrism' of the sociologist. Thoughts of the State intervened only in the course of the lectures on general sociology. Here Bourdieu's main point, mentioned on several occasions, was the difference between the categories of 'a sociologist who is independent, believing in his independence, and a bureaucratic State sociology like INSEE'.[129] Here he warns more than once of the risk of objectivism, which he associates with the temptation to adopt a technocratic posture, and pose as the 'sociologist-king'. By showing the place of the State at the origins, and thereby in the unconscious, of the discipline, the analysis of 1988 is much more explicit. Bourdieu can for instance henceforth announce – and offer a historical explanation for his observation – that 'the official representation that the discipline sociology gives of itself' tends to reproduce 'the official representation that the State gives of itself'. He also posits 'the antinomy of the social sciences': they can only assert their autonomy by relying on a State which is a source of constraint; they have to 'use against the State the relative liberty that the State allows them'. Bourdieu is thus led to highlight Durkheim's often repressed (or unnoticed) and potentially problematic relation to the State, whether the Third Republic or the Commune, and thereby to articulate, no doubt more explicitly than elsewhere, his difference from Durkheim, particularly in terms of reflexivity.[130]

Disinterestedness and the universal

The lectures of 1987–88 and 1988–89 were delivered under a title alluding to the State, but, as Bourdieu points out at one point, the problem of disinterestedness runs right through the lectures.[131] The first year starts with three lectures focused on the juridical field, 'a universe in which disinterestedness attracts interest'.[132] Later, Bourdieu examines theories of the State that describe a disinterested institution and others which on the contrary call into question the sincerity of disinterested service of the State. He finally raises, this time on the subject of the social sciences, 'the question of disinterestedness' that he says they are tempted to 'avoid'.[133] The following year, in Lyon as in Paris, but in different forms, he raises the question as to 'whether a disinterested action is possible'.[134] His argument turns above all on a 'bureaucratic field' whose law is 'the obligation of disinterestedness' or 'public service'; 'the social agents do not engage their personal interest [in it] and they sacrifice their own interests to the public, to public service, to the universal'.[135]

As the opposite of (individual) interest, disinterestedness is indeed on the side of the universal. The latter is another theme of philosophical origin that traverses Bourdieu's lectures, and he concludes his teaching for 1988–89 by speaking of 'a process in which the agents with an interest in the universal create a game in which the universal bears interest'.[136] The apparently rather disparate objects of study that he deals with – the State, the law, the genesis of the social sciences, the bureaucratic space, the 'professions' – tend to converge on the same family of problems. He sometimes draws the attention of his audience to this point, for instance in the Lecture of 14 April 1988 when he emphasizes the fact that 'one and the same problem', that of the 'universal class' and the 'free space', is posed in the case of the State, the 'juridical universe', 'the State thinkers' and the 'sociologist who claims to be a scientist'; indeed, jurists, technocrats and sociologists seem each in their turn to claim that they are situated at a point in the social space which is 'somehow outside the game',[137] bereft of individual interest, representing a 'position with the property of not being a position'.

The questions of disinterestedness and the universal did not suddenly burst into Bourdieu's thinking in 1988 out of nowhere, any more than did the question that he also raises in the lectures, namely that of the historicity of reason. This latter problem – which took a central place again in a later series of lectures[138] – was already present in one of his first articles on the scientific field.[139] As for disinterestedness, Bourdieu had already dealt with it, in particular in *The Logic of Practice* (1980), in a review of the debate on the gift instigated by Marcel Mauss.[140] He had already noted the profits that groups derive from 'the appearance of disinterestedness' and spoken of the need to 'escape the alternative of purely material, narrowly economic interest, and of disinterestedness', while still reaffirming the 'principle of sufficient reason, which means that there should not be any action without a reason'.[141] But these remarks remained fairly incidental: the terms 'disinterested' and 'disinterestedness' are used no more than a dozen times in *The Logic of Practice*.

The public lectures published here represent at the very least an expansion of the theme. As witness in particular the frequent developments they contain on the possibility of virtue and on pure moral action, which in a Kantian perspective should be inspired by respect for the moral law alone and not correspond to any interest (Lectures of 24 March 1988, 19 and 26 January 1989). Another sign of this development[142] is to be found in the references to the moralists of the seventeenth century (and Jansenism), authors that Bourdieu, normally, does not much quote. The lectures are almost placed under the sign of a maxim by La Rochefoucauld: 'hypocrisy is a tribute that vice pays to virtue'. For indeed, one central argument of the lectures – akin to the reasons which, at the start of his lectures in Lyon, Bourdieu cites to justify his usage of the notion of interest[143] – is modelled on the procedure of the moralists when they detect behind the mask of generosity the expression of 'self-love' or selfish interest. These lectures of 1988 show if not a renewal then at least an increase in the attention that Bourdieu pays to the ambivalence (or perhaps 'benefits') of hypocrisy. He attributes to Alain Bancaud the introduction of the formula 'pious hypocrisy', in the seminar discussion on law. He repeats it[144] and uses it, outside the context of the example of law,[145] in relation to a crucial element of his reflection: the 'pious but hypocritical' act whereby a social agent ('the jurists who cloak their decisions in a so-called juridical reasoning' are only one particular example), in placing himself in external conformity with the rule of logic of the group, brings us 'a little closer to the universal'.[146]

Returning to these questions, Bourdieu replies to those philosophers who are tempted to associate the social sciences once and for all time with utilitarianism or relativism (in some cases to be shot of them with the least effort). His analysis of disinterestedness can also be linked to the return in the 1980s of theories of the rational actor (the Chicago School for economics, 'methodological individualism' for sociology . . .), for whom disinterested actions and even 'collective action' are fundamentally self-contradictory. Bourdieu thus replied to those who, drawing on his frequent use of the notion of 'interest', assimilate his sociology to a form of utilitarianism.[147] In the case of the historicity of reason, the lectures suggest that Bourdieu reacted strongly to the publication (in 1981) and then the French translation (1987) of *The Theory of Communicative Action* by Jürgen Habermas, a thinker with whom Bourdieu had had points in common, as well as disagreements, since the 1960s.[148]

Contemporary debates or the feeling of being misread do not explain everything. The possibility of a virtuous action (which is a challenge for the social sciences since, as Bourdieu argued in Lyon,[149] it calls into question the principle of sufficient reason that orients scientific procedure), like the question of the historicity of reason (which implicates the very status of the 'truths' that sociology can hope to produce) are solicited by the very logic of Bourdieu's work. These lectures are part of a process of evolution which led him to progressively disentangle the implications of his research, a process which ten years later saw *Pascalian Meditations* mark a high point (with the questions broached in 1988 revisited). Bourdieu also explains[150] that a philosophical question like that of disinterestedness is one of the questions that a State sociology must raise, to avoid falling victim to one of the two visions of the State – diametrically opposed but in his eyes equally suspect – which are expressed for instance in Hegel and Marx. The terms 'disinterestedness' and 'universal', moreover, are in a sense no more than new ways of naming (and thereby apprehending) something that, in his earlier work, was designated by other words. Autonomy in the fields of cultural production thus corresponds to apparently disinterested actions, and 'the claim to universality' is, as Bourdieu noted in a lecture in 1986, one of the characteristics common to the fields of cultural production.[151]

Thus we can reasonably say that Bourdieu draws on his own work for solutions to the specific problems that he raises here, or that he uses the latter to explore new implications in his work on fields. What he brings to the fore in these lectures of 1988 and 1989 is the (not universal) existence of universes where agents fight for 'the monopoly of the universal' and help to 'promote [. . .] truths' that escape relativism. His demonstration leads him to put forward the idea of an 'interest in disinterestedness', an apparent paradox which enables him to avoid the opposition between individual interest and general interest.

In the universes where such an interest pertains, disinterested actions are objectively possible without the social agents necessarily being personally virtuous, without them obeying the call of duty exclusively. Bourdieu's demonstration also subsumes his analysis of the differentiation of the social world into associated fields, each with their own types of capital and interest. A last point – which he had not emphasized previously – is the affirmation that disinterestedness and the universal would tend to be universally rewarded.

Defending the universal

One final element may help to shed light on the lectures published here. At the end of the 1980s Bourdieu was nearly sixty, and was working and debating more and more on the international stage. He continued, as he had done for many years, to attend conferences in Europe, but he also spent two sessions (March–April 1987 and April 1989) in universities in the United States and visited Japan in October 1989. In the United States his contribution took as his object of study the international social field, although this now included him as an increasingly efficient participant himself. Bourdieu had kept up to date since the 1960s with the sociological production of the United States, but his elaboration of insights into the 'professions' (and the 'Capitoline triad'), his allusions to the relation of the American sociologists to the State, and his reference to the 'comparative history' of sociology that he produced in 1988, tend to locate the lectures of 1988 and 1989 squarely in an international scene. Moreover, the lectures include observations on the United States: the acknowledgement of the importance of a 'civic religion' in that country,[152] but also the comparison of French and American law, which marks an attempt, unprecedented in Bourdieu's work, to extend the concept of field to the American example.[153]

In France his fame had also been progressively growing since the beginning of the decade and his activities outside research strictly speaking were increasingly numerous. In 1985 he had been an active participant in the publication of a series of propositions on the educational system that the professors of the Collège de France had submitted to the President of the Republic, François Mitterrand. The 1988 lectures took place in the weeks preceding the election of Mitterrand in May and the nomination of Michel Rocard to the position of prime minister. If Bourdieu – despite his disappointment at the feeble effects of the 1985 report – agreed to be co-president of a commission on school syllabuses in 1989, his most striking political action during this period was the publication of an opinion piece in *Le Monde* on 16 September 1988.[154] Bourdieu's 'sole intervention in favour of a sitting government'[155] seems also to be the first article reacting to current affairs that he published in this paper.

Although it also ranges more widely, the article credits Michel Rocard's government, unlike its predecessor, with having sought a peaceful solution to the conflict separating partisans and opponents of independence in New Caledonia. This text is clearly in tune with Bourdieu's teaching at the Collège de France. Its title is 'Civic Virtue', a notion that Bourdieu mentions in passing in one of the lectures, attributing its invention to 'the civic humanism of the civil service'.[156] In another echo of the lectures,[157] the article opens with the observation that 'the gap between professionals and the profane in political matters has continued to grow, as has awareness of the specific logic of the game of politics'. Above all, he discusses disinterestedness and the opposition between 'decisions that are grounded in the interests fuelled by competition for some exalted post or other' and the 'demands for disinterestedness that are written into the democratic delegation of power'.[158] Bourdieu salutes as 'exemplary' the attitude of a government that prefers 'to put itself at the service of problems, at the risk of not lasting, rather than exploiting problems in order to survive at all costs'.[159] In addition to paying homage to this act of 'political courage', Bourdieu, drawing the consequences of the analyses he has been developing in his lectures, makes an appeal for 'objective mechanisms able in practice to impose a discipline of civic virtue on politicians',[160] since disinterestedness cannot safely rely on 'moral dispositions' alone.

The linguist Pierre Encrevé, at that time an adviser to Michel Rocard, reports that Bourdieu (the two men had known each other since at least the 1970s) was one of a group of intellectuals that Rocard invited to advise him in the winter of 1988–89, and that on several occasions in 1990–91 he met the prime minister or one of his counsellors to make observations on the exercise of power, drawing on his work in his lectures on the State.[161] This relative closeness to the left wing of the government soon came to an end. Bourdieu became increasingly critical of the Socialist Party, as witness his publication in 1993 of *The Weight of the World*, which draws up a balance sheet of fourteen years of 'socialism'.[162] A central thrust of Bourdieu's political interventions, which were now more numerous than in the past, was oriented, particularly after the social movement of 1995,[163] towards a critique of the politicians of neoliberal inspiration who were working away at dismantling the State and 'public service', those institutions whose genesis he had studied in his lectures at the Collège de France. In a way Bourdieu was finding a passage between the positive and the normative – the difficulty of which he recalls on several occasions in the lectures published here (10 March and 21 April 1988): the stances he adopted in favour of public service in the 1990s are based on the analyses of the State that he elaborated at the Collège de France from 1988 in very objective tones (there are only a few very rapid allusions to contemporary debates on the place of the State, and one or two parentheses where an obvious but discreet sympathy for d'Aguesseau shows through,[164] which escape this constative register).

The lectures of 1988 and 1989 occurred at a time which retrospectively appears important in the process that led Bourdieu to increase the number of his public pronouncements. Although *The State Nobility*, published in March 1989, was a scientific study destined by its subject and its size to attract a relatively limited public, its title was nonetheless a form of address to the media and to the political leaders who were preparing to celebrate in July 1989 the bicentenary of the abolition of privileges.[165] Bourdieu's opinion is that this 'State nobility', heir to the nobility of the gown that had invented the State, had converted itself radically to a liberal ideology which paradoxically promotes the withering away of the State institutions. The year 1789 was also marked in October by the launch of the first issue of *Liber-Revue européenne des livres*, a termly supplement published in five European papers (*Le Monde* in France), which Bourdieu hoped would 'broadcast to Europe and the world the cultural news that the journalists [no longer cover, preferring to] leave in the shadows everything "interesting", that is, "disinterested"'.[166]

The article on 'civic virtue' in September 1988 signalled his aspiration to invest more strongly in the public debate. Bourdieu concluded it with an invitation to 'citizens, or intellectuals, [. . .] who have the leisure and the means, to exercise their right to consider the political world', to 'participate, with others, in particular the journalists, in the exercise of civic vigilance' to 'help to establish a political world where the political authorities would be interested in virtue'.[167] He argued that it might be time to put an end to 'the silence of the intellectuals', a theme widespread in the 1980s when the left was in power, and the action he envisaged was none other than the control or cross-checking that he discusses in the lectures: within the field of power the relation between intellectuals and political authorities tends to be homologous with the relation which in the universe of law links the 'pure' jurists to those who are more oriented towards business. In 1988 Bourdieu hoped to associate the journalists with this vigilance. In the 1990s he became more pessimistic on this subject.

The lectures, then, were delivered at a time when Bourdieu was tending to adopt and theorize the role of the critical intellectual more intensely than at other periods in his career. The principal role he assigns to the intellectual is to defend and promote in political debate the 'universal' that he mentions in his lectures, that is, a historical conquest that is the outcome of the autonomization of the fields of cultural production. In May 1989 he delivered an address[168] which cited 'the particular reasons that today, with special urgency, call for a mobilization of the intellectuals' in order to 'defend the autonomy of the field'.[169] He called on cultural producers to 'be aware of their interests' and to place them at the service 'of the universal values that they promote, with the help of autonomy, in the protected universes of art, literature or science'.[170] On this subject he speaks of a 'corporatism of the universal', an alliance of contradictory terms of the same ilk as 'the interest in disinterestedness' and which implies a similar reasoning: just as, in a universe devoted to the public good, agents can serve the general interest while following their individual interest, so the intellectuals, acting in a universe oriented towards the universal, promote universal values in defending their individual interests.

The intellectual commitment recommended by Bourdieu from the end of the 1980s must be considered in conjunction with another central issue in the lectures of 1988 and 1989: the observation that the 'State nobility' which dominates today has imposed itself by choosing the universal as the orientation of its ends. In Lyon, Bourdieu drew the political conclusions:

> one of the difficulties of the political struggle today is that the dominants, technocrats or epistemocrats on the right or the left, are hand in glove with reason and the universal: one makes one's way through universes in which more and more technical, rational justifications will be necessary in order to dominate and in which the dominated can and must also use reason to defend themselves against domination, because the dominants must increasingly invoke reason, and science, to exert their domination.[171]

This is the source of Bourdieu's conviction that the social sciences have a specific role to play in contemporary political struggles and that they have a sort of duty to broadcast the knowledge they produce. This vision of things was in particular behind the creation of the publishing house Liber-Raisons d'agir in 1996.

Summaries of the Lectures
Published in the Annual of the Collège de France

1987–1988: On the State

In the first instance, a series of seminars was devoted to the discussion of research into the sociology of law.

Yves Dezalay, researcher at the Centre for Interdisciplinary Research at Vaucresson, presented for discussion a paper on the political and professional stakes of negotiated justice, showing, by way of a comparison of the different national traditions (Germany, France, United Kingdom, United States), that the credibility of justice depends largely on the complementary opposition between a technical and highly professional justice designed for the 'haves' and a negotiated, paternalistic justice designed for the 'have nots', and especially the poor, a justice which took on very diverse forms, depending on time and circumstance, from relying on local notables, such as justices of the peace, up to the establishment of a division of labour between a professional judge and expert auxiliaries in dealing with the minor disputes of everyday living.

Alain Bancaud, researcher at the Centre for Interdisciplinary Research at Vaucresson, analysed the art of interpretation, a technique specific to the Cour de cassation [Supreme Court of Appeal], and the 'pious hypocrisy' thanks to which politically and juridically novel decisions manage to espouse traditional forms; he also examined the social conditions of acquisition of the art of reading that is inseparable from an art of living and a whole vision of the social world. He continued all the while to take into account the position of the Supreme Court of Appeal in the sub-field of higher justice, where a subtle division of labour between 'pure' jurists and more 'political' jurists has been established.

Basing himself on recent changes in the juridical treatment of businesses in difficulty, Yves Dezalay analysed the redefinition of the division of labour between the business notable (the receiver), the jurist and the expert, caused by the crisis (with the increase in bankruptcies) and the importation of the American model of the professional management consultant.

According to Anne Boigeol, researcher at the Centre for Interdisciplinary Research at Vaucresson, the history of the confrontations and conflicts between different fractions of magistrates (who, because of their position in the hierarchy and their social and professional trajectory, do not share the same amount of interest in the establishment of an academic system of recruitment and training for the magistrature) leads us to interpret the creation of the National School of Magistrature as a response to the devaluation of the social capital of the magistrature compared to the other juridical professions – and indeed, compared to other leading positions in general, as a consequence notably of the creation of the ENA. But she also raises the very general question of the move from a mode of reproduction founded principally on the family transmission of an art to a genuinely academic mode of reproduction, aiming to transmit explicitly, that is, through a training pedagogically designed for the purpose, an expressly defined and designated competence.

Jacques Commaille, Director of Research at the Centre for Interdisciplinary Research at Vaucresson, showed that, if the diversity of forms of family justice, which oscillates between a juridical pole and a therapeutic pole (with for instance the abortive attempt to create family courts), can be interpreted in terms of struggles between diverse bodies of professionals, it should also be seen in the light of changes in the family as a political entity, especially if we want to explain developments linked with decentralization, as in the case of justice for minors. Antoine Garapon, Director of the Laboratory for Juridical Sociology in Paris, tried to show that the analysis of judicial practices could be based on three pairs of fundamental oppositions: between justice as ritual and justice as lawyers' practice; between justice negotiated and justice imposed; and between the equitable trial and the bureaucratic trial. The judge, taking into account the demands and constraints germane to each type of conflict or clientele, is then able to draw on the reservoir of multiple resources offered by this combination of possibilities.

The first part of [Pierre Bourdieu's] course of lectures was devoted to noting these seminars on the juridical field, which also served as an enquiry into the problem of the State. The notion of a juridical field, which was broached in some of the research presented at the seminars, has the initial advantage of enabling us to escape the alternative that seems to loom whenever we want to interpret a learned work (whether philosophical, literary, artistic or even scientific): an internal analysis which, like the history of law practised by the jurists, postulates the independence of juridical form from the social world, and which, particularly in Kelsen's work, seeks through a specific and absolutely irreducible mode of thought to found a pure theory, is opposed by an external analysis which reduces the law (as it does the State) to its function as an instrument of domination, aiming to establish relations of direct dependence between a 'juridical ideology' and the social groups whose interests it is supposed to serve, ignoring the actual structure of the juridical discourse. Breaking away from these two opposing positions inevitably implies a second break, indispensable for understanding the dual truth of 'juridical science': a break with the representation that the legal professionals offer to others and have of themselves; a break with the naively critical representation of the 'semi-learned' critics that describes the professional ethic as a 'professional ideology'. The agents engaged in the juridical field cannot avoid being caught up in their own game (*illusio*), if only by the logic of the 'pious hypocrisy' mentioned by Alain Bancaud, and, among other factors, the obligatory reference to a corpus of norms claiming universality, and to the values of righteousness appropriate for those who lay down the law, does have a real impact on practice.

The ideal values claimed by the juridical professions are the product of a collective work of invention which is inseparable from the process of constitution of a juridical field, an order separate and autonomous from the political powers and from the market, an order where certain ideals of disinterestedness are explicitly professed, and sometimes imposed as the norm for practice, in a quasi-judicial manner. Thus we analysed a certain number of texts (in particular the 'Discourse on the Independence of the Advocate' of 1693) in which the Chancellor d'Aguesseau, often invoked as one of the 'founding fathers' of modern justice, draws on a whole tradition of political philosophy to elaborate a representation of the magistrature as an agency able to affirm its independence from the political and economic powers, and its dedication to the 'public'. We also examined how this symbolic work of construction of a representation of the profession of magistrate or advocate developed, above all in the nineteenth century, into a process of codification of the 'rules of the profession of advocate', which was intended above all to regulate the conduct of advocates in matters of finance and business affairs. Even in cases where it is particularly weak, as in the United States at the end of the nineteenth century, autonomy from political and economic constraints and compromise is always claimed by the jurists and even by their clients. But from the end of the nineteenth century in the United States, and above all after the Second World War in France, the principles and rules designed to mark the distance between the juridical field and the economic field weakened. Like the literary field, the juridical field tends to be organized around a chiastic structure: at one pole we have the juridical theory, virtually monopolized by the professors, the 'pure' law of the superior agencies charged with safeguarding the letter and the spirit of the law, like the Cour de cassation [Supreme Court of Appeal], and finally the law traditionally practised in the courts, so many productions that procure more prestige than material profit; the other pole is occupied by business law which, directly engaged in the compromises and concessions of economic life, procures more material than symbolic profits. But it would be naive to conclude that the changes in the relations between the economic field and the juridical field resulting from the increasing reinforcement of the pole nearest to the economic world implies a weakening of the autonomy of the juridical field. In fact, in a universe dominated by reference to the values of universality and disinterestedness, competition engenders mutual checks and sanctions and tends to impose a respect for the fundamental norm of the juridical field, that is, the recognition of law, which does not depend on the individual's disposition towards virtue. So it is, for example, that the commercial jurists, often condemned by the 'integrists', can only fulfil their economic functions in negotiating contracts, founding companies, arbitrating or settling agreements between groups, on condition that they keep to their role as jurists and pay homage, even if purely verbal, to the guardians of the pure law. The 'temple merchants' can thus be perceived as the pioneers of the universal, who make the law advance on terrains where it was absent, as missionaries in heathen lands; who, as a Boston business lawyer said, fulfil a 'civilization function', a function of moralization of economic life. As the expression 'litigociation' – referring to legal negotiations entered into in order to avoid firms going to court – puts it so well, the economy penetrates the law, but as the law also penetrates the economy, the law changes while changing a changing reality, redefining ways of thinking of the company, which, as Yves Dezalay clearly shows, turns the intervention of a jurist in filing for bankruptcy, for instance, into an act of management.

In the end, we see that the juridical reason that emerges from a sociological analysis of the juridical field is opposed to the social philosophy of thinkers like Habermas who, like the Durkheimians, seek an objective ground for a normative reason and aim to base a normative and universal definition of reason on their positive analysis of communication. This 'well-founded fiction' or 'pious hypocrisy', which consists in passing off contingent and socially determined verdicts as the necessary conclusion of a deduction deriving from universal principles, finds the principle of its social existence and efficacy in the existence and operations of the juridical field: in this closed and regulated universe that is the contingent product of a long historical work of representation, representations and practices relatively independent of individual interests are produced and reproduced, thanks to struggles often fiercely 'interested' (in a sense that is not that of the utilitarians).

As a logical progression from this reflection on the historical genesis of a social microcosm (the juridical field) functioning under the sign of the universal, we moved on – much later than we had intended – to what was meant to be the principal object of the course this year: the analysis of the State and the bureaucracy. Of all 'social problems', the problem of the State is no doubt the one that is most difficult to convert into a sociological problem. In fact, as is shown by the fact that the public administrations and their representatives are great producers of 'social problems' which social science often merely ratifies in taking them on board without examining them, the State, as holder of the monopoly of legitimate symbolic violence, has the means to propose and impose an authorized mode of thinking of the social world and in particular of itself: the sociologist who undertakes to think on the State runs the risk of applying to the State categories of thought produced and guaranteed by the State (even more so when he is a State employee). To give himself some chance of clear thinking on a State that continues to think through those who are striving to think it, he must therefore proceed to a kind of radical doubt and attempt to call into question all the presumptions and preconstructions that are embedded both in the reality that needs to be thought and in the thought processes of the analyses themselves.

To this end, we undertook to analyse, treating them as exemplary anthropological documents, the two theories that map out the space of possibilities for considering the theory of the State, that of Hegel (and its variant in Durkheim) and that of Marx: on the one hand bureaucracy as a 'universal group' endowed with insight into the universal interest and the will to achieve it; on the other hand the corps of bureaucrats as usurpers of the universal, acting as private owners of public resources. (We note in passing how, as in the case of law, the naivety of the first theory in accepting the internal representation, and the naivety of the second in opposing that with its cynical, disenchanted vision, compound each other to prevent us from producing a representation that would combine a realistic description of the causes and effects of bureaucratic action and a reference to the values of impartiality and disinterested dedication to public well-being.) We only have to pass from Hegel to Durkheim (who, while sometimes professing the greatest prudence in the matter, treats the State as an 'organ of reflection' and a rational instrument charged with realizing the general interest) to see how difficult it is to escape the clutches of the State when thinking of the State: if the thinking of the State sociologist is riven through and through by official representations of the official, it is because, as we saw with the Chancellor d'Aguesseau, the State, and the civil servant conceived as servant of the 'public', are the culmination of a symbolic process aiming to produce and impose an official representation of the State as a site of universality at the service of the general interest.

Social science itself is part and parcel of this effort to construct a representation of the State, which is part of the actual reality of the State (as we can clearly see in the link between the State and statistics). All the problems that affect the study of bureaucracy also affect sociology when it claims to study the impartiality or disinterestedness of the bureaucracy, but at a higher degree of difficulty, since we can question its autonomy from the State and its professed claim to autonomy (as we see in the case of Durkheim making the sociologist the incarnation par excellence of the civil servant's reflexivity and universality).

We need then to question the relation of sociology to the State, and at least to lay out the plan for a social history of the genesis of the social sciences (trying once again to avoid the common alternative, which sees the social sciences either as an instrument of enlightened transformation, or else as an instrument of manipulation). Although we can locate its origins further back in time (by including the political philosophy of the counsellors of the prince), social science properly speaking was brought into existence by the 'social movements' and socialism, but only indirectly, through the will to counter them with the enlightened response of a social reformism. It found its first defenders in that sort of avant-garde of the dominant, the reformers and philanthropists, etc., who hoped that 'social economics' (an ancillary science, auxiliary to 'political economics') would help them find a solution to the 'social problems' posed by 'problem' groups and individuals. State sociology and the sociology of the relation between sociology and the State enjoy a relation of mutual dependence: to have some chance of thinking the State adequately, the sociologist has to think of the unthought relation with the State which, through an ensemble of social conditions that act to determine the possibilities of his activity, commands his first thinking on the State; and it is only from a history of the State that he can expect to draw a true comprehension of the truth of his relation to the

State. A brief comparative history of the development of the social sciences allows us to suggest that a model aiming to account for the state of the social sciences at different times and in different nations should take into account two fundamental factors: firstly, the form taken by the social demand for knowledge of the social world, particularly in the light of the dominant philosophy in the State bureaucracies (liberalism or Keynesianism, etc.), since a strong State demand is able to ensure the development of a social science relatively independent of economic forces (and the demands of the dominant), albeit strongly dependent on the State; and secondly, the degree of independence of the educational system and the scientific field from the economic and political powers, which is no doubt one of the major conditions for the development of a social science independent of these powers. Everything seems to indicate that the social sciences can only affirm their autonomy from the social forces by relying on the State, which means they are then at risk of losing their autonomy from it. And no doubt they can only become sciences like any other; that is, suffering no obligations or sanctions other than scientific – an independence which is particularly indispensable for them when they aim to apply it to the State that has made them possible – on condition that they use against the State the (relative) freedom that the State affords them.

1988–1989: On the State (sequel)

Before continuing with our project to examine the specific logic of a universe, the bureaucratic field, which has adopted as its official rule the obligation to be disinterested, we chose first to investigate (in the lectures given in Lyon) the anthropological roots of the notions of interest and disinterestedness. The notion of interest is a decisive instrument in the break with certain spontaneous representations of action, and in particular with the moralism of those fine souls who, above all when it concerns universes they belong to, reject as 'reductive' any attempt to 'explain away' practices or trace their 'necessary' dependency by tracking down their economic or symbolic determinants. But because of the connotations associated with the dominant use of this notion (as we see for instance in the expression 'interest understood'), the analyses that use it risk being submitted to a double reduction: firstly, interest may be reduced to specifically economic interest (following the everyday opposition between what is free or given away and what is lucrative); secondly, action associated with 'interest understood' may be reduced to an action consciously organized with a view to satisfying that interest. The combination of a narrowly intellectual view of action, which makes conscious, rational calculation the principle underlying all action (as for instance in the current vogue for 'rational action theory'), with an economism identifying all social economics with the specific economics of the economic field, leads to a form of utilitarianism which is utterly incapable of explaining the most ordinary human behaviour, even in the economic field strictly speaking. So we need to return to the relation (analysed in the previous course of lectures) between the habitus and the field (and more precisely the different fields that constitute a differentiated social world), seen as *illusio*, 'investment' in the game and interest in the game (as opposed to indifference, apathy and ataraxia), which is the foundation of the interests (in the sense of investments) that are at stake; and to analyse the temporal structure of this feel for the game as anticipation or pre-occupation, that is, as reference to a future inscribed in the immediate present (under the guise of 'something that needs doing', etc.), as opposed to a project or plan targeting the future, with one possibility seen as one among various other possibilities. Thus we see that an agent attuned to the constraints of the field – which a statistical analysis records as so many percentage probabilities – can attain objectives that he has not strictly speaking pursued; without the slightest hint of calculation, and even less of cynicism, he can attain objectives that he has not formulated as such. This is what occurs in a number of fields with which we very commonly associate the idea of disinterestedness, like the religious field, the artistic field, the scientific field or even the bureaucratic field: the agents there produce actions and discourse that are doubly 'disinterested' – in the ordinary sense of the word – since they are not motivated by a conscious intention or a rational calculation oriented towards obtaining economic profit (in the restricted sense).

This does not mean that they don't obey a particular form of interest or *libido*: just as a certain strain of religious reflection has questioned the validity of lives that are exemplary but suspect of being guided by a search for the profits accruing to a saintly reputation, so we may wonder whether the purest *libido sciendi* might not mask a certain *libido dominandi*, and likewise with all the specific forms of *libido* that are associated with the different fields. Having restricted the gambit of consciousness and calculation – in favour of the feel for the game – but meanwhile conversely expanding the influence of interest to include in particular all the forms of symbolic interest, we discover outside the economic sphere strictly speaking the existence of behaviour that, without being the product of a conscious calculation of interest, nonetheless obeys the laws of a certain form of interest. This is what is suggested for instance by the formula 'noblesse oblige': in fact nobility obliges the nobleman, it forces him to act nobly; incorporated in the form of dispositions left by a conscious or unconscious education, it becomes an unavoidable principle of practice, a habitus that, when confronted in a sustained and lasting manner with a universe equipped to reward his accomplishments ('glory', 'honour', etc.) and punish his failures ('shame', 'dishonour', etc.), can lead to extreme forms of sacrifice; the tendency of the habitus to perpetuate itself (even beyond the circumstances of its production) can even impose the obliteration of the body that serves as its vehicle (*pro patria mori*).

The question of a disinterestedness that rejects economic interest or more generally all kinds of selfish interest, material or symbolic, brings us to the question of the social conditions liable to generate social universes that would take as their law submission to the general interest or dedication to public service and which, in a word, would create the conditions favouring the emergence of an interest in disinterestedness and thereby of an altruistic habitus of abnegation and dedication. As is shown by the universal existence of strategies of universalization of individual interest (whereby agents aim to get the universal, that is, the group, on their side by getting on the right side of the rules that claim to be universal), we can admit that the universal is the object of universal recognition and that the sacrifice of selfish (especially economic) interests is universally recognized as legitimate (the collective judgement of the groups cannot fail to recognize in the transition from the selfish individual view to the point of view of the group a recognition of the value of the group and of the group as the foundation of all value, therefore a transition from 'is' to 'ought'). This implies that all the social universes tend to offer the symbolic profits of universalization to different degrees (the very same profits as those sought by strategies aiming to 'get on the right side of the rules'). And it also implies that the universes which, like the bureaucratic field, are most insistent in demanding submission to the universal are particularly disposed to produce such profits – and by the same token particularly exposed to suspicious eyes which see in all action claiming to be universal the universalization of a particular interest. It is significant that administrative law – which, in aiming to establish a universe of dedication to the general interest, takes as its fundamental law the obligation of disinterestedness – establishes suspicion of generosity as a practical principle for evaluating practices: 'the administration does not give presents'; the administrative action that benefits a private person in such personalized ways that it can seem to be the servant of private interest is suspect, or even illicit.

The profit of universalization is no doubt one of the historical motors of the advance of the universal. This is true insofar as it favours the creation of a universe where universal values (reason, virtue, etc.) are recognized, at least verbally, and where there is a process of mutual reinforcement between, on the one hand, the strategies of universalization aiming to obtain at least the negative benefits derived from conforming to the universal rules and, on the other hand, the structures of the universes officially dedicated to the universal. The bureaucratic field is one of these singular worlds that asks its agents to sacrifice their private interests for the obligations written into their function ('the agent owes himself entirely to his function') or, more realistically, for the specific interest that is rather vaguely indicated when we speak of 'the interests of the civil service'. And we can gain an idea of the real logic of the universes dedicated to the universal by confronting administrative law, the official norm of the universe of the official, with the reality of administrative practice as it is revealed (in particular) in a repertory of failures (which were in fact sanctioned) to observe the obligation of disinterestedness: these include for instance all the cases of 'private usage of a public service' (appropriation of public goods or services, corruption, or bribery, etc.) or, more perversely, the 'legal exceptions', waivers, influence peddling and the administrative blind eye, which amount to profiting from the non-application or the transgression of the law. Having thus revealed the essentially dual law of the bureaucratic universe (notably through comparison with the political field), we can submit to a critical examination the vast (and mostly Anglo-American) literature on the 'professions'; that is, in the terms we have been employing, the ensemble of agents or corps exercising, in the name of a technical competence guaranteed by the State, a political power, in denial. The majority of these studies, since in particular they fail to distinguish between field and corps, promote as a scientific description the idealized representation that the professionals make of themselves and their function (with notions such as 'collectivity orientation' in Parsons, or altruism and dedication to the 'common good'). But above all they forget that 'professional groups' depend doubly on the State, which guarantees their authority and their clientele, by assuring them of a protected market, through educational qualifications and the effect of the *numerus clausus*.

The dual logic (bordering on duplicity or schizophrenia) of the universes and agents dedicated to the universal is nowhere more clearly seen than in the history of the process of constitution of the bureaucratic field, which I have plotted in greater detail elsewhere. The nobility of the robe, whose inheritors, structurally speaking, are our contemporary technocrats, is a corps that came into being as it created the State; in order to construct itself as upholder of a new species of power and legitimacy, it was obliged to construct the State, which included, among other things, a whole philosophy of 'public service' as a disinterested activity oriented towards universal ends. In this way the *libido dominandi* developed into a principle of ethical progress, as much in discourse as in practice, by encouraging the establishment of universes in which civic virtue constitutes both an instrument and a stake in the struggles, and where, especially through the profits of universalization that they ensure, the development or perfection of an altruistic habitus can thrive. Unless we believe in miracles, or the possibility of ethical actions either gratuitous or having no motivation other than the resolution of pure will power (but the inability of 'rational action theory' to explain any kind of dedication to the collective is sufficient to cast doubt on this), we have to accept that the interest in disinterestedness or, to coin a phrase, the *libido virtutis*, provides no doubt the only, or at least the strongest, foundation of a socially durable order oriented towards what seems at every moment to be the universal.

Notes

Editorial Note

1 Pierre Bourdieu, *Science de la science et réflexivité* (Paris: Raisons d'agir, 2001); *Science of Science and Reflexivity*, trans. Richard Nice (Cambridge: Polity, 2004).
2 Pierre Bourdieu, *Sur l'État. Cours au Collège de France 1989–1992* (Paris: Seuil/ Raisons d'agir, 2012); *On the State*, trans. David Fernbach (Cambridge, Polity, 2014); Pierre Bourdieu, *Manet. Une révolution symbolique. Cours au Collège de France 1998–2000* (Paris: Seuil/Raisons d'agir, 2013); *Manet. A Symbolic Revolution*, trans. Peter Collier and Margaret Rigaud-Drayton (Cambridge: Polity, 2017).
3 Pierre Bourdieu, *Sociologie générale* (Paris: Seuil/Raisons d'agir, vol. 1, 2015; vol. 2, 2016). In English, the following five volumes translated by Peter Collier: *Classification Struggles* (2018), *Habitus and Field* (2020), *Forms of Capital* (2021), *Principles of Vision* (2022) and *Politics and Sociology* (2023) (Cambridge: Polity).
4 Pierre Bourdieu, *Anthropologie économique* (Paris: Seuil/Raisons d'agir, 2017).
5 Pierre Bourdieu, 'Intérêt et désintéressement', Cours du Collège de France à la Faculté d'anthropologie et sociologie de l'Université Lumière Lyon 2, 1 and 2 December 1988, *Cahiers de recherche du Groupe de recherche sur la socialisation*, no. 7, September 1989 [republished in 1993]; 'Un acte désintéressé est-il possible?', in *Raisons pratiques. Sur la théorie de l'action* (Paris: Seuil, 1994), pp. 147–67; *Practical Reason: On the Theory of Action*, trans. Randal Johnson (Cambridge: Polity, 1998), pp. 75–91.
6 The lectures seem to have been slightly shorter in 1988–89 than in the previous year. The recordings used here – which unfortunately include interruptions – last about an hour on average.
7 See the editorial note in *On the State*, pp. 7–9.

Lecture of 10 March 1988

1 This is no doubt an allusion to the sort of remark that opens Durkheim's lectures on the State: 'There are few words whose definition is less precise.' Émile Durkheim, 'L'État (1900–1905)', in *Textes*, vol. 3, *Fonctions sociales et institutions* (Paris: Minuit, 1975, p. 172).

2 See Émile Durkheim, *The Rules of Sociological Method*, trans. Steven Lukes (London: Palgrave Macmillan, 2013 [1895]), especially the preface to the first edition, and chapter II.

3 In an interview with Loïc Wacquant, where he discusses the start of his course of lectures on the State, Bourdieu relates it to 'negative theology'.

4 These lectures were delivered in 1988, twenty years after May '68. The heritage of that movement was already starting to be frequently challenged in the political and intellectual fields.

5 A few years earlier Bourdieu had used this formula in the title of one of his articles: 'Le hit-parade des intellectuals français ou qui sera juge de la légitimité des juges?', *Actes de la recherche en sciences sociales*, no. 52–53, 1984, pp. 95–100.

6 There must have been a first reference at the start of the lecture (in the passage that is missing from our recording) to the seminar devoted to the discussion of the sociology of law that Bourdieu had organized in the context of his teaching at the Collège de France in 1987–88, with the participation of Alain Bancaud, Anne Boigeol, Jacques Commaille, Yves Dezalay, Antoine Garapon and Irène Théry. No. 76–77 of *Actes de la recherché en sciences sociales*, 'Droit et expertise', March 1989, arose partly from this seminar.

7 Pierre Bourdieu, 'La force du droit. Éléments pour une soiologie de champ juridique', *Actes de la recherche en sciences sociales*, no. 64, 1986, pp. 3–19.

8 See in particular Georg Lukács, *The Theory of the Novel*, trans. Anna Bostok (Cambridge MA: MIT Press, 1974 [1916]); Lucien Goldmann, *Towards a Sociology of the Novel*, trans. Alan Sheridan (London: Tavistock, 1977 [1963]); Theodor W. Adorno, *The Jargon of Authenticity*, trans. Knut Tarnowski and Frederic Will (London: Routledge, 1973 [1964]).

9 On this point see Pierre Bourdieu, 'Le marché des biens symboliques', *L'Année sociologique*, no. 22, 1971, pp. 49–126. See also a later lecture by Bourdieu (27 May 1993) where he refers to a youthful project which would have aimed to establish 'a pure theory of sociology and a sociology of pure theory'; see *Anthropologie économique*, p. 165.

10 Hans Kelsen, *Théorie pure du droit*, trans. Charles Eisenmann (Paris: Dalloz, 1962 [1934]).

11 A reference to an episode in *The Adventures of Baron Munchausen*, a German tale from the end of the eighteenth century: the Baron on horseback extracts himself from quicksand by pulling himself up by his hair. This amusing metaphor is common in philosophy; Bourdieu had already used it in the context of a lecture on science; see Lecture of 19 June 1986, *Politics and Sociology*, pp. 203–4.

12 Louis Althusser, 'Ideology and Ideological State Apparatuses (Notes Towards an Investigation)', in *Lenin and Philosophy and Other Essays*, trans. Ben Brewster (New York: Monthly Review Press, 1971), pp. 85–126.

13 A reference to Marx's analysis of religion: '*Religious* suffering is at one and the same time the *expression* of real suffering and a protest against real suffering. Religion is the sigh of the oppressed creature, the heart of a heartless world and the soul of soulless conditions. It is the *opium* of the people.' Karl Marx, 'Critique of Hegel's Philosophy of Right. Introduction', trans. Rodney Livingstone and Gregor Benton, in *Early Writings* (London: Penguin, 1992), p. 244.

14 In fact Charles Renouvier had studied not at the École normale supérieure but at the École Polytechnique.

15 The philosophical tradition attributes to the scholastic philosopher Jean Buridan the paradox of the ass that dies of hunger because it can't choose between the trough of oats and the pail of water that are offered to it. Buridan was commenting on Aristotle, who described 'the man who, though exceedingly hungry and thirsty, and both equally, yet being equidistant from food and drink, is therefore bound to stay where he is'. Aristotle, *On the Heavens*, trans. J.L. Stocks, Global Grey ebook, 2018 [1922], §295b32.

16 See in particular the Lectures of 2 November 1982 in *Habitus and Field* (pp. 83, 361–2) and 22 March 1984 in *Forms of Capital* (pp. 102, 330).

17 Huizinga writes that the spoilsport 'robs play of its illusion, *illusio*, a pregnant word which means literally "in-play" (from *inlusio*, *illudere* or *inludere*)'. Johan Huizinga, *Homo Ludens: A Study of the Play-Element in Culture* (London: Routledge, 1949 [1944]), p. 11.

18 An allusion to Raymond Barre (an ex-prime minister who at the time of these lectures was a candidate for the presidential election). Originally an academic, Barre claimed to keep his distance from party politicking and the political world, which he sometimes treated as a 'microcosm'. Among other examples, *Le Monde* reported one of his declarations in 1979: 'It is this kind of gobbledegook that ultimately ruins their credit in the eyes of public opinion. The public understands these problems and does not react with the peculiar morals of a microcosm where what seems important has no relation to anything essential.' 'Le débat européen est plein d'arrière-pensées pour 1981, déclare M. Barre', *Le Monde*, 5 June 1979.

19 No doubt an allusion to the death of Archimedes, as related by Plutarch: 'Suddenly he found himself confronted by a soldier who ordered him to follow him to go to meet Marcellus. He refused to leave before he had concluded the demonstration of his problem. The Roman, irritated, drew his sword and slew him.' Plutarch, *Parallel Lives*, vol. V, trans. Bernadette Perrin (Cambridge MA: Harvard University Press, Loeb Clasical Library, 1917), vol. V, XVII, 'Marcellus', p. 479.

20 A reference to the notion of *épistémè* developed by Michel Foucault, in particular in *The Order of Things: An Archaeology of the Human Sciences*, trans. Alan Sheridan (London: Routledge, 2001) and *Archaeology of Knowledge*, trans. A.M. Sheridan Smith (London: Routledge, 2002).

21 For developments of this vision and Bourdieu's criticism of it, see in particular the Lectures of 9 November 1982 in *Habitus and Field* and 3 May 1984 in *Forms of Capital*.

22 'In every system of morality, which I have hitherto met with, I have always remark'd that the author proceeds for some time in the ordinary way of reasoning, and establishes the being of a God, or makes observations concerning human affairs; when of a sudden I am surpriz'd to find, that instead of the usual copulations of propositions, is, and is not, I meet with no proposition that is not connected with an ought, or an ought not.' David Hume, *Treatise of Human Nature* (Oxford: Clarendon Press, 1896 [1739]), vol. III, p. 244.

23 A reference to the analogy with Baron Munchausen's adventures (see above, note 11).

24 Bourdieu mobilizes this text in *Homo Academicus*, trans. Peter Collier (Cambridge: Polity, 1988), chapter 2, 'The Conflict of the Faculties', pp. 36–72; see also *Classification Struggles*, p. 108 and *Habitus and Field*, p. 165.

25 Immanuel Kant, 'The Conflict of the Faculties', trans. Mary J. Gregor and

Robert Anchor, in *Religion and Rational Theory* (Cambridge: Cambridge University Press, 2001 [1798]), pp. 233–327. 'The lower faculty is the rank in the university that occupies itself with teachings which are not adopted as directives by order of a superior, or in so far as they are not adopted . . . So the philosophy faculty, because it must answer for the truth of the teachings it is to adopt or even allow, must be conceived as free and subject only to laws given by reason, not by the government' (p. 255).

26 A reference to René Descartes' procedure in his *Discourse on Method* (1637), which posits the *cogito* and refers to the 'long chains of reason, all quite simple and quite easy, which geometers are wont to employ'. René Descartes, *Discourse on Method*, trans. Arthur Wollaston (Harmondsworth: Penguin, 1960), p. 50.

27 Bourdieu had reflected at length on the concept of 'culture' in the 1960s in his seminars at the École pratique des hautes études.

28 See Pierre Bourdieu, *The Rules of Art: Genesis and Structure of the Literary Field*, trans. Susan Emanuel (Cambridge: Polity, 1996 [1992]), in particular pp. 243 and 299–300.

29 This passage refers in particular to Niklas Luhmann's 'Theory of Systems'. See Luhmann, *Social Systems*, trans. John Bednatz Jr. (Stanford: Stanford University Press, 1995 [1984]); 'Die Einheit des Rechtsystems', *Rechtstheorie*, no. 14, 1983, pp. 129–54. Bourdieu reproaches Luhmann explicitly in his article 'La force du droit' (see note 7, above) with 'not distinguishing the properly symbolic order of norms and doctrines [. . .] from the order of objective relations between the agents and institutions in competition for the monopoly of the right to lay down the law'.

30 The argument of the 'cunning of reason' is associated with Hegel: 'The special interest of passion is thus inseparable from the active development of a general principle: for it is from the special and determinate and from its negation, that the Universal results. Particularity contends with its like, and some loss is involved in the issue. It is not the general idea that is implicated in opposition and combat, and that is exposed to danger. It remains in the background, untouched and uninjured. This may be called the *cunning of reason* – that sets the passions to work for itself, while that which develops its existence through such impulsion pays the penalty, and offers loss.' G.W.F. Hegel, *Reason in History*, trans. J. Sibree (Kitchener: Batoche Books, 2001), p. 47.

31 Bourdieu, 'La force du droit'.

32 This is one of La Rochefoucauld's maxims (*Réflexions ou sentences et maximes morales*, 1678, §218).

33 A reference to the intervention by Alain Bancaud in the seminar on sociology of law mentioned above (see note 6). This intervention (see below, p. 242) was no doubt similar to his article 'Considérations sur une "pieuse hypocrisie": la forme des arrêts de la Cour de cassation', *Droit et société*, 7, no. 1, 1987, pp. 373–87.

34 A reference to a passage in Cicero: 'We are familiar with this comment by Cato, who was surprised that the soothsayer didn't burst out laughing when he saw another soothsayer' (*De divisione*, II, 51). The soothsayers read the future in the entrails of animals.

35 We have not found this reference. It may be the memory of a passage from Robert Musil (whose work Bourdieu is likely to have known, if only through the intermediary of Jacques Bouveresse who quotes it more than once): 'The

course of history is not like a billiard ball which, once launched, follows a defined trajectory; it resembles rather the movement of clouds or the steps of a man wandering down the road, upset by a shadow here and a group of strangers or an unfamiliar row of houses there, and who finally ends up somewhere unknown where he didn't intend to go. The path of history often loses its way.' Robert Musil, *The Man Without Qualities* [*Der Mann ohne Eigenschaften* [1930], my translation].

36 It has not been proven, but it is said that the phrase (*Ageômetrètos mêdeis eisitô*) was engraved over the entrance to the Academy, the school founded by Plato.

37 Henri François d'Aguesseau, *Oeuvres du chancellier d'Aguesseau*, publiées par l'abbé André, son bibliothéquaire, 13 vols (Paris: Libraries associés, 1759–89) (republished in augmented form in sixteen volumes in 1819).

38 Henri François d'Aguesseau, 'Discours pour l'ouverture des audiences du Parliament. Premier discours, prononcé en 1693: L'indépendence de l'avocat', in *Oeuvres complètes du Chancelier d'Aguesseau. Nouvelle édition augmentée de pièces échappées aux premiers éditeurs, et d'un discours préliminaire*, vol. I (Paris: Fantin et Compagnie – H. Nicolle – De Pelafol, 1819), pp. 1–13.

39 At the time of this lecture course, the Lefevre-d'Ormesson family included in particular a General Inspector of Finance (Henry), an author-journalist and Academician (Jean) and a politician (Olivier).

40 Marcel Rousselet, *Histoire de la magistrature française, des origines à nos jours*, 2 vols (Paris: Plon, 1957).

41 D'Aguesseau, 'Trente-septième plaidoyer, prononcé en deux audiences, la dernière le 10 janvier 1696 dans la cause de M. Le prince de Conty et de Madame la duchesse de Nemours', in *Oeuvres complètes du Chancelier d'Aguesseau*, vol. 3, p. 113.

42 Ernst Hartwig Kantorowicz, *The King's Two Bodies* (Princeton: Princeton University Press, 1957).

43 Albert Hirschmann, *The Passions and the Interests: Political Arguments for Capitalism Before Its Triumph* (Princeton: Princeton University Press, 2013 [1977]).

44 Bourdieu went on to develop this argument in 1998 at the beginning of his lectures on Manet: *Manet. A Symbolic Revolution*.

45 D'Aguesseau, 'Discours pour l'ouverture . . .', p. 2.

46 A probable allusion to a famous statement by Philippe Pétain after France's military defeat by the German army in 1940: 'I make a gift of my person to France, in order to attenuate its misfortune' (radio broadcast of 17 June 1940).

47 D'Aguesseau, 'Discours pour l'ouverture . . .', p. 2.

48 Paul Bénichou, *Morales du grand siècle* (Paris: Gallimard, 1948); *Man and Ethics*, trans. Elizabeth Hughes (New York: Anchor, 1971).

49 A reference to the spelling of d'Aguesseau's name, mentioned above, p. 17

50 Norbert Elias, 'On the Sociogenesis of the Concepts of "Civilization" and "Culture"', in *The Civilising Process*, trans. Edmund Jephcott (Oxford: Wiley-Blackwell, 2000), pp. 3–44.

51 Monique de Saint Martin, 'Une grande famille', *Actes de la recherche en sciences sociales*, no. 31, 1980, pp. 4–21.

52 Perhaps: 'Troisième discourse, prononcé en 1699: Des causes de la décadence de l'éloquence', in *Oeuvres complètes du Chancelier d'Aguesseau*, vol. 1, pp. 31–46.

53 In the following quotations, the parentheses in italics between brackets are Bourdieu's commentary.
54 D'Aguesseau, 'Discours pour l'ouverture . . .', pp. 3–4.
55 Ibid., p. 4.
56 Ibid.
57 This is no doubt Thomas Crow, *Painters and Public Life in Eighteenth-Century Paris* (New Haven and London: Yale University Press, 1985).
58 *Fortuna* in Latin means 'fate', 'chance', 'destiny'.
59 'Next, "real" is what we may call a trouser-word. It is usually thought, and I dare say usually rightly thought, that what one might call the affirmative use of a term is basic – that, to understand 'x,' we need to know what it is to be x, or to be an x, and that knowing this apprises us of what it is not to be x, not to be an x. But with "real" (as we briefly noted earlier) it is the negative use that wears the trousers. That is, a definite sense attaches to the assertion that something is real, a real such-and-such, only in the light of a specific way in which it might be and might have been not real. "A real duck" differs from the simple "a duck" only in that it is used to exclude various ways of being not a real duck – but a dummy, a toy, a picture, a decoy, &c.' J.L. Austin, *Sense and Sensibilia* (Oxford: Oxford University Press, 1962), pp. 70–1.
60 Bourdieu and Monique de Saint Martin had studied the adjectives used by teachers in their assessments of dissertations. Pierre Bourdieu and Monique de Saint Martin, 'Les Catégories de l'entendement professoral', *Actes de la recherche en sciences sociales*, no. 3, 1975, pp. 68–93.
61 Plato, *The Republic*, book V.
62 For developments on the subject of 'epistemocratism' see in particular *Principles of Vision*, pp. 42–4.
63 On the 'oracle effect', see Pierre Bourdieu, *Language and Symbolic Power*, trans. Gino Raymond and Matthew Adamson (Cambridge: Polity, 1991), pp. 211–13.
64 D'Aguesseau, 'Discours pour l'ouverture . . .', pp. 5–6.
65 Ibid., p. 5.
66 See above, note 6. On the uprightness of jurists, see also Pierre Bourdieu, 'Les juristes, gardiens de l'hypocrisie collective', in François Chazel and Jacques Commaille (eds.), *Normes juridiques et régulation sociale* (Paris: LGDJ, 1991), p. 97: 'at the risk of reducing things to slogans, we might say that the uprightness of those who lay down the law is at once one of the foundations of the impact that the law has on the outside world, and a condition that the law applies to those who apply the law, who, in order to have the right to say what is right, must be "upright"'.
67 D'Aguesseau, 'Discours pour l'ouverture . . .', p. 7.
68 Ibid.

Lecture of 17 March 1988

1 The notion of the 'paradigm' became current in epistemology after the publication of Thomas Kuhn's book, *The Structure of Scientific Revolutions* (Chicago: University of Chicago Press, 1962).
2 Bourdieu returns to this comparison in the Lecture of 17 June 1993. *Phronèsis* is 'to be able to deliberate nobly about what is good and beneficial for himself

[the practically wise person], not in particular respects, such as what conduces to health or strength, but about what conduces to living well as a whole'. Aristotle, *Nicomachean Ethics*, trans. Roger Crisp (Cambridge: Cambridge University Press, 2014), book VI, chapter 5, p. 105.

3 A more helpful translation is the English 'practical wisdom'. See Roger Crisp's translation of the *Nicomachean Ethics*, p. 105 [translator].

4 *Le sens pratique* was translated into German by Günter Seib under the title *Sozialer Sinn. Kritik der theoretischen Vernunft* (Frankfurt-am-Main: Suhrkamp, 1993).

5 *Le sens pratique* [*The Logic of Practice*, trans. Richard Nice (Cambridge: Polity, 1990)] was published in 1980, but it is based on the research conducted in Algeria in the 1950s by Bourdieu, who started writing up in the 1960s, a decade when one of the works deemed to have founded 'ethnomethodology' appeared: Harold Garfinkel, *Studies in Ethnomethodology* (Englewood Cliffs: Prentice-Hall, 1967 [translated into French in 2007, after Bourdieu's lectures]).

6 Bourdieu developed new arguments on this point and the following analysis, in his lectures for 1992–93. See *Anthropologie économique*, p. 263.

7 See Wittgenstein's arguments on 'rule-following considerations'. Ludwig Wittgenstein, *Philosophical Investigations*, trans. G.E.M. Anscombe (Oxford: Wiley-Blackwell, 2009); *Remarks on the Foundations of Mathematics*, trans. G.E.M. Anscombe (Cambridge MA: MIT Press, 1981). See also Saul Kripke, *Wittgenstein on Rules and Private Language: An Elementary Exposition* (Cambridge MA: Harvard University Press, 1982).

8 See Pierre Bourdieu, *Le sens pratique* (Paris: Minuit, 1980), pp. 64–8; *The Logic of Practice*, esp. pp. 37–40.

9 The usage that Bourdieu makes of the notion of 'common sense' in the following argument is in part related to the (English-language) 'common sense' referred to by ethnomethodologists.

10 Pierre Bourdieu, 'Dialogue sur la poésie oral en Kabylie. Entretien avec Mouloud Mammeri', *Actes de la recherche en sciences sociales*, no. 23, 1978, pp. 51–6.

11 'Giving a purer sense to the words of the tribe' ('Donner un sens plus pur aux mots de la tribu') is a line from 'Le tombeau d'Edgar Poe' ('The Tomb of Edgar Poe') by Stéphane Mallarmé, in *Oeuvres complètes*, vol. 1 (Paris: Gallimard, 'Bibliothèque de la Pléiade, 1998), p. 70.

12 A reference to Max Weber's analyses of the rationalization and 'disenchantment of the world' (where the increasing importance of science is frequently mentioned), and perhaps in particular the 1917 essay on 'Science as a Vocation'. In this text, reconsidering the process of 'intellectualization and rationalization', Weber emphasizes the fact that, in modern societies, we are surrounded by products of science whose functions we do not personally control (he takes the example of the tramway), and also refers to the medical attention afforded the dying – the fact that this avoids the question of knowing whether 'life is worth the living, and in which cases'. Max Weber, 'Science as a Vocation', in *The Vocation Lectures*, trans. Rodney Livingstone (Indianapolis: Hackett Classics, 2004).

13 Pierre Bourdieu, *The Political Ontology of Martin Heidegger*, trans. Peter Collier (Cambridge: Polity, 1991).

14 This is no doubt Philippe Visser 't Hooft, 'La philosophie du langage ordinaire et le droit', *Archives de philosophie du droit*, XVII, 1972, pp. 261–84.

15 Pierre Bourdieu, 'Genèse et structure du champ religieux', *Revue française de sociologie*, 12, no. 3, 1971, pp. 295–334.

16 'There cannot be *primary* truths, there are only *primary* errors.' Gaston Bachelard, *Études de philosophie et d'histoire des sciences* (Paris: Vrin, 1970), p. 89.

17 'In the domain of political economy, free scientific enquiry does not merely meet the same enemies as in all other domains. The peculiar nature of the material it deals with summons into the fray on the opposing side the most violent, sordid and malignant passions of the human breast, the Furies of private interest. The Established Church, for instance, will more readily pardon an attack on thirty-eight of its thirty-nine articles than on one thirty-ninth of its income.' Karl Marx, *Capital*, vol. 1, trans. Ben Fowkes (London: Penguin/New Left Review, 1976), 'Preface to the First Edition', p. 92.

18 For further discussion of the relations between ethnomethodology and politics, and what follows here, see Lecture of 17 April 1986, *Politics and Sociology*, pp. 1–27.

19 See in particular Lecture of 18 January 1983, *Habitus and Field*, p. 299; Lecture of 19 April 1984, *Forms of Capital*, pp. 180–1; Lecture of 14 March 1985, *Principles of Vision*, p. 30; Lecture of 17 April 1986, *Politics and Sociology*, pp. 13–15.

20 The impact of ethnomethodology (which was developed in the United States in the 1950s and especially the 1960s) did not start to be felt in France before the 1980s.

21 See in particular Lecture of 2 November 1982, *Habitus and Field*, pp. 82–8; Lecture of 22 March 1984, *Forms of Capital*, pp. 103–4; Lecture of 24 April 1986, *Politics and Sociology*, pp. 36, 41–2.

22 D'Aguesseau, 'L'Amour de la patrie' (1715), in *Oeuvres complètes du Chancelier d'Aguesseau*, vol. 1, p. 229.

23 Ernst H. Kantorowicz, '*Pro Patria Mori* in Medieval Political Thought', *The American Historical Review*, 56, no. 3, 1951, pp. 472–92.

24 Bourdieu had worked on the State's higher civil service corps within the framework of inquiries that were published in 1989 in *The State Nobility: Elite Schools in the Field of Power*, trans. Lauretta C. Clough (Cambridge: Polity, 1996).

25 This is a reference to 'Traité de la co-naissance au monde et de soi-même', the second part of Paul Claudel's *L'Art poétique* (Paris: Mercure de France, 1907).

26 '[. . .] by mobilizing all available scientific expertise in an attempt to objectify our social milieu, far from exerting reductive violence or totalitarian imperialism – as is sometimes claimed, especially when the sociologist's study is applied to those who wish to objectify without being objectified – he offers a potential liberty; and he can at least hope that his treatise on the academic passions will be for others what it has been for him, a means of *socio-analysis*'. Bourdieu, *Homo Academicus*, p. 5.

27 The treatise is a philosophical genre; one of the titles given to *The Passions of the Soul* (1649) by René Descartes was 'Treatise of the Passions'.

28 See *Homo Academicus*.

29 See the previous lecture, pp. 5, 10, 254 note 11.

30 Wittgenstein, *Remarks on the Foundations of Mathematics*.

31 In accordance with the rules of the Collège de France, Bourdieu's lectures comprise a course of lectures (which for the years preceding the lectures repro-

duced here have been published in *General Sociology*) and a research seminar. Bourdieu is no doubt referring to a contribution to his research seminar here.

32 See in particular Bourdieu, *The Rules of Art*; and 'How to Read an Author', in *Pascalian Meditations*, trans. Richard Nice (Cambridge: Polity, 2000), pp. 85–92.

33 Marcel Proust, *Contre Sainte-Beuve* (Paris: Gallimard, 1954 [1908–9]).

34 The Musée d'Orsay had been inaugurated in 1986 and was part of a movement to rehabilitate 'pompier' art, which Bourdieu mentions on several occasions in his seminars on the artistic field during the 1984–85 year (see *Principles of Vision*).

35 Hans-Georg Gadamer, *Truth and Method*, trans. Joel Weinsheimer and Donald G. Marshall (London: Bloomsbury, 2013 [1960]).

36 Lucien Goldmann, *The Hidden God,* trans. Philip Thody (London: Verso, 2016); *Correspondance de Martin de Barcos, abbé de Saint-Cyran, avec les ditions de Port-Royal et les principaux personnages du groupe janséniste*, dition critique (Paris: PUF, 1956).

37 Étienne de la Boétie, *Discours de la servitude volontaire* (Paris: Gallimard, 1983 [1576]).

38 See above, note 22.

39 A classic analysis of the notion of *Beruf* has been offered by Max Weber in *The Protestant Ethic and the Spirit of Capitalism*, trans. Talcott Parsons (London: Routledge, 1992 [1904–5]).

40 'D'Aguesseau's work has been described as "an extensive commentary on Domat"'. Nannerl O. Keohane, *Philosophy and the State in France: The Renaissance to the Enlightenment* (Princeton: Princeton University Press, 1980), p. 6. The author refers to William F. Church, 'The Decline of the French Jurists as Political Theorists, 1660–1789', *French Historical Studies*, 5, no. 1, 1967, p. 24.

41 Bénichou, *Man and Ethics*.

42 'But now *we ourselves*, we philosophers of the present – what can and must reflections of the sort we have just carried out mean *for us*? [. . .] We have also become aware in the most general way that human philosophizing and its results in the whole of man's existence mean anything but merely private or otherwise limited cultural goals. In our philosophizing, then – how can we avoid it? – we are *functionaries of mankind*. The quite personal responsibility of our own true being as philosophers, our inner personal vocation, bears within itself at the same time the responsibility for the true being of mankind.' Edmund Husserl, *The Crisis of European Sciences and Transcendental Phenomenology*, trans. David Carr (Evanston: Northwestern University Press, 1970 [1954]), pp. 16–17.

43 Probably a reference to *Cinna or the Clemency of Augustus* by Corneille, and perhaps to Paul Bénichou's commentary: 'This clemency is certainly not without calculation, but it is a calculation of glory not of politics. It would be still more correct to say that it is a burst of glory that suddenly disarms the thirst for vengeance at the very moment when it reaches a fever pitch in the face of treacheries revealed in rapid succession. The unexpected announcement of the faithlessness of Maxime provokes suddenly, and contrary to all expectations, a burst of generosity surging up in defiance of fate and the temptation to punish.' Bénichou, *Man and Ethics*, p. 21.

44 'A frequent objection to monarchy is that it makes the affairs of the state

subject to contingency – since the monarch may be ill-educated or unworthy of holding the highest office – and that it is absurd for such a situation to be regarded as rational. But this objection is based on the invalid assumption that the monarch's particular character is of vital importance. In a fully organized state, it is only a question of the highest instance of formal decision, and all that is required in a monarch is someone to say "yes" and to dot the "i", for the supreme office should be such that the particular character of the occupant is of no significance. Whatever other qualities the monarch has in addition to his role of ultimate decision belong to [the sphere of] particularity [*Partikularität*], which must not be allowed to affect the issue. There may indeed be circumstances in which this particularity plays an exclusive part, but in that case the state is either not yet fully developed, or it is poorly constructed. In a well-ordered monarchy, the objective aspect is solely the concern of the law, to which the monarch merely has to add his subjective "I will".' G.W.F. Hegel, *Elements of the Philosophy of Right*, trans. H.B. Nisbet (Cambridge: Cambridge University Press, 1991), Addition to §280, pp. 322–3.

45 An allusion to 'the universal estate' (*Der allgemeine Stand*) which 'devotes itself to the service of the government' and has the universal as 'the end of its essential activity'. Ibid. §303, p. 343 (which Bourdieu will return to in his Lecture of 14 April 1988).

46 'Natural law has thus been the collective term for those norms which owe their legitimacy, not to their origin from a legitimate lawgiver, but to their immanent and teleological qualities. It is the specific and only consistent type of legitimacy of a legal order which can remain once religious revelation and the authoritarian sacredness of a tradition and its bearers have lost their force. Natural law has thus been the specific form of legitimacy of a revolutionarily created order. The invocation of natural law has repeatedly been the method by which classes in revolt against the existing order have legitimated their aspirations, in so far as they did not, or could not, base their claims upon positive religious norms or revelation.' Max Weber, 'Sociology of Law', in *Economy and Society*, trans. Guenther Roth et al., 2 vols (Berkeley: University of California Press, 2013), vol. 2, p. 867.

47 An allusion to the anti-racist movement that developed in the left in the 1980s, which started with the March for Equality and against Racism in 1983.

48 This remark seems to be fairly common. The hypothesis of an 'influence' of d'Aguesseau on Montesquieu, or even a relation between the two men (born twenty one years apart), has even sometimes been evoked.

49 The Greek word *pléonexia* designates 'the fact of having more than others'. Plato uses it in particular in a passage in *The Republic*: 'those who know nothing of wisdom and human excellence, who are always engaged in things like feasting . . . are like cattle, their gaze constantly directed downwards. Eyes on the ground – or on the table – they fatten themselves at pasture, and rut. The struggle for these things [*pléonexia*] makes them kick and butt – with horn and hoof of iron – until they kill one another. But they cannot be filled, since they do not fill the part of them which truly is, the retentive part, nor do they fill themselves *with* what truly is.' Plato, *The Republic*, trans. Tom Griffith (Cambridge: Cambridge University Press, 2000), book 9, §586a–b, p. 305.

50 D'Aguesseau, 'L'Amour de la patrie', p. 229.

51 Ibid., p. 230.

52 Bourdieu may be thinking of authors published by Minuit in his series 'Le sens

commun': Louis Marin, *La Critique du discours. Sur la Logique de Port Royal et les Pensées de Pascal*, in 1975; Jean-Claude Pariente, *L'Analyse du language à Port Royal. Six études logico-grammaticales*, in 1985.

53 Bourdieu sometimes refers to Pascal when developing his theory of the social world. He does so explicitly in 1997 in *Pascalian Meditations*.

54 The idea, if not the exact formula, may be found in passages such as: 'For each new class which puts itself in the place of one ruling before it, is compelled, merely in order to carry through its aim, to represent its interest as the common interest of all the members of society, that is, expressed in ideal format has to give its ideas the form of universality and represent them as the only rational, universally valid ones.' Karl Marx and Friedrich Engels, 'Ruling Class and Ruling Ideas', in *The German Ideology*, trans. Tim Delaney and Bob Schwarz, at marxists.org.

55 'On comparing the Primitives to the masters of the Renaissance and the painters of Siena to those of Florence, I gained an impression of deterioration: what did the latter achieve, other than precisely what they should not have done? And yet they remain admirable. The grandeur that attaches to beginnings is so sure that even their mistakes, as long as they were new, still overwhelm us with their beauty.' Claude Lévi-Strauss, *Tristes Tropiques*, trans. John and Doreen Weightman (London: Penguin, 2011), chapter XI [my translation].

56 Bourdieu had made an exceptionally detailed study of the cases of Manet (Lecture of 14 March 1985, *Principles of Vision*, pp. 26ff.; and, after the lectures, *Manet. A Symbolic Revolution*) and Flaubert (*The Rules of Art*).

57 *Propositions pour l'enseignement de l'avenir élaborées à la demande de Monsieur le Président de la République par les professeurs du Collège de France* (Paris: Collège de France-Presses du Palais Royal, 1985).

58 François-Etienne Mollot, *Règles de la profession d'avocat: suites des usages, lois et règlements*, 2e édition revue et augmentée, vol. 1 (Paris: Durand, 1866), p. 29.

59 Ibid., p. 30.

Lecture of 24 March 1988

1 The *Science Citation Index* appeared, on the initiative of Eugene Garfield, in the 1960s. Scientometry developed in its wake.

2 Bourdieu returned to discuss at greater length the question of quotation and scientometry in his lectures on science in 2000–1 (*Science of Science and Reflexivity*).

3 Bourdieu had taken these agents as an object of study at the beginning of the 1970s: Pierre Bourdieu, 'Les doxophobes', *Minuit*, no. 1, 1972, pp. 26–45; 'L'opinion publique n'existe pas', *Les Temps modernes*, no. 318, 1973, pp. 1292–1309 (reprinted as 'Public Opinion Does Not Exist', in *Sociology in Question*, trans. Richard Nice (London: Sage Publications, 1993), pp. 149–57. In 1990 Minuit published in the series 'Le sens commun' Patrick Champagne's *Faire l'opinion. Le nouveau jeu politique* (reprinted in 2016).

4 *Actes de la recherche en sciences sociales*, no. 71–72, 1988, 'Penser la politique 1' (issue no. 73, which appeared after the lecture, dealt with the same theme: 'Penser la politique 2'.

5 Patrick Champagne, 'Le cercle politique. Usages sociaux des sondages et

nouvel espace politique', *Actes de la recherche en sciences sociales*, no. 71–72, 1988, pp. 71–97.
6 Bourdieu returned to these questions at much greater length in his lectures for the year 1992–93 (*Anthropologie économique*).
7 Bourdieu may be thinking in particular of the readings of his work that had been presented since the 1980s by the MAUSS (Mouvement anti-utilitariste en sciences sociales) and its leader, Alain Caillé. See in particular Alain Caillé, *Don, intérêt et désintéressement. Bourdieu, Manet, Platon et quelques autres* (Paris: La Découverte/MAUSS, 1994).
8 Bourdieu published his analyses of Flaubert and Mallarmé in 1992 in *The Rules of Art*.
9 See in particular *The Logic of Practice* and the lectures on economics that Bourdieu went on to give in 1992–93 (*Anthropologie économique*).
10 See for instance its formulation in Leibniz's *Monadology* (1714) §31: 'Our reasoning is based upon *two great principles*: first, *that of contradiction*, by means of which we decide that to be *false* which involves contradiction and that to be *true* which contradicts or is opposed to the false.' §32: 'And second, the *principle of sufficient reason*, in virtue of which we believe that no fact can be real or existing and no statement true unless it has a sufficient reason why it should be thus and not otherwise. Most frequently, however, these reasons cannot be known by us.'
11 For developments of this analysis of delinquency, see in particular the Lecture of 19 April 1984, *Forms of Capital*, pp. 171 ff.
12 An allusion to the following quotation: 'Philosophy is written in this grand book – I mean the Universe – which stands continually open to our gaze, but it cannot be understood unless one first learns to comprehend the language and interpret the characters in which it is written. It is written in the language of mathematics, and its characters are triangles, circles, and other geometrical figures, without which it is humanly impossible to understand a single word of it; without these, one is wandering around in a dark labyrinth.' Galileo Galilei, *The Assayer*, trans. Stillman Drake, web.stanford.edu, p. 4 (*Il Saggiatore*, 1623).
13 Georges Frêche, 'Un chancellier gallican: Daguesseau', in Georges Frêche and Jean Sudreau, *Un chancelier gallican: Daguesseau, et un cardinal diplomate: François Joachim de Pierre de Bernis* (Paris: PUF, 'Travaux et recherches de la faculté de droit et des sciences économiques de Paris', 1969), pp. 1–94.
14 Weber, *Economy and Society*, vol. 1, pp. 445–6.
15 'The capitalistic economy of the present day . . . forces the individual, in so far as he is involved in the system of market relationships, to conform to capitalistic rules of action. The manufacturer who in the long run acts counter to these norms, will just as inevitably be eliminated from the economic scene as the worker who cannot or will not adapt himself to them will be thrown into the streets without a job'. Weber, *The Protestant Ethic and the Spirit of Capitalism*, pp. 19–20.
16 'All the glory of greatness has no lustre for those engaged in intellectual pursuits. The greatness of intellectuals is invisible to kings, to the rich, to military leaders and to all such worldly folk. The greatness of wisdom, which is nothing unless it comes from God, is invisible to the carnal minded and to intellectuals. These are three orders differing in kind.' Blaise Pascal, *Pensées*, trans. John Warrington (London: Dent, 1960), §585, p. 168 [Lafuma, §308].
17 'But obedience is the constant will to execute that, which by law is good, and

by the general decree ought to be done.' Baruch Spinoza, *Treatise of Political Authority* (1677), chapter 2, 'Of Natural Right', §19.

18 Julien Sorel, the main character in Stendhal's *Scarlet and Black* (1830), is sentenced to the guillotine by a class-based justice which cannot forgive the means he has employed to escape his fate as a carpenter's son.

19 This sentence had already been quoted at the end of the previous lecture; see above, p. 52.

20 Bourdieu took these analyses further in his lectures for 1992–93 on the social foundations of economic action (*Anthropologie économique*).

21 A reference to the notion of a *Grundnorm* ('basic' or 'fundamental' norm) introduced by Hans Kelsen (*Théorie pure du droit*) and mentioned by Bourdieu in the previous lecture.

22 See the 'Summaries of the Lectures', below.

23 See Lecture of 2 May 1985, *Principles of Vision*, pp. 163–5, and *The Rules of Art*.

24 Bourdieu is no doubt referring to James Willard Hurst, *The Growth of American Law: The Law Makers* (Boston: Little, Brown and Company, 1950).

25 An allusion to the passage where Marx finally defines religion as 'the opium of the people': 'Religion is the general theory of this world, its encyclopaedic compendium, its logic in popular form, its spiritual *point d'honneur*, its enthusiasm, its moral sanction, its solemn complement and its universal basis of consolation and justification.' Marx, 'A Contribution to the Critique of Hegel's Philosophy of Right. Introduction', in *Early Writings*, p. 244.

26 See the chapter 'Cultural Goodwill', in Pierre Bourdieu, *Distinction: A Social Critique of the Judgement of Taste*, trans. Richard Nice (London: Routledge, 1984), pp. 318–71.

27 Svend Ranulf, *The Jealousy of the Gods and the Criminal Law of Athens: A Contribution to the Sociology of Moral Indignation* (London: Williams, 1913–14); *Moral Indignation and Middle Class Psychology* (Copenhagen: Lewis & Munksgaard, 1938).

28 Jean-Paul Sartre, *Anti-Semite and Jew*, trans. George J. Becker (New York: Schocken Books, 1948), pp. 32–3. Bourdieu may be thinking of a passage where Sartre explains that defending 'pure virtue' and 'morality' masks 'a curiosity fascinated by Evil', giving the example of a Protestant in Berlin whom 'the sight of women in bathing suits . . . aroused . . . to fury [but who] passed his time at swimming pools'.

29 See note 44 in the previous lecture, pp. 261–2.

30 On social ageing, see *Distinction*, pp. 110–11.

31 These lectures were delivered during the 1988 presidential election campaign. The candidate declaring 'late in the day' was doubtless the outgoing president, François Mitterrand, who declared his candidature only one month before the first round of voting (and two days before this lecture).

32 Michael Polanyi, *Personal Knowledge* (London: Routledge, 1958). An extract from this book entitled 'Les contrôles croisés et la transitivité de la censure' figured in 1968 in Pierre Bourdieu, Jean-Claude Chamboredon and Jean-Claude Passeron, *Le Métier de sociologue,* 4th edition (Paris: Mouton, 1983 [1968]), pp. 322–3; 'Cross-checks and the transitivity of critiques', in *The Craft of Sociology: Epistemological Primaries*, trans. Richard Nice (Berlin and New York: Walter de Gruyter, 1991). The author was the brother of the anthropologist Karl Polanyi, whom Bourdieu often refers to.

33 See Lecture of 9 June 1982, *Classification Struggles*, p. 111.

34 Bourdieu speaks of this inverted world the following year (below, pp. 143–4), and of the 'economic world overturned' in *The Rules of Art*, pp. 141–6.

35 On 'communism' in science, see Robert K. Merton, 'The Normative Structure of Science' (1942), in *The Sociology of Science: Theoretical and Empirical Investigations* (Chicago: University of Chicago Press, 1973), pp. 273–5.

36 The analysis of a 'functional' social world proposed by the 'structuro-functionalism' to which Robert Merton belonged tended to justify American society in conservative terms. Bourdieu often commented ironically (see below, **pp. 188–9, 193–6**) on the 'Capitoline triad' (Lazarsfeld, Merton, Parsons) who dominated sociology in the United States in the postwar decades (he returns to Merton in his lectures on science; see *Science of Science and Reflexivity*, esp. pp. 9–14).

37 Jürgen Habermas, *The Theory of Communicative Action*, vol. 1 (Cambridge: Polity, 1984 [1981]).

38 Lucien Lévy-Bruhl, *La Morale et la Science des moeurs* (Paris: Alcan, 1903).

39 This is the argument of the empiricists, sometimes called 'Hume's law', that Bourdieu often refers to (he returns to it in the next lecture).

40 Herbert Paul Grice (ed.), *Studies in the Way of Words* (Cambridge MA: Harvard University Press, 1989).

Lecture of 14 April 1988

1 The date of this session has not been established for certain. The most likely hypothesis is that the lecture was delivered on 14 April 1988, after a break of two weeks between lectures because of the Easter vacation in the Paris region.

2 A probable allusion to the electoral context (the lecture was delivered ten days before the first round of the presidential elections).

3 The affair of Martin Heidegger's Nazi commitment took on a new dimension in autumn 1987 with the publication of a book by Victor Farias, *Heidegger et le nazisme* (Paris: Verdier). The literary critic and television personality Michel Polac contributed to the development of the 'affair' in the written press addressing members of the general public interested in culture. He reviewed the book in October 1987 in the weekly review *L'Événement du jeudi*, and was attacked by certain media-savvy philosophers (Alain Finkielkraut and Luc Ferry) who, unlike Polac, were academically qualified, and who denounced his incompetence and some of his formulae (such as: 'Might Heidegger's obscurity be hiding some Le Pen-type banalities?'). Bourdieu in turn republished in book form in March 1988 the article that he had written on Heidegger in 1975: *The Political Ontology of Martin Heidegger*. [Jean-Marie Le Pen was the leader of the far-right political party in France, Le Front National (translator).]

4 The reference is to Matthew 7:1–5 [translator].

5 See above, Lecture of 10 March 1988, note 22, p. 255.

6 Hegel for instance writes: 'The task of *upholding*, within these particular rights, *legality* and the *universal interest of the state*, and that of bringing these rights back to the universal, need to be performed by delegates of the executive power, i.e. the executive *civil servants* and the higher consultative bodies.' He adds that although individuals and lower authorities 'know and have before them their own distinct interests and affairs, they have a less complete grasp of

the connection between these and more remote conditions and universal points of view.' Hegel, *Elements of the Philosophy of Right*, §289, pp. 329–30.

7 These examples refer to research by Bourdieu into housing policies (*Les structures sociales de l'économie* [Paris: Seuil, 2000]) and by Abdelmalek Sayad into policies on immigration (*L'Immigration ou les Paradoxes de l'altérité* [Paris: Raisons d'agir, 3 vols, 2006–2014]).

8 Most probably an allusion to the 'Commission of the Sages' established in June 1987 by the minister of justice, after the government had been obliged to withdraw a draft law attempting to reform the regulations concerning French nationality.

9 On the distinction between monumental history, antiquarian history and critical history, see Friedrich Nietzsche, 'On the Use and Abuse of History for Life' (1874), in *Untimely Meditations* (Cambridge: Cambridge University Press, 1997).

10 We have not found the article referred to.

11 Gaston Bachelard, *La formation de l'esprit scientifique. Contribution à une psychoanalyse de la connaissance objective* (Paris: Vrin, 1970).

12 In particular Georges Canguilhem, *Idéologie et rationalité dans l'histoire des sciences de la vie* (Paris: Vrin, 1977).

13 Niklas Luhmann, *Soziale Systema. Grundriss einer allgemeinem Theorie* (Frankfurt-am-Main: Suhrkamp, 1984).

14 Montesquieu, *Cahiers (1716–1755)*, textes recueillis et présentés par Bernard Grasset (Paris: Grasset, 1941).

15 Bourdieu may be thinking of the chapter on 'The Working Day' (pp. 340–416), and in particular of the passage on the 'Ten Hours Act' of 1847 (pp. 393–8), in Marx, *Capital*, vol. 1.

16 This formula is used – if not by Leibniz himself – by Merleau-Ponty: 'Our perception ends in objects, and the object once constituted, appears as the reason for all the experiences of it which we have had or could have. For example, I see the next-door house from a certain angle, but it would be seen differently from the right bank of the Seine, or from the inside, or again from an aeroplane: the house *itself* is none of these appearances: it is, as Leibniz said, the geometrized projection of these perspectives and of all possible perspectives, that is, the perspectiveless position from which all can be derived, the house seen from nowhere.' Maurice Merleau-Ponty *Phenomenology of Perception*, trans. Colin Smith (London: Routledge, 2002 [1945]), p. 77.

17 On other occasions, Bourdieu refers to this passage: 'Because a labor leader has been successful in several rounds of collective bargaining, he may have the false impression that he is an expert in matters of wage economics. The manager of a firm who has "balanced the books" may, wrongly, consider his opinions on price control to be irrefutable. A banker who has managed to consolidate his funds may conclude (wrongly) that he knows everything there is to know about the creation of wealth [. . .] When he composes a general introductory treatise, the economist is considering the functioning of the economy as a whole rather than from the point of view of any particular group or unit.' Paul A. Samuelson, *Economics* (New York: McGraw Hill, 2009 [1948]).

18 For developments of this, see Lecture of 19 October 1982, *Habitus and Field*, p. 55; Lecture of 28 March 1985, *Principles of Vision*, pp. 42–4.

19 Émile Durkheim, *On the Division of Labor in Society*, trans. George Simpson (Illinois: The Free Press of Glencoe, 1933 [1893]), p. 68.

20 Émile Durkheim, *The Rules of Sociological Method*, trans. W.D. Halls (New York: The Free Press, 1982 [1895]), pp. 65–6.

21 Durkheim, 'Débat sur les syndicats de fonctionnaires' (1908), in *Textes*, vol. 3, pp. 202–17, esp. p. 205.

22 Durkheim, 'Débat sur le rapport entre les fonctionnaires et l'État' (1908), in *Textes*, vol. 3, pp. 189–202, esp. pp. 192–3.

23 This reference indicated by Bourdieu probably refers to the following quotation: 'If we again borrow biological terminology . . . This system, in current parlance, is designated by the name, State).' Durkheim, *On the Division of Labor in Society*, p. 219.

24 An allusion to his research with Luc Boltanski in the 1970s on 'the dominant ideology'. Pierre Bourdieu and Luc Boltanski, 'La production de l'idéologie dominante', *Actes de la recherche en sciences sociales*, no. 2–3, 1976, pp. 3–73, republished by Raisons d'agir/Demopolis, 2007.

25 This is probably Louis Guillermit, *L'Élucidation critique du jugement de goût selon Kant. Suivi d'une traduction nouvelle de la* Critique du jugement (Paris: Éditions du CNRS, 1986).

26 A right-wing politician and minister during the 1970s, Michel Poniatowski was one of the authors of the essays included in the corpus that Pierre Bourdieu and Luc Boltanski used to create an 'Encyclopaedia of received wisdom and commonplace ideas in use in neutral spaces' ('La production de l'idéologie dominante').

27 To refer to a book that Bourdieu often cites, this is the case with Albert Hirschman's *The Passions and the Interests*.

28 Bourdieu may be thinking of passages where Hegel writes that the 'higher viewpoints of the state' are opposed to 'civil society' which is 'the field of conflict in which the private interest of each individual comes up against that of everyone else', but 'the spirit of the corporation . . . is at the same time inwardly transformed into the spirit of the state, because it finds in the state the means of sustaining its particular ends'. Hegel, *Elements of the Philosophy of Right*, §289, p. 329.

29 This comment, often made by Bourdieu, is inspired by the following passage: 'a truly philosophical criticism . . . does not however consist, as Hegel thinks, in discovering the determinations of the concepts of logic at every point; it consists in the discovery of the particular logic of the particular object.' Marx, 'Critique of Hegel's Doctrine of the State', in *Early Writings*, pp. 158–9. (One French translation is closer to the wording quoted by Bourdieu: 'Ce n'est pas la Logique de la Chose mais la Chose de la Logique qui est le moment philosophique.' Karl Marx, *Critique du droit politique hégélien*, trans. Albert Baraquin (Paris: Éditions sociales, 1975), p. 51 [translator].)

30 For developments of this point, see an article published after these lectures: Pierre Bourdieu, 'Le mystère du ministère. Des volontés particulières à la volonté générale', *Actes de la recherche en sciences sociales*, no. 140, 2001, pp. 7–11.

31 Bourdieu is probably referring to the following passage: 'The particular functions and activities of the state *belong to it* as its own essential moments, and the *individuals* who perform and implement them are associated with them only by virtue of their universal and objective qualities. Consequently, the link between these functions and particular personalities as such is external and contingent in character. For this reason, the functions and powers of the state

cannot be *private property*.' Hegel, *Elements of the Philosophy of Right*, §277, p. 314.

32 'Der dritte, denkende Stand hat die allgemeinen Interessen zu seinem Geschäfte; wie der zweite hat er eine durch die eigene Geschicklichkeit vermittelte und wie der erste eine aber durch das Ganze der Gesellschaft geicherte Subsistenz.' 'The third, "thinking" estate has for its business the general interests; like the second it has a subsistence procured by means of its own skill, and like the first a certain subsistence, certain, however, because guaranteed through the whole society.' G.W.F. Hegel, *Encyclopedia of the Philosophical Sciences*, Part 3: *Philosophy of Mind*, trans. William Wallace (Oxford: Clarendon Press, 1971), §528.

33 See for example §257 of Hegel's *Elements of the Philosophy of Right*.

34 On the notion of exemption (and the example below), see an article published after these lectures: Pierre Bourdieu, 'Droit et passe-droit. Le champ des pouvoirs territoriaux et la mise en oeuvre des règlements', *Actes de la recherche en sciences sociales*, no. 81–82, 1990, pp. 86–96.

35 Bourdieu has in mind a quotation from Hegel that he will use a little later.

36 An allusion to the origin of the word 'statistic', forged in the eighteenth century from the Italian word *statista*, 'statesman'. Bourdieu will return at greater length to the relation between the development of statistics and the formation of the State in his lectures for the year 1990–91; see *On the State*.

37 See Sébastien Le Prestre de Vauban, *Projet d'une Dîme royale* (1707), in particular p. 158: 'The Chinese, according to the report by the Jesuit father Le Comte and other authors who have written about it, observe a very straightforward and seemingly well-organized method of counting their population, which we would find useful.'

38 On the notion of the 'oblate', see in particular Pierre Bourdieu, 'Le mort saisit le vif. Les relations entre l'histoire réifiée et l'histoire incorporée', *Actes de la recherche en sciences sociales*, no. 32–33, 1980, pp. 3–14. 'The further we move away from the ordinary functioning of fields as fields of struggle to move towards their marginal states, no doubt never to be reached, where [. . .] the field becomes ossified, reducing itself to a "totalitarian institution" [. . .] or [. . .] an apparatus, which is able to demand everything without conditions or concessions and which, in its extreme forms – barracks, prison or concentration camp – has the means to symbolically and physically annihilate the "man of old", the more the institution tends to consecrate agents who give everything to the institution (to the "Party" or the "Church", for instance), and who accomplish all the more easily this oblation the less capital they have outside of the institution, and therefore the less freedom from it and from the specific capital and benefits it has to offer' (pp. 10–11). In the 1980s, the notion of the 'oblate' was used by Bourdieu and/or researchers working with him in analysing, for example, the Communist Party (Jeannine Verdès-Leroux, 'Les invariants du parti communist français', *Actes de la recherche en sciences sociales*, no. 36–37, 1981, pp. 65–81), the Catholic Church (Pierre Bourdieu and Monique de Saint-Martin, 'La Sainte famille. L'épiscopat français dans le champ du pouvoir', *Actes de la recherche en sciences sociales*, no. 44–45, 1982, pp. 2–53) or the university institution (*Homo Academicus*). See also *Habitus and Field*, p. 163; *Forms of Capital*, p. 268; *Principles of Vision*, p. 216.

39 This research was published in 1990 in the issue 'L'économie de la maison' of the journal edited by Bourdieu. See Pierre Bourdieu and Rosine Christin, 'La

construction de marché. Le champ administrative et la production de la politique du logement', *Actes de la recherche en sciences sociales*, no. 81–82, 1990, pp. 65–85 (republished in *Les structures sociales de l'économie*, pp. 145–94).

40 Bourdieu may be thinking of a passage like the following: 'The three forces operative within the laity with which the priesthood must come to grips are: (a) prophecy, (b) the traditionalism of the laity, and (c) lay intellectualism. In contrast to these forces, another decisive factor at work here derives from the necessities and tendencies of the priestly enterprise as such.' Weber, *Economy and Society*, vol. 1, p. 456.

41 Doubtless a reference to §324 of Hegel's *Elements of the Philosophy of Right*, pp. 360–2.

42 Émile Durkheim, *Leçons de sociologie* (Paris: PUF 'Quadrige', 1990 [1950]), p. 87.

43 Spinoza opposed sensible perception and convictions acquired by 'hearsay' (the first kind of knowledge) and the objective knowledge derived from the use of reason (the second kind) to an intuitive 'third kind of knowledge', accessible to the philosopher alone, which 'proceeds from the adequate idea of certain attributes of God to the adequate knowledge of the essence of things'. Baruch Spinoza, *Ethics*, trans. Andrew Boyle (London: Dent/Everyman, 1986 [1677]), Part V, proposition xxv, pp. 214–15.

44 See above, note 23.

45 Durkheim, *Leçons de sociologie*, p. 87.

46 'To counter all the inequalities and injustices which necessarily result from this, there must therefore be, above all these secondary groups and all these particular social forces, an equal (sovereign) force that is higher than all the others and which consequently is able to contain them and prevent their excesses. This force is that of the State.' Durkheim, 'L'État (1900–1905)', *Textes*, vol. 3, p. 177.

47 'Nothing in the content of this typically professorial aesthetic could stand in the way of its being recognized as universal by its sole ordinary readers, the professors of philosophy, who were too concerned with hunting down historicism and sociologism to see the historical and social coincidence which, here as in so many cases, is the basis of their illusion of universality. And the formalization which is required in order for social impulses and interests to be expressed within the limits of the censorship of a particular form of social propriety can only help to encourage this illusion, so that a discourse which makes art a criterion of an ethical and aesthetic distinction which is a misrecognized form of social difference can be read as a universal expression of the universality of art and aesthetic experience.' Pierre Bourdieu, 'Towards a Vulgar Critique of Pure Critiques', *Distinction*, pp. 485–500 (p. 493).

Lecture of 21 April 1988

1 Gottfried Wilhelm Leibniz, *Animadversiones ad Cartesii Principia Philosophiae* [*Remarks on the general part of the principles of Descartes*] (Palala Press, 2016 [1692]). In 1953, when he was a student, Bourdieu had made a translation of this text with a preface and commentary, under the direction of Henri Gouhier.

2 Marx, 'Critique of Hegel's Doctrine of the State', and 'A Contribution to the Critique of Hegel's Philosophy of Right', in *Early Writings*, pp. 57–198 and 243–57.

3 See Neil L. Wilson, 'Substances without Substrata', *The Review of Metaphysics*, 12, no. 4, 1959, pp. 521–39.

4 In the previous lecture Bourdieu had already made a brief allusion to the chapter 'The Working Day' (pp. 340–416), and in particular to the passage on the 'Ten Hours Act' of 1847 (pp. 393–8), in Marx's *Capital*, vol. 1.

5 These inspectors were instituted by the Factory Act of 1850: 'Certain guardians of these laws are appointed, factory inspectors, directly under the Home Secretary, and their reports are published every six months by order of Parliament. They therefore provide regular and official statistics of the voracious appetite of the capitalists for surplus labour.' Marx, *Capital*, vol. 1, p. 349.

6 Bourdieu is no doubt drawing conclusions (which do not seem very explicit in Marx's text) from the detailed account in part 6 of the chapter (pp. 389–411), of the evolution of the 'English factory legislation of 1833–1864', while drawing on the general remarks that Marx formulates in other sections, such as this: '*Après moi le déluge!* Is the watchword of every capitalist and of every capitalist nation. Capital therefore takes no account of the health and the length of life of the worker, *unless society forces it to do so.*' Marx, *Capital*, vol. 1, p. 381. [A footnote reproduces extracts from *The Times* and from a report by the Registrar General in 1861.]

7 Bourdieu may be thinking of the key passage in the previous note, and of a longer passage where Marx mentions the London dailies which, in June 1863, all had as their headline the 'Death from simple overwork' of a [twenty-year-old] woman employed in a very respectable workshop run by a lady with the gentle name of Elise, a supplier of ballgowns to the Court. Marx, *Capital*, vol. 1, pp. 364–5.

8 See the previous lecture.

9 Here Bourdieu is probably referring to the following passage: 'The bureaucracy holds the state, the spiritual essence of society, in thrall, as its *private property*. The universal spirit of bureaucracy is *secrecy*, it is mystery preserved within itself by means of the hierarchical structure and appearing to the outside world as a self-contained corporation. Openly avowed political spirit, even patriotic sentiment, appears to the bureaucracy as a *betrayal* of its mystery. The principle of its knowledge is therefore *authority*, and its *patriotism* is the adulation of authority [. . .] As for the individual bureaucrat, the purpose of the state becomes his private purpose, *a hunt for promotion, careerism.*' Marx, *Early Writings*, p. 108.

10 See above, Lecture of 14 April 1988 (section on 'The organicist metaphor').

11 Bourdieu had often discussed 'nomination' in his lectures on general sociology; readers may check under 'nomination' in the indexes of the earlier volumes of *General Sociology*.

12 See Lecture of 9 May 1985, *Principles of Vision*, pp. 167–81.

13 The verb 'to certify' comes from the Latin *certifico*, and Bourdieu recalled that this may be broken down into *certus-facio*, 'I certify as true'. Ibid., p. 167.

14 See Bourdieu, 'The Twofold Truth of Labour', in *Pascalian Meditations*, pp. 202–5.

15 Japan's economic growth was very strong in the 1980s, and the 'Japanese model' gave rise to many commentaries and analyses.

16 An allusion to Pascal's 'Imagination', in Pascal, *Pensées*, §81, pp. 26–7.

17 'Wives, children, and goods must be had, and especially health, by him that

can get it; but we are not so to set our hearts upon them that our happiness must have its dependence upon them; we must reserve a backshop, wholly our own and entirely free, wherein to settle our true liberty, our principal solitude and retreat. And in this we must for the most part entertain ourselves with ourselves, and so privately that no exotic knowledge or communication be admitted there; there to laugh and to talk, as if without wife, children, goods, train, or attendance, to the end that when it shall so fall out that we must lose any or all of these, it may be no new thing to be without them.' *Essays of Michel de Montaigne, Complete*, trans. Charles Cotton, book 1, chapter XXXVII, 'Of Solitude' (Project Gutenberg ebook 3600).

18 See the notions of the 'wings' or the 'back region' in the chapter 'Regions and Region Behaviour', in Erving Goffman's *The Presentation of Self in Everyday Life* (Penguin: Harmondsworth, 1959), pp. 109–40.

19 Erving Goffman's parents, whose origins were Ukrainian and Jewish, had set up store in a town in Manitoba. Yves Winkin, who worked in collaboration with Pierre Bourdieu, had published (a few weeks before this lecture) a text establishing links between Goffman's biography and his sociology: 'Portrait du sociologue en jeune homme', in Erving Goffman, *Les moments et leurs hommes* (Paris: Seuil/Minuit, 1988).

20 See for example the passage on the Shetland Hotel in Goffman, *The Presentation of Self in Everyday Life*, pp. 123–4.

21 Robert Bellah, *The Broken Covenant: American Civil Rights in Time of Trial* (New York: Seabury Press, 1975).

22 Mithridates, king of Pontus, an enemy of Rome and the hero of a play by Racine, cultivated an immunity to poisons by regularly ingesting sub-lethal doses; this practice, now called 'mithridatism', is named after him [translator].

23 The title of the 'New Sorbonne' goes back as far as the reforms that at the beginning of the Third Republic supported the sciences to the detriment of the traditional literary culture and religious influence. Towards 1910, the defenders of traditional literary culture attacked Émile Durkheim, Gustave Lanson and Charles Seignobos, who personified in their eyes 'the spirit of the New Sorbonne'. Agathon, *L'Esprit de la Nouvelle Sorbonne. La crise de la culture classique. La crise du français* (Paris: Mercure de France, 1911).

24 Bourdieu had referred to Nietzsche in the previous lecture.

25 On the notion of socio-analysis, see in particular 'La sociologie comme socio-analyse', in Pierre Bourdieu and Loïc J. Wacquant, *Réponses* (Paris: Seuil, 1992), pp. 45–70.

26 In the 1980s Bourdieu had already attracted a lot of attention from the press. Obtaining the chair in sociology at the Collège de France led to increased interest from journalists.

27 There had been much debate after the decision in 1960 to demolish the Baltard market pavilions ['les Halles'] in the centre of Paris in order to construct on their site (nicknamed, during the period of works in the 1970s, 'le Trou des Halles') the commercial centre of the Forum des Halles, which opened in 1979.

28 An allusion to the 'provisional morality' adopted by Descartes in his *Discourse on Method* (Part 3).

29 The *licentia docendi* was one of the first grades that was awarded by the medieval university. It gave the authorization to teach.

30 Kant, 'The Conflict of the Faculties', in *Religion and Rational Theology*, pp. 233–93. See also Bourdieu, *Homo Academicus*, chapter 2, 'The Conflict of the Faculties', pp. 36–72.

31 A reference to Immanuel Kant, 'Religion within the Boundaries of Mere Reason' (1793), trans. George di Giovanni, in *Religion and Rational Theology*, pp. 39–215.

32 In the second half of the 1980s, a series of articles appeared in Bourdieu's review, *Actes de la recherche en sciences sociales*, on the condition and the characteristics of national sociologies in Europe: Mihai Dinu Gheorghiu, 'La sociologie roumaine contemporaine', no. 55, 1984, pp. 68–70; Louis Pinto, 'Un regard sur la sociologie en Hongrie', no. 61, 1986, pp. 48–51; Johan Heilbron, 'Particularités et particularismes de la sociologie aux Pays-Bas', no. 74, 1988, pp. 76–81; Patrick Champagne, 'Notes sur quelques développemements récents de la sociologie en Union Soviétique', no. 83, 1990, pp. 68–72.

33 See in particular Bourdieu's articles from the early 1980s; for example, 'A Science that Makes Trouble' and 'The Sociologist in Question', in *Sociology in Question*, pp. 8–35.

34 This article is no doubt Daniel Lerner, 'Social Sciences: Whence and Whither', in Daniel Lerner (ed.), *The Human Meaning of the Social Sciences* (Cleveland and New York: Meridian Books, 1959), pp. 13–39.

35 Michael Pollak, who wrote his thesis under Bourdieu's supervision, had worked on this period. See in particular his 'La planification des sciences sociales', *Actes de la recherche en sciences sociales*, no. 2, 1976, pp. 105–21.

36 These may be quotations from Daniel Lerner, but they are not to be found in the article that Bourdieu appears to be referring to.

37 Lerner, 'Social Sciences: Whence and Whither', p. 29.

38 Daniel Lerner, *The Passing of Traditional Society: Modernizing the Middle East* (New York: Free Press, 1958).

39 See Pierre Bourdieu, 'Structures sociales et structures de perception du monde social', *Actes de la recherche en sciences sociales*, no. 2, 1975, pp. 18–20. The heading to the article is the quotation: 'They would like, by all means, to convince themselves that the striving after English happiness, I mean after COMFORT and FASHION (and in the highest instance, a seat in Parliament), is at the same time the true path of virtue; in fact, that in so far as there has been virtue in the world hitherto, it has just consisted in such striving.' Friedrich Nietzsche, *Beyond Good and Evil*, trans. Helen Zimmern (Project Gutenberg ebook 4363).

40 Bourdieu often uses this ironic term to designate what certain American researchers call 'cosmopolitan' academics in their typologies. See Alvin W. Gouldner, 'Cosmopolitans and Locals: Toward an Analysis of Latent Social Roles', *Administrative Science Quarterly*, 2, no. 3, 1957, pp. 281–306; and Bourdieu, *Homo Academicus*.

41 Hans Maier, *Politsche Wissenschaft in Deutschland. Aufsätze zur Lehrtradition und Bildungspraxis* (Munich: R. Piper and Co., 1969).

42 Bourdieu might be addressing Johan Heilbron, for instance, who at this time was working on the 'prehistory' of sociology: *Het ontstaan van de sociologie* (Amsterdam: Prometheus, 1990); *Naissance de la sociologie*, trans. Paul Dircks (Marseille: Agone, 2006); or Éric Brian, who in 1990 submitted a thesis entitled 'La mesure de l'État, recherches sur la division social du travail: statistique aux XVIIIe et XIXe siècles'.

43 At the end of the previous lecture, Bourdieu had mentioned 'an interest specifi-
    cally linked to the existence of the bureaucracy' (see above, p. 106).
44 The name is not audible. It may be Edward Shils. In which case the book
    could be his collection of essays on intellectuals, universities and the history of
    sociology, *The Calling of Sociology and Other Essays on the Pursuit of Learning*
    (Chicago: University of Chicago Press, 1980), which starts with the following
    affirmation: 'The concerns of counselors to princes, of philosophers who would
    be kings, of disenchanted and optimistic moralists, of rueful critics of conquest
    and revolution, and of reformers alarmed at the state of their societies provided
    the rudiments of the sociological outlook' (p. 3). It might also be the anthology
    that Shils had co-edited (Talcott Parsons, Edward Shils, Jesse Pitts and Kaspar
    Naegele [eds.], *Theories of Society: Foundations of Modern Sociological Theory*,
    2 vols [New York: The Free Press, 1961]), which opens with extracts from
    Niccolò Machiavelli, Thomas Hobbes, John Locke and Adam Smith.
45 The creation in 1975 by Bourdieu and his team of researchers of the journal
    Actes de la recherche en sciences sociales was a practical consequence of this
    reflection on social science journals. See in particular Pierre Bourdieu, 'Secouez
    un peu vos structures!', in Jacques Dubois, Pascal Durand and Yves Winkin
    (eds.), *Le Symbolique et le Social. La réception Internationale du travail de
    Pierre Bourdieu* (Liège: Éditions de l'Université de Liège, 2005), pp. 325–41.
46 This lecture was delivered at a time before the massive influx of electronic
    information and computers into laboratories and more generally into office
    life.
47 Althusser, 'Ideology and Ideological State Apparatuses', in *Lenin and
    Philosophy and Other Essays*, pp. 85–126.
48 For further developments of this point, see Lecture of 5 June 1986, *Politics and
    Sociology*, p. 168.
49 For references see Lecture of 18 January 1983, *Habitus and Field*, pp. 295 and
    386, note 12.
50 See Hegel, *Reason in History*, on the distinction between 'three manners of
    writing history: original history; reflective history; philosophical history'.
51 See the development on the 'double-voiced discourse' with its 'divided inten-
    tion' 'facing two ways at once', in Lecture of 23 November 1982, *Habitus and
    Field*, pp. 153ff.
52 See previous lecture, 14 April 1988, above, p. 98.
53 On this point (and the Arab proverb quoted) see Lecture of 17 April 1986,
    Politics and Sociology.
54 Gadamer, *Truth and Method*.
55 Frédéric Le Play attracted renewed interest among historians and sociologists
    in the 1970s and 1980s. In the years following these lectures the following
    were republished: *La Méthode sociale. Abrégé des 'Ouvriers européens'* (Paris:
    Méridiens-Klincksieck, 1989) and *Les Mélouga. Une famille pyrénéenne au
    XIXe siècle* (Paris: Nathan, 1994).
56 Bourdieu is alluding to his work on the Béarn peasantry in *The Bachelors' Ball*,
    where he cites Frédéric Le Play, *L'Organisation de la famille salon le vrai modèle
    signalé par l'histoire de toutes les races et de tous les temps* (Tours: A. Mame et
    fils, 1884 [1871]). Pierre Bourdieu, *The Bachelors' Ball: The Crisis of Peasant
    Society in Béarn*, trans. Richard Nice (Cambridge: Polity, 2008).
57 *The Defiant Ones* (1958) is an American film on the escape of two prisoners,
    one black and one white, chained to each other.

58 Bourdieu's formula ('his colleagues and professors') should be understood in the context of the 'republic of the professors', unless it designates the senior civil servants of the public educational system, who were very receptive to the 'operational' character of the sociology that Durkheim was promoting.

59 Dominique Damamme, 'Genèse sociale d'une institution scolaire', *Actes de la recherche en sciences sociales*, no. 70, 1987, pp. 31–46.

60 See the discussion of the 'modernizing bourgeoisie' in France after the war, in Pierre Bourdieu, 'Dominant Ideology and Scientific Autonomy', in *Political Interventions: Social Science and Political Action*, trans. David Fernbach (London: Verso, 2008), pp. 98–102; see also Bourdieu, *Distinction*.

61 From 1946 onward, successive French governments took advice on planning economic activity from a planning body founded by Jean Monnet. Its original aim was to lead from capitalism to a kind of moderate socialism. 'Le Plan' took on a life of its own, accumulating ministerial credibility and power, leading to disputes between President François Mitterrand, elected in 1981, his minister of finance, Michel Rocard (previously a commissioner of the Plan), and prime minister, Pierre Mauroy. Bourdieu thinks that although Commissioners of the Plan sought advice from academics, that advice was not necessarily followed, and yet both bodies were attempting to analyse and rationalize society.

62 In France it was particularly in the 1960s that the general commissioners of the Plan started to call on sociologists. See Pollak, 'La planification des sciences sociales'.

63 Between 1958 and 1970 the Jean Moulin club brought together senior civil servants, business managers, trade unionists and academics.

64 Max Weber had joined the Verein für Sozialpolitik in 1888. His enquiry into agricultural workers, which Bourdieu made known in France, is linked to this association: 'Enquête sur la situation des ouvriers agricoles à l'est de l'Elbe. Conclusions prospectives', *Actes de la recherche en sciences sociales*, no. 65, 1986, pp. 65–69.

65 Durkheim, *Leçons de sociologie*, pp. 114–17.

66 Bourdieu is no doubt thinking of his own experience. See Pierre Bourdieu, *Sketch for a Self-Analysis*, trans. Richard Nice (Cambridge: Polity, 2007).

67 See Pollak, 'La planification des sciences sociales'.

68 A reference to the 'Observation continue du changement social et culturel', a section of the CNRS created particularly on the initiative of the sociologist Henri Mendras, which functioned between 1977 and 1981.

69 On the EHESS, see in particular Bourdieu, *Homo Academicus*, and also Brigitte Mazon, *Aux origins de l'École des hautes études en sciences sociales. Le rôle du mécénat américain (1921–1960)* (Paris: Le Cerf, 1988), and Bourdieu's preface to this book.

70 Referring to the Frankfurt Institut für Sozialforschung (Institute for Social Research) that Horkheimer refounded on his return to Germany after the Second World War.

71 In the year after this lecture, one of the researchers at Bourdieu's centre published a text on this question: Remi Lenoir, 'Objet sociologique et problème social', in P. Champagne et al., *Initiation à la pratique sociologique* (Paris: Dunod, 1989), pp. 53–100.

72 Bourdieu had developed this point on several occasions in his *General Sociology*. See in particular: Lecture of 9 May 1985 and Lecture of 23 May

1985, *Principles of Vision*, p. 172, and pp. 212–13; and Lecture of 17 April 1986, *Politics and Sociology*, p. 26.

Lecture of 19 January 1989

1 Pierre Bourdieu, 'Intérêt et désintéressement. Cours du Collège de France à la Faculté d'anthropologie et de sociologie de l'Université Lumière Lyon 2 les 1er et 8 décembre 1988', *Cahiers de recherche du Groupe de recherche sur la socialisation*, no. 7, 1989 [republished in 1993]; 'Is a Disinterested Act Possible?', in Pierre Bourdieu, *Practical Reason: On the Theory of Action* (Cambridge: Polity, 1998 [1994]), pp. 75–91.
2 In the 1980s these two writers often contributed political commentary to the national daily press or certain radio or television broadcasts. Pierre Rosenvallon, who was Director of Studies at the École des hautes études en sciences sociales, was known as the founder in 1982 of the Saint-Simon Foundation (many of whose members were senior civil servants). In 1990 he published *L'État de France de 1789 à nos jours* (Paris: Seuil, 1990). Alain Minc was an inspector of finance who had worked notably at the Saint-Gobain glass factory.
3 One aspect of the research that Bourdieu started in the 1980s on the Impressionist revolution focuses on the reception of Manet by contemporary critics. He had presented the first results of this research in the framework of his teaching at the Collège de France in 1984–85. See *Principles of Vision*, pp. 26–224.
4 See above, Lecture of 24 March 1988, note 24, p. 265.
5 Laurent Richer (ed.), *L'Activité désintéressé, réalité ou fiction juridique?* (Paris: Economica, 1983). The book derives from a colloquium organized by the Faculty of Law, Economics and Social Sciences of the University of Angers held on 15 and 16 October 1981 at Fontrevaud.
6 The passage quoted is from the beginning of the article. The passages between square brackets are comments by Bourdieu.
7 *Droit administratif*, 11th edition, 1927, p. 884.
8 Catherine Teitgen-Colley, *La Légalité de l'intérêt financier dans l'action administrative* (Paris: Economica, 1981).
9 Pierre Bourdieu, 'Droit et passe-droit. Le champ des pouvoirs territorial et la mise en oeuvre des règlements', *Actes de la recherche en sciences sociales*, no. 81–82, 1990, pp. 86–96.
10 The notion of the 'inverted world' is used by Hegel in 'Force and the Understanding: Appearance and the Supersensible World', in *The Phenomenology of Spirit*, trans. Terry Pinkard (Cambridge: Cambridge University Press, 2018), chapter III, pp. 95–7.
11 See Immanuel Kant, *Groundwork of the Metaphysics of Morals*, trans. Mary Gregor and Jens Timmermann (Cambridge: Cambridge University Press, 2012 [1785]); *Critique of Practical Reason*, trans. Mary Gregor (Cambridge: Cambridge University Press, 2015 [1788]).
12 See in particular *The Logic of Practice*.
13 Marcel Mauss and Henri Hubert, 'Esquisse dune théorie générale de la magie', in Marcel Mauss, *Sociologie et Anthropologie* (Paris: PUF, 1997 [1950]), pp. 1–141; here p. 119 [my translation]; *A General Theory of Magic,* trans. Robert Brain (London: Routledge, 1972 [1904]).

14 Bourdieu is certainly thinking primarily of the French Communist Party (PCF). For articles which appeared in the journal he founded, and which mobilize the notion of the 'oblate', see Bernard Pudal, 'Les dirigeants communistes. Du "fils du people" à "l'instituteur des masses"', *Actes de la recherche en sciences sociales*, no. 71–72, 1988, pp. 46–70; Jeannette Verdès-Leroux, 'Champ scientifique et champ politique', 'Une institution totale auto-perpétuée' and 'Les invariations du Parti communiste français', *Actes de la recherche en sciences sociales*, no. 36–37, 1981, respectively pp. 25–31, 33–63 and 65–81.

15 In 1913 Charles Péguy called primary school teachers the 'black hussars of the Republic', since they were involved in a battle against the Church to impose the free, compulsory lay education introduced by the State following Jules Ferry's laws of 1881 and 1882 [translator].

16 Robert Park, one of the founders of the 'Chicago School' and who in addition had been very influential in the education of one of Goffman's professors, Everett C. Hughes, often attacked the 'damned do-gooders'. Winifred Raushenbush, *Robert E. Park, Biography of a Sociologist* (Durham NC: Duke University Press, 1979), p. 96. Bourdieu could have come across the word while reading or listening to Goffman, but he might also have been struck by a phrase of Yves Winkin's in a text on Goffman published in 1988: 'Robert Park was repelled by the "do-gooders", those delicate souls who intrude into sociology in the guise of philanthropists and missionaries.' Winkin, 'Portrait du sociologue en jeune homme', p. 46.

17 To the best of our knowledge Bourdieu never elaborated this notion, which remains subjacent in certain passages of *Distinction* (see the following note).

18 In *Distinction* (pp. 317, 352 ff.) Bourdieu explains that, like the Puritans at the beginning of capitalism, the rising petite bourgeoisie 'supplements the absence of capital' by a 'surfeit of "moral" resources', by 'moral guarantees', by a 'strict and rigorous' morality. Asceticism is one condition of its rise. 'Morality' is the 'strong point', 'the favourite terrain' of this class which 'has an interest in morality'.

19 Most likely a reference to an anecdote recounted by Norbert Elias that Bourdieu sometimes quotes: 'This obligation to spend on a scale befitting one's rank demands an education in the use of money that differs from bourgeois conceptions. We find a paradigmatic expression of this social ethos in an action of the Duc de Richelieu related by Taine. He gives his son a purse full of money, so that he can learn to spend it like a grand seigneur, and when the young man brings the money back his father throws the purse out of the window before his eyes. This is socialization in keeping with a social tradition that imprints on the individual the duty imposed on him by his rank to be prodigal.' Norbert Elias, *The Court Society*, trans. Edmund Jephcott (New York: Pantheon Books, 1983 [1933]), p. 74.

20 An allusion to the phrase, 'You are trembling, Carcasse, but you would tremble all the more if you knew where I am going to take you', that the Viscount de Turenne (from the old house of the Tour d'Auvergne) is said to have spoken to his mare, Carcasse, in 1675 just before the battle where he met his death.

21 For a comparable study, almost contemporary with these lectures, in understanding a 'petite bourgeoisie [which] does not spontaneously inspire the sympathy, pity or indignation that the harsh conditions of the industrial proletariat or sub-proletariat inspire', see Pierre Bourdieu, 'Un signe des temps', *Actes de la recherche en sciences sociales*, no. 81–82, 1990, p. 2.

22 See Paul Nizan, *Antoine Bloyé* (Paris: Grasset, 2005 [1933]).
23 See in particular Pierre Bourdieu, Alain Darbel and Dominque Schnapper, *The Love of Art: European Art Museums and their Public*, trans. Caroline Beattie and Nick Merriman (Cambridge: Polity, 1991 [1966]).
24 Kantorowicz, '*Pro Patria Mori* in Medieval Political Thought'. Bourdieu had developed this point at greater length the previous year (see above, pp. 35–6).
25 See in particular 'Morality', in Hegel, *Elements of the Philosophy of Right*, pp. 133–86.
26 Kant writes, for example, that 'One need not even be an enemy of virtue, but only a cold-blooded observer who does not at once take the liveliest wish for the good as its actuality, to become doubtful at certain moments [. . .] whether any true virtue is actually to be found in the world at all.' He evokes the possibility that there might 'never have been actions that have sprung from such pure sources [. . .], actions of which the world so far has perhaps not yet given an example.' See Kant, *Groundwork of the Metaphysics of Morals*, p. 22.
27 For example: 'Firstly, a being capable of nothing but unegoistic actions is more fabulous than the phoenix; it cannot even be imagined clearly, if only because under strict examination the whole concept "unegoistic action", when closely examined, vanishes into thin air. No man has ever done anything that was done wholly for others and with no personal motivation whatever; how, indeed, should a man be *able* to do something that had no reference to himself, that is to say lacked all inner compulsion (which would have its basis in personal need)? How could the ego act without the ego?' Friedrich Nietzsche, *Human, All Too Human*, trans. R.J. Hollingdale (Cambridge: Cambridge University Press, 1996), §133, p. 71.
28 A probable reference to Hegel's analysis of the Terror in 'Absolute Liberty and the Terror', in *The Phenomenology of Spirit*, pp. 454–7. Hegel does not use the term 'fanaticism' here, but he does later (see in particular *Elements of the Philosophy of Right*, addition to §5, p. 39).
29 An ironic allusion to the Parisian café *La Coupole*, frequented by bourgeois intellectuals like Sartre and Simone de Beauvoir, far removed from the Renault factory in Boulogne-Billancourt (which is the subject of a famous maxim from Sartre's 1955 play *Nekrassov* [often misquoted]: 'il ne faut pas désespérer Billancourt' ['we mustn't deprive the workers of all hope']).
30 Pierre Bourdieu, 'Case Study: Parallel Cousin Marriage', in *Outline of a Theory of Practice*, trans. Richard Nice (Cambridge: Cambridge University Press, 1973), pp. 30–71.
31 See above, Lecture of 24 March 1988, p. 65.

Lecture of 26 January 1989

1 Max Weber, 'The Meaning of "Ethical Neutrality" in Sociology and Economics', in *Methodology of Social Sciences*, trans. Edward A. Shils and Henry A. Finch (London: Routledge, 2011 [1917]), pp. 1–48.
2 At the time of this lecture, the 'Pechiney affair' had been attracting much interest in the media for some weeks. The events dated from two months earlier: a large quantity of shares in a company called Triangle had been bought (which made the value of its shares rise sharply) just before a public enterprise, Pechiney, announced that it was going to purchase a branch of

this company (American National Can). Very soon some people close to the president and some members of the government were suspected of a 'conflict of interest'.

3 Having detected abnormal operations on shares in American National Can before Pechiney's announcement, SEC then launched an enquiry with the Commission des opérations de la Bourse (COB) on 9 December.

4 Pechiney is a public enterprise and the suspicions concerned in particular the cabinet secretary of the socialist minister of finance, Pierre Bérégovoy, and various people close to him and/or the President of the Republic, François Mitterrand (such as Roger-Patrice Pelat).

5 The Conseil supérieur de l'audiovisual was created in on 17 January 1989. It followed on from the Haute autorité de la communication audiovisuelle (1982–86) and the Commission national de la communication et des libertés (1986–89). The role of this agency of regulation was much discussed in the 1980s, a period when the monopoly of public television came to an end.

6 An allusion to two journalists, André Fontaine, director of *Le Monde* from 1985 to 1991, and Jean Daniel, co-founder and director (until 2008) of *Le Nouvel Observateur*.

7 A theme often treated by Bourdieu, in particular in the lectures on general sociology that he gave between 1982 and 1986 (see *General Sociology*).

8 Bourdieu, 'A "Book for Burning"', in *Homo Academicus*, pp. 1–35.

9 Probably a reference to *Le Monde* of 25 January 1989, where there was in particular an article entitled 'La COB au défi' ('Challenge to the COB'). 'Will the investigators of the COB suffer political pressure? In the case of the Pechiney affair, paradoxically, this seems impossible. In fact, the French institution, which has been assigned to this enquiry by its American counterpart, the SEC – which disposes of much more considerable resources – finds itself placed in the fearful situation of little continental challenger.'

10 During the month of January 1989 several big names on the right used the facts of the Pechiney affair against the government of the day. Raymond Barre denounced their 'political commerce', Charles Pasqua, 'the mixture of commerce and socialism', Philippe Séguin, a 'Louis-Philippish odour', Alain Juppé approved the 'more vocal' voices of the opposition, etc.

11 The Greek word *scholè* means 'leisure' and the place of leisure, opposing the 'school' (*schola* in Latin) to a practical occupation.

12 On the subject of *libido*, see Lecture of 2 November 1982, *Habitus and Field*, p. 83; Lecture of 22 March 1984, *Forms of Capital*, pp. 104–5; Lecture of 18 April 1985, *Principles of Vision*, pp. 81–2; Lecture of 22 May 1986, *Politics and Sociology*, p. 90.

13 Bénichou, *Man and Ethics*.

14 See note 19 in the previous lecture.

15 Bourdieu is most probably thinking of the careers he analysed in the article on the bishopric that he co-authored with Monique de Saint-Martin. The case of Monseigneur Robert de Provenchères, for example, inspired the following remark: 'the acceptance of a charge both fraught and in the public eye represents perhaps the only solution for someone who stems from an aristocratic family and accedes to the bishopric relatively late'. Bourdieu and Monique de Saint-Martin, 'La Sainte famille', p. 16.

16 Bourdieu had discussed this point in particular in his lectures at the Collège de France (see for example the Lectures of 9 November and 14 December

1982, *Habitus and Field*, pp. 122–3, 250). See also *Distinction*, esp. pp. 424 and 511.

17 See *General Sociology*.

18 *Habitus* is the Latin word that scholastic philosophers in the Middle Ages used to translate the Greek word *hexis* in Aristotle. The two words have their origin in the verb 'to have' (*ékho* in Greek, *habere* in Latin).

19 *Eu prattein* is the formula of greeting used at the beginning of the letters attributed to Plato. Plato, *Epistles* (Cambridge MA: Loeb Classical Library, vol. VII, 1929).

20 'Attempt to Introduce the Concept of Negative Magnitudes into Philosophy' (1763), in Immanuel Kant, *Theoretical Philosophy, 1755–1770*, trans. David Walford (Cambridge: Cambridge University Press, 1992), pp. 207–41.

21 Bourdieu returns to this debate in his lectures for 1992–93 (*Anthropologie économique*, pp. 235–6).

22 Mancur Olson, *The Logic of Collective Action* (Cambridge MA: Harvard University Press, 1965).

23 A reference to Jon Elster's arguments on 'the weakness of the will' (*Ulysses and the Sirens: Studies in Rationality and Irrationality* [Cambridge: Cambridge University Press, 1984]. The example given by Bourdieu of the individual who takes the decision to stop smoking comes from here, as does that of the landlord, borrowed by Elster from Derek Parfit (who had made it up): 'Let us take a nineteenth-century Russian who, in several years, should inherit vast estates. Because he has socialist ideals, he intends, now, to give the land to the peasants. But he knows that in time his ideals may fade. To guard against this possibility, he does two things. He first signs a legal document, which will automatically give away the land, and which can only be revoked with his wife's consent. He then says to his wife, "If I ever change my mind, and ask you to revoke the document, promise me that you will not consent." He might add, "I regard my ideals as essential to me. If I lose these ideals, I want you to think that *I* cease to exist. I want you to regard your husband, then, not as me, the man who asks you for this promise, but only as his later self. Promise me that you would not do what he asks." Derek Parfit, 'Later Selves and Moral Principles', in Alan Montefiore (ed.), *Philosophy and Personal Relations* (London: Routledge & Kegan Paul, 1973), p. 145.

24 'Suppose that someone has ten degrees of passion – miserliness, say – and that this is sufficient, under certain circumstances, to conflict with the rules of duty. Let him apply twelve degrees of effort, and let them be exercised in accordance with the principles of benevolence. The result will be two degrees in magnitude, and that will be the extent to which he will be benevolent and beneficent. Imagine another person who has three degrees of miserliness and seven degrees of capacity to act in accordance with the principles of obligation. The action will be four degrees in magnitude, and that will be the extent to which he will benefit another person after the conflict of his desires. But what is indisputable is this: in so far as the passion in question can be regarded as natural and involuntary, the moral value of the action performed by the first person will be greater than that performed by the second, even though, if one were to assess the actions by reference to the living *force*, the consequence of the latter case exceeds that of the former. For this reason, it is impossible for us, with certainty, to infer from another person's actions the degree of that person's virtuous dispositions. He who sees into the inmost chambers of the

heart has reserved for Himself alone the right to pass judgement on others.' Kant, 'Negative Magnitudes', pp. 237–8.
25 Bourdieu will return to this recurrence of the *homo economicus* theory 'in the forefront of the intellectual scene in the form of what we call "rational action theory"' at the start of his 1992–93 lectures on the 'social foundations of economic action'. *Anthropologie économique*, p. 13.
26 A reference perhaps to the *Nicomachean Ethics*. Dealing with the essential nature of each creature, Aristotle writes in particular that 'Each animal seems to have its own proper pleasure, as it has its own characteristic activity, since its proper pleasure will be that in line with the activity it engages in' (book X, chapter 5, p. 189), and says of the horse (mentioned a little later by Bourdieu) that 'the virtue of the horse makes a horse good – good at running, at carrying its rider and at facing the enemy' (b0ook II, chapter 6, p. 29).
27 A tentative reading of this comment (since the recording is unclear here).

Lecture of 2 February 1989

1 See above, Lecture of 24 March 1988, p. 65 and note 17.
2 The source cited has not been identified. Nowadays one of the conditions under which a civil servant may leave their post for a position in the private sector is the absence of any link between 'the functions exercised during the past three years' by the leaver and 'the enterprise that they wish to join'.
3 An allusion to the analysis of the gift (the counter-gift, in particular, becomes insulting if it intervenes too soon – and therefore explicitly – after the initial gift) that Bourdieu had returned to in his Lecture of 19 January 1989 (see above, pp. 145–6). See also 'The Work of Time', in *The Logic of Practice*, pp. 98–111.
4 Jacques-Sylvain Klein, 'La procédure des fonds de concours ou l'art de tourner les règles budgétaires', *La Revue administrative*, no. 203, 1981, pp. 466–71.
5 Ibid., p. 468.
6 Here (and in what follows) Bourdieu is drawing on a passage from Klein's article: 'What are the heads under which the 1,700 millions of competitive funds available for salary credit have been allocated? A small proportion were used to remunerate titular civil servants (3.2%) or assistants (7.4%). But for the most part (nearly 90%) they were used to give bonuses or indemnities, as shown in the following table.' Ibid., p. 470.
7 Ibid., p. 471.
8 As far as we are aware, this analysis has never been published.
9 See above, Lecture of 14 April 1988, pp. 96–106 and note 6.
10 This might be Richard Crossman, who was twice a minister (for Housing and Social Services) in Harold Wilson's Labour government (1964–70).
11 Pierre Bourdieu, 'La représentation politique. Éléments pour une théorie du champ politique', *Actes de la recherche en sciences sociales*, no. 36–37, 1981, pp. 3–24.
12 This passage contains allusions that were transparent for the lecture audience, referring to the political switch that occurred in May 1981 with the election of François Mitterrand, the first President of the Fifth Republic to emerge from the left. Pierre Mauroy had been appointed prime minister. Their electoral victory occurred in the context of a political alliance, sometimes referred to

as the 'union of the left', between the Socialist Party (home to Mitterrand and Mauroy), the Communist Party (then represented by Georges Marchais) and the Radical Left Movement.

13 The cover of the issue reproduces a photograph of François Mitterrand shaking hands with Georges Marchais, who is seated at a rostrum in front of a banner calling for 'victory for the union of the left'.

14 Bourdieu, 'La représentation politique . . .', p. 3. Pierre Mauroy was a member of parliament for the Nord department, and mayor of Lille. He was an eminent figure in the Socialist Party. The exact slogan was: 'Rejoin the Socialist Party, it is fighting for you.'

15 'It is enough to judge well to do well.' Descartes, *Discourse on Method*, p. 17.

16 See above, Lecture of 14 April 1988, p. 93 and note 16.

17 This text has not been identified. In his 1913–14 lectures on pragmatism, Durkheim says something similar: 'The individual minds are finite, there is not one that could place itself at all the points of view at once'; 'scientific truth' (which 'is [therefore] not incompatible with the diversity of minds') enables us to totalize these 'partial truths'. Émile Durkheim, *Pragmatism and Sociology*, trans. J.C. Whitehouse (Cambridge: Cambridge University Press, 1963), p. 186.

18 I say then, first, that privation is not the act of depriving, but simply and merely a state of want, which is in itself nothing: it is a mere entity of the reason, a mode of thought framed in comparing one thing with another. We say, for example, that a blind man is deprived of sight, because we readily imagine him as seeing, or else because we compare him with others who can see, or compare his present condition with his past condition when he could see; when we regard the man in this way, comparing his nature either with the nature of others or with his own past nature, we affirm that sight belongs to his nature, and therefore assert that he has been deprived of it.' Benedict Spinoza, Letter XXXIV (XXI) to Willem van Blyenbergh, in *On the Improvement of the Understanding. The Ethics. Correspondence*, trans. R. Elwes (New York: Dover, 1955), pp. 336–44.

19 See in particular Lecture of 28 April 1982, *Classification Struggles*, pp. 13–14.

20 Bourdieu and Boltanski, 'La production de l'idéologie dominante'.

21 See above, Lecture of 14 April 1988, p. 94 and note 17.

22 See Bourdieu and Christin, 'La construction du marché . . .'.

23 Bourdieu adds a comment that is barely audible in the recording (it might be: 'perhaps [a hand] in the till as well'), which makes the audience laugh.

24 The RPR (Rassemblement pour la République), which existed between 1976 and 2002, was then the main party on the right. During this period the left was dominated by the Parti Socialiste.

25 See in particular Claude Lévi-Strauss, *Mythologiques*, trans. John and Doreen Weightman, 4 vols (Chicago: University of Chicago Press, 1964–71).

26 Bourdieu is thinking of some of the research that he accomplished in Algeria. See in particular the article originally destined for *Mélanges offerts à Claude Lévi-Strauss*: 'La Maison ou le monde renversé'. See 'Structures and the Habitus', in *Outline of a Theory of Practice*, pp. 72–95.

27 See Bourdieu and Boltanski, 'La production de l'idéologie dominante'. Also Pierre Bourdieu, 'Un jeu chinois', *Actes de la recherche en sciences sociales*, 2, no. 4, 1976, pp. 91–101, and 'The Racism of "Intelligence"', in *Sociology in Question*, pp. 177–80.

28 No doubt an allusion to the absenteeism among members of the National Assembly (parliament).
29 A reference to an argument by Callicles in *Gorgias*: 'we mould the best and strongest among us, taking them from their infancy like young lions, and utterly enthral them by our spells and witchcraft, telling them all the while that they must have but their equal share, and that this is what is fair and just'. Plato, *Gorgias* §484a, in *Lysis. Symposium. Gorgias*, trans. W.R.M. Lamb (Cambridge MA: Harvard University Press, 1925), p. 387.
30 On this point (and the previous one), see a text arising from a conference almost contemporary with these lectures, 'On the Possibility of a Field of World Sociology', trans. Loïc Wacquant, in Pierre Bourdieu and James Coleman (eds.), *Social Theory for a Changing Society* (Boulder: Westview, 1991), pp. 373–87. See also Pierre Bourdieu, 'Le champ scientifique', *Actes de la recherche en sciences sociales*, no. 2–3, 1976, pp. 101 ff., and 'La cause de la science', *Actes de la recherche en sciences sociales*, no. 106–107, 1995, pp. 3–10.
31 Talcott Parsons, 'Professions', in David L. Sills (ed.), *International Encyclopaedia of the Social Sciences* (New York: Macmillan, 1968), pp. 536–46.
32 Canguilhem, *Idéologie et rationalité dans l'histoire des sciences de la vie*, pp. 33–45. On these analyses by Georges Canguilhem, see Bourdieu, *Habitus and Field*, pp. 183 ff.
33 Pierre Bourdieu, 'Le Nord et le Midi. Contribution à une analyse de l'effet Montesquieu', *Actes de la recherche en sciences sociales*, no. 35, 1980, pp. 21–5.
34 It was only in the 1980s that the sociology of professions started to be imported into France. For instance, works by Eliot Freidson (*La profession médicale* [Paris: Payot, 1984]; 'Les professions artistiques comme défi à l'analyse sociologique', *Revue franchise de sociologie*, XXVII, no. 3, 1986, pp. 431–43) were translated, and several French sociologists started to sign up to this sociological specialism, including Claude Dubar and Pierre Tripier, who published ten years later the first synthesis in French: *Sociologie des professions* (Paris: Armand Colin, 1998). This period also corresponds to the moment when interactionist sociology became more widely translated in France (for instance, Howard Becker's study of jazz musicians).
35 'Every scientific investigation concerns a specific group of phenomena which are subsumed under the same definition. The sociologist's first step must therefore be to define the things he treats, so that we may know – he as well – exactly what his subject matter is.' Durkheim, *The Rules of Sociological Method*, p. 74.
36 Austin nowhere uses the expression 'true philosopher' or the equivalent. It is possible that Bourdieu had in mind the passage in *Sense and Sensibilia* on the different meanings of the word 'real', which he had already mentioned the previous year (Lecture of 10 March 1988): what Austin says of the expression 'real duck' (see above, pp. 23–4 and note 59) is equally valid for the expressions 'true philosopher' or 'true artist'.
37 The reference is probably: Geoffrey Millerson, *The Qualifying Associations: A Study in Professionalization* (London: Routledge, 2003 [1964]).
38 Bourdieu is probably referring to the table entitled 'Showing an Analysis of Elements Included in Various Definitions of Profession' (Millerson, *The Qualifying Associations*, p. 5). The retranscription here is not integral, because of a brief interruption to the recording (to change the tape), but Bourdieu clearly mentions only the first few of the twenty-three criteria recorded in the

table: '1. Skill based on theoretical knowledge, 2. Requires training and education, 3. Competence tested, 4. Organized, 5. Adheres to a professional code of conduct, 6. Altruistic service, 7. Applied to affairs of others, etc.'

39 A reference to the interactionist sociologists from Chicago, often pupils of Everett Hughes, who conducted in-depth investigations into professional groups: Howard Becker, Anselm Strauss, Blanche Geer . . .

40 David J. Hickson and Matthew W. Thomas, 'Professionalization in Britain: A Preliminary Measurement', *Sociology*, 3, no. 1, 1969, pp. 37–53.

41 Louis Guttman, 'Relation of Scalogram Analysis to Other Techniques', in Samuel A. Stouffer et al., *Measurement and Prediction* (Studies in Social Psychology in World War II, vol. IV) (Princeton: Princeton University Press, 1950), pp. 60–90.

42 'Among these elements, no means were devised for "Skill based on Theoretical Knowledge", "Altruistic Service", "Affairs of Others". All others were operationalized, including representation of "Requires Education and Training", "Competence Tested", "Organized", and "Adheres to a Code of Conduct". So the scale verifies the assumption that possession of more of these characteristics signifies greater professionalization.' Hickson and Thomas, 'Professionalization', p. 46.

43 'Professionalization is very likely to be a long drawn out process in which the early starters hold an advantage over late comers in the number of professional characteristics they can boast.' Ibid., p. 49.

Lecture of 9 February 1989

1 Bourdieu, Chamboredon and Passeron, *Le Métier de sociologue*, pp. 73–4.
2 Hickson and Thomas, 'Professionalization'.
3 See Bourdieu, Chamboredon and Passeron, *Le Métier de sociologue*, chapter 2, pp. 51–80.
4 See in particular above, Lecture of 21 April 1988, pp. 120–1; see also Lecture of 29 March 1984, in *Forms of Capital*, p. 132.
5 Bourdieu discusses this point at length in his lectures over the following three years: *On the State*.
6 No doubt an allusion to Michel Foucault, *Discipline and Punish: The Birth of the Prison*, trans. Alan Sheridan (London: Penguin, 1991).
7 Theodore Caplow, *The Sociology of Work* (Minneapolis: University of Minnesota Press, 1954).
8 Harold L. Wilensky, 'The Professionalization of Everyone', *American Journal of Sociology*, 70, no. 2, 1964, pp. 137–58.
9 'It's not even wrong' is apparently a note that Éric Weil – whom Bourdieu knew during his time teaching in Lille (1961–64) – sometimes wrote in the margin of a dissertation he was correcting.
10 'When a man who is happy compares his position with that of one who is unhappy, he is not content with the fact of his happiness, but desires something more, namely the right to this happiness, the consciousness that he has earned this good fortune, in contrast to the unfortunate one who must equally have earned his misfortune. Our everyday experience proves that there exists just such a need for reassurance as to the legitimacy or deservedness of one's happiness, whether this involves political success, superior economic status,

bodily health, success in the game of love, or anything else. What the privileged classes require of religion, if anything at all, is this psychologic reassurance of legitimacy.' This theodicy of 'good fortune' is opposed to a 'theodicy of disprivilege'. Max Weber, *The Sociology of Religion*, trans. Ephraim Fischoff (Boston: Beacon Press, 1964 [1920]), pp. 107, 113.

11 G.W. Leibniz, *Theodicy* (Whithorn: Anados Books, 2019 [1710]).

12 On the forceful position held by functionalist sociology in the American and international space, see above, Lecture of 14 April 1988, p. 107.

13 Bernard Barber, 'Some Problems in the Sociology of the Professions', *Dedalus*, 92, no. 4, 1963, pp. 669–88.

14 Bourdieu is drawing on the following passage: 'Professional behaviour may be defined in terms of four essential attributes: a high degree of generalized and systematic knowledge; primary orientation to the community interest rather than to individual self-interest; a high degree of self-control of behaviour through codes of ethics internalized in the process of work socialization and through voluntary associations organized and operated by the work specialists themselves; and a system of rewards (monetary and honorary) that is primarily a set of symbols of work achievement and thus ends in themselves, not means to some end of individual self-interest.' Ibid., p. 672.

15 On this point, see the previous lecture.

16 For discussions of Merton's sociology of science, see Bourdieu, 'Le champ scientifique', and, after these lectures, *Science of Science and Reflexivity*.

17 See above, the Lectures for 1987–88.

18 For developments of the two notions of field and corps, see in particular Pierre Bourdieu, 'Effet de champ et effect de corps', *Actes de la recherche en sciences sociales*, no. 59, 1985, p. 73; *Manet. A Symbolic Revolution*.

19 William Goode, 'Encroachment, Charlatanism and the Emerging Profession: Psychology, Sociology and Medicine', *American Sociological Review*, 25, no. 6, 1960, pp. 902–14.

20 'Admissible', 'bi-admissible' and 'inadmissible' are terms applied to teachers who have passed the first stage (written tests) but not the second (oral examination) of a competitive examination for entry into the teaching profession (such as the *agrégation*).

21 Probably an allusion to the protest movement by teachers which had started on 18 January 1989 after the announcement by the minister of education, Lionel Jospin, of a set of proposals to 'revalue the teaching function'.

22 See Johan Heilbron, 'La professionalisation comme concept sociologique et comme stratégie des sociologues', in *Historiens et sociologies aujourd'hui* (Paris: Éditions du CNRS, 1986), pp. 61–73.

23 See in particular Bourdieu, 'La cause de la science'.

24 Magali Sarfatti Larson, *The Rise of Professionalism: A Sociological Analysis* (Berkeley: University of California Press, 1977).

25 Possibly an allusion to debates linked to the reforms of the health service in the United Kingdom under Margaret Thatcher (one aspect of these reforms was the new role given to administrative managers).

26 'It is my view that the professional complex, though obviously still incomplete in its development, has already become the most important single component in the structure of modern societies. It has displaced first, the "State", in the relatively modern sense of the term, and more recently, the "capitalistic" organization of the economy. The massive emergence of the professional complex,

not the special status of capitalistic or socialistic modes of organization, is the crucial structural development in twentieth century society.' Parsons, 'Professions', p. 545.

27 See for example Peter B. Evans, Dietrich Rueschemeyer and Theda Skocpol, *Bringing the State Back In* (Cambridge: Cambridge University Press, 1985). Bourdieu says more about Theda Skocpol's research in his lectures *On the State* and published a translation of one of her texts: Theda Skocpol, 'Formation de l'État et politiques sociales aux États-Unis', *Actes de la recherche en sciences sociales*, no. 96–97, 1993, pp. 21–37.

28 Published between 1974 and 1993, the journal *Actes. Cahiers d'action juridique trimestriels* was created by magistrates who had 'chosen to call the judicial institution into question'.

29 This challenge was strong enough in the 1970s for the suppression of the Order of Doctors to be one of the '110 propositions for France' advanced by François Mitterrand during the presidential campaign of 1981.

30 An article dealing with this question had been published in Bourdieu's journal: Pierre Elzière, 'À propos des "médecines naturelles"', *Actes de la recherche en sciences sociales*, no. 64, 1986, pp. 79–80.

31 David D. Bien, 'Les offices, les corps, et le crédit d'État: l'utilisation des privilèges sous l'Ancien Régime', *Annales. Économies, sociétés, civilisations*, 43, no. 2, 1988, pp. 379–404.

32 Yvette Delsaut, 'Carnets de socioanalyse 2 – Une photo de classe', *Actes de la recherche en sciences sociales*, no. 75, 1988, pp. 83–96 (republished in *Carnets de socioanalyse. Écrire les pratiques ordinaires* [Paris: Raisons d'agir, 2020], pp. 101–52).

33 Here and in the following discussion Bourdieu is probably referring to the work on the sociology of education that he pursued from the 1960s onward at the Centre for European Sociology. See in particular the first lines of the article 'The School as a Conservative Force: Scholastic and Cultural Inequalities', trans. J.C. Whitehouse, in J. Eggleston (ed.), *Contemporary Research in the Sociology of Education* (London: Methuen, 1974), p. 32–46; also in R. Dale et al. (eds.), *Schooling and Capitalism: A Sociological Reader* (London: Routledge/ The Open University Press, 1976), p. 192–200: 'It is doubtless through an effect of cultural inertia that we are able to continue to see the educational system as a factor of social mobility, according to the ideology of "the school as liberator", whereas on the contrary everything tends to show that it is one of the most efficient factors of social conservatism and that it furnishes an appearance of legitimacy to social inequalities, and that it gives its sanction to cultural heritage and the social gift, treating them as natural' [my translation].

34 The opposition between 'ascription' and 'achievement' (or in French, between *qualité attribuée* and *performance*) is, along with some other dilemmas (neutrality vs affectivity, universalism vs particularism . . .), one of the 'pattern variables' through which Parsons proposes to characterize each social action. See Talcott Parsons, Edward Shils et al., *Toward a General Theory of Action* (Cambridge MA: Harvard University Press, 2001 [1951]).

35 The transcription is problematic (Bourdieu seems hesitant and the recording used is of poor quality at this point), but Bourdieu seems to be talking about his own research (and drawing attention to the fact that the idea of a comparison with the nobility did not strike him at first).

36 We should remember that these lectures were given in the year of the bicen-

tenary of the French Revolution. The celebration of this anniversary in 1989 was often accompanied by the idea that the nobility and its privileges had been definitely 'abolished' in 1789.

37 See for instance Lecture of 17 April 1986, *Politics and Sociology*, p. 50.
38 Pierre Bourdieu and Monique de Saint-Martin had studied the episcopate ('La Sainte famille . . .') and in particular proceeded to compare (successive) generations of bishops.
39 See above, Lecture of 10 March 1988, p. 18.
40 For a development of this point, see Bourdieu, *The State Nobility*, pp. 377–82.

Lecture of 16 February 1989

1 See Bourdieu, *On the State*. The main points of this lecture often overlap with Part V of *The State Nobility* (pp. 371–89), where they are treated sometimes more concisely, sometimes in more detail.
2 In other places Bourdieu criticizes the analyses of power proposed in the 1970s by Michel Foucault, Gilles Deleuze, Pierre Legendre and Pierre Clastres . . .
3 Bourdieu quotes (and criticizes) Michel Foucault's words according to which 'power comes from below' (see in particular Lectures of 17 April and 15 May 1986, *Politics and Sociology*).
4 Jan Goldstein, '"Moral Contagion": A Professional Ideology of Medicine and Psychiatry in Eighteenth- and Nineteenth-Century France', in Gerald L. Geison (ed.), *Professions and the French State, 1700–1900* (Philadelphia: University of Pennsylvania Press, 1984), pp. 181–222.
5 Several measures taken during the French Revolution (the night of 4 August 1789 and the abolition of privileges, the Allarde decree, the Le Chapelier law of 1791) attacked the '*ancien régime* corporations', which were increasingly seen as an obstacle to the freedom of enterprise and a direct relationship between the State and its citizens.
6 Since 1945 in France a medical convention has linked independent doctors to the health service: doctors who sign up to it are committed to aligning their charges with the rates of reimbursement set by the health service.
7 The reference to this book has not been found.
8 See the research on Manet in *Principles of Vision* (for instance, Lecture of 14 April 1985, pp. 28–9), and for a later, more fully developed version, *Manet. A Symbolic Revolution*.
9 A reference to the orientation taken by the Catholic Church after the Vatican II Council (1962–65). For notes on this *aggiornamento* (an Italian word meaning 'updating'), see Bourdieu and de Saint Martin, 'La Sainte famille . . .'.
10 This was a conference paper that Bourdieu had given in January 1971 to the Noroît circle in Arras and first published in *Noroît* (no. 155–156, 1971): 'L'opinion publique n'existe pas', *Les Temps modernes*, no. 318, 1973, pp. 1292–1309, reprinted as 'Public Opinion Does Not Exist', in *Sociology in Question*, pp. 149–57.
11 [The editors list various later translations into French.] The standard English version is: Max Weber, 'Bureaucracy and Education', in *Economy and Society*, vol. 2, pp. 998–1001.
12 Bourdieu frequently pointed out the gaps in the French editions of Max Weber (see Lecture of 1 March 1984, *Forms of Capital*, pp. 4, 314–15). At the time of

these lectures the first wave of translations of Weber into French (between 1959 and 1971) was already past history. It was from the middle of the 1980s and above all the 1990s that the translations were resumed.

13 This reference has not been found. It is perhaps in Hildred Geertz and Clifford Geertz, *Kinship in Bali* (Chicago: University of Chicago Press, 1978).

14 'The peculiarity of modern culture, and specifically of its technical and economic basis, demands this very "calculability" of results. When fully developed, bureaucracy also stands, in a specific sense, under the principle of *sine ira ac studio*. Bureaucracy develops the more perfectly, the more it is "dehumanized", the more completely it succeeds in eliminating from official business love, hatred, and all purely personal, irrational, and emotional elements which escape calculation. This is appraised as its special virtue by capitalism. The more complicated and specialized modern culture becomes, the more its external supporting apparatus demands the personally detached and strictly objective *expert*, in lieu of the lord of older social structures who was moved by personal sympathy and favour, by grace and gratitude.' Weber, *Economy and Society*, vol. 2, p. 975. [The editors give the German original, since a French translation was not available (translator).]

15 'Without anger or passion'. This formula, borrowed from Tacitus, is used by Weber in the passage quoted above.

16 See in particular Weber, 'Legal Authority With a Bureaucratic Administrative Staff', *Economy and Society*, vol. 1, pp. 217–26.

17 A reference to a passage in Weber (which Bourdieu had commented on in his lectures for 1984–85, in particular the Lecture of 10 May 1984, *Forms of Capital*, pp. 249–53): 'The ideal example of this type of rational administration of justice is the "kadi-justice" of the "Solomonian" judgment as it was practised by the hero of that legend – and by Sancho Panza when he happened to be governor.' Weber, *Economy and Society*, vol. 2, p. 845. The reference to Sancho Panza concerns the chapter in *Don Quixote* entitled 'How the Great Sancho Panza Took Possession of His Island, and How He Started to Govern". Miguel de Cervantès, *Don Quixote*, trans. John Rutherford (London: Penguin, 2003 [1605–15]), Part 2, chapter 45.

18 No doubt a reference to the Lecture of 10 May 1984, *Forms of Capital*, pp. 249–53.

19 See the passage previously quoted in note 14: 'The more complicated and specialized modern culture becomes, the more its external supporting apparatus demands the personally detached and strictly objective *expert*, in lieu of the lord of older social structures who was moved by personal sympathy and favour, by grace and gratitude.'

20 An allusion to the 'textual analysis' practised in light of the deconstruction developed by Jacques Derrida. See in particular *Of Grammatology*, trans. Gayatri Chakravorty Spivak (Baltimore: Johns Hopkins University Press, 1998 [1967]).

21 Weber, 'Bureaucracy and Education', *Economy and Society*, vol. 2, p. 1000.

22 Bourdieu, *Distinction*, especially pp. 23 ff.

23 A more literal translation would be: 'The function is eternal'.

24 Kantorowicz, *The King's Two Bodies*.

25 'State Magic', in *The State Nobility*, pp. 374–7.

26 No doubt a reference to the Lecture of 9 May 1985, *Principles of Vision*, pp. 166 ff.

27 Mauss and Hubert, *A General Theory of Magic*.

28 See Pierre Bourdieu and Yvette Delsaut, 'Le couturier et sa griffe: contribution à une théorie de la magie', *Actes de la recherche en sciences sociales*, no. 1, 1975, pp. 7–36.

29 This formula, still frequently used in the 1980s, was used to refer to couples who had been 'cohabiting', when they got married, making their life in common official by having it recognized by the State.

30 A reference to the commentary on Kafka that Bourdieu had undertaken during his lectures for 1983–84. See in particular the Lectures of 8 March 1984 and 22 March 1984, *Forms of Capital*, pp. 53–4 and p. 121; and the Lecture of 30 May 1985, *Principles of Vision*, pp. 251–3.

31 Marcel Mauss, *The Gift*, trans. Jane I. Guyer (Chicago: Hau, 2016 [1902–3]).

32 This formula was used by Maoists, but may have been borrowed from Lenin: 'We all know now that the economists have bent the stick in one direction. To put it right, we had to bend it in the other direction, and that is what I have done'. V.I. Lenin, 'Discours sur la question du programme du parti. 22 juillet (4 août)', in Lenin, *Oeuvres*, vol. 6 (Paris/Moscow: Éditions sociales/Éditions du progrès, 1966), p. 515. The 'theory of bending the stick', that Lenin owed to his 'grandfather, a peasant and woodsman', is also known through a quotation by Louis Althusser ('Soutenance d'Amiens', in *Solitude de Machiavel* [Paris: PUF, 1998], p. 205).

33 John Wakeford, *The Cloistered Elite: A Sociological Analysis of the English Public Boarding School* (London: Macmillan, 1969).

34 'Sacred things are those things protected and isolated by prohibitions; profane things are those things to which such prohibitions apply and which must keep their distance from what is sacred.' Émile Durkheim, *The Elementary Forms of Religious Life*, trans. Carol Cosman (Oxford: Oxford University Press, 2001), p. 40.

35 Arnold Van Gennep, *Les Rites de passage* (Paris: Émile Nourry, 1909; republished, Paris: Maison des sciences de l'homme, 1969).

36 Owen Lattimore, *Inner Asian Frontiers of China* (Boston: Beacon Press, 1962), p. xlvi.

37 Bourdieu is thinking of the main character, Frédéric Moreau, 'an "inheritor" who wants to inherit without being inherited [and who] lacks what the bourgeois call a serious side, that aptitude to be what one is'. See Pierre Bourdieu, 'L'invention de la vie d'artiste', *Actes de la recherche en sciences sociales*, no. 2, 1975, pp. 67–93, and *The Rules of Art*, pp. 9–20, esp. p. 11.

38 See Bourdieu, *The State Nobility*, pp. 73–93 and 102–27.

39 Bourdieu no doubt derives this definition of the clergy from the link that Durkheim establishes between separation and the clergy, the sacred being separated from the profane by prohibition and the idea that priests are privileged persons who seem to possess some powerful spirit and whom society tends to protect. See Durkheim, *The Elementary Forms of Religious Life*, pp. 36–41.

40 Bourdieu developed this point at greater length in his lectures on domination in 1998. See also 'La noblesse: capital social et capital symbolique', in Didier Lancien and Monique de Saint Martin (eds.), *Anciennes et nouvelles aristocracies de 1880 à nos jours* (Paris: Éditions de la Maison des sciences de l'homme, 2007), pp. 385–97.

41 For development of this point, see Bourdieu's comments made at the time of

these lectures: Pierre Bourdieu and Loïc Wacquant, *An Invitation to Reflexive Sociology* (Cambridge: Polity, 1992), p. 114.

42 Bien, 'Les offices, les corps, et le crédit d'État', p. 381.

43 On these points see Bourdieu, *The State Nobility*, pp. 116–17, 263–95, 377–86.

44 Weber, *The Protestant Ethic and the Spirit of Capitalism*, pp. 39 ff.

45 Keohane, *Philosophy and the State in France*, pp. 83–6.

46 See above, Lectures of 10 and 17 March 1988.

47 See above, p. 45.

Pierre Bourdieu at the Gates of the State

1 Pierre Bourdieu, *General Sociology*, trans. Peter Collier (Cambridge: Polity), vol. 1, *Classification Struggles* (2018); vol. 2, *Habitus and Field* (2020); vol. 3, *Forms of Capital* (2021); vol. 4, *Principles of Vision* (2022); vol. 5, *Politics and Sociology* (2023). Abbreviated in the following notes as: CS, HF, FC, PV and PS.

2 These sessions were not transcribed or recorded, but are summarized in the *Annuaire du Collège de France* (see below, pp. 242–3).

3 Pierre Bourdieu, 'Intérêt et désintéressement. Cours du Collège de France à la Faculté d'anthropologie et de sociologie de l'Université Lumière Lyon 2 les 1er et 8 décembre 1988', *Cahiers de recherche sur la socialisation*, no. 7, 1989; 'Is a Disinterested Act Possible?', in *Practical Reason*, pp. 75–91. Lyon was chosen because one of Bourdieu's former students, Philippe French, was teaching there. Also, the buildings of the Collège de France in Paris were under repair in the middle of the 1990s, so Bourdieu moved all of his lectures out.

4 The three following years have been published: Bourdieu, *On the State*.

5 We can gather from certain indications (for instance 'I might in a year or two . . .', above, p. 42), that Bourdieu was already in 1989 planning to devote several years to the State, but the titles under which the lectures would be given, and which on two occasions announced a false 'conclusion' ('À propos de l'État' in 1987–88; 'À propos de l'État (suite)' in 1988–89, 'À propos de l'État (suite et fin)' in 1989–90; 'L'État: conclusion' in 1990–91; and 'Sur l'État' in 1991–92), seem to show that he did not know at the outset how many years the lectures would last.

6 Unpublished interview with Loïc Wacquant, Fonds Pierre Bourdieu (Documentary archives of the Condorcet campus). Bourdieu continues: 'That is why I started with a long study in "negative sociology" (by analogy with "negative theology") aiming to call into question all prevailing presumptions on the State, whether naive or scholarly.'

7 Lecture of 14 April 1988.

8 'Position of the Lectures on the State in Pierre Bourdieu's Work', in *On the State*, pp. 378–81.

9 'Strikes and Political Action' (1975), in *Sociology in Question*, pp. 168–76.

10 The only exceptions, perhaps, are an insert in *Distinction*, which, observing that 'the Parisian grande bourgeoisie' has reappropriated no doubt more completely than ever the commanding positions in the economy and the senior administration of the State' (pp. 309–15), anticipates the analyses in *The State Nobility*; and, in *The Logic of Practice*, a reference to *obsequium*

or a passing parallel drawn between the economic redistribution operated by modern States and the logic of the gift in traditional societies (pp. 122–3).
11 Pierre Bourdieu, *Ce que parler veut dire* (Paris: Fayard, 1982).
12 CS 102, 113.
13 CS 103. See also in particular pp. 97, 125.
14 CS 126.
15 CS 131.
16 PV 252.
17 PV 253.
18 FC 49, 137.
19 FC 49.
20 PV 207.
21 CS 127; see also in particular PV 45, 87, 104.
22 CS 125. On this formula, see above, p. 267, note 16.
23 CS 125, HF 224, FC 49, PV 64, 178–9, 206. Bourdieu sometimes reminds us that this monopoly is still liable to be challenged, at least virtually (CS 126).
24 He wrote later that 'one could, following medieval theologians, choose to give the name of "state" to the last (or to the first) link in the long chain of official acts of consecration'. *Practical Reason*, p. 51.
25 PV 250.
26 PV 104.
27 FC 166.
28 PS 160–2.
29 PV 180.
30 PV 180.
31 PV 64.
32 PV 28.
33 CS 129, HF 120.
34 FC 136–7.
35 *Practical Reason*, p. 41. The journal *Actes de la recherche en sciences sociales* also published issues on 'Histoire de l'État' (no. 116–117, 1977) and 'Genèse de l'État moderne' (no. 118, 1997).
36 *Practical Reason*, p. 51.
37 Bourdieu, 'Du champ national au champ international', in *Les structures sociales de l'économie*, pp. 339–53.
38 Since the State is a collective, Bourdieu also speaks of the 'mystery of the incarnation of the State in a person', the civil servant (CS 111, 121, and also HF 16 and CS 114).
39 HF 19.
40 CS 105.
41 FC 49.
42 PV 175.
43 HF 119.
44 On these points see CS 105, HF 106–7, 118, PV 180, PS 68.
45 HF 119.
46 PV 180.
47 In 2000, issue no. 133 of *Actes de la recherche en sciences sociales* was entitled 'Science de l'État'.
48 PV 151.
49 PV 208.

50 CS 132. This antagonism is also a question of *obsequium* (Lecture of 2 February 1989). In the 1980s, writing more about the State, Bourdieu also uses the word *obsequium* (which he owes to Spinoza and his commentator Alexandre Matheron) to 'designate the relation that links the citizen to the State' (HF 177).

51 CS 83.

52 See in particular Alain Desrosières, 'Bourdieu et les statisticiens: une rencontre improbable et ses deux héritages', in Pierre Encrevé and Rose-Marie Lagrave (eds.), *Travailler avec Bourdieu* (Paris: Flammarion, 2003), pp. 209–18.

53 This research led to a report in 1988 (Pierre Bourdieu, Rosine Christin, Claire Givry and Monique de Saint Martin, 'Éléments d'une analyse du marché de la maison individuelle', Paris: Centre de sociologie européenne, 1988), then to an issue of the journal ('L'économie de la Maison', *Actes de la recherche en sciences sociales*, no. 81–82, 1980, pp. 2–112).

54 The first four parts of *The State Nobility* had been pre-published in the journal *Actes de la recherche en sciences sociales*: the first part in Pierre Bourdieu and Monique de Saint Martin, 'Les catégories de l'entendement professoral' (no. 3, 1975, pp. 68–93); the second part in Pierre Bourdieu, 'Épreuve scolaire et consécration sociale. Les classes préparatoires aux grandes écoles' (no. 39, 1981, pp. 3–70); the third part in Pierre Bourdieu and Monique de Saint Martin, 'Agrégation et ségrégation. Le champ des grandes écoles et le champ du pouvoir' (no. 69, 1987, pp. 2–50) and in Pierre Bourdieu, 'Variations et invariants. Éléments pour une histoire structurale du champ des grandes écoles' (no. 70, 1987, pp. 3–30); the fourth part in Pierre Bourdieu and Monique de Saint Martin, 'Le patronat' (no. 20–21, 1978, pp. 3–82).

55 Pernelle Issenhuth, 'La "clef de voûte de toute sociologie de la culture". Enjeux des premières enquêtes "Éducation"', in *Pierre Bourdieu et l'art de l'invention scientifique. Enquête au Centre de sociologie européenne (1959–1969)* (Paris: Classiques Garnier, 2022).

56 For a probable example, see above, p. 219.

57 PV 179.

58 FC 276. See also HF 64.

59 PV 204.

60 PV 170.

61 FC 209. See also PV 117.

62 FC 210.

63 PS 182.

64 Edward P. Thompson, 'Modes de domination et révolutions en Angleterre', *Actes de la recherche en sciences sociales*, no. 2–3, 1976, esp. p. 140.

65 Ibid., p. 139. See also E.P. Thompson, *Whigs and Hunters: The Origin of the Black Act* (New York: Pantheon, 1975).

66 Pierre Cam, 'Juges rouges et droit du travail', *Actes de la recherche en sciences sociales*, no. 19, 1978, pp. 7–27.

67 Jean-Pierre Mounier, 'Du corps judiciaire à la crise de la magistrature', and Rémi Lenoir, 'Groupes de pression et groupes consensuels. Contribution à une analyse de la formation du droit', *Actes de la recherche en sciences sociales*, no. 64, 1986, respectively pp. 20–9 and 30–9.

68 Bourdieu, 'La force du droit'.

69 Reading the lectures reminds us that Bourdieu's interest in the 'force of form' goes further than the simple case of law. His work on Heidegger in particular

(*The Political Ontology of Martin Heidegger*), which he republished in 1988, draws attention to the operation of formalization in the case of the philosophical field.

70 CS 77, 95 and PV 114.
71 On the particular interest in Weber that Bourdieu seems to have had in this period, see 'Situating the Later Volumes of *General Sociology* in the Work of Pierre Bourdieu', PV 254–71, especially 262–3.
72 Lecture of 16 February 1989.
73 FC 82 and 252–3.
74 FC 249–51. See also FC 75.
75 CS 10. See also FC 242.
76 CS 60.
77 CS 75.
78 FC 90, PV 117.
79 PV 118.
80 CS 74–5.
81 PV 118.
82 PV 118.
83 PV 119.
84 HF 223–4.
85 CS 91.
86 FC 208.
87 CS 73.
88 On this point, see 'Situating the Course on General Sociology in the Work of Pierre Bourdieu', in CS 134–54.
89 PV 118.
90 Ibid. Bourdieu alludes to his point again in his Lecture of 19 January 1989.
91 CS 73.
92 Ibid.
93 PV 117. In return, we might note some reactions from jurists to Bourdieu's sociology of law. On this point see in particular Liora Israël, 'À qui de droit', in Pierre Bourdieu, *La Force du droit* (Paris: Éditions de la Sorbonne, 2017), pp. 7–15; Antoine Vauchez, 'Droit', in Gisèle Sapiro (ed.), *Dictionnaire international Bourdieu* (Paris: CNRS Éditions, 2020), pp. 262–4.
94 Lecture of 10 March 1988.
95 Lecture of 10 March 1988.
96 Letter of 29 March 1978 from Pierre Bourdieu to Gérard Lyon-Caen, on the subject of Pierre Cam's article, Fonds Pierre Bourdieu.
97 Yves Dezalay recounts his trajectory in 'Une leçon de réflexivité', in Gérard Mauger (ed.), *Rencontres avec Bourdieu* (Boissieu: Éditions du Croquant, 2005), pp. 233–8, and in 'Enquêter sur l'internationalisation des noblesse d'État. Retour réflexif sur des stratégies de double jeu. Entretien avec Yves Dezalay. Propos recueillis par Didier Bigo et Antonin Cohen', *Cultures & Conflits*, no. 98, 2015, pp. 15–52. Yves Dezalay's thesis gave rise to the publication of *Marchands de droit. La restructuration de l'ordre juridique international par les multinationales du droit* (Paris: Fayard, 1994).
98 Dezalay, 'Enquêter sur l'internationalisation . . .'.
99 On this point, see ibid. Bourdieu remarked that, 'In the eyes of the jurists, the absolute limit was [. . .] the sociology of law. Since the law sees itself as the discourse of legitimacy there is no justification for trying to study how it

comes to be produced, because the law proclaims how things should proceed' (PV 118).

100 Pierre Bourdieu, 'The Invention of the Artist's Life' (1975), trans. Eric R. Koch, *Yale French Studies*, no. 73, 1987, pp. 75–103.
101 Lecture of 17 March 1988.
102 Lecture of 24 March 1988.
103 Lectures of 10 March 1988 and 19 January 1989.
104 Lecture of 17 March 1988.
105 Bourdieu, Seminar of 28 March 1985, not yet published.
106 Pierre Bourdieu, 'La production de la croyance', *Actes de la recherche en sciences sociales*, no. 13, 1977, p. 9.
107 Lecture of 2 February 1989.
108 Lecture of 24 March 1988.
109 Ibid.
110 Ibid.
111 Ibid.
112 Ibid.
113 Bourdieu, *On the State*; 'De la Maison du roi à la raison d'État. Un modèle de la genèse du champ bureaucratique', *Actes de la recherche en sciences sociales*, no. 118, 1997, pp. 55–68.
114 These reflections led to an issue of *Actes de la recherche en sciences sociales* (no. 101–102, 1994) devoted to 'the stranglehold of journalism'. The issue includes in particular an introductory text (pp. 3–9) where Bourdieu mentions 'the case of the jurists' (and refers implicitly to his analyses of the juridical field in previous years) and two articles on the relations between the press and the juridical world (Michael J. Powell, 'La nouvelle presse juridique et les métiers du droit', and Remi Lenoir, 'La parole est aux juges', respectively, pp. 63–76 and 77–84). In 1993 Bourdieu seems to have discussed with several researchers working on law (Denis Ardisson, Alain Bancaud, Anne Boigeol, Dominique Khalifa, Remi Lenoir, Lygia Sigaud . . .) the question of 'how the press changes the law', how 'the body of the jurist is penetrated by the journalists' (source: documents shown to the author by Remi Lenoir).
115 Lecture of 17 March 1988.
116 Lecture of 2 February 1989.
117 Lecture of 21 April 1988.
118 Bourdieu, Chamboredon and Passeron, *Le Métier de sociologue*, pp. 95–106.
119 Bourdieu, 'A Science that Makes Trouble', in *Sociology in Question*, p. 10.
120 See Bourdieu, *Homo Academicus*; *The Political Ontology of Martin Heidegger*; 'Le champ scientifique'.
121 Bourdieu, 'For a Sociology of Sociologists', in *Sociology in Question*, pp. 49–53.
122 Ibid., p. 50.
123 See in particular 'Histoire sociale des sciences sociales', *Actes de la recherche en sciences sociales*, no. 106–107 and no. 108, 1995.
124 Lecture of 21 April 1988.
125 Bourdieu, Chamboredon and Passeron, *Le Métier de sociologue*, p. 103.
126 Bourdieu, 'The Sociologist in Question', in *Sociology in Question*, p. 28.
127 See Bourdieu, *The Rules of Art*, p. 248.
128 Lecture of 26 January 1989.
129 Lecture of 21 April 1988.

130 Lecture of 14 April 1988.
131 Lecture of 17 March 1988.
132 Ibid.
133 Lecture of 21 April 1988.
134 Lecture of 19 January 1989; and 'Is a Disinterested Act Possible?', in *Practical Reason*, pp. 75–91.
135 Bourdieu, 'Is a Disinterested Act Possible?', pp. 84, 88–91.
136 Lecture of 16 February 1989.
137 Lecture of 14 April 1988.
138 Bourdieu, *Science of Science and Reflexivity*.
139 Pierre Bourdieu, 'La spécificité du champ scientifique et les conditions sociales du progrès de la raison', *Sociologie et sociétés*, 7, no. 1, 1975, pp. 91–118.
140 He returned to discuss this debate in detail in his teaching for the year 1992–93 (*Anthropologie économique*).
141 Bourdieu, *The Logic of Practice*, pp. 98–111.
142 We could mention other themes, more briefly evoked here, such as sacrifice for the country (Lectures of 17 March 1988 and 19 January 1989) or the question of sainthood ('Is a Disinterested Act Possible?').
143 'Is a Disinterested Act Possible?', in *Practical Reason*, pp. 75–6.
144 Lecture of 24 March 1988.
145 A reference to a talk by Alain Bancaud at the Lyon seminar on Law. See note 6 to Lecture of 10 March 1988, above p. 254, and Summaries of Lectures, below p. 242.
146 Lecture of 10 March 1988.
147 This was the case with the Anti-Utilitarian Movement in the social sciences (MAUSS) that published a journal from 1981.
148 See Ingrid Gilcher-Holtey, 'Jürgen Habermas', in Sapiro (ed.), *Dictionnaire international Bourdieu*, pp. 385–6.
149 Bourdieu, 'Is a Disinterested Act Possible?', p. 75.
150 Lecture of 19 January 1989.
151 PS 202.
152 Lecture of 21 April 1998.
153 Lecture of 24 March 1988.
154 Pierre Bourdieu, 'La vertu civile', *Le Monde*, 16 September 1988, pp. 1–2, republished in *Interventions 1961–2001. Science sociale et action politique* (Marseille: Agone, 2002), pp. 235–8.
155 Éric Aeschimann, 'Bourdieu venait voir Rocard à Matignon . . .' Un entretien avec Pierre Encrevé, *L'Obs*, 4 January 2012, https://bibliobs.nouvelobs.com /essais/20120104.OBS8066/bourdieu-venait-voir-rocard-a-matignon.html.
156 Lecture of 16 February 1989.
157 See 'Is a Disinterested Act Possible?', pp. 75–91, and the Lecture of 2 February 1989.
158 Bourdieu, 'La vertu civile', p. 254.
159 Ibid., p. 237.
160 Ibid., p. 238.
161 Aeschimann, 'Bourdieu venait voir Rocard à Matignon . . .'.
162 Sylvain Bourmeau, 'Défataliser le monde. Entretien avec Pierre Bourdieu', *Les Inrockuptibles*, no. 99, 1997, pp. 22–9.
163 See Pierre Bourdieu, *Acts of Resistance: Against the New Myths of Our Time*, trans. Richard Nice (Cambridge: Polity, 1998).

164 A certain sympathy for this magistrate does indeed seem to show through, for instance on the subject of the humanists' refusal to retreat into the bookshops, or when Bourdieu recognizes in d'Aguesseau's writings his own preoccupations as a sociologist (the idea that 'we can only fight a passion with another passion', or on the problem of 'radical historicism', or again when he suspects the sociologists of being in certain respects 'below the level of Chancellor d'Aguesseau'.

165 See Pierre Bourdieu, 'Naître à Normale', *Le Monde de la Révolution française*, no. 3, 1989, p. 25: 'The right to an education is without any doubt one of the most difficult to contest in theory; but also one of the most difficult to impose as a fact.'

166 Pascale Casanova, '*Liber*', in Sapiro (ed.), *Dictionnaire international Bourdieu*, p. 510.

167 Bourdieu, 'La vertu civile', p. 238.

168 Lecture delivered in Turin in May 1989, 'Pour une Internationale des intellectuels', *Politis*, no. 1, 1992, pp. 9–15, republished in *Interventions*, pp. 257–66 (revised version: 'Postscript. For a Corporatism of the Universal', in *The Rules of Art*, pp. 337–48).

169 Bourdieu, 'Pour une Internationale des intellectuels', p. 262.

170 Florence Dutheil, 'L'intellectuel dans la cité. Un entretien avec Pierre Bourdieu: "Il faut restaurer la tradition de vigilance"', *Le Monde*, 4 November 1993, p. 29.

171 Bourdieu, 'Is a Disinterested Act Possible?', p. 90.

Index